CD-ROM
Fundamentals to applications

CD-ROM
Fundamentals to applications

CD-ROM

Fundamentals to applications

Edited by
Charles Oppenheim
Manager, Database Products, Reuters Ltd, London, UK

Butterworths
London   Boston   Singapore   Sydney   Toronto   Wellington

First published 1988

© **Butterworth & Co. (Publishers) Ltd, 1988**

British Library Cataloguing in Publication Data

CD-ROM: fundamentals to applications.
 1. Computer systems. Read only memory: Compact discs
 I. Oppenheim, Charles
 004.5′6

 ISBN 0-408-00746-X

Library of Congress Cataloging in Publication Data

CD-ROM fundamentals to applications.

 Includes bibliographies and index.
 1. CD-ROM.   I. Oppenheim, Charles.
 TK7882.C56C33   1988   004.5′6   88-19386

 ISBN 0-408-00746-X

Cover photograph by courtesy of Hitachi New Media Products, Hayes, Middlesex
Filmset by BC Typesetting, Exeter EX2 8PN
Printed and bound in Great Britain at the University Press, Cambridge

621.3819′5833
CDR

Preface

Until very recently, only consultants, conference organizers and publishers of books on the topic were making money out of optical disc technology. Now, some years after the first launch of videodiscs, the technology is maturing, one type of product (CD-ROM) is clearly in the forefront, and commercial CD-ROM products are coming on the market. There are already more than 200 CD-ROM 'publications' available worldwide and hundreds of thousands of CD-ROM discs have been manufactured. Most of the progress has been made in the USA, with Europe (with the notable exception of Italy) lagging well behind.

Why has CD-ROM proved to be so interesting whereas other optical technologies have apparently failed to fulfil their promise? There are several factors, including its high storage capacity, the imposition of agreed standards, the ability to link to standard personal computer hardware, and the benefits of mass production, as CD-ROM can be stamped out at the same manufacturing plant as CD audio.

CD-ROM is not by any means the only optical storage memory system available. A plethora of technologies, including digitally encoded video-discs, CD-I, OROM, WORM, DVI and erasable optical discs, have either been launched or are the subject of active R and D investigation. It is not surprising, therefore, that both publishers and users of information are confused and are cautious about committing themselves to CD-ROM technology that may be superseded.

In its early days, CD-ROM was the victim of considerable hype. Market research reports were published with wildly over-optimistic forecasts of sales of CD-ROM. The immediate demise of the online industry was forecast. It is now clear that CD-ROM rarely provides an adequate substitute for an online database. Its strengths lie elsewhere, and it should be viewed as complementing online rather than competing with it.

Although the growth of the industry has been slower than originally predicted, there can be no question that the technology is the most important change to the electronic information market since the introduction of online information retrieval in the early 1970s. Quite where the technology will have its greatest impact is not clear, although distribution of software, databases, encyclopaedias, catalogues, standards, training manuals and legal guides seem to be most popular at the moment.

The most promising CD-ROM products are those that add value over traditional online services, for example by combining multiple sources of data on a single disc, by the implementation of user friendly software, or by integration with personal computer software such as wordprocessing and spreadsheet applications.

The fact remains, however, that for all its promise, users of CD-ROM face problems. Publishers face an uncertain marketplace, high start up costs, lack of an installed base of players and uncertainty about the precise 'shape' of the product to be created. Users face investment decisions when standards are still being set, new hardware products are threatening the existing product, and a lack of published products at the moment. It is a classic 'chicken and egg' problem, and one requiring skill and deep pockets to solve. Nonetheless, Link Resources predict a CD-ROM market worth $900 000 000 pa by 1991, of which Europe would be $100 000 000.

This book is aimed at both potential publishers of data on CD-ROM, and potential users. A series of chapters, contributed by leading experts in the field, review CD-ROM and its place in the optical technology market-place and discuss the product available and the procedures for putting data onto this exciting new medium. The costs of CD-ROM publishing, some case studies, and the role of the EEC are also reviewed.

I am grateful to all the authors who so willingly contributed material to the book. The choice of authors and subjects was mine, and complaints about either should be addressed to me, not the authors themselves. I am also grateful to Ann Berne of Butterworths for her ideas, enthusiasm and persistent reminders, which ensured a vague idea translated into this final publication.

Charles Oppenheim
Reuters

Contributors

Christine Baldwin, Product Manager, Pergamon Compact Solution, London, UK

Martin Brooks, Executive Editor, Bowker Electronic Publishing, New York, USA

Patrick Gibbins, Managing Director, Pergamon Compact Solution, London, UK

Robert Campbell, Managing Director, Blackwell Scientific Publications, Oxford, UK

Tony Hendley, Head of Research and Consultancy, The Centre for Information Media and Technology (CIMTECH), Hatfield, Hertfordshire, UK

Franco A. Mastroddi, Directorate-General, Telecommunications, Information Industries and Innovation, Commission of the European Communities, Luxembourg

Charles Oppenheim, Manager, Database Products, Reuters Ltd, London, UK

Gordon Priestley, BRS Europe, London, UK

David Rosen, Link Resources, New York, USA

Barrie T. Stern, ADONIS, Amsterdam, Netherlands

Raymond V. Walsh, Electronic Publishing Services Ltd, London, UK

Martin S. White, Managing Director, European Technology Services Group, International Data Corporation, London, UK

Robin Williamson, Director, Mandarin Communications Ltd, London, UK

Contents

ix

Chapter 1

An introduction to the range of optical storage media

Tony Hendley

Introduction

The Centre for Information Media and Technology (CIMTECH), set up at Hatfield, UK, in 1967 and sponsored by the British Library's Research and Development Department, has specialized in monitoring new technologies, media and systems for capturing, storing, retrieving and distributing information, both structured and unstructured. Its prime focus has always been on the new storage and distribution media becoming available, and the way in which the introduction of a new medium enables new information products and services to be developed. Throughout its twenty year lifetime, CIMTECH has advised our members — publishers, librarians, records managers and data processing specialists — on the potential of microform as a storage and publishing medium and has taken an active role in developing standards and evaluating equipment for producing and retrieving the various formats of film that emerged. CIMTECH has also closely monitored the development of magnetic storage media and, in particular, the limitations of magnetic tapes and discs for the long-term storage and wide distribution of information. By the late 1970s and early 1980s it became obvious to CIMTECH and its members that the existing storage and distribution media were simply not capable of meeting the increasing demands being made by the burgeoning information industry.

The need for a new digital storage medium

The widespread availability of low cost mini- and microcomputers and the introduction of word processing packages, text retrieval systems and database management systems that could run on minicomputers and microcomputers as well as mainframes has led many to predict a future where the vast majority of human knowledge and information would be created electronically and vast databases could be accessed 'online' and searched interactively. Today, personal computers and desktop publishing packages enable more and more material to be created electronically. However, while a large percentage of material is created electronically today, very little of it is stored or distributed electronically for a number of reasons.

1

The first has to do with standards. In the early days, every word processing system was incompatible so reports produced on one system could not be read on another system. Reports produced on a word processing system were printed out and kept in hardcopy for long term storage. Today we have some *de facto* standards at the personal computer end of the market and moves towards open systems. Generally speaking, however, these have had little effect.

The second key issue is the storage media available. Depending on the size of computer used, there is a choice of removable floppy discs, fixed hard discs or removable magnetic tapes.

Floppy discs come in a wide range of sizes, have a relatively short storage life and a relatively small storage capacity so they are far from ideal as a long-term storage medium or as a distribution medium for all but small files.

Hard discs or Winchester discs are fixed and hence long-term storage on Winchester disc is an expensive option as more and more drives or drives with higher storage capacity have to be purchased to cope with growing storage requirements. Hence, in most organizations, Winchester discs are used to store current files and are backed up on floppy discs or tape.

Magnetic tapes are removable and have a higher storage density than floppy discs. There are some data interchange formats being standardized. Tapes, however, suffer from wear and tear and need to be stored in controlled environments and only offer very slow serial access so they are far from ideal for the storage of active files or files that need to be searched at random. Organizations with large tape files report that they are extremely expensive to maintain.

Hence, while an increasing amount of text is created electronically, the lack of standards in the computer environment and the limitations of the magnetic storage media are major obstacles to storing and distributing it electronically. The situation is set to deteriorate even further and the gulf between user requirements and the capabilities of magnetic storage media will be further exposed by the introduction of image and voice processing facilities into the office automation and publishing environment.

Already, in the desktop publishing market, we are seeing the introduction of facsimile type scanners that scan the contents of a document and store it in bit mapped form as an electronic 'image' of the contents of that document. These systems also have enormous potential in the records management area where they form the input to an electronic document filing system with many advantages over existing paper and microfilm based systems but they create tremendous demands for digital storage. While the text of an A4 page typed on a word processor and held in 'coded' form on a computer occupies approximately 1 kilobyte of storage, the contents of an A4 page scanned and held in 'bit map' or facsimile form can occupy 50–60 kilobytes of storage, so a file of 20000 page images would require some 1 gigabyte or 1000 megabytes of storage.

The last information element that needs to be captured in the office and publishing environment is voice, and here there is yet another order of magnitude of storage required. One A4 page read into a computer can occupy some 500 kilobytes of storage. So, while magnetic media is struggling to cope with the storage requirements of data and text processing systems, it will prove totally incapable of dealing with the growing demand for image and voice storage as well.

At present, inhouse users creating large files of information electronically have to choose between making files available online by keeping them on hard disc or archiving them on tape or Computer Output Microfilm (COM) that is far less accessible. Publishers have the option of putting their databases up online via a host company who is able to place the database on Winchester disc, and provide access to it via a mainframe with sufficient ports to allow a wide range of users to gain online access to the database via the telephone network, and carry out searches from their own terminal. Alternatively, they can distribute it on magnetic tape for large users to put it up on their mainframes, or they can print out subsets of the database on paper or microfilm.

While the market for commercial online information services is growing rapidly, it still has a number of major limitations due to the limitations of existing communication links and, of course, the requirements of the host and publisher to recoup the costs involved in putting databases up online. The limitations of the communication links mean that it is still impractical to hold large image databases online and there are still limitations to the type of user interface available online. The main emphasis is on economy and speed and hence commands are terse and coded and not easily mastered by novice users. The result is that online searching has traditionally been a specialized activity carried out by trained intermediaries.

This trend is encouraged by the fact that, due to the cost of holding databases online and the fact that access is via the commercial telephone network, users searching online databases incur relatively high costs both for accessing the commercial databases and for the time they are connected to the network. This again militates against the widespread acceptance of online services by end users who need time to formulate enquiries and browse through databases if they are ever to be persuaded to choose online instead of printed reference works.

One other regrettable result of the economics of online systems is that publishers have to try to appeal to as wide a market as possible, so most online databases tend to be targetted at a very generalized audience. It is not economic to create and put up a very specialized database unless it is of such great value that the relatively small number of potential users would be prepared to pay a large premium for accessing it.

Therefore there are growing problems related to the long-term storage of the ever-growing volume of electronically generated information and in the distribution of that information in electronic form. The records manager and publisher may say that has always been the case and that is why we have paper and microform that, because they are analogue media, can be read by anyone and overcome problems of standards and longevity. Historically this is true but no-one has ever really liked using microfilm and, when one is dealing with large amounts of information, paper is impractical too.

The fact of the matter is that this generation has become used to the speed of access offered by electronic information systems and the ability to search databases interactively and intelligently. They are not therefore prepared to spend hours rifling through paper files or winding through reels of microfilm unless there is absolutely no alternative. Microfilm is an extremely cost effective, space saving medium. It is widely used in academic libraries and by records managers and archivists. For most users of electronic information systems, however, microfilm can be no more than a backup medium as it cannot meet their requirement to search data intelligently and to reprocess that data once they have retrieved it.

Therefore, from the late 1970s onwards there was a growing, often ill-articulated, demand for an electronic alternative to microfilm and paper — a storage and distribution medium that, like microfilm and paper, could be universally accessed without locking users into proprietary standards, that had enormous storage density to cater for the storage of text, data, voice and image files, and, most importantly, that was as durable as paper and microfilm and was easily removable and transportable. Could there ever be such a panacea or was this just the electronic equivalent of the holy grail?

The potential of optical storage

Back in the 1970s, the one candidate appeared to be a form of optical storage device that made use of a laser beam to both record and read back data stored on a disc. These devices were being researched both by the computer industry, in the search for an alternative to magnetic storage media, and by the consumer electronics industry who were looking for a way of distributing prerecorded programmes to the growing number of television owners. Alan Horder and Professor Barrett of Hatfield Polytechnic, together with experts from the US, Europe and Japan, began to take a close look at these developments and before moving on to outline the range of optical storage and distribution media that have emerged from this work and match their capabilities against the requirements listed above, a very brief account of the history of optical storage research and development follows.

Optical storage research and development

Over the past 25 to 30 years, there has been a remarkable resurgence of interest in applied optics that has extended to include many areas hitherto considered the exclusive preserve of electronics. Fibre optics are already employed in communication systems and optical devices are being developed for use as internal computer memories. It is, therefore, not surprising that considerable research has been carried out into optical storage devices.

Today's optical disc storage devices are actually the result of a merger of two seemingly unrelated lines of development. On the one hand, the computer industry was developing optical data storage systems while, on the other hand, the television manufacturers were developing optical recording systems alongside mechanical and capacitive recording for a new generation of video disc systems. These were designed to enable domestic customers to play back pre-recorded television programmes and films on their television sets.

Since the early 1960s the computer industry, aware of some of the limitations of magnetic storage media, has devoted a great deal of research and development effort to the investigation of alternative high-density recording technologies, paticularly optical data storage systems. This research centred around the use of the laser, which was introduced in the 1960s, to record digital data onto a photosensitive medium. The initial aim was to develop a very fast-access but relatively low-cost storage system that would bridge the gap between very expensive main memory and the much slower magnetic disc or tape-based external storage systems. It was also hoped that optical memory systems would prove much more reliable than magnetic tape systems as initial research indicated that there would be no need for any contact between the laser and the storage medium. There was much optimistic speculation concerning the storage capacity obtainable with optical systems although, as research progressed, it became evident that the limits of optical methods in most cases are determined by material properties and not by light properties, like wavelength or light velocity.

The key to the development of suitable optical data storage systems was the availability of appropriate storage materials and a wide range of materials and recording techniques were experimented with. The main requirements of the storage material were: high optical and mechanical stability, simple handling, large recording sensitivity with small recording energy, short recording time, high optical resolution, easily erasable and rewritable, easily duplicated and low cost. It was recognized, however, that these were very demanding and, in some cases, conflicting requirements and that some compromises would be needed. Research effort focused on holographic and 'bit-by-bit' recording techniques with holographic storage regarded by many as the most attractive option for permanent data storage for the following reasons.

With magnetic media, the presence of dust can cause information to be lost but with holographic storage systems the presence of dust or scratching would result only in a slight loss of resolution as the data is recorded throughout the entire recording medium. Also, for retrieving data on magnetic media, extreme accuracy is required in the location of the read head but the holographic system is very tolerant of positional inaccuracies. Finally, holographic storage systems were thought to have an enormous potential storage capacity.

In practice, however, this storage capacity could only be obtained using three-dimensional holograms as opposed to two-dimensional holograms, and the use of three-dimensional holograms has never proved a practical proposition. With two-dimensional holograms, the storage capacity is quite limited. Also, any digital holographic information storage system would depend upon the availability of a relatively high power laser, a number of complex electro-optical components including a deflection system, page composer and photodiode array, and the development of a suitable storage medium. Whilst most of these essential components were produced in the laboratory, it proved extremely difficult to create an erasable and fast switchable holographic storage material and, as a result, interest in holographic memories gradually declined.

Thus, in the early 1970s attention switched from holographic systems to 'bit-by-bit' systems where individual bits of information are recorded in a serial fashion using a low-power laser beam. A requirement of the laser was that it would have to have a small spot size for high data density and the semiconductor laser seemed the most promising. It was also decided that the ideal storage medium needed to be self-developing so that images could be viewed immediately after recording (a facility which became known as Direct Read After Write, DRAW) and at the time ablative thin films and organic dyes seemed the most promising.

At about the same time, it was also realized that the initial requirements made of optical storage systems were no longer relevant. With the development of semiconductor storage, the capacity of internal memories had increased a thousandfold, reducing the gap between internal storage and magnetic disc systems. Experts began to see that the main area of application for optical storage was not as an intermediate form of storage between internal and magnetic disc storage, but rather as a very large capacity mass storage medium to rival magnetic tape. At the same time it was realized that, in order to store these vast amounts of data, some form of mechanized storage unit would inevitably be needed.

This led manufacturers to experiment with a wide range of formats and mechanical systems for optical data storage. Precision Instruments produced their System 190 based on data strips mounted on rotating drums while Plessey developed a system using optical tape. The fact that the majority of systems available or under development today are now disc-based, however, is largely due to the realization that another new medium — the optical video disc — could be adapted for computer data storage and retrieval.

Readers interested in the history of the development of the optical videodisc should consult an earlier report (Hendley, 1985). This introduction will also look at videodiscs in more detail later. Suffice it to say here that in the 1960s, in addition to mechanical, magnetic and capacitive videodiscs, considerable work was going into the development of optical videodisc systems.

An experimental videodisc system designed and built at the Stanford Research Institute in the early 1960s with the support of the 3M company used optical principles. A high-resolution photographic plate was used as the recording medium and a high-pressure mercury vapour lamp with a Kerr-cell modulator was used as the light source. Although this work was not followed up at the time, it served to demonstrate the feasibility of using optical techniques for the recording of video signals. Using analogue techniques, it proved possible to record a 30 minute black-and-white television programme on a 305 mm diameter disc.

Another early videodisc development using optical techniques was the OROS (Optical Read-Only Storage) conceived and developed by the Teletron Data Corporation under contract to the US Office of Naval Research. In this system, analogue or digital data stored on a conventional audio disc could be read by a non-contacting optical read head, tracking being controlled by a pair of photocells straddling the image of the groove in the head.

Since then, all significant work on optical videodisc systems has been centred around the use of laser recording and, in most cases, laser playback systems. All the optical videodisc systems that have been launched in the past five years (with the exception of the McDonnell Douglas system) make use of a mastering technique based on Philips technology but there have been a number of different replication systems employed and a number of different playback systems.

The range of optical storage products

So optical storage devices were developing along several parallel tracks, geared for different sectors of the market. Today, some 10 years on, this research has spawned a comprehensive family of optical storage systems that, like magnetic media before them, are beginning to have a major impact in the consumer video and audio playback market, the education and training field, electronic publishing, data distribution and the rapidly converging areas of office automation, data processing and records management.

As major names launch products, there is considerable interest in the potential of these optical storage devices and the impact they will have on current video cassette recording systems, phonographic records, audio cassettes, microforms and magnetic media. However, there is also a lot of confusion, with many potential users and suppliers of systems unaware of the many different types of optical discs, cards and tapes becoming available and the benefits and limitations of each one.

There are a number of ways of dividing up the range of optical media. The simplest, and the one adopted here, is to distinguish firstly between three functional varieties of optical media: read-only opical media, write-once optical media, and erasable/rewritable optical media.

Read-only optical media

Read-only optical media are, by their very nature, publishing or distri-bution media because, as their name implies, all the end user receives is a replicated read-only disc that he places in a player in order to read the data, text, audio or video information contained on the disc. There are no facilities for the user to record his data onto a read-only disc. In that sense, read-only discs are like gramophone records or books. They are produced in quantity from a master copy and distributed to end users who read the information off the discs with the aid of a mechanical player. The pro-duction techniques employed for each category of read-only optical media are described in more detail below.

In chronological terms, the first read-only optical disc to become avail-able commercially was the 12 inch optical videodisc in 1978, followed by the 8 inch optical videodisc and the 4.72 inch (12 cm) compact audio disc in 1982, hybrid 12 inch videodisc systems in 1984, the 4.72 inch CD-ROM in 1985, the 12 inch Laservision ROM in 1986, the 4.72 inch CD-video in 1987 and in future CD-Interactive and many more CD derivatives plus the 5.25 inch OROM and optical cards from companies such as Drexler Technology and Dai Nippon Printing. The main types of optical read-only media on the marketplace, their strengths and weaknesses and their application areas are described below.

Write-Once Read-Many (WORM) optical discs

The second category of optical storage media — WORMs — owes more to research in the computing industry than in the consumer electronics industry and are primarily storage media rather than publishing media, although they can be used for low-volume data distribution. With WORM discs, it is possible for the end user to record data on the discs inhouse. The term Write-Once Read-Many is slightly misleading as it tends to imply that all the data has to be written onto the disc at the same time. This is not the case. In fact users can continue to record data onto sections of the discs over a period of time measured in years until the disc is full. In effect they are 'write many times and read many times' discs. However, the key point is that any one sector of the disc can only be written on once. It is not possible to overwrite data onto a sector that has already been used or to erase and rerecord data on the same sector, so in that sense each sector of the disc is 'write once read many times'.

This characteristic makes WORM optical discs an ideal archival storage medium and they are already challenging magnetic tape in a number of applications such as a data archiving medium. They are also challenging microfilm as a medium for the storage of facsimile scanned images of documents where their high storage capacity, random accessibility and write-once nature are major advantages.

There are already 5.25 inch, 8 inch, 12 inch and 14 inch WORM optical discs on the market. Write-once optical cards and a write-once version of a CD-ROM called CD-PROM are under development. The main application areas for write-once optical media are in the professional marketplace.

Erasable/rewritable optical media

The third category of optical media is erasable rewritable media. These are not yet commercially available but have been demonstrated in prototype form by major companies including 3M and Sony. They use a range of recording techniques including magneto-optic and phase change. The main difference between erasable and WORM optical media is that with WORM systems the act of recording the data is irreversible. A pit is formed or a bubble created or an irreversible chemical change effected. With erasable optical media, the recording process can be reversed, the data deleted and new data rerecorded on the same sector, just as with magnetic media. While erasable optical media have been a long time in development, considerable efforts are being poured into their research because long term they offer all the functionality of existing magnetic discs, cassettes, tapes etc., but with added advantages of removability, higher storage densities and greater durability. Erasable optical media will find applications in the consumer and professional marketplace.

A review of the range of optical media on the market or under development

Table 1.1 lists the main optical storage and distribution media under one of the above three functional categories. All the major optical storage and

Table 1.1 Optical disc functional varieties

Read-only media (publishing /distribution)
Videodiscs
Hybrid discs
LV-ROM
CD audio
CD-ROM
CD-I
CDV
CD-IV
OROM

Write-once read-many (WORM) media (storage, archiving)
CD-PROM
Recordable videodiscs — OMDR
5.25 inch digital optical discs
8 inch
12 inch
14 inch

Erasable/rewritable media (consumer and mainstream computing applications)
Phase change/magneto-optic
3.5 inch
5.25 inch
2 inch?

---

distribution systems that are either on the market, or about to be launched into the marketplace, are now described in order to help put CD-ROM in context and get a feel for the scope and breadth of applications for optical storage products.

Videodiscs

Videodiscs were originally developed by consumer electronic companies looking for an alternative to video cassette recording systems for the lucrative domestic video playback market. The majority of commercially available videodiscs are read-only media used for the distribution and display of pre-recorded video, still-frame images and, in some cases, digital information. Production of a videodisc involves three main stages: pre-mastering, mastering and replication/dissemination. Pre-mastering refers to the process of recording video, still-frame or digital information onto a master videotape that is used as the input to the mastering process. Mastering involves transferring the information contained on the video-tape onto a master videodisc. Replication then involves the creation of a number of sub-masters or stampers from that master videodisc and the production of large volumes of duplicates from these sub-masters using a mix of techniques including pressing, injection moulding and optical duplication.

Establishing a videodisc mastering or replication facility involves the investment of millions of pounds due to the sophisticated equipment involved and the need to maintain 100% clean room conditions and there are, therefore, relatively few videodisc mastering and replication facilities available worldwide. Most of them are owned and operated by the manufacturers of the discs and the players themselves.

Videodiscs were primarily developed to compete with the video cassette recorder for a share of the lucrative consumer market for video recording and playback systems. Videodiscs, it was felt, would compete with video cassette recorders (VCRs) in the same way that audio records compete with audio cassettes. Advantages claimed for the videodisc systems were that disc replication costs were low and hence the discs would be cheap to buy, the players would be cheaper than VCRs, the image quality offered by videodiscs would be superior to cassettes, there would be far less wear during playback and the videodisc systems would be far more flexible, offering facilities such as freeze-frame, random access and slow speed forward and back. The main drawback with the videodiscs, as with the audio discs, is, of course, that they are playback-only devices which means that the user must either buy or hire all the films and other material that he wants to view. He cannot simply buy a blank videodisc and record onto it from the television, as he can, of course, with VCR systems.

This lack of a record facility has, to a large extent, prevented videodiscs taking off as a consumer system. However, the many extra features offered by some laser-based optical videodisc players compared to VCRs have made videodisc systems very attractive in the more specialized institutional audio-visual field where they are being used for education, training, point-of-sale promotion and simulation exercises.

While video recording has much in common with audio recording, video recording requires some 210 times more bandwidth than audio recording. This means that video recording makes greater demands on the capacity of the recording system. Therefore, one of the main aims of those companies who were developing videodisc systems was to invent recording systems capable of the very high packing density needed to store this very much greater amount of information. One other major requirement was for a relatively cheap recording medium. A number of recording and playback techniques were experimented with including mechanical, magnetic, capacitive and optical (see *Figure 1.1*) but the only two to be widely used commercially were capacitive systems and optical systems.

The term capacitive is applied to those videodisc systems in which changes in capacitance between the tip of an electrode carried on a flat surface of a stylus and a metallic coating on a videodisc are used to tune an electronic circuit to reconstruct a recorded signal. The two main pioneers of this technique were RCA with their Selectavision CED system and JVC with their VHD (Very High Density) system. RCA targetted their system at the consumer market but sales were disappointing due to the lack of a record facility and they eventually pulled out. The VHD system was launched later in the UK by Thorn EMI and was targetted at the institutional market for interactive training and promotional video systems. Although the use of a stylus limits the degree of interactivity that can be achieved on the system, the low cost of the system enabled Thorn to capture a part of this market. However, there is little scope for improving the facilities offered on the VHD system and industry observers do not expect that the system will ever be used for mainstream storage of digital information.

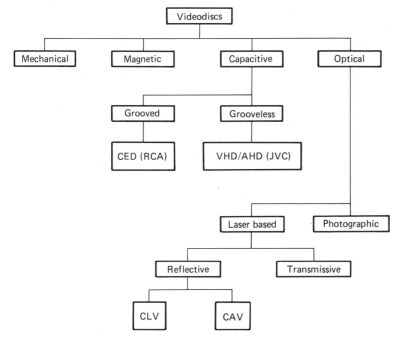

Figure 1.1 Recording and playback techniques

This leaves optical systems based round the use of a laser beam for both recording and playback. These form the basis for all the other videodisc, compact disc and digital optical disc systems that will be described in this chapter (see *Figure 1.2*). As pointed out above, all the optical videodisc systems launched in the past five years make use of a mastering technique developed by Philips; this will be briefly described as it is also used for the creation of most of the other optical disc systems. All that basically differs is the amount and type of material that is recorded onto the master disc and the type of coatings placed on the discs once they have been created.

For videodisc mastering, the program information which can be stored on film or tape, is read by a helical scan videotape unit and used to modulate the intensity of a laser beam that is focused on a rotating glass master disc coated with a thin film of photoresist. Once recording is completed, the exposed areas of photoresist are etched away to leave a master disc containing video information encoded in its periodicity and length as pits. The master's recording surface is then metallized using an evaporated coating and becomes the source for generating identical submasters; these are used to produce stampers, which in turn produce hundreds or thousands of identical copies of the master videodisc for distribution to users with videodisc players and television monitors.

To playback the replicated videodiscs, all the major laser optic videodisc systems make use of the same basic playback technique, which involves using a low-power laser as a stylus and a photo-detector to collect the light reflected by the disc. Such systems are called reflective systems. The Philips

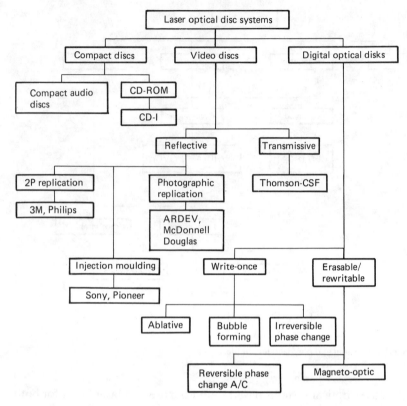

Figure 1.2 Laser optical disc systems

discs have a diameter of 20 cm (12 in) and the information is encoded on the disc as a series of pits or holes, which vary in length and spacing, arranged on a spiral track. A single track of pits or flats (lands) contains all the information necessary for a colour video programme with stereo sound or two separate sound channels plus control data for playback operations. There are some 54 000 tracks per disc side and the disc rotates at 1800 rev/min for US 60 Hz 525-line systems and 1500 rev/min for European 50 Hz 625-line systems. The information on the disc is read by pointing a laser beam onto the underside of the disc and focusing it directly into the bottom of the pits. The light is then diffracted and reflected back through servo-tracking mirrors to a photodiode.

The information can be recorded on the disc in two different ways to cater for two different markets. For the consumer market, where all that is required is the serial playback of feature films etc., the chief aim is to provide the maximum playback time per disc side. Hence Philips abandoned the principle of one video frame per revolution of the disc and varied the velocity of the disc to give Constant Linear Velocity (CLV) mode or long-play mode. This involves expanding the playback time of each side of the disc by placing two or even three frames on the outer tracks of the disc where the circumference of the disc is greater and one frame on the inner, shorter tracks. The result is that a 12 inch CLV mode videodisc can hold 60 minutes of video on each side, a total of two hours per disc.

The alternative mode is Constant Angular Velocity (CAV) mode or active play mode where one frame is allocated to each track. The disc rotates at a constant velocity with linear tracking velocity increasing from the innermost track where it is least to the outermost track where it is greatest. As each track holds one video frame, a single frame can be frozen on the screen by directing the laser beam read head to scan one track continuously. The speed and direction of the read head can be exactly controlled and each frame on each disc (54 000 per side) can be numbered. The read head can be required to go and read one at speeds measured in fractions of a second. The CAV discs have proved successful in interactive training and point-of-sale systems. A hierarchy of players and systems have evolved to meet differing market requirements:

- *Level 0* players offer basic serial play facilities.
- *Level 1* players offer additional still-frame, forward and reverse play facilities under remote keypad control.
- *Level 2* players have their own internal microprocessor controllers and hence can be programmed to display frames in a set sequence.
- *Level 3* systems comprise a level 2 player connected to and controlled by a microcomputer.
- *Level 4* systems are available now with a number of players controlled by a computer and a range of graphic overlay and simulation facilities.

Hybrid videodiscs

Professor Barrett at Hatfield Polytechnic was one of the first people in the UK to take delivery of a level 2 player in the UK, courtesy of a grant from the British Library's Research and Development Department. The player was shown at a number of library and publishing conferences. The level of interest was phenomenal with both librarians and publishers quick to grasp the potential of such optical publishing media once digital data could be recorded on the discs alongside video information.

Hybrid videodiscs are those videodiscs that have been used to store digital data in analogue form or, more usually, a mixture of digital data and analogue information. Given the figures for CAV videodiscs, it was not surprising that a number of companies should investigate the potential of standard videodiscs for distributing digital data. Although videodiscs are an analogue recording medium, there are very few limitations placed upon the type of signal that can be stored on a videodisc as the channel is clean and wideband. Any signal that can be segmented for insertion of TV-type synchronization bursts and that fits within a 4.2 MHz 40 dB band can be recorded onto a videodisc and recovered by a standard player and some form of outboard decoder, e.g. digital data, audio and very high resolution video. Digital data can be impressed on the lines of a composite video frame as well as analogue video signals. In theory, some 400 bits can be written on each TV line and with approx 500 lines per frame, one frame per track and 50 000 tracks per side that gives a theoretical storage capacity of at least 1 gigabyte of data per side, making the videodisc a potentially low-cost, high-density, data distribution medium.

The development of a range of different recording techniques for encoding digital data onto standard videodiscs by a number of US companies, including Laserdata, Reference Technology and TMS, allowed a number of publishers and database providers to take their first tentative steps into optical publishing. Provided the publisher had the material in machine-readable form, all he had to do was send it on half-inch magnetic tapes to one of the above companies and they would encode the data, arrange for it to be recorded onto a master videodisc, stamp out replicate discs containing the data and provide the publisher's clients with the relevant hardware and software needed to read the data back from the discs.

One major problem with these hybrid videodisc based information delivery systems was a lack of standardization. All three companies used proprietary encoding techniques and different hardware at the workstation with the result that TMS videodiscs could not be played back on a Laserdata workstation etc. Laserdata themselves offered the end user a workstation comprising an industrial videodisc player linked to a decoder/ controller unit that was in turn linked to an IBM PC. The user searched the data via the keyboard on the microcomputer, the data was read off the videodisc, a frame at a time, converted in real time from analogue to digital format, passed through the error detection and correction system and then displayed on the computer screen. Reference Technology, on the other hand, opted not to use a standard videodisc player and developed their own Datadrive 2000, a high-specification drive with millisecond access speeds, integral error detection and correction (EDAC) system and a number of outlet ports so that it could be accessed by multiple users at their own microcomputers.

A second problem was the relatively high price of the hardware. The Laserdata end user workstation would cost £8000 and could only be used by one person at a time.

These two factors — the lack of standards and the relatively high cost of the hardware — have tended to restrict the number of applications where hybrid systems have been used. Hybrid systems are not generally popular with generic publishers who are looking for a standard medium, like paper or microfilm, that everyone can access and that libraries and businesses will invest in the hardware to access. However, hybrid systems have been used by a number of specialist information providers who have a closed user base so they can opt for one particlar system and major on it. One major advantage of hybrid systems is, of course, the ability to store a range of different types of information on one disc including text, data and high quality video.

Recently, a major new player in the hybrid arena has been Philips themselves, with their Laservision ROM system. This is a new generation Laservision player, designed specifically for the BBC, that can accept discs holding the standard 54 000 frames of video on each side plus a further 324 megabytes of digital data per side, recorded in the twin audio tracks on the disc. The player can be connected to a standard television set and microcomputers from Acorn and Research Machines and the BBC have developed their Domesday discs to play on a Laservision ROM player. Domesday occupies three sides of the 12 inch hybrid discs and comprises approx 150 000 frames of motion and still-frame video plus approximately 1 gigabyte of digital data. The hardware package for accessing the Domesday discs is available for approximately £3000.

Compact discs

Compact discs (CDs) were later on the market than optical videodiscs. Optical videodiscs were first shown in 1973 and became commercially available in the US in 1978. Compact discs were first shown in 1980 and were launched commercially in 1983. However, sales of compact disc players to the consumer market have already outstripped sales of videodisc players in what has been described as one of the most successful launches of a consumer electronic product ever. It has been estimated that approximately one million videodisc players have been installed worldwide whereas already some 15 million CD players have been installed worldwide.

CDs are designed to compete with gramophone records for a share of the audio playback market. CD systems are all standardized on the format and digital recording techniques designed by Philips and the error detection and correction systems jointly developed by Philips and Sony. These are embodied in what is known as the Philips and Sony 'Red Book', which is made available, on the payment of a small licence fee, to companies who wish to have a license to produce discs or drives that meet the standard. The main aim of the standard is to achieve total compatibility so all CDs produced to the standard can be played on all CD players designed to meet the standard. It is this compatibility that has led to the CD's success in the consumer marketplace.

The physical processes involved in producing a CD are virtually identical to those for a videodisc except that the material recorded on the disc is in a different format and the master and replicate discs are single sided with a 12 cm (4.72 inch) diameter rather than 12 inches.

Production of a CD is a three-stage process comprising pre-mastering, mastering and replication. At pre-mastering, audio information is recorded onto digital tape to provide a standard input to the mastering process. At the mastering stage the audio information stored on tape is recorded onto a glass master CD using a laser beam. The replication stage involves the creation of a number of sub-masters from the master CD and the production of large volumes of replicate discs from these sub-masters.

The key difference between CDs and videodiscs, other than their size, is that the audio information is stored on the CD in digital form. CDs are a digital storage medium while videodiscs are essentially an analogue storage medium. With CDs, the audio information is digitally encoded prior to storage on the discs and is read off the discs as a bit stream at rates in excess of 4 megabits per second. At the output stage the digital information on the CDs is passed through a digital to analogue converter for output as a series of audio signals that can then be replayed on standard consumer high-fidelity systems making use of the same amplifier and loudspeaker systems as would be used to replay the signals picked up from a record or cassette deck.

For CD replication, the basic raw material used is a polycarbonate called macrolon that is liquidized and injected under high pressure and heat into the injection moulding machines. After moulding, the single disc surface that carries the pits is coated with a thin layer of aluminium to produce a reflecting surface for the laser beam. The surface itself is coated with a protective layer that is dripped on the rotating disc. Before labelling and packaging the disc is centred and the centre hole punched in.

Like analogue records, CDs are produced with a run-in section, a music section and a run-out section, all of which contain information in digital form. In the run-in section, CDs have a table of contents and details of the number of recorded tracks and the time from the start of the disc to each track. Data is recorded onto each CD master in a spiral of tracks starting at the inside of the disc and working outwards. There is provision for dividing each CD into a maximum of 99 tracks. The standard 12 cm disc contains some 20 000 spirals in the programme area and in these are recorded a series of laser cut pits. Using this recording technique, one 12 cm CD can store over 60 minutes of high-quality stereo. When error correction and detection codes are taken into account, this represents a storage capacity of 7 gigabits.

Playback of the discs in a CD player involves the use of a laser optical system that has to be positioned accurately over the relevant track on the disc and accurately focused on the disc's recorded surface. The CD player uses the same reflective system as the videodiscs to read the data from the discs. A low-power laser beam is shone onto the disc's recorded surface, and the intensity of the reflected laser beam is less when the laser reads a pit than when the laser beam reads a land. The different intensities of reflected light are detected by photocells and constitute the raw digital signal.

The CDs are played back at a constant linear velocity of 1.25 metres per second from the inside to the outside, which means that the rotational speed varies from 430 to 200 rev/min. CLV mode is employed to maximize the storage capacity and hence the playing time, but access is slower than with CAV discs. In practice, a particular piece of music on the disc is accessed not via its track number (1–99) but by its position on the disc spiral counted in terms of the time it takes to reach it in normal playback from the beginning of the disc. This is not a significant limitation when storing audio information, but it limits the applications for CDs as a computer storage peripheral (see the next section on CD-ROM). The final significant point about CDs is that, since they are a digital storage medium, they are supplied with a sophisticated error detection and correction system devised by Philips and Sony that serves as the basis for the error detection and correction system used on CD-ROMs.

Because of their success in the consumer market, the price of CD players has come down dramatically from £700 when they were first launched to £100–£200 depending on the features included. This is because development costs can now be amortized over large sales volumes and components can be bought in bulk and mass produced. It is extremely significant as it means that any computer peripheral based around the CD format (e.g. CD-ROM) can take advantage of the low-cost components.

CD-ROMs (Compact Disc Read-Only Memories)

The section earlier on hybrid videodiscs described how an analogue consumer product was adapted and used by a number of companies to develop information delivery systems based on hybrid videodiscs. It was not surprising, therefore, that when a digital consumer product — the compact disc — was introduced, computer manufacturers, software suppliers, publishers and database providers should take a considerable interest in the potential of this new medium as a computer storage peripheral and an electronic publishing medium.

The result was that, within two years of the launch of the first commercial CD player and the availability of the Red Book standard, Philips showed a CD-ROM player that was, in essence, a direct adaptation of the CD system for publishing and data processing applications. The worldwide Red Book standard was extended in the CD-ROM Yellow Book standard to cover the requirements of the data processing environment so the new CD-ROM drives and discs could benefit from the use of proven technologies.

CD-ROMs and CDs are both mass produced using the same physical mastering and replication processes. Plant designed to master and replicate CDs can be adapted to master and replicate CD-ROMs. The discs have the same physical dimension and chemical composition, the CD-ROM drives rotate at the same speeds as the CD players, and both CD and CD-ROM discs are recorded and read in CLV mode. The CD-ROM drives and CD players use the same modulation systems and error detection and correction systems, defined in the Red and Yellow Books as EFM (eight to fourteen modulation) and CIRC (cross-interleaved Reed Solomon coding). However, CD-ROMs are primarily designed to store digital data whereas CDs are designed to store digitally encoded audio information; hence the CD-ROM Yellow Book standard has made provision for more accurate addressing of data blocks and for an extra level of error detection and correction.

Both CDs and CD-ROMs use the same basic control and display (subcoding) systems for locating/addressing information. As we have seen, the subcoding system for CDs and CD-ROMs divides the disc into three parts: the lead-in area, the programme area and the lead-out area. With CDs and CD-ROMs, the programme area can be divided into a maximum of 99 tracks. For CDs storing only digitally encoded audio information, this is sufficient to enable any section of audio to be addressed quickly. With CD-ROM, as defined in the Yellow Book, such a division is not sufficient and there is a need to add a facility to access specific data more precisely and to provide for extra error correction. Hence, in the Yellow Book, provision is made for every one of the 99 tracks or programmes to contain either digitally encoded audio information or pure digital data. The two types of information are handled in different ways and are referred to as two different modes. In practice, most CD-ROMs produced today contain just one data programme but the standard will support mixed-mode discs holding both pure data and digitally encoded audio and a range of other types of information.

The error detection and correction specified in the Red Book standard is adequate for storing audio information, where one lost bit will not affect the sound reproduction and data, to quote Philips, tends to degrade gracefully, but it would not be adequate for storing pure digital data, where one uncorrected bit error could mean the difference between a plus or a minus sign on your bank balance. The result is that CD-ROM drives require a further level of error detection and correction than CD players.

To achieve this, the Yellow Book standard divides the data programmes on a CD-ROM into logical units — 2 kilobyte blocks — one of which is stored in each physical sector on the CD-ROM. One CD-ROM is divided up into 60 minutes of playback; 60 seconds within each minute of playback and 75 fractions of a second within each second of playback. Each 75th of a second of playback represents one physical sector on the CD-ROM and hence each CD-ROM has a storage capacity of $270\,000 \times 2$ kilobytes = 552.96 megabytes.

Each sector on the CD-ROM disc actually contains some 98 CD frames, each of 24 bytes, to give a total sector capacity of 2352 bytes of data of which 2048 bytes are always for user data and the remaining 304 bytes are used for data that the drives need to locate data on the disc, additional error correction systems or additional user data, as illustrated below:

Synchronization field	12 bytes
Header field	4 bytes
User data field	2048 bytes
Auxiliary data field	288 bytes
Total	2352 bytes

At present, in the Yellow Book standard, mode 1 is defined for computer data storage where, as explained above, the additional error correction is required and hence the 288 bytes in the auxiliary data field are used for another level of error detection and correction. A second mode is defined for information which will degrade gracefully, and here the existing EDAC system specified in the Red Book is adequate. With mode 2 the 288 bytes in the auxiliary data field are used to store more user information, and hence in mode 2 the CD-ROM has a total storage capacity of $270\,000 \times 2336$ bytes = 630 megabytes.

The result is that, in future, the same basic CD-ROM drive could be used for both audio playback and data retrieval. Already a number of combined audio/data CD-ROM drives have been shown.

In CD-ROM production, the disc mastering and production facilities that are already well established for the CD audio system can also be used to produce CD-ROMs. The only process that differs significantly is the data preparation/pre-mastering required to produce the master tape. The effort involved at the data preparation stage will depend on a number of variables, such as whether the data is already in machine readable form, whether it is in a database format, how it is to be organized and presented on the screen, and what retrieval software is required. These aspects of CD-ROM production are dealt with in more detail below.

Basically, if a CD-ROM is being used to distribute a database, the database has to be organized, indexed and formatted by a data preparation facility or the publisher; suitably formatted magnetic tapes are then sent to a mastering facility where the tapes carrying the customer's database, divided into 2 kilobyte blocks, are processed in order to add the necessary synchronization patterns, headers and error detection and correction codes required to form CD-ROM sectors. During recording, the information is encoded into the CD format and the process follows as for the CD audio.

With a user storage capacity of 550 megabytes, CD-ROM has the equivalent storage capacity of approximately 500–1000 floppy discs, 27 twenty-megabyte Winchester discs, 10–20 magnetic tapes and 3–500 COM microfiche. Putting it another way, it would theoretically be possible to store some 200 000 pages of text created on a word processor on one CD-ROM, or approximately 10 000 raster-scanned facsimile page images. This should serve to highlight CD-ROM's potential as an electronic publishing medium. Its strengths and weaknesses as a publishing medium are looked at in more detail below.

The question of CD-ROM standards is a complex one and has been the subject of several reports (Schwerin and Hendley, 1988; Schwerin, Lightbourn, Bailey and Kaikow, 1988). When dealing with CDs, it was stated that the Red Book standard ensured that all CDs could be played on all CD players. Physically this is true with CD-ROMs too; any CD-ROM disc produced to the Yellow Book standard can physically be placed into any CD-ROM drive and can be read. However, because CD-ROM drives are computer peripherals and users need a computer to access and process the data stored on the CD-ROMs, a number of other factors militate against total compatibility of all CD-ROMs and all CD-ROM retrieval stations.

The first and most critical factor is the volume and file structures used on the CD-ROM discs — the logical format — or, in other words, how the data is organized on the disc. The Yellow Book standard does not address this issue because it is directly linked to the operating system environment where the CD-ROM is likely to be used. Hence for CD-ROMs to be readable on a range of computer systems by a range of operating systems, there was a need to define a CD-ROM volume and file structure standard. A group of computer companies, software companies and CD-ROM system integrators met together in the US and formed the High Sierra Group (HSG); they attempted to cater for this requirement by producing a 'Working Paper for Information Processing — Volume and File Structure of Compact Read Only Optical Discs for Information Interchange'. This standard has now been endorsed by ECMA, the European Computer Manufacturers Association, and was on its way to becoming an ISO (International Standards Organization) standard as this chapter was completed.

The logical format is one of the three key components of a CD-ROM file management system. The file management system stands between the application software running on the computer and the controller that controls the disc drive. A file management system basically comprises software and data structures designed to convert the physical, sector-oriented view of the disc held by its controller into a logical view that the application program can use. In CD-ROM drives, a CD-ROM drive controller views the CD-ROM disc as a sequence of 2 kilobyte sectors spread over 60 minutes of recording time with 75 sectors in each second of the recording, a total of 270 000 sectors. Viewed logically, however, a CD-ROM is a collection of files, each with its own unique name. The application program needs to be able to call for a file by name and, once the file is open, read it, however long it is, regardless of the fact that the information in the file has to be read in 2 kilobyte blocks or that each sector has a precise physical address.

A CD-ROM file management system, therefore, is designed to allow users to view the disc as a collection of files. A complete CD-ROM file management system comprises three major components: the structure or logical format of the data, the software that writes the data in that format (origination software), and the software that reads and translates the logical format for use (destination software).

The logical format of the CD-ROM disc will determine where to put identifying data on the disc, where to find the directory or directories of files on the disc, how the directory is structured, whether subdirectories are supported, how many files can be stored on a CD-ROM, the performance cost of storing large numbers of files, how large a file can be, whether files can span multiple volumes, and whether files must consist of sequential consecutive sectors. The logical format must be clearly distinguished from the physical format of the disc, defined in the Philips/Sony Yellow Book, which is considered as given by the file management system.

The origination software component of a CD-ROM file is dealt with in more detail below when looking at the stages involved in producing a CD-ROM product. Basically, before mastering a CD-ROM, the files that are going to be recorded on the disc must be assembled and a directory created according to the rules of the logical format. Origination software does this work, effectively providing the writing component of the file system.

The destination software component is the software, running on the end user's computer, that understands the logical format and can use it to provide access to the files on the disc. The destination software is effectively the reading component of the file system.

To fully appreciate the need for a CD-ROM volume and file structure standard, compare what is involved in mounting a database on CD-ROM to what is involved in mounting a database on magnetic disc. If the database files were being loaded onto a standard random-access erasable magnetic disc then a reserved segment of the disc containing the volume directory would be updated to indicate their arrival, their location and other information. In addition to the volume label or name, the volume directory would contain information about every file on the disc including the file name, the start address, the file length and, if required, information about creation data, file organization and access privilege. The construction of the volume directory and the maintenance of its entries is, of course, the responsibility of the computer system's operating system and the procedures would be proprietary.

In the case of CD-ROM, however, while it is of course necessary to construct a similar directory and insert the various statistics that describe the files to be loaded on the disc, this is not the responsibility of any particular operating system. Rather, it is the responsibility of the disc producer or data preparation facility to define the volume directory and to ensure that correct entries are inserted.

To create the volume directory and the file structure, the disc producer must write a file structure creation program. Currently there are a number of proprietary programs designed to create a number of proprietary file structures. Any volume directory structure can be defined, but it is then the responsibility of the disc producer to produce CD-ROM device drivers and file servers to interpret the directory correctly so that the required data can be transferred to the search program running under a particular operating system.

Now that the HSG and ECMA have outlined a working file format standard, the disc producers can devise one file structure creation program that complies with the format specified by the HSG. This should pave the way for the CD-ROM drive manufacturers and operating system suppliers to cooperate and provide the necessary device drivers and file servers so that operating systems can deal with CD-ROM drives as yet another standard peripheral.

The second factor relates to the CD-ROM drives. Drives have different controllers, and the commands that controllers accept and the format they must be supplied in are not standardized. Then there is the physical/logical connection between the host microcomputers and the controller. This is another area where, now the file structure standard is agreed, *de facto* standards will need to be worked out.

The third factor relates to the choice of retrieval software. If a publisher wishes to provide free text retrieval facilities — an almost essential requirement when dealing with such large databases — then a retrieval software supplier such as BRS or Harwell has to be chosen and the data organized according to the requirements of that supplier. In addition, the publisher will have to supply versions of that retrieval software package with the database, either on the CD-ROM itself or on a separate floppy disc. This will immediately limit the range of computer/operating systems that the CD-ROM can be used on. The limiting factors will be how many versions of the software package there are, which operating systems they run on, and what is the minimum RAM and magnetic disc storage required on the PC to support the destination software.

Stages in the production of CD-ROM databases

The stages involved in the production of a CD-ROM are now briefly outlined before concluding this overview of CD-ROM with a look at the retrieval workstations that users need to purchase to access CD-ROM databases. Both these areas will be covered in more detail in later chapters, so here it is sufficient to provide information to enable CD-ROM to be compared with the other optical storage media described in this introduction.

The type and volume of data that is being and will be placed on CD-ROM varies dramatically, and the way in which that data is organized will also vary widely depending on the application. It is not surprising, there-fore, that the software vendors and data preparation companies who specialize in preparing the data prior to recording it on CD-ROM are developing a range of different services based around software that runs on a wide range of hardware, to cater for all requirements.

Anyone producing a CD-ROM database has to follow three sets of rules. At the base level, the Yellow Book defines the physical characteristics of the disc and the data format and provides for a basic level of physical compatibility. The second level is the organizational or logical level, where the High Sierra Group standard lays down a logical format standard that provides for data to be organized on CD-ROM in a form which, given the necessary hardware and software interfaces between drives, computers and operating systems, will enable it to be accessed by multiple operating systems running on a range of computer hardware. The third level is the publishing or database level, where the publisher cooperates with a vendor of retrieval software, organizes and indexes his database to their specifications, and makes available the retrieval element of the software package to users to access the database on CD-ROM as efficiently as possible via a PC.

Bearing in mind these three sets of requirements, there are actually eight stages involved in the production of a CD-ROM database.

The first stage is to choose an existing database or collection of data that is well suited to distribution on CD-ROM, or to step back and plan a new database or publication that takes full advantage of the strengths and weaknesses of CD-ROM as a distribution medium.

Having identified the data the second stage is to capture and place it in a format that can be accepted by the software vendor/system integrator who is going to organize and index the database for the publisher.

The third stage is database creation where, once the relevant data has been captured, it is organized into a database format so that the data is easily accessible and meets the search requirements of potential users. Many of the processes involved in planning, organizing, indexing and inverting a database for CD-ROM publication today will simply follow the processes established for creating an online database. The first step is to ensure that the data exists in ASCII coded form on magnetic tape. The second step is for the information provider and the software vendor to consult together and plan the database. The third step is to divide the database or data file into a series of logical constructs — records or documents — that will then be divided into fields, the size and shape of which will also be designed to meet the requirements of the application. The records then need to be structured to meet the requirements of the application, screen formats are designed, decisions are made on whether fixed or variable length fields or both are required, and a set of descriptors or headers is defined to identify the records retrieved as the result of a search.

The next step is to define whether all or just a part of each record is to be searchable and within each area of the record which is to be searchable to define a stop word list. The final step covers application-specific requirements such as the handling of non-standard character sets, computer graphics and digitized images.

Once the planning has been done, the database will need to be formatted prior to being loaded. The formatted data is inverted using a specific software program running on anything from a PC to a powerful mainframe, depending on the size of the database. Each record in the database is processed and every significant word in each searchable field is extracted and stored, along with a corresponding record number, field identifier and a location identifier for that word, in order to build up an occurrence list or inverted file. Once the conversion is complete and the desired user interface/screen format has been designed then we move on to the fourth stage in the CD-ROM production process.

The fourth stage is data preparation. With the data captured and the database designed, data preparation involves creating the directory structure and mapping out the database onto the master magnetic tape from which the master CD-ROM will be produced.

The first three stages have to be gone through whatever medium the database was designed to be recorded on. At the data preparation stage, however, the process has to be geared specifically to the requirements of CD-ROM. The data preparer, publisher or system integrator has to construct a volume directory and insert the vital statistics that describe the files to be loaded on the disc. As we have seen above when discussing standards, currently they have a choice of using their own proprietary file structure creation program to create the volume directory and file structure or of using a file structure creation program that complies with the format specified by the High Sierra Group. Once the directory has been constructed, the final part of this process is for the various files that constitute the database to be concatenated together and, with the directory, to be re-blocked into 2 kilobyte blocks of data. The output from this process will then be recorded onto high-quality 1600 bits/inch magnetic tape ready for pre-mastering.

The fifth stage, pre-mastering, can either be done by the data preparation facility or, more commonly, by the CD-ROM mastering facility. Basically, pre-mastering comprises taking the database in 2 kilobyte blocks and adding the 12 bytes of synchronization data, 4 bytes of header data and the 288 bytes of additional error detection and correction coding that are specified in the Yellow Book standard. The pre-mastering process is fully covered by the standard, and the result of the process is a ¾ inch VCR tape that essentially contains the original data in a high-quality audio format.

The sixth stage is the actual creation of a CD-ROM master disc, as described above. The seventh stage is the replication process, also described above. The eighth stage relates to the packing and distribution of the CD-ROM discs, an area that needs to be investigated before large-scale commercial distribution of CD-ROM discs becomes a reality.

It is extremely difficult to quote an overall price for producing a CD-ROM as it depends on whether the data was already in coded form, the size of the database, the retrieval software chosen, the timescale required, the number of replicates produced, etc. The cost of capturing the data and placing it in a format that can be accepted by the software vendor must remain a variable. After that, database creation can cost from £10 000 to £50 000 depending on the size of the database and the sophistication of the database; data preparation and pre-mastering can cost from £5000 to £20 000 depending on the size of the database; mastering costs from £2000 to £3000; and the price per replicate disc ranges from £5 to £25 depending on volume. In addition, the software supplier will charge the publisher a royalty or licence fee for using the software.

CD-ROM workstations

Hardware

CD-ROM drives are computer peripherals and can either be attached to an installed base of host computers or supplied as part of a complete workstation package comprising a host computer, the physical and logical interface and the CD-ROM drive. The main target market for CD-ROM products is the growing number of PC users in business, government etc., so the first generation of CD-ROM workstations are all based around the IBM PC/XT/ AT and compatibles. Looking to the future, the IBM PC range, its clones and future upgrades, such as PS/2, will continue to form the basis of the majority of professional CD-ROM workstations, but inevitably, as the market for CD-ROM systems develops and specialized applications emerge, CD-ROM drives will be attached to a wide range of host computers. Already mainframe and minicomputer suppliers are looking at distributing user manuals and documentation on CD-ROM. Digital Equipment Corporation has developed links from the MicroVAX range of computers to CD-ROM. In the educational and publishing sectors, interfaces are being developed from CD-ROM to the range of Apple microcomputers.

There are an increasing number of CD-ROM drives coming onto the market and each new drive brings with it some advance. The two major suppliers in Europe at present at Hitachi and Philips, but Sony, JVC, Toshiba, Panasonic, Denon and many others are also now shipping CD-ROM drives. The first CD-ROM drives to be made available were stand-alone units, using the same casings as consumer CD players with top or front loading facilities. These were placed to one side of the PC or under the monitor. Hitachi then launched their CDR2500 front loading full-height 5.25 inch CD-ROM drive for integration into the PC. Recently Philips has introduced a half-height 5.25 inch CD-ROM drive that will use the PC's power source. The development of such drives means that portable CD-ROM viewing stations will become available based around lap-top size PCs; it also means that, whereas early CD-ROMs were supplied in the jewel boxes used for consumer CDs, CD-ROMs destined for use in half-height units will be supplied in plastic cartridges or caddies, akin to those used for the WORM optical discs, and there will be vertically loaded CD-ROM drives.

As the size of the CD-ROM drives comes down, so too does the price. When first introduced the CD-ROM drives plus interface cards and cables were priced at £1500–2000 but already they are priced at under £1000 in the UK; in the US, where they are sold by PC dealers and volumes are beginning to rise, it is possible to obtain CD-ROM drives for approximately £500.

The performance of the drives is also set to improve as smaller, lighter read lasers and better drive motors are employed. The first CD-ROM drives offered average access speeds of 1 second and worst-case access of 2 seconds. With the latest drives, this is down to 0.5 second average access and 1 second worst-case.

As mentioned earlier, most of the early products targeted the IBM PC base, specifying an IBM PC with the Intel 8086 microprocessor, the PC DOS version 2.0 or later, 256 kilobytes of RAM, dual floppy disc drives and a monochrome display. Two types of interface are common with the IBM PC. The *de facto* IBM PC bus interfaces can be used with a CD-ROM drive linked by a proprietary interface to a host resident controller card with a PC bus interface and with CD driver software. Alternatively the SCSI (Small Computer Systems Interface) standard I/O bus is used with the CD-ROM drive plus SCSI controller linked optionally with other CD-ROM drives, via the standard I/O SCSI interface to an SCSI host adapter with a PC bus interface and SCSI driver software with a CD-ROM module.

Software

There are four areas that need to be considered here. The first is the host computer's operating system; the second is the file structure creation program used to structure the files and build the directory on the CD-ROM; the third is the device drivers that act as a link between the file server software and the CD-ROM controller; the fourth is the application software.

The operating systems are given, and will partly determine the design of the device driver and file server software needed to control a CD-ROM drive and handle it as a peripheral of the host computer. For most applications, at present, MS DOS or PC DOS is assumed.

The role of the file structure creation program has already been described in the sections on standards and CD-ROM production. It is expected that each data preparer will be able to produce one file structure creation program, which will structure the files and produce directories that meet the provisions of the HSG standard.

The device driver is the next key element. If the operating system does not offer a device driver for a CD-ROM drive then the drive supplier or the software supplier must provide a specific device driver for each of the CD-ROM drives on the market or as many as they wish to support. The device driver provides a link between the file server software and the CD-ROM controller. For the foreseeable future, device drivers will be operating system and drive specific although, of course, combination device drivers can be designed that serve a number of drives or operating systems. When developing a device driver for Microsoft's MS DOS or PC DOS, until recently the software supplier had to supply additional software to overcome the 32 megabyte file size limit of current versions of MS DOS/PC DOS. However, Microsoft has recently introduced extensions to MS DOS that allow PC users running versions 3.1 and 3.2 onwards to read data from any CD-ROM disc that conforms to the final version of the HSG standard. The extensions allow the PC user to overcome the 32 megabyte file size limitation and access the full 550 megabytes stored on a CD-ROM or even on multiple CD-ROMs. The Microsoft extension aims to make the CD-ROM drive appear like any other magnetic disc drive to the user and to the application software. The MS DOS CDEX CD-ROM extension is classed as a separate product by Microsoft, so a separate licence fee is required and they are distributing it via CD-ROM drive suppliers and system integrators.

Looking to the future, one can expect a steady reduction in the price of CD-ROM drives, the development of dedicated CD-ROM workstations including portable CD-ROM readers, the development of specialized CD-ROM workstations for accessing images stored on CD-ROM (which will need to provide high-resolution monitors and laser print facilities), and the launch of CD-ROM type jukeboxes capable of loading one of a number of CD-ROMs into one of a number of CD-ROM drives.

On the software side, the High Sierra Group standard is expected to be widely adopted for new versions of PC and, indeed, most computer operating systems will be designed to support very high density read-only and write-once storage media as well as erasable media.

CD-Interactive (CD-I)

Just over a year after the launch of CD-ROM, on 24 February 1986, Philips and Sony announced plans for the CD-I specification that would be embodied in the Green Book standard. It was a rushed announcement at the Microsoft Conference and led to considerable confusion with some people seeing it as an alternative to CD-ROM and others as a development of CD audio. In effect, CD-I represents a logical development of the CD-ROM Yellow Book standard and is one of many CD variants provided for within the standard. Again, CD-I will be described in more detail later. Here it is only necessary to differentiate CD-I from CD-ROM, while at the same time showing the links between the two.

The CD-ROM Yellow Book standard is the basis for CD-I. CD-ROM is not outmoded by CD-I. CD-I is not a subset of CD-ROM. Instead it is a special use of CD-ROM that has several key components. Special use means that the CD-ROM data records can contain data in specific formats, including sixteen kinds of audio, two video resolutions, one microprocessor object code and one file system. CD-ROM is the foundation of all CD data format standards. These are like a tree where the trunk is CD-ROM and the branches, like CD-I and other new CD versions to follow, are all application specific. CD-I, as defined by Philips and Sony, is the consumer entertainment and education branch and attempts to meet all the requirements of that marketplace. The High Sierra Group proposed standard could equally be regarded as CD-C for CD-Commercial, aiming to meet commercial data processing requirements.

In summary, the CD-I recording format is identical to CD-ROM. CD-I simply gives the user some standard ways in which to represent common forms of information that they can use when the forms are appropriate for their application.

CD-I attempts to define a complete system because it is aimed at the consumer market. The requirement there is seen to be for an appliance that provides a particular function or set of functions and that is as simple to use as a record player or CD player. CD-I has to be a simple system and hence, while CD-I is logically an extension of the CD-ROM standard, conceptually CD-I also represents an extension of the CD audio concept of a consumer product offering total compatibility of discs and players by defining both the way in which information is recorded on the disc and the equipment needed to read the disc.

With CD-I, therefore, as with CD, Philips and Sony have defined not only the medium but also the equipment that will be needed to read it, the audio processes, the video processes, the choice of microprocessor and the operating system so they can achieve their goal of being able to play all CD-I discs on all CD-I players.

In addition, because CD-I players will be used in the home, it is a requirement that CD audio discs can be played on CD-I players too. It is also expected, and claimed by Philips, that, following the work of the HSG, data recorded on CD-ROM according to the provisions made by the HSG standard would also potentially be readable on a CD-I player. Certainly Philips are committed to using the volume and file structures defined by the HSG working standard in their CD-I discs. However, for a database on CD-ROM to be usable on CD-I, the software vendor would need to have developed his software specifically to run on the CD-I player and use the CD-I player's operating systems. Although this could potentially be done in the future, very little standard retrieval software, particularly free text retrieval software, would be able to run on the CD-I player.

In effect, therefore, while CD-I is still a computer peripheral and computer interfaces to link a CD-I player to other computer systems will be available, a computer itself will be incorporated in the CD-I player so there will be no need to attach a CD-I player to a computer system to access the data. All that is required will be to link the CD-I player to a standard television set or monitor and control it via a keypad or mouse device. The CD-I player will not have any magnetic disc drives so all the information (including the application program, the additional information needed for the operating system and all the data) must be on the CD-I disc itself, as that will be the only medium used to run the complete application.

CD-I is a complete self-contained specification based on three basic requirements: there should be full compatibility of CD-I discs and all CD-I players; CD-I should be a single media system; CD-I must be based on and piggyback on existing mass-produced electronic products (CDs and televisions).

Philips are initially targetting five application areas: in-car, education and training, entertainment, creative leisure, and work at home. It is expected that the first CD-I players will become available in 1989.

CD-Video (CD-V)

The next product to be launched is Compact Disc-Video (CD-V) which was introduced at the Consumer Electronics Show in Chicago in June 1987. CD-V is a gold-coloured 4.72 inch CD that carries a six-minute analogue video/digital audio clip together with a further 20 minutes of full CD audio. According to Philips some 250–300 CD-V titles will be available when the product is launched commercially, and what they describe as CD-V long forms (8 inch and 12 inch version) will also be introduced in time.

At present there is no way of supporting high-quality, full motion video from a CD-ROM or CD-I disc. The conventional wisdom has always been that the CDs do not revolve fast enough and hence the transfer rate is not fast enough to refresh a video screen. Hence there would always be a market for videodisc systems, hybrid videodisc systems, CD-Vs and combination players capable of playing back both analogue videodiscs and CD-ROMs.

However, at the 1987 Microsoft Conference, the RCA subsidiary of GE in the US launched what they call DV-I (Digital Video Interactive), which is an integrated video and graphics technology based on two chips that handle pixel and display processing. Data is stored on CD-ROM in compressed form, and is decompressed during playback fast enough to allow 24 frame per second motion video at a resolution of between 256 and 768 pixels by 512 pixels. The DV-I system can use existing CD-ROM players, existing microcomputers and existing television standards, but can also be adapted to other storage media such as WORM discs etc.

DV-I is currently only in the prototype stage but it does indicate that eventually the development of digital video techniques may enable us to replace the analogue videodisc entirely and introduce one fully integrated digital publishing medium. It should also serve to make the point that the next ten years will see the introduction of many more techniques designed to maximize the potential of optical publishing on yet more variants and extensions of the CD and CD-ROM standards.

Optical Read-Only Memory (OROM)

The key advantages of CD-ROM as a publishing medium, as outlined above, are standardization, high storage capacity, the availability of mastering and replication facilities, and the relatively low cost hardware. One drawback with CD-ROM is its use of CLV mode recording, which results in relatively slow access times of 1–2 seconds in current drives. A second potential drawback is that, in addition to using CLV format, the CD-ROM is 12 cm or 4.72 inches in diameter and hence not compatible with the emerging 5.25 inch (13 cm) standard diameter for WORM and erasable optical discs, which tend to use the CAV mode of recording.

A number of companies, including 3M and Sony, have therefore floated the concept of a 5.25 inch CAV mode read-only optical disc that they variously call OROM (Optical Read-Only Memory) or Data ROM. This could play in a new generation of multifunction 5.25 inch optical disc drives capable of accepting read-only, write-once and erasable rewritable optical discs. The benefits of OROM would be that it was compatible with future optical media standards, had faster access times and data transfer rates, would be easily adaptable to higher storage densities as they became feasible, and would serve the high-end computer marketplace where multi-user access is a requirement, leaving the low-end publishing marketplace to CD-ROM.

Assuming that such universal drives were produced, what effect would OROM have on CD-ROM? The effect would appear to be very little at this stage for commercial publishers keen to launch CD-ROM products or librarians and end users wishing to buy CD-ROM drives to access these products. In commercial publishing applications, the emphasis will be on low-cost workstations, standards and the widespread availability of mastering and replication facilities and CD-ROM is already here and meeting those requirements. Similarly, for many technical publishing applications where CD-ROM is in competition with existing paper and microfiche-based systems the key requirements will be low-cost workstations and low replication costs for the media.

However, for software distribution and the distribution of raw data and graphics libraries for use in particular computer systems, and for a number of corporate data distribution applications, then OROM looks potentially very attractive. If it receives the right backing from IBM and others then it could be widely adopted by mainstream computer users.

OROM would offer fast access of 100 msec or less to support multi-user access and compatibility with other formats so users would only need one drive for read-only, write-once and erasable storage. 3M and Sony can master OROM/Data ROM media already and other mastering facilities could be adapted for OROM if demand grew.

However, this is purely speculation; at present there are no standards for OROM or Data ROM.

Optical cards

Our review of read-only optical storage products concludes by looking at optical cards and, in particular at the Drexon laser card developed by Drexler Corporation. There are a number of other companies researching optical cards but Drexler are the pioneers of this technology. The Drexon laser cards, like optical discs, can be read-only or write-once and are basically plastic credit cards with the optical recording medium applied in a strip as a replacement to the magnetic strip used in so called 'smart cards'. Drexler have sold non-exclusive licences for the technology to over 30 major companies including British Telecom and Maxwell Communications Corporation in the UK and a number of applications have been announced for the cards, e.g. Blue Cross Blue Shield where client's medical details are recorded on read-only cards and hospitals are issued with card readers for reading the details into PCs.

A 35 × 80 mm Drexon recording strip has a storage capacity of 2 megabytes, and 10 megabyte versions have been shown. The cards can be pre-recorded in the factory for ROM applications where many copies of permanent identical data are required, e.g. software distribution etc. Alternatively there are recordable cards, also with a storage capacity of 2 megabytes or approximately 800 pages of text, for cardholder data, transaction data, digitized photographs or fingerprints etc. The cards will be laser recordable at a secure point of issue or at point of use for cumulative record keeping or debiting and a standard blank recordable card could sell for approximately $2 in high volume.

A number of companies have shown card readers and reader-writers. The Toshiba reader is priced at £100 and the read-write unit at £1500. The reader offers a transfer rate to a PC of 32–64 kilobits/second, while the read/write unit offers a write speed of 10 kilobits/second. Clearly optical cards are not going to challenge CD-ROMs for the distribution of large databases but they could prove useful for software distribution and for updating data distributed on CD-ROM.

WORM optical discs

The processes involved in producing Write-Once Read-Many (WORM) optical discs are very similar to those for read-only optical media, but there are also a number of key differences that will restrict the potential of recordable optical disc systems for publishing applications.

The first is the mastering process. With read-only media, all the information (video, audio, digital data etc.) is recorded onto the master disc at this stage together with formatting and indexing data and, in some cases, retrieval software. With recordable and erasable media, only the formatting data is recorded at this stage, leaving the rest of the disc blank for users to record their own data onto it at a later stage.

After mastering, the blank formatted WORM discs are not just coated with a reflective layer and a protective coating — as is the case with videodiscs and all the CDs. The WORM optical discs are first coated with a sensitive recording layer; then a number of different protective treatments are applied and the discs are usually loaded into plastic cartridges to provide further protection from damage during handling. Hence, in a very real sense, each WORM optical disc is actually a master disc.

Thirdly, at the playback stage, users of WORM optical disc systems require a combined recorder/player rather than simply a player. In the recorder/player or drive the optical head comprises either two separate lasers — a high-power write laser and a lower-power read laser — or one laser that can operate at different levels of intensity.

Fourthly, while there is one physical standard for CDs and one *de facto* standard for videodiscs, there are currently no standards relating to WORM optical discs. They are available in a range of diameters including 5.25 inch, 8 inch, 12 inch and 14 inch and they make use of a wide range of substrates (base materials) including glass, aluminium and plastic. They use a wide range of different recording mechanisms (pit forming, bubble forming, phase changing and dye ablative), a range of protective measures, single, dual, trilayer and even quadrilayer recording surfaces, and grooved or non-grooved tracking.

The result is that each commercially available WORM optical disc is designed to play in one particular WORM drive and is not recordable or readable in drives from other suppliers. This point relates primarily to 12 inch WORM discs, the first WORM discs to be launched on the market, and to the first generation of 5.25 inch WORM discs. Suppliers were so far advanced with commercialization of incompatible 12 inch WORM discs that it was impossible to try and impose standards. However, with 5.25 inch discs considerable efforts are being made to introduce physical standards.

The organizations involved include the British Standards Institution, the American National Standards Institution and the Japanese Industrial Standards Committee at the national level, and the International Standards Organization, the European Computer Manufacturers Association and the International Electro-Technical Commission at the international level. There are four main aspects to the 5.25 inch WORM standard. The first aspect is definitions and environment, and this is agreed. The second aspect is mechanical, physical and dimensions, and this is almost complete. There was controversy here over whether magnetic or mechanical clamping should be endorsed, but magnetic won the day. The third aspect relates to optical characteristics; there are two schools, favouring continuous and sampled servo-tracking techniques respectively. The fourth relates to formats, where there is still considerable work to be done. While it appeared as if it would be possible to support two standards in early 1987, this position has changed since the launch of IBM's 5.25 inch WORM optical disc, which is sourced from Matsushita. This uses mechanical clamping rather than magnetic and effectively creates a third standard.

Hence, while progress has been made and there is a perceived requirement for 5.25 inch WORM discs and drives to be interchangeable, there is a long way to go before an equivalent to the Philips/Sony Yellow Book could be agreed for 5.25 inch WORM optical discs.

The final key difference between read-only and WORM optical discs is in pricing. The read-only media are publishing media and hence, while there is a relatively high mastering cost, replicate discs can be produced very cheaply and the players are relatively inexpensive. With WORM optical discs there is, of course, no commercial mastering cost as the data is recorded on the discs by users inhouse. However, the discs are relatively expensive at present because they are all effectively master discs, the coating process is critical and they have to be supplied with cartridges. Current prices for 12 inch WORM optical discs range from £200 to £400 for single- or double-sided discs. The IBM 5.25 inch WORM disc is priced at £60. In addition, the WORM drives are more expensive as they include record capabilities and are built to a higher specification. A 12 inch WORM drive with controller is approximately £10 000–15 000 end user price, while a 5.25 inch WORM drive is priced at £2500–3000.

The above points should indicate that although WORM and read-only optical discs are similar in many respects, there are also significant differences that help determine the market area each will serve. CD-ROM is well suited to the distribution of digital databases to a large number of customers for access via a low-cost PC-based workstation but it is not suited to the inhouse creation and storage of databases as users would have to have a magnetic tape drive on their computer system, send the tape to an intermediary and have them reformat it, produce a master CD-ROM and one or two replicates and then send them back to the user company if they wanted to use CD-ROM as an archiving medium. This would prove a very expensive and time-consuming exercise and could not be justified unless hundreds of copies of the database were required.

By contrast, a WORM optical disc would be ideal for archiving inhouse databases as the user would simply download data from their computer system onto the recordable disc and it would be stored and instantly available. A number of companies, including Aquidneck Data Systems in the US and Data General, Kenda and AM Programmers in the UK offer WORM optical disc data storage subsystems that are designed to emulate tape drives and link with a range of host processors. The Central Computing and Telecommunications Agency in the UK recently conducted a major study to prove the viability of such systems.

However, if the user then wanted to make multiple copies of that database available to other users there would be a problem. The only way to copy WORM optical discs at present is serially by reading the data from one WORM disc and writing it onto another. This is a slow process, akin to copying a video cassette and demands, at a minimum, the availability of two WORM optical disc drives and while it can be used for making one or two backup copies, it would not be attractive for largescale copying of hundreds of copies of a database. The high cost of the media would also militate against this approach to the distribution of data in commercial publishing applications.

In future, if the physical and logical structures of 5.25 inch WORM optical discs are standardized (either internationally or *de facto*) and different discs can therefore be played on different drives, then 5.25 inch WORMs could be used for the exchange of database information. They would not compete with CD-ROMs for publishing to a mass market but they could complement them. For example, users of online databases can, in future, expect to be offered the option of purchasing all or a portion of their databases on CD-ROM for a fixed yearly subscription and end users would then be able to search the databases locally on their PCs. However, if the database is widely used in the organization this could necessitate the purchase of a large number of subscriptions to the same CD-ROM database. An alternative would be for large organizations to purchase, at a higher price, the entire database on a 5.25 inch or 12 inch WORM and then run it on their host mainframe to provide multi-user access to the database and the ability to download major sections of the database, just as today some organizations purchase databases on magnetic tape.

One other way in which WORM optical discs will complement CD-ROM publishing systems and be used alongside them is demonstrated by systems launched by Laserdata and Plexus Computers. They are document image processing systems comprising a host computer, document scanners, standard computer terminals, WORM optical disc storage subsystems, laser printers and high-resolution terminals plus sophisticated relational database management systems that allow images to be treated as another data element. The Laserview system from Laserdata is a PC-based system which allows users to build up image databases on WORM optical disc and then gives them the option of distributing copies of the database on other WORM discs via serial copies or on CD-ROM via a tape drive output option on the system. The Plexus system is a larger scale super-microcomputer-based system which they call their Extended Data Processing System. It can be used in electronic publishing to handle mixed-mode documents containing images and text; one system is being used to compile yellow pages directories in the US. Another system is being developed for University Microfilms to enable them to compile mixed image and textual databases that they can then distribute on a choice of paper, microfiche or CD-ROM depending on the application.

Such combined optical publishing or republishing systems will have a major impact on current microform publishers and governmental organizations such as NTIS, the Patent Offices, the US Government Printing Office and others who are obliged to maintain very large stocks of publications, reports etc. and make copies available on demand.

In conclusion, therefore, WORM optical discs are for inhouse capture, storage and retrieval of coded data, text, scanned images and eventually voice and are not primarily a publishing medium. They will function primarily as an enabling medium, enabling publishers and inhouse records managers, archivists and data processing managers to build up and maintain large mixed, online databases inhouse, comprising both data and text and voice and images where previously the costs of the equivalent amount of magnetic storage would have proved prohibitive. They (or, in future, erasable optical discs) may prove the answer to the requirement outlined at the beginning of this chapter, for high density, removable, durable electronic filing cabinets.

This section closes by giving a brief indication of the specification of WORM media and drives. The OSI Laserdrive 1200 WORM drive is a relatively typical 12 inch WORM drive. It can accept double-sided discs with a storage capacity of 1 gigabyte (1000 megabytes) per side and can be supplied with an ISI or SCSI interface and offer a sustained transfer rate of 250 kilobytes/second and average access times of 480 rev/min. Because the media is removable, the OSI media and drives can be supplied in a number of WORM optical disc automatic handling devices or jukeboxes capable of holding from 1 to 7 drives and from 16 to over 100 discs. Such devices allow users to store several hundred gigabytes of data and retrieve any file automatically within 30 seconds to 1 minute. To place this in context, 1 gigabyte represents approximately 400000 pages of coded text and approximately 25000 scanned A4 page images held in bit-map form.

The 5.25 inch WORM drives on the market from Optotech, ISI, IBM, Toshiba and others offer storage capacities of from 100–400 megabytes per side, data transfer rates of 2–3 megabits/second and average access times of 100–300 milliseconds. There are not currently any jukeboxes commercially available for 5.25 inch WORM drives but they are under development.

Finally, within a year or two there may be a recordable CD-ROM called CD-PROM from Philips that would make use of irreversible phase change recording techniques and would offer the same storage capacity, access speeds and data transfer rates as current CD-ROM drives. The CD-PROM would not be readable in current CD-ROM drives but current CD-ROMs would be readable in future CD-PROM drives.

Erasable optical discs

Erasable optical discs, as described earlier, are the third functional category of optical discs and the third generation of optical storage device. They will potentially give users all the advantages of optical storage plus the ability to not just read data from the discs or record data onto the discs once, but also the ability to record, erase and rerecord data on the same sector of a disc many thousands or even millions of times, just as they can with magnetic media today.

This latter facility is essential for many active computer applications where files need to be retrieved, modified and rewritten on a regular basis and the majority of operating systems and application software packages assume the use of such erasable media. Hence, whereas read-only and write-once optical storage media are destined to open up new markets and compete with paper, microfilm and magnetic tape, erasable optical disc suppliers will be aiming to compete directly with both flexible and hard magnetic discs for a share of the mainstream computer storage peripheral market.

The four main advantages that erasable optical discs should offer over magnetic discs are:

● high storage capacity;
● low-cost drives;
● removable media, so the off-line storage capacity is unlimited and jukebox-type devices could offer automatic disc handling facilities;
● durability, as the use of non-contact record/read heads should avoid the danger of headcrashes and mechanical wear.

As can be seen from *Figure 1.3*, the processes involved in mastering and replicating erasable optical discs are almost identical to those for WORM discs, and also bear many resemblances to the processes used with read-only optical discs. However, at the coating stage the chemical structure of the recording layer is different from that used with WORM optical discs so that the recording/erasure process can be repeated on a cyclical basis and not be a single unalterable process.

Although working prototypes of erasable digital optical disc systems have been shown by companies such as Verbatim and 3M, no erasable

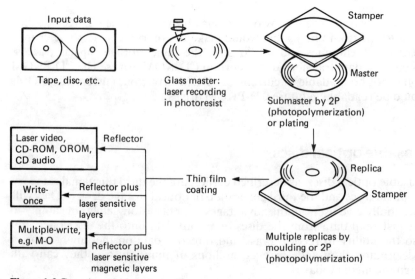

Figure 1.3 Generic optical media outline

systems were commercially available at the time of writing and hence exact specifications cannot be given. 3M is one of the leading media suppliers together with Matsushita, KDD and Verbatim.

Two basic techniques are employed, phase change and magneto-optic. Latest estimates are that erasable disc systems using one or other of these two techniques will be commercially available by 1990.

Phase change systems are based around the fact that certain tellurium-based alloys can exist at room temperature in either the crystalline or the amorphous form and can be switched reversibly between each state. The optical properties of the film — its reflectivity — are different for the crystalline and amorphous states and this forms the basis for the optical read-out of the stored data. Matsushita is one of the leading proponents of this recording technique.

The recording of data in magnetic-optic systems involves the use of a laser to provide heat and a magnetic coil to provide the magnetic field. Prior to recording the entire recording layer of the disc is perpendicularly magnetized. Then, at the recording stage, a micrometre-sized region on the disc is heated up by the write laser to a point above the so called Curie point; as the material cools in the presence of an external magnetic field oriented antiparallel to the initial direction of magnetization, a small region (one micrometre) is formed that is reverse polarized. This region is the equivalent of a pit or bubble in WORM optical discs and playback is accomplished with a low-power laser using either the Kerr effect or the Faraday effect.

The first generation of erasable optical discs are likely to be 5.25 inches in diameter and will be recorded in CAV mode to provide fast access times and high data transfer rates. They will be compatible with existing 5.25 inch WORM discs and drives, and combination players will be made available capable of playing WORM, Erasable and possibly also OROM discs. In addition, Verbatim have shown a 3.5 inch diameter erasable optical disc and, as the media is erasable, it will certainly prove feasible to produce discs of as little as 2 inches in diameter for use in portable computers.

Summary

In this introduction to the requirements for a new generation of storage media, the potential of optical storage and the wide range of optical media currently available or just coming onto the marketplace, the aim has been to give the reader a brief survey of the potential of these media and to dispel any misconceptions or confusion concerning the range of acronyms and the differing applications for these systems. It will also, hopefully, explain why many industry experts consider WORM optical discs to be an ideal storage medium for the future and CD-ROM to be the most promising of the optical storage media for publishing applications. The rest of this book is devoted to various aspects of CD-ROM as a publishing media, so no attempt will be made here to describe all the potential application areas for CD-ROM. Instead, to conclude this chapter, here is a brief list of some of the areas where CD-ROM is already being used, and a summary of the apparent strengths and weaknesses of CD-ROM as a publishing medium.

Applications

CD-ROM is already being used inhouse by a range of public and private organizations for data distribution, distributing procedures manuals, telephone directories, reference works, technical manuals, parts catalogues etc. It is being tested in a wide range of technical publishing applications in the aerospace, aircraft, automotive, ship-building and many more manufacturing environments for distributing parts catalogues; training manuals etc.

CD-ROM is already being tested to distribute software and user documentation by the computer companies and third parties and is being used to distribute graphics databases in the CAD, desktop publishing and scientific computing fields.

Perhaps the most publicized application for CD-ROM to date has been the distribution of commercial databases that were previously made available online. There are close to 100 such databases now available on CD-ROM and suppliers are developing terminals that can be used to search online databases and backfiles of the same database stored locally on CD-ROM in so-called hybrid workstations. In addition, a number of innovative publishers are making available subsets of a number of databases that relate to a particular topic or discipline on one CD-ROM with a common search software, and are targetting them at particular groups of professionals in the financial and medical marketplaces.

Bibliographic databases are now distributed on CD-ROM for retrospective cataloguing in libraries or for bibliographic checking and book ordering functions, as with Whitakers' *British Books in Print Plus* and Bowkers' *Books in Print*.

Reference works are also being published on CD-ROM including trade directories, telephone directories, dictionaries, textbooks and technical encyclopedias. Lastly products targetted at the domestic marketplace are appearing, including Microsoft's *Bookshelf* and Grolier's *Encyclopedia*.

Advantages and disadvantages of CD-ROM as a publishing medium

Advantages
(1) Its high storage capacity (550 megabytes or 200000 pages of coded text) is, on balance, a major advantage, offering the potential for considerable consumable savings when compared with large microform or paper publications. Clearly, however, the economics of CD-ROM publishing are such that one would not contemplate using CD-ROM to distribute a very small database of a few pages. Also, it can be expected that the storage capacity of optical media will increase dramatically over the next few years and this will pose strains on the standard. Could there be a 1 gigabyte CD-ROM?
(2) CD-ROM is based on an established mass-produced audio consumer medium and hence drive and media costs can be kept low, the technology is proven, and mastering and replication facilities already exist.

(3) The physical specifications are standardized in the Yellow Book, and the computer and information industries have cooperated to develop a file format standard for CD-ROMs.

(4) The economics of CD-ROM publishing mirror CD music publishing, book publishing and newspaper publishing; the more you can sell, the lower the per unit production costs. Hence the most popular material can be produced very cheaply.

(5) CD-ROM is a digital storage medium. Hence data stored on CD-ROM can be searched interactively, just like online databases, and the data retrieved as the result of a search can be downloaded into other programs for processing. This is perhaps the most significant benefit of CD-ROM over paper and microfilm reference material. The latter are island systems with no link to existing computer systems. Once that reference material is available on CD-ROM, fully integrated systems can be developed. For example, parts manuals can be linked to stock control and part ordering systems, and bibliographic listings can be linked to online book ordering and stock control facilities.

(6) CD-ROM media, being based on CD audio discs, are rugged, portable media capable of being transported via postal services.

(7) CD-ROM, like all optical storage media, is just at the beginning of its life and hence further improvements in storage capacity, drive performance, price reductions and additional facilities such as DV-I, CD-V and others can be expected.

Disadvantages

(1) Currently the data preparation, pre-mastering, replication, checking, packaging and distribution cycle is a long and complex one; particularly in Europe, the infrastructure needed to support serious CD-ROM publishers is not yet fully in place. This should only be a question of time, however.

(2) Mastering and replication facilities are extremely expensive to set up, so they cannot be installed by publishers themselves or large corporate users of CD-ROM. This is a disadvantage when dealing with confidential information or when fast turnaround is essential and the publisher wants full control of the distribution cycle. However, work is progressing on simpler mastering techniques for CD-ROMs.

(3) The CD-ROM is a computer peripheral. Although that brings many advantages in terms of the user's ability to search the data on CD-ROM, it also brings some uncertainty. The PC market is volatile and competitive and unless the publisher also supplies the user with the hardware it is difficult to control what version of DOS the user is working with or how compatible his PC is, what hard disc he has etc.

(4) CD-ROM is recorded in CLV mode and hence access times, in computing terms, are relatively slow. This puts the onus on the publisher and software supplier to organize the database in such a way as to optimize search performance. It also poses the question of how practical it is to use CD-ROM drives on a network basis. This is a common requirement with academic libraries etc. and will need to be addressed in the context of specific system requirements.

(5) CD-ROM may be challenged in certain data distribution applications

in future by other read-only formats — notably OROM — or by 5.25 inch WORM discs if a standard is agreed and speedy copying procedures are developed.

(6) Finally, the point must be made that, while CD-ROM has an enormous storage capacity and can be mass produced, it is nevertheless just a storage medium. CD-ROM in itself does nothing to reduce the cost of data capture or database organization. If it was not economic to create an online database, it may not be economic to create a CD-ROM database either.

Equally, while many are predicting that CD-ROM will replace microfilm in most technical and academic micropublishing systems, one must bear in mind that most of the figures relating to the storage capabilities of CD-ROM and the cost of workstations assume coded text. If we compare CD-ROM with microfilm for the distribution of images, e.g. facsimile images of old journals or collections of photographs etc., then CD-ROM begins to look a very expensive medium at present. One can only store approximately 10000 facsimile scanned images on one CD-ROM and, in addition to a PC one needs a high-resolution display terminal and a laser printer, bringing the price of a CD-ROM graphics workstation to over £10000 at current prices. No doubt eventually CD-ROM will be used to distribute facsimile images and mixed mode documents, but it will take time before prices drop and compression techniques improve.

Overall, it should be clear that CD-ROM does meet most of the requirements made at the beginning of this section for a high density, removable, low cost, digital publishing medium, and the following chapters will amply illustrate its potential in many key application areas.

References

HENDLEY, A. (1985) Video discs, compact discs and digital optical discs, *Cimtech report 23*, Hatfield, UK

SCHWERIN, J., LIGHTBOWN, P., BAILEY, C. and KAIKOW, H. (1988) *CD-ROM standards: the book*, Learned Information, Oxford and New Jersey

SCHWERIN, J. and HENDLEY, A. (1988) *International initiatives for CD-ROM standards: a report prepared for the director-general information market and innovation (Commission of the European Communities)*, Learned Information, Oxford and New Jersey

Further Reading

HENDLEY, A. (1987) CD-ROM and optical publishing systems, *Cimtech report 26*, Hatfield, UK

HENDLEY, A. (1988) A comparison of the archival storage potential of microfilm, magnetic media and optical data discs, *Cimtech report 19*, Hatfield, UK

Chapter 2

Current CD-ROM products

Raymond V. Walsh

Introduction

CD-ROM is beginning to take hold as a medium for the delivery of electronically accessible information. The sheer storage capacity of the medium is what originally attracted technicians, but the flexibility of presentation and access that this allows is what particularly attracts publishers and consumers.

As with all new products, some time must pass and some experimentation in the marketplace be conducted before the combinations of information content, flexibility of the medium and price of the product begin to define a

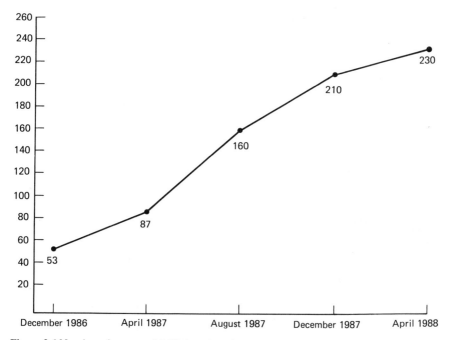

Figure 2.1 Number of commercial CD-based products

new marketplace. This is certainly happening more quickly with CD-ROM than it did with online databases, but CD-ROM will owe some of its expected success to appetites created by its predecessors. An appetite among librarians for electronic access to large collections of information was created by online databases. PCs have created an appetite for easy-to-use and WIMP (Windows, Icons, Mouse, Pull-down menus) software. CD-ROM provides an opportunity to bring these features and facilities together.

The increase in sheer numbers of commercial CD-ROM based products available is one indication of success. *Figure 2.1* shows how this has increased over the 12 months from December 1986 to December 1987. While the number of products has increased by fourfold there are still barely more than 200 commercial products available and few of these have sold more than 200 copies.

In order to identify the trends in CD-ROM products, it is necessary to look at a number of the characteristics of those products. Among the characteristics to be considered here are the product content, intended audience, product type, update cycles, 'bundled' hardware and price. From this data, it will be possible to estimate the current state and direction of CD-ROM market development.

Content and intended audience

At present (1988), there are 230 information products commercially available on CD-ROM, most of which are US-developed. In addition to

Table 2.1 Current CD-ROM products

Investment data	Library catalogues
Company accounts	Addresses and postal codes
Hazardous chemical data	Spare parts catalogues
Economic statistics	Educational encyclopedia
Maps	Chemical deffraction data
Bibles	Veterinary drug details
Patents	Career opportunities data
Trademarks	Industrial statistics
Pharmaceutical details	Medical dictionary
Geographic data	Engineering encyclopedia
Computer products and suppliers	Public policy literature
Chemical encyclopedia	Agricultural literature
Legal encyclopedia	Medical abstracts
Book reviews	Medical diagnosis data
Scientific abstracts	Toxicology data
Author's reference material	Engineering abstracts
Table and capsule identification	Broker's reports
Aeronautics abstracts	Educational abstracts
Audio-visual materials catalogue	Chemical suppliers directory
Newspaper archieves	Educational test questions
Dissertation abstracts	English dictionary
Navigational data	Psychology abstracts
Travel statistics	Multi-lingual dictionary
Software	Curriculum objectives
Sociology abstracts	
Demographic data	

this, there are many companies using CD-ROM for internal publishing (computer documentation, engineering manuals, etc.). This latter group is beyond the scope of the current review. Among the commercially published products, there is a broad range of subjects covered (see *Table 2.1*).

At first glance this list of products appears to be quite varied and to cover a wide range of subjects. Upon closer examination it can be seen that the majority of products fall into a few general categories with a limited breadth of audience.

Libraries

A large part of the list is aimed at libraries and librarians. This certainly formed the bulk of the earliest CD-ROM products. At the moment, there are no fewer than 21 products containing book or serials reference data aimed at those involved in book-buying and archiving. In addition to this there are more than 20 products containing abstracts of literature as well as bibliographic references. While this latter group may have some appeal beyond libraries, that is their main constituency since the products do not contain the full text that an end-user would usually require.

Library products continue to appear in substantial numbers but they represent a declining percentage of all new products. This is primarily due to the increase in other products rather than a decline in the volume of library products. These library products are well-suited to CD-ROM in that they contain millions of very brief, highly structured records that can be accessed from the workstations that are becoming common in libraries.

Libraries will continue to be a major market for CD-ROM products whether these products are specifically aimed at librarians or not. CD-ROM allows libraries to overcome a number of problems. The most obvious one is the limited amount of storage space but it can also contribute to the efficiency and security of libraries. Hardware developments to assist in this area are discussed in the last section of this chapter.

Medicine, pharmacy and veterinary science

Medical and veterinary literature and reference materials also constitute a substantial proportion of the extant CD-ROM products. The abstracting services are of some value to end users but these are primarily library products as described above. There are at least 15 other medical, pharmacological and veterinary products on CD-ROM. Most are general reference works for the bookshelf but several are designed to be used as interactive aids in diagnosis or treatment. The 'bookshelf' and reference works outnumber the more immediately applied products. More of these are due to appear in the near future than are interactive aids. The appearance of CD-ROM products in the surgery may indicate a softening of doctors' views to the applicability of computer-based products to general diagnostic and treatment work. It also says a good deal about the medium's suitability for these applications.

Science and engineering

There is a range of scientific and engineering products that contain biblio-graphic data and hence fall within the librarian's sphere of influence. In addition to this, there are approximately a dozen products which are non-bibliographic. These contain technical and analytical data, product details and sources, etc. Several leading scientific encyclopedias are also available on CD-ROM.

The non-bibliographic science and engineering products are relatively recent developments and it appears that more will be produced in the near future. Several products providing sophisticated interfaces are under development including those with 'expert' front ends and those allowing searching via chemical structures and other non-text methods of access.

Finance and business

Finance and business are currently the areas of fastest growth in the production of CD-ROM based products. A few products began to appear in 1986 but 1987 has seen a rapid increase in the number of new products. At this time, there are 20 products available and at least two dozen more under development.

This category includes databases of company accounts, business direc-tories, broker reports, prices of bonds and equities, financial news, economic and industry statistics, etc. These services are linked to analytical software (including popular spreadsheets), online databases, newswires, etc. The products are aimed directly at end users who wish to quickly apply or analyse the data retrieved. The services are also aimed at a broad range of business users who do not require access to 'real time' prices and news.

Types of product

As noted, many of the original CD-ROM products were aimed at the library community and other information intermediaries. Consequently bibliographic and abstracting products predominated. Recently a great number of non-bibliographic products have appeared. As can be seen from *Table 2.2*, bibliographic references and abstracts continue to constitute a significant number of the available CD-ROM products and this is likely to continue. However, the proportion of the total that they represent is declining and will decline sharply during 1988 as more products for end users appear (see *Table 2.2*).

In this context, 'reference' refers to those materials that may be directly applied by the end users including products where the individual records

Table 2.2 Types of CD-ROM product

	Bibliography	Abstracts	Reference	Full text
January 1987	30%	30%	20%	10%
January 1988	25%	25%	50%	5%

do not contain large amounts of text. This includes statistics, corporate data and encyclopedias.

'Full text' refers to records that are largely textual such as law reports, legislation, book reviews, postal codes, etc.

The trend described here is remarkable for a number of reasons. It implies a wider distribution of CD-ROM players than has been seen heretofore which may encourage other publishers to begin to produce products for this audience. It also implies that a greater number of end users will be able to make direct use of information technology. Finally, it might be inferred that full text archives are not yet considered suitable for CD-ROM.

This last point deserves further consideration as it has often been assumed that large scale text-based publishing, such as legal publishing, was ideal for CD-ROM. While law publishing is appearing on CD-ROM, it primarily consists of legislation and legal encyclopedias rather than full-text case law, which is the heartland of legal research in English language countries. CD-ROM does not offer sufficient storage capacity to be immediately attractive for the publishing of case law. Subsets of case law databases will appear on CD-ROM during 1988 but the early emphasis on the sheer capacity of CD-ROM for text storage was clearly misplaced.

Update cycles

The creation of an update for a CD-ROM can be done in several ways. As it is a 'read-only memory', the currently issued disc cannot itself be amended or added to. The disc can be updated by creating a new master and pressing replacement or supplemental discs or by providing updates that can be read from a different medium in conjunction with the CD-ROM.

CD-ROM was originally seen as a medium for publishing relatively static data or data for which updates were not highly time-sensitive. The early products tended to fit within these parameters (see *Table 2.3*).

The products that were never to be updated were largely promotional. Quarterly updates predominated with a sprinkling of products following shorter or longer update cycles.

The trend is now towards shorter update cycles. The majority of new products are settling for monthly updates through the issuance of new discs incorporating all the required additions and changes (see *Table 2.3*).

Only one product is now updated weekly through the issuance of new discs. The data carried on this disc is weekly financial data, which is delivered 10 days after the week's data that makes up the addition (and is

Table 2.3 Update cycles

	Continuously	*Weekly*	*Monthly*	*Quarterly*	*Semiannual*	*Annual*	*Never*
January 1987	1%	0%	12%	60%	12%	10%	5%
January 1988	4%	2%	20%	46%	9%	13%	4%

supplemented by a floppy disc during the intervening week). This is quite an unusual approach and has been successful within a relatively small market (about 150 subscribers) at a high price (up to US$26000 per year). The supplier of this product is developing new products with similar update cycles. It will be interesting to see if others follow this lead.

'Continuously' updated services are those designed to work together with an online service. The disc is used for archival data (usually on monthly updates) and a newswire or online database is accessed for more recent data. There are half a dozen products (mostly business and financial) taking this approach.

The vast majority of CD-ROM products follow the more typical 'hard copy' publishing schedules and appear monthly or quarterly. This follows established editorial and production schedules. It also makes the delays in disc production due to lack of industry capacity less obvious to the consumer. The recent introduction of 'stand alone' pre-mastering workstations, designed to be used on the publisher's premises, will reduce the impact of delay by third parties. It will be interesting to see if this freedom encourages publishers to publish more time-sensitive information on CD-ROM.

Prices

Pricing of CD-ROM products covers a broad range. Factors affecting price include the update cycle, general availability of the information, perceived value to users, links to hard copy, features of the software, pricing of competitive products and the hardware included. *Table 2.4* shows the distribution of products across the range of prices. Several products are included free of charge with the purchase of a CD-ROM reader. Others charge nearly US$30000 per year for a subscription. One medical abstracts database (in slightly varying forms) could be bought from four different integrators/suppliers at four different prices with a range of US$1000 from the lowest to the highest.

Table 2.4 CD-ROM product prices at January 1988 (US$)

<1000	1–3000	3–5000	5–10000	10–15000	15–20000	>20000
26%	34%	21%	6%	4%	3%	1%

The majority of products are priced below US$5000. Library products (as defined above) typically fall in the two categories of price ranging from US$1000 to $5000, including reader. Business and financial products are usually in the price brackets well above those of library products. Medical and engineering products are priced slightly below the business and financial services.

The pricing of electronic information products has always been difficult. A great range of pricing policies was seen with online databases. This is also an important issue with CD-ROM products. The particular problem with CD-ROM is that it requires a special piece of equipment in order to be used. This equipment is expensive (as compared to a modem for example) and very few potential customers already own one. Most publishers overcome this by quoting a price that includes lease/purchase of the reader. Most of the products in the middle bands of the figure above include such a charge in their prices. As the installed base of readers develops the pricing pattern will change. Interestingly, many of the higher-priced products do not include lease/purchase costs.

The most highly-priced product is updated weekly. Production costs continue to be relatively high but the price of this product is not dictated solely by its frequency of update. It also reflects the supplier's view of the value of his product to his customers.

The future of CD-ROM products

The trends in CD-ROM products point in a number of directions. End-user-oriented products will begin to predominate both in numbers and in delivered services. That is to say, the products will begin to be designed to be integrated into the users work pattern rather than set outside it as a secondary resource. This is possible through the proliferation of PCs as multi-use workstations.

The emphasis in use of CD-ROM will be less on its mass storage capacity as an archive. The space will be used to make the products more flexible and adaptable to the user's requirements. This will include software to manipulate the retrieved data.

There is likely to be a rapid reduction in product prices during 1988. Prices will reach a plateau during 1989 and then fall again steeply in 1990. The lowering of price will be made possible by a drop in pre-mastering costs (as publishers take this inhouse) and reproduction costs (as pressing capacity for CD-audio exceeds demand). It will also be influenced by the economies of scale as the market for CD-ROM products grows.

Even with production costs falling, there is a plateau or 'floor' price below which they will not fall in 1988. This price relates not to the cost of editorial input (always a relatively modest cost in publishing) but to the perceived product value and this should be higher on CD-ROM than on paper or online. Merely putting information on CD-ROM can add to its value but the majority of this added value will come from the tools for access, navigation and manipulation of the information which the publisher provides. It is in this added value that products appearing in 1988–89 will differ from most of those currently available. This floor price is likely to be somewhere around 150% of the price of the equivalent printed product.

The plateau or floor price will drop in 1990 because of the pressures introduced into an increasingly competitive market. There will be a lot of room to move in reducing prices in 1990. The room is created by the fact that the costs of producing, storing and distributing CD-ROM will be well below those of printed products and the costs of entering the CD-ROM market will begin to be recovered. This means that the profit margins will be 2–3 times that of current margins on equivalent printed products.

As more publishers produce more products on CD-ROM for the same markets, price will become an important competitive issue and prices will fall sharply.

Updates through issue of new discs will move toward a monthly schedule. This will be supplemented by updates from optical and 'smart' cards, online access and magnetic media. The restrictions on updates introduced by reliance on third parties will become less significant. As stated above the move to inhouse pre-mastering and the excess of production capacity should remove all barriers to fast updating by 1989, and reduce the premium which is now added to products requiring fast production turnround.

The future of CD-ROM technology

As noted earlier, one of the limitations of CD-ROM is its lack of sufficient capacity to handle really large databases on a single disc. Great advances have been made with techniques for compressing data so that it can occupy one-fifth or less of the space it would require in uncompressed form (depending on the data being stored). This increased capacity will make CD-ROM attractive for many more applications.

Most products come with their own retrieval software integrated into the product. This is sensible as it requires little of the user who need only boot the operating system (MS DOS or similar), load the retrieval software from the CD-ROM and commence using the product. As the reader or drive contains no processing power the software must be loaded onto the PC from disc.

This means that only one product can be used at a time. If the user wishes to look at two products dealing with the same subject he must do so consecutively. With each change he must 'dump' the current product's software and load the second product's software. If done once this is quite tolerable but research often requires several iterations and where three or more products must be searched, this can cause considerable delay and frustration.

One way around this problem is to standardize the retrieval software. This is unlikely to suit professional products as a very low level of flexibility in product design and function will be achieved. This approach is being taken with the consumer-oriented version of the technology being promoted by Philips in the form of CD-Interactive (CD-I).

What is required is the placement of processing power in the reader itself. This would allow a different retrieval software to be loaded in each drive and to be accessed via the PC alternatively and quickly via a suitable multi-drive interface. In a network, this would allow each workstation to have access to all products attached to the network merely by nominating the product(s) to be searched.

Several companies have developed drive stacks to allow all of the discs to be stored centrally. This is a step in the right direction but each drive is linked to only one PC. They are now extending these products to allow PCs on a network to access any of the discs on the stack. The problem is not yet solved, however, as each PC on the network must still load the application software from the disc and then dump it before accessing another product in the stack.

This network of PCs and disc stacks does have its own attractions, particularly in libraries. It allows for the creation of a central 'host' for all of the discs held in stock. All PC users will have access to all CD-ROMs held without having physical access to the discs. The discs never need be borrowed as they will always remain accessible to all users and the risks of damage or loss will be reduced.

Chapter 3

The role of the systems integrator
Patrick Gibbins

With the rapid growth in the application of CD-ROM, the need has emerged for specialist services and software that enables the transfer of information onto CD-ROM. In the absence of any better term, suppliers of these services have been labelled 'systems integrators'. It is an unfortunate and confusing label. The data processing industry has used the term systems integrator for several years, to describe organizations that combine together hardware and software from multiple sources in order to create a computer system that is then offered for sale as a package. This has little similarity with the work undertaken by the CD-ROM systems integrator. Better parallels exist in the print and publishing industries; the job of preparing data and programs for distribution on CD-ROM is similar to the role played by the typesetting service (disc replication is parallel to printing). Alternatively, there are specialist companies that provide the facilities and skills needed to prepare audiovisual material for distribution on interactive videodisc. These companies are simply 'production service' companies. Although the author would prefer to use the label 'production service', for the purposes of this book the label 'systems integrator' will grudgingly be adopted to comply with common usage.

Whilst dealing with the matter of definitions, a label is also needed that succinctly describes the type of organization that originates the creation of a CD-ROM based information product. The organization may own the information, distributing it already through other media such as paper, microfilm or online. Alternatively, the organization may be licensing information from multiple sources, bringing it together to make a new product. Whether the initiator is already a primary or secondary publisher, a software house or an operation set up just for this purpose, the author will describe them simply as 'the publisher'. Assigning the title of publisher carries with it many responsibilities, both legal and commercial. It is well to be aware what these responsibilities are. As technology and the shading of traditional industrial divisions result in more and more organizations becoming involved in publishing, the role of the publisher needs clear statement. Although it is not within the scope of this book to enter in this debate, it is worth asserting the basic principle that *the publisher takes ultimate responsibility for the form and content of a publication*. The systems integrator's job is to advise the publisher and to provide the technical resources needed to realize the publisher's conception of the product that the publisher wishes to bring to the market.

One further definition: data is material that can be processed by a computer; what customers are offered is information. Information is made up of data organized in a carefully selected way to meet the perceived needs of a customer. A CD-ROM is a delivery medium for an information product, whether that product comprises words, numbers, pictures or sound.

So we have the initiative being taken by a *publisher*, who employs a *systems integrator* to provide skills and resources in order to create an *information product* that the publisher will then market or otherwise distribute. The publisher need not be a commercial publisher. Indeed it is likely, over time, that the bulk of applications that use CD-ROM will come from corporate publishing or other 'closed loop' publishing activities such as technical documentation and maintenance manuals. Although the mix of skills and resources may vary, the pattern of relationships remains the same.

The history of CD-ROM is short. It is therefore difficult to present a stable picture of the services available and the type of organization that provides these services. So far systems integrators have emerged from two backgrounds. Firstly there is the software house that has developed proprietary software products which it then offers for use with CD-ROM As they have better understood the needs of publishers, these software houses have had to extend their range of support services to include consultancy, data conversion, preparation of data for mastering on CD-ROM, programming to meet the special requirements of the planned product and so on. All these support services are provided because without them few products could be made and copies of software would not be sold. There are also systems integrators which have their origins in the design and implementation of computer software but which do not necessarily have a proprietary software package developed for the CD-ROM market. In this case, they may enter into licensing agreements with owners of software (either for a single product or for a range of complementary software products). The systems integrator in this case will have to acquire a detailed understanding of the functionality and the operation of the software packages they are handling. However, they may bring other skills such as expertise in certain types of application, knowledge of the design of electronic information products and access to computer resources. Whatever the origins of a systems integrator, the publisher will have to base its selection of a contractor on confidence that the integrator understands what the publisher is trying to achieve, and on the software offered by the integrator. The importance of choosing the right software cannot be overstated. Although it is not dealt with in any detail in this chapter, it is important to make the point that the published information product is a combination of information and software. The two elements must be closely integrated to make the product as effective and usable as possible. One of the great benefits offered by CD-ROM, over other forms of electronic delivery, is the ability to tailor software to match the characteristics of the information being delivered and to meet the needs of the ultimate user of the product. Without the right software, it is impossible to create a well-designed product.

In this chapter, the role of the systems integrator will be defined simply by describing the tasks that the integrator carries out when undertaking the job of disc production. Every product is different, so it is only possible to generalize about the activities that typically take place. The main production steps are described in the order in which they occur. In the author's view, the main contributions that a systems integrator can make towards the production of a CD-ROM based product (outside software provision) are, initially, contributing to the preparation of a detailed product design. Whilst the publisher may know generally what they wish to achieve, it will require the systems integrator's detailed knowledge of what can be achieved and the techniques available, in order to prepare an effective specification. Secondly, the systems integrator should have the skills needed to analyse the available source data and to develop techniques for processing this data into a form in which it can provide input to the CD-ROM production process. The poor state of availability of data in a suitable form is one of the major barriers to publishers adopting CD-ROM technology. For this reason a disproportionate amount of this chapter is devoted to discussing typical sources of data and the problems encountered in processing them.

Production overview

Producing an information product for distribution on CD-ROM is achieved through a number of production stages. Each of these stages will be described in detail. However it will be useful to first give an overview of the production process and to provide some perspective on the problems likely to be encountered.

Product design

There is a direct analogy that can be drawn between the services that a publisher obtains from a printer and the services provided by a systems integrator. Most publishers treat the business of typesetting and printing as a discrete operation separate from the preparation of manuscripts and marketing the finished book. Similarly, CD-ROM production can be treated by a publisher as a service that is contracted out. The publisher may also take the view, as with typesetting and printing, that they need not become involved in the mechanics of production or with the technology that is being used. And here the analogy can be used to emphasize the ways in which CD-ROM production differs from print production. The range of choices open to a publisher in selecting the way a printed product appears are well established and limited. The size of the page, the layout and typography, the type of illustrations and the binding selected are issues decided by the publisher with regard to cost and the nature of the market the book is aimed at.

The nature of an electronic information product, particularly using a distributable electronic medium such as CD-ROM, must be determined prior to the production process. It involves decisions not only about the content, but about how the contents are going to be used. Decisions have to be made about the nature of the device the product is aimed at (screen resolution, requirements for hard disc, integration with an online service). How a product will be used, and by whom, should determine the selection of software. Software adds value to information and affects the 'look and feel' of the product. There is no direct analogy here with print production. Publishers who wish to use CD-ROM must therefore involve themselves closely in how the information will appear to the user, what software features are needed to provide the required forms of access and what equipment needs to be available for the product to be used.

These, and other considerations, add up to a new step in production that can be called product design. Publishers of books and magazines for the consumer market are familiar with the idea of 'designing the product'. It is less of a conscious requirement for publishers of professional and technical material. There is a significant risk that because the publisher may not be aware of the need for product design, decisions get made by default, determined not by the need to make an effective product, but by what the software supplier has on offer. The working relationship between the publisher and the systems integrator is vital during the product design phase. Publishers must recognize that product design in this context is an iterative process. Objectives and ideas must be shared between the systems integrator and the publisher. Undoubtedly some compromises will have to be made. The publishers should have developed their own thoughts about how they want the CD-ROM based product to work. These objectives have to be viewed in the context of what can sensibly be done with the present generation of computer technology and with off-the-shelf software. For example, there is no point in a publisher demanding high-quality full-colour illustrations, if the finished product is targeted at owners of standard PCs, or proposing the development of complicated expert systems as front ends to their planned product. This is not to say that the publisher should accept whatever the systems integrator offers. The publisher who has no views on market requirements and product design cannot be surprised by subsequent lack of sales.

Source data

The role of the systems integrator in handling a wide variety of source data will be discussed in detail later. Any review of the production process must acknowledge the significance of the form in which data is available. Whilst CD-ROM technology continues to address specialist markets, such as libraries (with well structured bibliographic databases offered as an alternative to online) or the market for financial information, the fundamental problems remain hidden. As the technology begins to be adopted as a widespread alternative to print, the magnitude of the problem of converting data from printers' tape to database will begin to emerge. There are, of course, significant differences between countries in the degree of sophistication of print and publishing technology. The UK is probably more backward than many countries, because of the long history of industrial relations problems and the reluctance of publishers to face up to the need to come to grips with new technology.

In the author's experience, the form in which the source data of printed publications are held is a major barrier to publishers who wish to exploit new sources of revenue from electronic delivery. The costs of automatically converting from a typesetting tape into a recognizable database that the systems integrator can use may be as great as rekeyboarding the entire collection of information. This initial production stage is notoriously difficult to cost accurately, giving the publisher a major problem in deciding on the economic viability of a proposed product.

Where publishers have anticipated a requirement to supply data in a neutral database format, few problems are encountered. File loading is done using standard software modules that expect standard forms of input. The simple translation of one tag in a publishers database, into another tag required by the file loading software, is a simple process, requiring no manual intervention. Where the source data is a typesetting tape, conversion may be straightforward, if the structure of the data is simple and a consistent set of editorial rules have been applied. In either case, one of the most important jobs undertaken by a systems integrator is to advise the publisher on the feasibility of using source data held in electronic form. The systems integrator will also provide the specialist knowledge to advise, and possibly carry out, the required preprocessing. Where processing can be carried out using existing software utilities, costs can be controlled. Where purpose-written (bespoke) software is required, costs escalate along with the period of time required to bring about a successful conclusion.

Paper and microfilm based products are not, of course, limited to text data. Indeed one of the strongest arguments for adopting CD-ROM technology, instead of other forms of electronic delivery, is its ability to distribute graphical and numeric data. The limitations on how graphics can be stored and represented will be discussed later in this chapter. It should be pointed out, however, that technology for capturing and storing graphics in machine readable form is less advanced and less standardized than it is for text and numbers. A further major barrier to the adoption of CD-ROM, particularly in areas such as technical documentation, is the lack of graphical information already held in machine readable form and the high cost of recreating a drawing in digital form.

File loading

Every software package distributed for use with CD-ROM requires data to be organized within a file structure specific to that package. Because CD-ROM is a read-only medium, the process of file loading takes place prior to disc mastering. It is worth making this obvious point because it is in contrast to the way in which most database management systems, written for the general data processing market, are designed to work. Indeed most database management systems go to considerable lengths to deal with the requirements of online updating, such as ensuring the latest version of a record is displayed and handling conflicts where two users try to update the same record at the same time. The requirements of file loading software for CD-ROM distribution are, first and foremost, that it can process input data as efficiently as possible, in batch mode, with minimum manual intervention. Speed of processing is significant because input files may be large and may need to be rerun in order to create accurate loaded files prior to mastering.

Typically, file loading will be offered as a service by systems integrators. Publishers who anticipate repeated use of the software (for example, for regular updating) will need to consider whether they should license the file loading software for inhouse use. The ease and cost of doing so may be a factor in a publisher's selection of software to be distributed as part of their product.

File loading is carried out using normal data processing equipment. The result of completing the file load stage is a copy of the finished information product, stored on a magnetic disc. At this stage, and prior to being transferred to CD-ROM, the selected user software can be used to test the product. Testing is important because once the disc master has been made no changes can be made. Testing should be carried out by the publisher and the systems integrator. Software is available that simulates the performance the product will give, once it has been put on compact disc. This is valuable because of the engineering characteristics of CD-ROM players and the effect these have on access times. Publishers should expect that at the end of a period of testing, the systems integrator will seek to obtain their approval that the work has been completed to the agreed specification. This again has a parallel with print production, where publishers' approval of final proofs is required before copies are printed and bound.

Pre-mastering

A further and final processing step is required before files can be sent to the disc mastering and replication facility. The files that have been loaded to create the structure required by the applications software must be formatted for layout on compact disc. CD-ROMs are not like magnetic discs. Data is recorded as a continuous spiral, rather than in sectors. Where data is put on a compact disc this can affect access times and subsequent performance. Pre-mastering is also the step at which file layout standards are imposed. As described in Chapter 1, agreement on a standard for the way files are held on CD-ROM was a vital prerequisite for its development as a medium for electronic publishing. Publishers should ensure that their discs are made to High Sierra standard (ISO 9660), because this provides forward compatibility with new versions of the target PCs operating system and ensures that the disc can be played on any standard combination of PC and CD-ROM player.

Output from the pre-mastering stage is a copy of the software and data files on magnetic tape in a standard format specified by the mastering and replication plant operators.

Mastering and replication

The process of mastering and replication is carried out at specialized facilities that are normally set up to produce compact audio discs. Building a compact disc manufacturing plant is expensive (of the order of US$20 million), because of the need to create a 100% clean environment. CD-ROM production piggybacks on the manufacture of compact audio discs in the same way that the manufacture of CD-ROM players depends heavily on the economies of scale achieved in the production of components for audio players. At present no replication plants exist solely for the production of CD-ROMs. Conversely not all CD audio plant can produce CD-ROM masters. Making a master CD-ROM requires a higher standard of error correction than audio disc mastering. Unlike audio recordings, files for mastering on CD-ROM are supplied on industry compatible magnetic tape and need to be transferred into the recording medium required for production of a master disc.

The systems integrator plays a minimal role in the disc mastering and replication process. Publishers may wish to contract directly with the suppliers of mastering and replication services. However, a systems integrator will have experience of dealing with those suppliers and resolving any difficulties which occur. A systems integrator may also have negotiated preferential terms, because of their regular use of the services, that can be passed on to the publisher. For these reasons many publishers prefer to place a single contract with the systems integrator, covering the entire production process.

Packaging and labelling

Unless otherwise instructed, disc replication services will supply discs with the name of the disc or the publisher printed in one colour. Discs for stand-alone drivers are supplied in clear plastic 'jewel cases' (with the introduction of integral drivers the new style of caddy for holding discs will become standard). Publishers need to specify the design and colours required on the disc. They also need to consider what material needs to be printed for insertion in the jewel case (for example, instruction booklet, statement of copyright and software licence terms). This is a further job that the publisher may wish to contract to the systems integrator. The publishers of information in electronic form have much to learn from the PC software industry about packaging and presentation. This area is often regarded as an irritating detail, but is essential as more and more CD-ROM products are produced for end user markets.

Beyond disc production

The job of the systems integrator may extend beyond providing disc production services. Participation in the commercial risk of bringing a disc-based information product to market is discussed elsewhere in this chapter. Keeping within the role of provider of systems and software, the systems integrator may need to support the publisher in developing the market for its products.

Every publisher launching a CD-ROM based product needs to consider whether a CD-ROM player, and possibly a PC, needs to be bundled with the price of the information product. PCs are easily acquired (although still with a relatively low installed base in some industries). Less than 70000 CD-ROM players were shipped worldwide in 1987. With the possible exception of the US library market a publisher cannot expect to find an installed base of players in its selected market. Furthermore, in Europe at least, distribution mechanisms and retail outlets for CD-ROM players are still at an early stage. For these reasons a publisher may well decide that pricing the information product to include a player is the only sensible marketing strategy. But publishers are traditionally wary of supplying hardware. This includes specialist secondary publishers with databases as well as primary publishers familiar only with print media. The systems integrator has a part to play filling the hardware component of the publishers' information product sale. The systems integrator can handle the purchase, inventory handling and shipment against orders received by the publisher. The systems integrator may negotiate an agreement with the player manufacturer that grants discounts on volume purchases, which could not be achieved with the more limited sales potential of a single CD-ROM based product. Supply by systems integrators of CD-ROM players brings the added benefit of technical support. Publishers are generally not geared to handling client's technical queries about equipment (How to instal it? Why won't the disc go round?). The systems integrator's greater level of technical expertise should ensure a happier base of clients. It is significant that Philips forecast the bulk of CD-ROM players they sell in Europe over the next 12–24 months being sold through systems integrators.

There is one further reason why the systems integrator may become involved in the supply of hardware. While many CD-ROM based information products require just the display of text and numbers on a screen, an increasing number of graphics-based information products will emerge. The demands of graphics display are many and various, and until a widespread standard evolves (possible through the upper range IBM PS/2 and its derivatives) special screens and special graphics boards may need to be supplied. Components have to be sourced and shipped to customers. Instructions need to be given (and frequently telephone support) to help with installation. Adequate post-sales support must be provided.

The same situation exists with CD-ROM products that require online telecommunications access in order to obtain the most up-to-date information. Where the product is aimed at a market without the necessary telecommunications boards and modems, the same problem of hardware supply, installation and support exist.

Systems integrators must offer the full range of technical expertise and resources needed to support the initial product specification. Their experience can be invaluable in helping publishers avoid technical pitfalls and achieve customer satisfaction.

Sources of data

Introduction

As the realization emerges that CD-ROM will become a widely-used publishing medium, so the variety in sources of data will extend to include holders of highly-structured data processing files, through to the publisher who arrives with a lorry load of printed copies. Systems integrators will inevitably specialize in handling different types of data and different sources of data. Initially however, and whilst applications for CD-ROM technology are still emerging, the systems integrator must offer a wide spectrum of services and ideally have a broad understanding of how information is organized and stored.

A fundamental problem exists with information that has been selected for electronic publishing. It has rarely been collected and organized in a manner that anticipates electronic distribution. The way information is organized is largely dictated by the anticipated uses to which it will be put. For example, most printed material, where it is available in machine readable form, is held in a form suitable for driving a typesetting system. Engineering drawings are usually held in the form dictated by the software used to create them (e.g. a computer-aided design system). Numeric data are stored using file structures expected by the computational software used to operate on them. It is only where database technology has been adopted that data files are likely to be held in a form independent of their source of input, or of a specific output technology. Even then, the way that data is organized within a database management system reflects the uses anticipated for the data. The systems integrator has a major part to play in analysing how data is currently held and identifying ways in which it can be transformed to be usable for electronic publishing.

Where source data is not available in machine readable form, or where the machine readable source is unusable, data capture techniques have to be employed.

Given the diversity of potential sources of information, it would be foolish to attempt a comprehensive classification. Instead, the following section reviews some broad classes of information and thus indirectly deals with the formats in which information can be made available to the systems integrator.

Structured text

Structured text is taken to include text-based information collections that are organized as discrete units of information (such as records) that can be broken down into smaller components (typically fields). Perhaps the most common example of a structured text database is the bibliographic database of the type that provided the initial impetus for the development of online systems during the 1970s. These often very large collections of information were converted into computer readable form at an early stage. The ability of computer software to automatically create indexes contributed to the early cost-justification of adopting computer-based typesetting systems. The use of database maintenance systems contributed substantially to the efficiency with which these information collections could be updated and maintained. Other examples of structured text are found in patents and standards databases, both of which contain data that looks in many ways like bibliographic data, and in directory type information. Company and product directories have already been targeted as candidates for CD-ROM distribution. Many of the larger directory publishers store and maintain their collections using similar techniques to those used by the producers of bibliographic databases. In addition, there are a great variety of lists of one type and another (dictionaries, address lists, catalogues) all of which fall under the heading of structured text.

Confusing though it may seem, structured text files often also contain numeric data. For example, numeric classification schemes, as in the case of business directories and numeric data on company financial performance. The major difference from a purely numeric database is the fact that text remains one of the key entry points to the information.

There are a few basic characteristics of structured text files that are significant. Individual records (entries) are separate entities. In the case of many bibliographic type files, an entry may have no relationship with entries that are contiguous with it in the database. They are next to each other just because they were added to the database one after another. Typically records will be broken into subrecords or fields. All records tend to have the same list of possible fields. Fields are defined to contain different types of information with the aim of reducing ambiguity between BROWN author and BROWN colour. The type of data held in a field will vary from short (a date) to long (a summary or abstract about the original item that the record describes), and from text to numeric. The ability to efficiently handle structured text data with software depends on flexibility (handling different types of data) and retrieval efficiency. However, the general functionality required is perhaps better established than for any other type of software designed to support electronic delivery. This is because of the well-established technology of online distribution of bibliographic type information.

A structured text file is amongst the easiest type of source data to process for distribution on CD-ROM. Each new record is clearly identified with a unique internal identifier. Fields within a record are separated and each field has its own unique tag that is used throughout the database. Well-organized databases will be supported by documentation that defines the editorial rules applied when entering data into a field. This documentation is important and valuable to the systems integrator. Changes in editorial practice over time have little effect on printed serial publications; they have a profound effect once a file is loaded under an information retrieval system. If a classification scheme is expanded and new headings added, how will a retrieval system match up items which fall into both the new and old classification? A change in convention about the use of punctuation in personal names can have a disastrous effect when the indexes are being built, unless they are first normalized. A well-documented file will record changes that have taken place over time in editorial rules and how they are applied.

Having understood the rules applied in creating the file, and having normalized data for internal consistency, the first stage of file loading should be simply a matter of translating the output format of the source file into the input format required by the file load software. This will often be possible using standard programs.

If the client wishes the data to appear differently on the CD-ROM product, it can be achieved at this stage by the systems integrator. It may be decided, during product specification, that a numeric classification should be replaced or supplemented by the text equivalent of the classification. The format of a date may be changed from a machine-friendly representation to a human friendly form. But again, if editorial rules have been applied consistently during file creation, and well documented, the application of simple algorithms can achieve the required effect.

In some tightly controlled file production and maintenance operations, software will have been used to validate data on entry. It is impossible to write programs to check that data entered into a file is sensible, but it is easy to check that a date follows the required format, that a numeric field contains only numbers, and that the record identifier is unique. Software checks of this type reassure the systems integrator that they are dealing with a 'clean' database, reduce the costs of dealing with inconsistent data, and increase confidence in the finished product.

The output formats in which structured text files are produced from a database maintenance system tend to follow common and well established rules. There are three common formats which the systems integrator should be familiar with:

● Continuous text stream. Data is supplied as a continuous stream of text, broken only by record delimiters and field tags and delimiters. Care must be taken to use delimiters that will never occur in the text, otherwise the software used to process the file will break a record or a field in the wrong place.
● Card image records. Using the most basic of computer input media, the 80-column card image, specified columns contain field tags and possibly one column to show where a field's contents continue over more than one line.
● Directory-based record structures. At the start of each record is a directory that specifies where a field starts and ends. This type of structure is the basis of the internationally agreed MARC format (also adopted by the International Standards Organization). The structure is more complex than the other two examples but has the benefit that more complex data structures (such as subfields) can be represented.

A systems integrator should have access to standard software that will read each of these common formats and convert data into the format required by the file loading programs.

Unfortunately not all structured text files are held using database maintenance systems. They may exist only in hard-copy form, with a common source being the ubiquitous card index catalogue. Smaller information providers, or organizations without access to professional data processing skills or equipment, may opt to use word processing software to create and maintain structured text files. The files involved are likely to be small because of the implicit limitations of PCs (limited storage, single data entry station). Word processing files themselves can create significant problems for the systems integrator. Word processing software is designed to show a screen representation of the text and to control a limited range of printers. Internally files are held in a format that is highly specific to the word processing software, including special control characters used by the software to control the screen. Multiple blanks, tabs and hard carriage returns are added by users to make the data look as though it is structured when displayed. Control characters and other unwanted formatting characters have to be removed before the file can be processed. Utilities are usually provided with word processing software that converts the word processed file into a file of neutral ASCII characters. But tabs, multiple blanks and hard carriage returns will have to be removed using specially written software, which at the same time will have to infer the structure of the data from the layout applied by the person using the word processor.

Handling 'databases' created using word processing software should not present the systems integrator with any substantial problems, but the fact that further processing is needed to reorganize the data underlines the benefits of using DBMS software, which is now widely available for PCs as well as far larger shared systems.

Continuous text

Continuous text differs from structured text in that it is not easily divided into discrete records with a repeating structure. The most obvious example of continuous text is a book. Most books contain information organized to reflect the author's or editor's ideas about how topics within the subject of the book should be grouped together. With some obvious exceptions, such as encyclopedias, books normally have a hierarchical structure: Volume, chapter, section, paragraph. A contents list is a map of this structure that gives the reader immediate insight into how the author has treated the subject.

Techniques of book production, and particularly of typesetting, have become more efficient with the introduction of computers. Most photo-typesetting systems now incorporate computers as front ends, to aid in the process of calculating how many words can be fitted on a line, how many lines to a page, and the automation of other, previously manual tasks. The fact that text and other information is being captured in a form in which it can be processed by a computer leads many publishers to believe that they therefore automatically have a usable source for the creation of electronic information products. They have not.

There are a number of fundamental problems facing the systems integrator who is presented with a typesetting tape as the source of data for a proposed product. These problems have been familiar to online operators over many years, who ventured into putting printed directories online. They are being rediscovered by suppliers of software and services for using CD-ROM, but with greater impact because of the emphasis on CD-ROM as an alternative to print. It must also be stressed that not all continuous text comes on typesetting tapes; some alternative and preferable formats are discussed later.

But, in the author's experience, a vast gulf remains between the technology, procedures and assumptions used in typesetting systems and the requirements of the electronic publishing data processing specialist. There is a basic problem, that the way information is captured and organized is dictated by the perceived end product. If a publisher is producing a printed book then it is not surprising if the technology used is specific to print production. It takes a far-sighted publisher to spend more than the cost of straight typesetting, in anticipation that the text may need to be processed for electronic delivery. Those publishers who have anticipated the future benefits are now in a stronger position to exploit the new delivery technologies. Those publishers who have continued to use 'standard' typesetting technology will now have to consider the costs of reprocessing, or, at worst, rekeyboarding the text of the selected product.

It is probably helpful to explain the nature of problems encountered by the systems integrator in converting data on typesetting tapes into a form where it can be used as input to file loading software.

When continuous text (or for that matter any text) is searched or displayed using a computer, it is necessary for software to differentiate between different types of information held within the text. It is also necessary for the structure of the text to be clearly identified to the software. In print, both the structure and the difference between types of information are indicated using typography. The weight of a type font (font size, emboldening) and the layout of text on a page are essential clues to the reader. Chapter headings are set in larger type, section headings are set in bold type to distinguish them from the body text. Other types of information, such as footnotes, figure captions and references are laid out on the page to make it clear to the reader that they are not part of the continuous text. Typography has a rich repertoire of type styles and layout that the typesetter and designer use to make the information clear and easy to read.

The typesetter controls the selection of fonts by inserting special commands to the typesetting system that cause it to change font, indent from the side of the page and so on. The typesetting tape therefore contains both the text of the publication and the control characters that control the phototypesetting machine. In order to use a typesetting tape the *implicit structure of the information has to be inferred from the typographic control codes*. This in itself does not represent a difficult programming challenge, provided that the codes used by the typesetting system are known. Unfortunately typography can either be ambiguous (using the same typographic convention for different types of information, e.g. italics for both footnotes and captions) or rely on a combination of font and position on page to indicate the type of information being presented (for example, using the same point size for two types of heading, with the less important heading indented). The examples given here are simplistic, but a brief examination of any complex technical book will illustrate how hard it is to derive a consistent set of rules about how typography has been applied. Human readers are always able to use the additional clue of context when dealing with typographic ambiguity. The reader understands what the text says. Computer programs that try to derive rules using syntax and grammar are very difficult to write, and rarely achieve the required level of accuracy.

Two important types of information are particularly difficult to process when presented without structure in a stream of continuous text. Cross references are widely used in scientific and technical publications. Ignoring cross references would mean degrading the quality of information, yet the editorial conventions for citing a cross reference are rarely applied consistently. They can vary from 'see Section 1.3.2' to 'readers might wish to refer to the second paragraph on page 173'. The function of a cross reference in a book is exactly matched by the use of 'hot spots', a software function that allows a sideways jump from one point to another in a file of information. But this software function can only be used where the start and the target of a cross reference can be unambiguously identified. The systems integrator has, therefore, to write software that reads the text held on the typesetting tape, looking for all possible variants in the form of cross references. Since there is a chance of creating spurious cross references in this process, this often means going through an editorial check after the source data has been processed.

A further class of problematic information is a table. Tables can vary enormously in complexity, limited only by the amount of information that can be fitted on a printed page. Whether large or small, simple or complex, the same difficulties are encountered. A table is understood by a reader because rows and columns are labelled; in order to know what a particular value relates to, the reader has only to inspect the labels in the relevant row and column. What appears on the typesetting tape is just the number of spaces between values inserted to ensure the characters line up under the appropriate heading. The values are not linked in any clear or logical way to the names of the row and column in which they fall. In other words, the typesetting system is only concerned with putting the right characters in the right place on the page, not with retaining a link between the characters in a cell and what information the cell is meant to contain. To make matters worse, there is rarely consistency between groups of tables in the way they are laid out in a book or journal. The way a table is composed for print is based purely on the information content and the space available, not in accordance with fixed editorial rules. This means that to process them may require several bespoke programs or reinputting the contents of the table.

Fortunately tables are relatively infrequent (they are complicated and expensive to typeset as well). If it is not cost effective to automatically convert from the source typesetting tape, the table can be rekeyed directly into a form in which it can be handled by the selected software. Indeed, this may prove to be a benefit in disguise. One characteristic of a PC is the very limited number of characters that can be fitted on a screen. Twenty-four lines of 80 characters gives a maximum of around 2000 characters, allowing for no blank spaces and no blank lines. This is less than a third the number of characters that fit on a normal printed page. Print is already a limited medium for communicating complex tabular information (forcing publishers sometimes to have pages that fold out). Given a page that is one-third normal size, there is a real problem displaying anything more than the simplest table. In order to resolve this dilemma we must ask ourselves 'what is the table trying to do?'.

A table is primarily a mechanism for retrieving a unit of data, using the X-Y coordinates of the rows and columns. This is in fact something that computers are very good at doing. It is supported by existing software packages (such as spreadsheets) and is very easy to program. A table, stored in a computer, can be infinitely wide and infinitely deep (limited only by the amount of online storage available). Therefore once the data contained in a printed table has been processed or reinput, it becomes easier to access using software than on the printed page. The user can scroll sideways across the columns and down through the rows until the desired area is displayed. Alternatively the software could support user selection of a specific combination of a row and column, with the data held in that cell being displayed directly.

This is one area that, if properly handled, can significantly improve user access to complex information, beyond what can be achieved in printed form. Better still if the data held in a table is amenable to subsequent processing, the computer can be used to manipulate, reformat or use the data as input to other computational software. A simple example might be using the facilities of a spreadsheet package to create a graphical representation of selected numeric data.

Giving structure to continuous text

So far this section has concentrated on some of the problems faced by a publisher and a systems integrator when dealing with tapes generated directly from typesetting systems. An alternative and much preferred solution is for the publisher to capture and store their products in a neutral format independent of any specific output device or delivery medium.

Over the last ten years a major internationl effort has been under way to define and standardize generic mark-up languages. A generic mark-up language is a language used by the subeditor preparing a manuscript, to describe the different types of information explicitly, rather than in terms of the desired typographic characteristics. Instead of marking a first-level heading for setting, say, in 12pt bold, the subeditor will add a code 'H1' contained within a pair of escape codes that distinguish the mark-up from the text. By using this technique, all the different classes of information held within the text (headings, footnotes, captions, cross references and so on) can be described in a neutral and unambiguous form. Most importantly this language can be understood by a computer, which can then impose on the different types of information the characteristics required of it for a particular form of output. Typesetting can be automatically performed using a set of rules, e.g. 'all first-level headings are set in 12pt bold'. Processing the same text to be used with retrieval software on CD-ROM, the rule might be 'mark every word between this first-level heading and the next as belonging to the same section'. In other words, at the data capture stage, a single source is created that can then be automatically processed without further significant manual effort in editing or rekeying. The use of generic mark-up gives the publisher a genuine resource of information for repackaging into various forms.

The adoption of generic mark-up by publishers in the UK has been slow, despite a lot of educational effort on the part of industry associations. To be fair, the cost of retraining editorial staff and the effort required to impose more rigorous editorial standards are a very real barrier to change. Unfortunately there is also some disagreement on generic mark-up standards, which has led to the UK adopting slightly different standards from the US. However, any SGML (Standard Generic Mark-up Language) is better than no SGML. Even if a publisher develops its own variant on SGML, it will still achieve flexibility and cost savings in subsequent reuse of information.

In addition to adopting generic mark-up, additional disciplines must be imposed on the production process. Whether the information is held in a neutral form on a computer using SGML or whether it is available only in the form of a typesetting tape, the publisher must ensure that *all* the information is stored in its final form. With the normal pressures to hit deadlines for production, last-minute errors are often corrected by cut and paste directly on to the composed text. These changes must be incorporated into the master copy of the information. Few controls exist to impose this discipline, but without it errors will persist in subsequent reuse of the information.

Sources of graphics

It is difficult to generalize about sources for graphical information. The diversity of types of graphic and the different approaches used within different industries mean that the systems integrator will either have to specialize or to assemble a wide range of expertise in different aspects of graphics handling. Graphics are, however, of great significance, particularly in the use of CD-ROM for delivering scientific, technical and medical information products. One of the major reasons why online delivery has generally failed to meet the requirements of the primary publisher is the inability of that technology to sensibly handle anything more than the crudest graphics. The large storage capacity of CD-ROM, combined with increased processing capacity in the PC and wider availability of high-resolution screens, make the delivery of graphics a realistic option. Indeed a new range of purely graphical information products is being stimulated by the convergence of these technologies.

The use of computers to capture and store graphics is less widespread and less standardized than with text and numbers. Computer-Aided Design (CAD) systems are used extensively in certain industries (for example, the aerospace and automotive industries, the design of electrical circuits and in the construction industry). CAD systems are almost unknown in the print and publishing industries. Very few primary publishers use computer technology to originate line drawings. These are still normally produced by hand on the drawing board. Photographic illustrations are normally merged with the typeset text only at the final stage in production. On the rare occasions that photographs are transferred into machine readable form, it is done for organizational purposes (for example, to ensure that illustrations are correctly placed in text in very large publications) with little attention paid to long-term archiving. Systems integrators, working with publishers to create electronic products that combine text and graphics, will in most cases need to organize the electronic capture of graphics from the original sources. It is also worth observing that publishers who have not anticipated the reuse of information may be casual in the preservation of the original material. Photographs and drawings may get left around the production office until someone notices them and throws them away in a moment of tidiness.

Assuming the source material is still available what are the technical options available to the developer of the electronic product?

Raster vs vector
Computer graphics technology is fundamentally split. Prior to the emergence of scanner technology, vector-based graphics representation dominated. This technology depends on recording the points between which lines are subsequently drawn. As the drawing is input each new

point is recorded. Software controls the creation of lines, curves and fills. This is basically how a CAD drawing is captured and stored. There are two basic advantages to vector-based systems. Firstly, the storage required is minimized since all that is recorded is the X and Y coordinates of each new point. Secondly, because the computer 'knows' about the points that make up the drawing, software can be used to manipulate the drawing. It can be scaled, rotated, stretched or compressed. It can also be edited to produce a modified drawing by again using CAD software facilities. The main disadvantages of vector representation are that photographs cannot be processed and the high cost of recreating line drawings. The technology required to go from a scanned (raster) representation of a drawing to a vector-based representation is still embryonic and not widely available. This means that a line illustration has to be redrawn using a selected CAD system (or in the case of less demanding applications using one of the draw package available with the new generation of software environment such as Windows or GEM).

One of the main barriers to the widespread adoption of CD-ROM technology as an alternative to the use of microfilm by the automotive and aerospace industries is the high cost of recreating huge volumes of complex drawings and the need to adopt CAD technology for the future creation of maintenance manuals and illustrated parts catalogues.

Raster-based representation of graphics is a newer technology that emerged with the development of the laser printer (the engines used are fundamentally the same as those used in scanners). The technology works by scanning a drawing or a photograph by moving a point of light backwards and forwards across the image, recording light levels. The closer the scanned lines are together, the better the resolution of the captured image. Because of the standards used by laser printers, 300 dot per inch (dpi) has become a widely accepted norm.

Scanned images are cheaper to capture than are vector-based drawings although some manual intervention is necessary: handling, cropping and in some cases cleaning up the illustration. The fundamental disadvantages of scanned images are that they are not intelligent — they cannot be edited or otherwise manipulated by software — and that they require larger amounts of storage. The latter disadvantage is ameliorated by the wide availability of compression techniques that can typically reduce the amount of storage used by a factor of 10 to 1. But a compressed image has to be decompressed at display time. This can be done reasonably quickly by the use of special hardware (an additional board in a PC) or slowly using software. Fast and slow in this context are very variable because of the difference in the density of pictures and the number of lines that may have been used in scanning.

The use of scanned images has been accelerated by the development of facsimile machines for the transmission of documents. The Group 3 fax standard can be used to capture and compress an image at low cost. The boards developed for fax machines can then be used to decompress the image after it is retrieved from the disc. A number of electronic publishing experiments have been mounted using Group 3 fax as a standard (namely, ADONIS and as part of the European Commission DOCDEL programme). In both these applications, both the text and illustrations have been scanned and the resulting image stored electronically for delivery on demand to a remote facsimile machine. This approach has the immense advantage of removing the need to reprocess the original machine readable sources. No more typesetting tapes, no special programming, no additional editing. The great disadvantage of storing an information product as an image is that no value can be added by providing computer software to access or process the information. The image is not intelligent, just a large array of bits that have to be displayed in exactly the same way they are stored.

Display technology

All PCs can display text and numbers on a standard screen. Once the product adds illustrations, consideration must be given to the type of display screen needed, the availability in the market place of the selected display technology, and the cost of upgrading where necessary. Manufacturers promoting their products all describe the PCs they offer as incorporating a high-resolution screen. This is simply untrue. The first generation of IBM PCs and their clones use very low-resolution screens. Screens start to offer better quality resolution at 100 dpi and over. Expensive CAD systems work at over 500 dpi. However a publisher will be unrealistic if he believes that customers will rush out and spend over US$1000 for a special screen in order to view the illustrations held in a CD-ROM based product. The only exception is high-value graphics applications such as the delivery of CAD drawings libraries or high quality mapping data.

For the bulk of CD-ROM based publications, developers have to work within the limits of the technology that is already installed and in the marketplace. The most common standard at the time of writing are IBM's CGA and EGA graphics and the similar Hercules board. All boards are widely available or can be added to existing PCs at low cost. But, working at this level, it is difficult to display much more than a simple line drawing with much success. Once the drawing becomes too complex, lines will be too close together and merge and captions will become unreadable. This is irrespective of the resolution at which the image was originally captured. This standard of graphics adaptor is inadequate to display photographs. It does not offer any grey scales on the screen and therefore the picture is reduced to patches of black and white (or phosphor green and black).

Depending on the type of illustration required, the choice of preparing a product for delivery to an EGA/Hercules standard screen may decide the producer in favour of redrawing illustrations. Control can then be exerted over the density of lines and the size of captions, rather than using scanning technology, where the results on the user's screen will be variable depending on the scale and complexity of the original drawing.

Those developers who want to deliver photographs (and ideally colour photographs) on CD-ROM should not despair. It is already possible to demonstrate high-quality colour photographs stored on CD-ROM and displayed using special graphics boards and high quality colour monitors. The newly announced PS/2 range of PCs from IBM includes higher resolution displays and standard boards capable of driving them. These computers will start to replace the existing generation over the next few years, creating a market to which high quality graphics can be delivered on CD-ROM.

Moving pictures

Some comment is needed on the feasibility of using moving pictures as part of CD-ROM based products. CD-ROM technology as currently available is not capable of supporting video sequences. It is however capable of providing low-quality animation (low quality in the sense of not producing smooth movement of animated figures, but rapid redrawing of a series of pictures can achieve pseudo-animation of the type used in the computer games industry). The fundamental limitation lies in the speed at which the disc rotates and hence the rate at which the digitized version of the image can be read off the disc. This limitation is being addressed in the CD-I specification (albeit initially using only one-seventh of the screen area). The limitation of CD-ROM technology is capable of being overcome by using extremely high compression factors, of the order of 100 to 1. Digital Video Interactive (DV-I) technology, which achieves this, has been demonstrated, but is a few years away in terms of production volumes of chips and realistic pricing levels.

Product design

One important factor that distinguishes the development of an electronic information product from the production of a printed product is the considerable attention that must be given to product design. A book is designed from the point of view of typography, layout and content. By contrast, an electronic product must be designed to 'work' in a way that the user will find useful and yet simple. The systems integrator should bring to the task of product design, wide-ranging experience of electronic information products. A publisher has a concept of what the CD-ROM product should do, what information it contains and what market it is aimed at. The integrator's job is to interpret that concept in terms of software and interface design. The first step towards developing a product is to prepare a detailed functional specification by combining the publisher's objectives, the systems integrator's knowledge of what can realistically be achieved, and as much information as possible about how the product is likely to be used.

But even before work can begin on this functional specification, the systems integrator will need to carry out a detailed analysis of the proposed sources for the information. Previously, in this chapter, the author has commented on some of the difficulties that may be encountered in using existing machine readable sources as input to the production of a CD-ROM based product. The level to which a computer-readable source is documented varies widely. In general, it is only those organizations with a mature data-processing operation that document their systems fully. Where a publisher has used an outside agency such as a typesetting bureau, documentation tends to be poor in quality and communications between the publisher, the typesetter and the systems integrator are likely to be slow. Where documentation exists, it is fragmented. The publisher may document the editorial rules applied. The typesetter will have detailed documentation on how their typesetting system works, but not necessarily on how it has been used to interpret the editorial rules. Ideally documentation should cover:

- the structure of the information,
- coding systems employed,
- editorial rules applied (and changes over time),
- updating rules and policies,
- how the data is held,
- physical tape formats.

The availability of documentation reduces the amount of time the systems integrator will need to spend on analysis. In all cases, systems integrators must familiarize themselves with the contents of the information, the markets envisaged for it by the publisher and the way the finished product is likely to be used. Where no documentation is available, substantial amounts of effort may have to be spent with publishers and with any outside organizations used in capturing and storing the data. The final product of this activity should be a report back to the publisher that documents the form in which the information is held and the feasibility of using existing machine readable sources. This report should be of value to the publisher even if the publisher decides not to use the production services offered by the systems integrator. Having completed the data analysis, the systems integrator should be able to give an indication of the cost of processing the source data into the required form or for the cost of recapturing the information.

The systems integrator can also support the publisher in its effort to position the planned CD-ROM product for the market. A systems integrator's ability to provide consultancy in the area of publications planning will, of course, depend on the range of experience of the staff. Evidence that the systems integrator has worked in similar areas in the past is a good criterion for selection.

Product planning includes research to establish facts about the proposed market, such as the present distribution of PCs, the availability of CD-ROM players and the value that the ultimate purchaser is likely to put on the finished product. It can also include an analysis of how the information can be integrated into existing computer based activities. Investigation in these areas can be based on past experience, access to published sources and discussion with potential customers. If it is considered necessary to carry out a full market survey, the systems integrator should be involved in preparing the survey and analysing the results.

With the analysis of the source data completed and some clear ideas about the proposed market, the systems integrator and the publisher can set about the task of designing the desired product. The primary objective of product design should be to find ways in which software can be used to enhance the value of information. The opportunities that exist will be dictated by the nature of the information and the working environment in which it will be used. In the case of a bibliographic type database, the use of software may be limited to providing fast and precise access to relevant information. Where the information collection is large or complex, computer-based search techniques may be the primary function of the product, but in many cases designers need to consider what further processing the user may wish to carry out on that information.

In a library environment, further processing may mean merging retrieved information with other information sources. It may be desirable for a bibliographic record to be imported into the library cataloguing system, or made available in a neutral format so that it can be incorporated in a printed bibliography. Designers of full text products will need to consider providing links to word processing, so that having found a relevant passage, the user can extract the text and incorporate it into a report. In the case of information that includes financial data, the user may wish to use a spreadsheet package to analyse the figures or to present them in a graphical form. Each of these options involves making design decisions about the units of information that can be retrieved (a record, a paragraph, a line) and designing software that will easily download the selected information into the target software.

All products, but particularly those designed for end user markets, should be implemented to minimize the amount of work needed to switch between information access and the programs used for subsequent processing. Designers should be sensitive to the potential frustrations for the user of, step by step, having to select information, download on to a hard disc, stop the program that accesses the information, start up the target applications software, tell the software the name of the file that holds the downloaded information and then reverse the process to get back to the CD-ROM access software. As far as possible, designers should try to integrate the information product into the general PC environment. A good example of how this can be achieved exists in the Microsoft Bookshelf product, which allows the user to access information held on the CD-ROM whilst remaining inside wordprocessing software.

The availability of Windows and GEM provides a straightforward route to achieving these design objectives. The advent of multi tasking on PCs will make simultaneous access to multiple information sources an achievable reality.

Integration of an information product with an established PC application is one of the keys to the successful development of an electronic information product. The publisher can target a precise market and sell the product on the strength of improved productivity and effectiveness for an established activity.

Understanding how an information product is going to be used, whether integrated with other PC applications, or as a 'stand alone' reference product, informs the product designer about the selection and use of applications software. The functionality required for the finished product must be matched to available software options. Because of the overwhelming benefits of selecting from the wide range of existing CD-ROM software, the publisher is well advised to work with a systems integrator that offers a suitable software package. If the product is to contain graphics, the integrator should offer software able to support the display of graphics. If the product incorporates statistical data, a different profile of software functions is needed. This may be an obvious principle to state, but online technology has survived for fifteen years on the premise that a single centrally-operated software package is capable of handling widely different collections of information. One of the great opportunities offered by CD-ROM is to develop information products incorporating software tailored to the requirements of the information and to its application.

It is to be hoped that developers of CD-ROM based products avoid some of the mistakes made by operators of online services, particularly avoiding the complexity of search languages and the inflexibility of user interface design.

In order to provide the desired software functionality, it is likely that the selected applications software will need some tailoring and possibly the implementation of special software features. Those additional features may be specific to the types of information being handled or to the requirements of a specific market. This is likely in the case where CD-ROM applications software needs to be integrated with some existing PC application. The more flexible the CD-ROM software, the more easily special features can be impiemented by the systems integrator. The systems integrator should be in a position to estimate the time and cost elements required for undertaking software development following the completion of an agreed product specification.

A well-designed CD-ROM software package should combine the required functionality with a flexible set of tools for designing the user interface. A complicated or confusing user interface will result in poor sales and undue frustration. It is impossible to generalize about user interface design. Different considerations apply to different products and different markets. If the author was pressed to offer nine golden rules to be observed, they would be:

- Avoid cluttered and over complicated screens.
- Always let the user know when input is required.
- Show the user the options available.
- Where long response times are inevitable, provide feedback that the system is still working.
- Try to match the way information is presented to the user's intuitive view of the contents.
- Always provide a consistent and simple route back to the start of an operation.
- Never display incomprehensible system error messages.
- Try to do a few things well, and avoid adding too many complicated options.
- Provide clear and concise help messages.

A good systems integrator should be able to advise the publisher on user interface design and have the technical resources to implement the desired result. User interface design is likely to go through several iterations of testing before the optimum solution is achieved.

Product design does not end with the specification of software functions and information organization. Attention must be given to making the product easy to access for the user who has just unwrapped the packaging and sits in front of the PC wondering how to get started. The majority of sales of CD-ROM products will be to inexperienced users. They will not be willing to attend training courses or read complex manuals end to end. The product designer has probably no more than five minutes of the user's attention in which the product has to be loaded and used for the first time. Beyond five minutes, frustration and anger will set in, and it will be directed at the supplier. Simple procedures and a clear set of initial instructions are vital. Ideally telephone support should be available to help the confused new user through his first faltering steps. Building the user's confidence in his or her ability to use the product is a vital component of successful design.

The design and specification of the planned product is a crucial step in the production process. Without it neither the publisher nor the systems integrator will know where the product is going. When completed, the systems integrator can proceed with implementation and file loading.

File loading

Whatever software is chosen for distribution as part of a CD-ROM based information product, input data will have to go through a 'file loading' process before it can be transferred to CD-ROM. Everyone who uses a PC knows that a spreadsheet package cannot access text entered using a word processing package (unless the two are linked in some way by software). This is because each applications software package has its own specific file structure that only it can use. PC users are not normally conscious of the existence of this file structure (except when they try to read a file using the wrong software by accident) because data is structured as it is input.

Everyone also knows that computer software handles both input and output. Because of the read-only nature of CD-ROM, these two functions have to be separated. Data held in files has to be processed into the structure and format expected by the applications software that will access it, before the files are transferred to CD-ROM. This step in the production process is referred to in a number of different ways: database build, data preparation, file inversion, indexing etc. For the purposes of this book, the term file loading has been adopted.

What actually happens during file loading is specific to the type of application and the software used to support it. The process required to load a graphics file for access by a CAD package is quite different to the processing required for, say, a collection of statistical data. Because most of the initial applications of CD-ROM are for retrieval from large databases of text and numeric data, only this type of data will be covered in this section. At least with retrieval software, there is a multiplicity of software packages that all work in more or less the same way. Other types of applications software (mapping, CAD, statistical etc.) are more heterogeneous in the way they work and therefore in the basic rules for file loading.

Information retrieval software

The theory of information retrieval is extensively documented in the literature and will not be dealt with here. It is necessary to make clear that most information retrieval software works on an inverted file principle. Information retrieval systems were developed some twenty years ago to deal with large files of bibliographic data within which a few specific entries had to be located and rapidly retrieved. The first attempts at solving this problem were based on serial searching in batch mode, where the selected subjects or terms were matched against the characteristics of each entry in the database. The serial searching approach could not support interactive access, therefore indexing techniques were developed that enabled the applications software to find a route, from a term entered by a user, directly to all the entries containing that term. The simplest and still most successful solution to this problem is to create an index containing all the words, phrases and numbers in the input file, and to invert that index so that it is sorted in some sort of alphanumeric order. It is much simpler for software to find an entry in an alphabetic list that matches the user's query, than it is to scan the original file end to end. The inverted index not only contains the terms, but it also contains pointers to the records from which this term derives, a count of the number of times the term occurs in the database and usually information about the position of the term in relation to other terms (in order that retrieval can take place on 'nuclear' within three words of 'resonance'). Despite significant advances, over the last 15 years, in hardware that does multiple parallel searches of a database, the inverted file software approach remains the best proven and most widely-used solution to the problem of rapidly locating a single unit of information in a large collection of data. This approach is ideal at finding a needle in a haystack (it is not necessarily the best approach for those wishing to view the whole of the haystack from end to end, but that is a different discussion).

The disadvantages of inverted file information retrieval systems include the amount of processing which has to go into creating the index, the amount of storage the index requires and the problem of updating the index, as the file is updated.

Alternative approaches

The reader should not be left with the idea that inverted file retrieval software is the only way to offer electronic information products on CD-ROM; it is simply the best known and longest established. Information theory has developed along several paths over the last twenty years. Some of the most interesting approaches have emerged from the efforts of designers of computer systems for use by non-specialists. Although this work began a long while ago, it has only started to influence the design of software products over the last two or three years. Perhaps the most dramatic breakthrough was the launch of the Apple Macintosh followed by the general development of the WIMPS environment (Window, Icon, Mouse, Pointer).

The same theorists behind the development of this new type of user interface have been concerned with the problem of organizing quantities of text and graphics in a way that allows fast and easy access without the need for specialist training in retrieval command languages and Boolean logic. They have developed the view that complex information is best represented as a network of inter-related units, rather than a simple linear structure. Paper-based products tend to be linear because of the difficulty of jumping around from place to place in a book. Software does not suffer from the same limitation. There is now a new type of software product based around a concept called 'hypertext'. Hypertext assumes that within a unit of information (which may be words, numbers or pictures) there are jumping-off points to further information. For example, within a diagram of an engine there will be points that will lead the user to a more detailed diagram or some explanatory text. Within a text passage, there will be words behind which further explanation or information exists. These jumping-off points are referred to as 'hot spots'. Moving the cursor over a hot spot gives the user some feedback that further information is available if they wish to see it.

Whilst this approach is exciting, allowing the creation of new types of information product that provide better models for human knowledge than can be achieved with linear organization, it implies the creation of those new products from scratch. Since the bulk of published knowledge is on paper, and paper implies linear organization, there is no easy route from an existing publication to a hypertext-based electronic information product on CD-ROM. Technical documentation, for example, would have to be re-authored and reorganized in order to work in this way. The one area where this view of information has so far had an impact is in the handling of cross references. The paper-based equivalent of a hot spot is a cross reference, which is a vital tool in the hands of the scientific and technical author and editor. Cross references cannot be handled in any sensible way by conventional inverted file retrieval packages (there is very limited connectivity within a bibliographic database). A few packages are now available that incorporate hot spots with conventional retrieval techniques. These packages are appropriate for use with electronic versions of full text publications. So a further processing stage has to be added in file loading, to identify a cross reference and its target and to build a pointer from one to the other, allowing the user of the retrieval software to jump to a cross-referenced point and back again.

Indexing

Creating the index for an inverted file system determines the form and scope of the access that will be available to the user. If a certain class of data is indexed then an entry or entries can be retrieved using a term in that index. If the decision is taken not to index on a particular class of data then the only means of accessing entries through that class of data will be by a serial search if the applications software permits this. For example: an inverted file information retrieval system would be a good way to handle a telephone directory on CD-ROM. Although subscribers' names are sorted alphabetically in a printed directory, the name of the street is not. If both were indexed then it would be much easier to find a particular Mr Jones, by combining his name with the name of the street he lives in. Now, the product designer has the choice of indexing the telephone number. This would mean that using a phone number it would be possible to retrieve the name and address of the subscriber. As a means of protecting subscribers, some telephone service operators (British Telecom in the UK) will not allow look-up by telephone number. The product designer may decide not to index on a certain class of data for a multiplicity of reasons, but in general the decision goes in favour of indexing, because of the potential increase in utility of the finished product, at low cost.

How a class of data is indexed is also an important decision for the product designer. This topic comes close to the questions related to software selection and therefore will not be dealt with in detail in this section. It is sufficient to make the point that different applications software provides different indexing facilities and it is important to consider those capabilities in relation to the type of information product the software will be used with. For example, formal chemical names are more effectively retrieved by software and indexes that support left-hand truncation; full text applications benefit from being able to keep information in the index about the co-occurrence of terms within a sentence or a paragraph.

A crucial step in the development of a CD-ROM based product is a careful analysis of the different types of data held in a file, an informed consideration of what types of retrieval users will wish to carry out, and a trial run of the indexing rules adopted on a subset of the file. Once the rules have been developed and tested the full file has to be automatically processed through a number of steps that together make up the file load process. Each software package varies in how these steps are divided and performed, but in summary the logical steps are:

(1) Break out the index terms from the entries in the input file.
(2) Sort the index terms into the order required by the retrieval software (this may be a single alphanumeric sorted file or several files each sorted alphanumerically).
(3) Process the sorted index terms to count the occurrences of a particular term, compress the index terms so the text of the term occurs the minimum number of times (deduplication), and build the structure, complete with pointers to the entries in the linear file.
(4) Process the input file to build the structure required by the software to allow access and display in the required order.

Processing considerations

The amount of processing required to complete the file load will increase, at best, linearly to the size of the input file. In fact, it will tend to get worse the larger the file because of the increasing difficulties of sorting larger files. If the application involves very large files that will fill a CD-ROM (or indeed flow over several discs), the processing time required can be substantial. Depending on the efficiency of the software and the speed of the computer used, elapsed time can stretch from hours to several days. Any computer job that runs over several days poses special problems (like making sure no one unplugs the computer while the job is running) and the ability to stop and restart jobs is a special consideration in software selection.

The sorting stage particularly will require a significant amount of magnetic storage space. Typically, this will be between 2.5 and 4 times the size of the input file. There are sort techniques that use less file space, but at the cost of increasing the amount of processing time required.

Running a file through the file load process the first time may need several attempts in order to ensure the processing completes correctly and the procedures surrounding the processing are correctly set up. When a file has been processed through several updates the procedures should 'bed down' and processing become routine and automatic. An operation that is processing many different types of often new products (such as a bureau service) may encounter procedural problems and the frustration of having to rerun work several times.

Updating

Because of the read-only nature of CD-ROM, updating requires some specific comment. In a conventional magnetic storage environment, it is possible to add new data or amend existing data with relative ease. Updating an inverted index does cause some special problems but these are overcome by following special procedures supported by most file load software. When a CD-ROM based product requires updating the product developer has a limited range of choices. Indeed the selection of CD-ROM as a delivery medium should be dictated by the updating frequency of the product. It is possible to issue a new CD-ROM on a weekly cycle. Mastering and replication facilities are offering premium services for mastering and pressing within 24 hours. However, the cost of making a new master each week and the production operation needed to support this make it feasible only for products that appeal to a large, high-value market.

Alternatives to reissuing a new updated CD-ROM are either providing online access to updated data (with the associated need for software that links to the online service and makes the updates appear transparent to the user) or by delivering updates on some other medium such as floppy disc or tape cartridge. Both techniques are employed by existing CD-ROM products, but both have the disadvantage of additional operating costs and increased complexity for the user. It is likely that in the future, the most successful and more widespread applications of CD-ROM will be those that require less frequent updating (monthly, quarterly, annually) or those which do not require updating at all.

Testing

Once a file has been fully loaded on the production computer system, it must be reviewed and tested before the data is sent for mastering on to CD-ROM. It is less costly to correct a file on magnetic storage than it is to re-master the CD-ROM. Testing is difficult, particularly in the case of large files where it is not feasible to proofread the product from end to end. Normally testing must be limited to checking out functionality and examining sample data from within the file. Where the file loading is being carried out under contract by a systems integrator, the systems integrator will normally require the publisher placing the contract to sign an under-taking that they approve the file as loaded on magnetic storage and accepting responsibility for the cost of remastering and replicating, in case this proves to be necessary as a result of errors discovered in the final product.

During the test phase, it may be desirable to run a simulation of the performance of the product as it will appear when available on CD-ROM. The positioning of files on a disc can have a significant impact on retrieval performance. Specialist software exists that will simulate the slow access time characteristic of CD-ROM technology, allowing the product developers to make adjustments to layout in order to give improved retrieval performance.

Processing software

The software that performs the file load is supplied by the same organization that has developed the retrieval software. In the normal data-processing world it would be unnecessary to make this point clear, because the input and output operations are tightly integrated (you can display the results of a change to a word processing file immediately the change has been made). Preparation of files for distribution on CD-ROM is a separate process from users retrieving information from those files. The markets for the two components of the applications software are clearly different. The retrieval software is distributed to every user of the CD-ROM based product and probably with every copy made of the CD-ROM. It therefore has to have a lower unit cost and contains none of the functions associated with the file load process. The file load software, on the other hand, is designed to be used by specialist technical staff concerned with production. It needs extensive functionality to allow the product developer to tailor the product to his/her perception of the market. It will also sell to a much smaller market (there are many more readers than publishers). Since file load software is essentially production software, it will be priced accordingly, probably in tens of thousands of dollars rather than tens or low hundreds of dollars charged for each copy of the retrieval software.

Bureau services or inhouse operation

The file loading tasks described in this section can be undertaken by an external systems integrator who offers a bureau service. Most suppliers of software are willing to provide these services to publishers and other owners of information, as an integral step in the process of developing a CD-ROM based product. There are clear advantages to using a service run by staff who are expert in the use of the selected software. Chances are better of developing a successful product in the shortest time and at the lowest cost. However these benefits reduce once the initial design and development are completed and operations move into a routine production phase. The publisher will need to consider the frequency with which discs will be produced, whether updating existing products or creating new products on CD-ROM. The cost of developing the necessary expertise inhouse, and acquiring software and hardware, will have to be spread over the anticipated levels of use.

Many information owners who are adopting CD-ROM feel that in the longer term they need to be in control of the complete production process. On the other hand, many print publishers are uncomfortable with the idea of increasing the number of computer staff on their payroll. Publishers have also traditionally farmed out other specialist tasks such as typesetting and printing. In order to keep their full range of options open, the publisher/information owner should investigate the availability of file load software for licensing, the costs involved and the types of computer equipment required. They should also satisfy themselves about the attitude and commitment of the systems integrator towards transferring technical knowledge along with the software. As with all computer operations, after sales technical support is an important factor in the selection of software products.

Pre-mastering

At the end of the file loading process, an operational and tested copy of the product (both software and data) will be available on magnetic storage. A further production step has to be performed before files can be passed to the mastering and replication facility. CD-ROM is not like a magnetic disc. Data is stored on the disc as a continuous spiral, with physical areas measured in seconds and minutes as opposed to kilobytes. Therefore files have to be processed in order to determine how they will be laid out on the CD-ROM. Effectively the disc is a blank sheet of paper. Files and headers could be put anywhere. However, the benefits of standardization of file layout were recognized by developers during the early stages of CD-ROM technology. The High Sierra standard ensures that all discs prepared to this standard can be read using any software designed to read High Sierra. In due course, High Sierra file layout will be recognized by PC operating systems like MS DOS. Until these are available, extensions to MS DOS are available through a number of routes including drive manufacturers.

Pre-mastering firstly requires processing all the files to be included on a CD-ROM, including applications software, to the High Sierra file layout specification. There are standard systems that are designed to perform this task. Software is available that runs on mainframe computers. Processing is performed on the file serially as a single batch process. Run times, even on large files, are short relative to the amount of processing required for file loading. Alternatives to the purely software approach are offered by systems like CD Publisher, manufactured by Meridian Data. These dedicated systems use a high-specification microcomputer with a large disc drive and a tape unit for input and output. The main proprietary element remains software, but the manufacturers test the disc drives to minimize the occurrence of disc errors that over time could reduce the amount of space available. CD Publisher in particular offers the additional advantage, over the purely software approach, of allowing the systems integrator to simulate the performance of the finished information product as it will appear when accessed on a CD-ROM. The product can therefore go through further stages of performance tuning, either through improvements in software or by revising the layout of files on the disc.

Output from the pre-mastering process is a magnetic tape that contains the files to be placed on disc laid out in accordance with the High Sierra specification, and in the format specified by the disc mastering facility. In the near future, it will be possible to use a digital optical disc (a WORM device) as the medium for transferring files to the mastering facility.

Mastering and replication

Mastering and replication is carried out at specialist facilities that are designed to meet the stringent production requirement of compact disc manufacture. These facilities are primarily built to meet the demands of the compact audio disc market. As the amount of CD audio plant moves into overcapacity, so the plant operators have taken a greater interest in CD-ROM. CD-ROM discs are produced in smaller volumes than CD audio discs. However the higher unit price charged for replicating a CD-ROM makes it an attractive area for the operator.

Mastering and replication are two discrete steps. Some operators such as Philips DuPont combine the two operations at a single plant. Other operators have a specialist facility for making CD-ROM masters with replication undertaken at a CD audio replication plant. CD-ROM masters require an extra level of error correction coding to be applied. CD audio can tolerate a higher level of error because the human ear cannot detect the effect. An error in a file or a program could render the disc unusable by computer. The addition of the error correction coding (ECC) and the transfer from magnetic tape to the recording tape used in the audio disc production process are confusingly also referred to as pre-mastering by the mastering and replication facilities. The equipment used in applying the ECC is coming down in price, with several sources becoming available. Initially this means that more CD audio plants will be able to offer CD-ROM production services. In the longer term, it may be feasible for the systems integrator to operate the equipment with the output, recording tape, being sent to the facility able to offer the lowest price and fastest turnaround at the time.

Turnaround time on disc mastering and replication has been a major concern for systems integrators and publishers alike. During the early days in which services became available, the time taken to make a master and produce the first discs varied widely. Most plants now regularly achieve the quoted turnaround time. Most plants offer a range of turnaround times, from two weeks down to three day turnaround, with a higher mastering charge applied the shorter the turnaround time required. At the time of writing, both Philips DuPont and 3M offer one day turnaround albeit at a premium price. CD-ROM production is now a routine activity with production facilities better able to support the requirements of their customers in this area.

Another early cause for concern was the quality of the copies made. Integrators were finding a significant number of discs supplied would not play because physical imperfections corrupted files held on the disc. In one case, a rejection rate as high as 50% was quoted. Plant operators have improved their quality control procedures. They claim the faults were caused by problems in maintaining a clean environment in the pressing plant, and as a result of impurities in the plastic coatings. The larger plant operators now undertake a 100% check on each disc copy made with only a low level of rejects being detected.

The systems integrator can offer the publisher two choices. Either the integrator can contract with the publisher to supply finished discs, effectively subcontracting disc mastering and replication, or the integrator can supply the publisher with the finished magnetic tape version, and the publisher contract separately with the plant operators. The former option is normally selected unless some special conditions give a publisher preferential access to a plant. The systems integrator will have established a good working relationship with one or more plant operators. The integrator knows which technical staff to deal with in the case of a problem. The production flow from the integrator to the plant will have become well established. And the integrator is likely to be able to negotiate better terms of service from the plant operator by virtue of the larger volume of work being handled.

Packaging

Discs are supplied from the replication plant in a standard plastic case and with a monochrome label. Normally the publisher will want to give his product a more attractive appearance by producing an insert for the plastic case and by specifying the labelling on the disc. The system integrator has a role to play, advising the publisher on what options are available, although it is likely the publishers will wish to involve their own designers.

However well-designed a compact disc product, some instruction will need to be supplied, firstly to tell the user how to load the disc, and then how to use the programs and information held on the disc. Preparing technical documentation is a specialist activity and outside the scope of this publication. The systems integrators may provide a service to prepare the required user documentation or they may call in an organization specializing in preparing this type of material. Most importantly, the need for good packaging and effective documentation must not be underestimated. Planning for it needs to start at the outset of the project. Adequate budgets must be allocated.

Conclusion

The role played by the systems integrator today is central to the successful exploitation of CD-ROM. It will be some time before publishers can develop sufficient expertise inhouse to allow them to directly operate the file loading and pre-mastering services themselves. Even then the issue of capturing information at source in a suitable format for onward processing will remain.

Where publishers do move production operations inhouse (a move that should be encouraged where regularly updated products are involved) there will be a continuing need to use external software and development services to enhance existing products. The world of the personal computer will experience radical change over the next three to four years with multi-processing, improved user interface design and networking. The publishers will need the support of specialist skills if they are to properly exploit these developments. As CD-ROM publishing grows, the scope of applications will become broader and the need for more diversified products increase. The main change likely to occur is the specialization of systems integrators. Focus on different fields of application (financial information, mapping, full text products, software distribution and so on) will lead to the emergence of organizations with a mix of skills and resources specific to those applications.

But until this change takes place the publisher must choose a systems integrator on more generalized criteria. There are three factors which the publisher must consider:

(1) Does the systems integrator display an understanding of the publisher's requirements and objectives? The publisher should not be intimidated by demonstrations of advanced technology, nor by the salesman who tries to persuade the publisher to change requirements to meet what the salesman has on offer. The publisher is carrying the burden of financial risk and will have to sell the product at the end of the day. The systems integrator should be able to understand what the publisher wants to do, refine the publisher's views with experience gained by developing other products and propose practical routes to achieving the agreed objectives. Ultimately, the publisher has to decide whether the proposals sound convincing and rely on the experience of the systems integrator in developing other similar products.

(2) Does the systems integrator have the right software available? Choosing software is difficult for the publisher. Functionality, performance, look and feel, flexibility and cost are all factors that have to be assessed. The publishers may have their own fixed ideas about the factors that govern software selection. These ideas may need to be modified in discussions with potential systems integrators. Ultimately, selection of software is likely to be based on the best fit between design objectives and what can be achieved with existing and well supported software.

(3) Do I like the look of similar products produced by the systems integrator? The successful implementation of other similar products should give the publishers confidence in their selection of a systems integrator, particularly where existing products incorporate features that the publisher may wish to emulate. Publishers considering the design of CD-ROM based products for specific niche markets should look at other products already launched in that market. Unlike book production, electronic products need to exploit established familiarity with the way software works and the way information is organized. Indeed, the systems integrator can act as a bridge between publishers who would not otherwise consider cooperating in the design of their products.

Using a systems integrator for the first time will always be risky. Whilst the publisher and the systems integrator have to build a good working relationship, the publisher is well advised to break up a project into several discrete steps, with commitment to proceed following only on the satisfactory completion of the previous stage.

When contracting for a systems integrator's services, as with all other aspects of developing CD-ROM based information products, enthusiasm needs to be tempered with judicious application of common sense.

Chapter 4

The cost of becoming a CD-ROM publisher

Robin Williamson

Introduction

A CD-ROM publisher is anyone who undertakes the task of collecting data and disseminating it on CD-ROM. A CD-ROM publisher may be an information department within a large corporation, an existing print publisher, or a new entrepreneurial venture set up to exploit the new technology.

In this chapter, the stages through which a CD-ROM publication passes from initiation to delivery to the final end user are defined. Not all these stages are relevant to every type of publisher; for example, an inhouse publication may not need to be marketed, and an existing publisher disseminating his own works on CD-ROM will not need to consider negotiating for publishing rights.

In discussing the costs of CD-ROM publishing, a distinction is made between inhouse resources and bought-in resources. The former are resources controlled directly by the publisher; for example, editorial and marketing resources. The latter are resources acquired from external suppliers; for example, data conversion, CD-ROM integration and reproduction. Different publishers will control different resources, and some of those categorized as inhouse or bought-in in this chapter will differ with different organizations. For the purpose of the discussion in this chapter, bought-in resources include most of the services currently available to publishers from third parties.

In providing cost estimates, inhouse resources have been calculated in terms of effort, and no monetary figure has been given, since the method of allocating internal costs will vary from organization to organization. Bought-in costs are derived from current published prices for services, but remain a guide only, and should be checked against supplier estimates before embarking on any actual development programme.

The publishing cycle

This section provides an outline description of the development stages through which a CD-ROM publisher will pass in launching a CD-ROM product. Each of these stages is described in more detail in the following sections.

Market assessment

A CD-ROM is a product and, like any other product, it has to find a market. Probably the most important task facing the CD-ROM publisher is assessing the market for the product. CD-ROM is a medium for delivering a large mass of information, together with added value in the form of its internal structure and the access software used to search the data. These three factors, the information *content, structure* and *access software* will be determined by the proposed market. Markets can be divided into a number of broad categories. Niche markets for high-value products aimed at well-defined professional users will normally be met with relatively high-priced products selling in relatively low volumes. Mass markets for lower-priced, higher-volume products will require different forms of added value, exploiting mass consumer market features, with emphasis of ease of use, colour, graphics, etc.

The CD-ROM publisher must at an early stage in the production process make an assessment as to where his product is targeted. This assessment process may involve commissioning formal market research, as well as reviewing published market research reports and studying competitive products.

Outline product design

Once the overall market for the product has been identified, the next stage is to produce an outline design. As mentioned earlier, the three key elements in a CD-ROM product are the information content, the structure and the access software. At an early stage in the development process, the basic requirements for each of these design elements must be defined.

Information content will include the subject matter of the product, related to the overall requirements of the chosen market, and an initial assessment of likely sources for the information. The CD-ROM publisher will need to decide to what extent material will come from sources he/she controls already and how much material will be acquired from third parties. Some early assessment is required as to the technical format of the source material. For example, how much material is likely to be in electronic format already, what coding standards apply, how much will have to be converted into electronic format from print, and what conversion techniques are likely to be applicable? Another important consideration when defining information content is the volatility of the information and the need for up-to-dateness. Information that changes very rapidly may be unsuitable for CD-ROM; if change is inherent, then consideration must be given to the frequency of updating the information content and the way updates will be delivered to the customer.

Structure is the basis of the added value offered in an electronic data product. Structure design includes identification of the categories into which the information is subdivided (the electronic equivalent of chapter, section, paragraph, reference, footnote, etc.), and the links between elements (the electronic equivalent of contents list, index, bibliography). The richer and more complex the structure, the greater the added value of the product, but high added value implies high production costs. Structure design needs to take into consideration the amount of structuring inherent in the source material and its reusability, as well as the intellectual effort needed to add structure not present at source.

Access software is the means by which the user interfaces with the information content and structure. However comprehensive the information, however rich the structure, if access software is ineffective or difficult to use the value of the product is diminished. Few CD-ROM publishers will be in the business of designing and developing access software, so a choice will have to be made from available products, or special software development will need to be considered. Criteria to be applied in selecting software will include the ease with which a user interface can be made to fit the expectation and skills of prospective users and its ability to handle the structure of the data, as well as considerations of technical quality and the commercial terms on offer.

Market research

The first two stages of product development will have resulted in an initial assessment of the market for the product, and an outline design in terms of information content, structure and access software. While in some cases these initial stages will have given the publisher a sufficient basis for proceeding with detailed planning and development, it is important to consider the benefits of conducting more thorough research into the market, in order to be able to assess the revenue potential of the product and hence build up a sensible financial case for going ahead. Market research into a CD-ROM product is complicated by the need to research both the value of the information itself and the acceptability of the medium for delivery. The latter must not be allowed to get in the way of the former. While CD-ROM technology provides the mechanics for the delivery of the product, the key element is market research into the information and the way it can be put to use. The publisher must define the requirements for a piece of market research very carefully and be sure that the final results will provide feedback into product design as well as giving a view as to revenue.

It may be necessary to produce a demonstration of the product for the research organization to use in conducting interviews, as this prevents a waste of time trying to explain how the information will be made available.

Another important element of market research is to determine product pricing and delivery policy. There are a number of alternative strategies for the publisher to consider: Should the publisher supply the CD-ROM player and computer as well as the disc itself? Should the product be sold outright or on subscription? How will updates be paid for? Research can help determine the strategy that will meet the expectation of the marketplace and maximize product profitability.

Project plan

Preliminary work on outline product design and on market assessment and research will have brought the CD-ROM publisher to the point where a

Expenditure items

Development   This section of the plan will cover all aspects of product development, including detailed product design, identification and security, all development resources including agreements with third parties, collection of data from source, conversion into a standard electronic format, addition of editorial input including the structuring of the data, conversion to the product's format, development of any special access software, integration of access software with the database, testing of the product, including the production of a demonstration version, product approval and finally the process of reproducing the product on CD-ROM.

Marketing   This section of the plan will cover the process of defining a price and packaging policy, deciding how the product will be sold, planning a product launch, assembling and training sales staff, and producing sales support material, e.g. sales manual, brochures, user guides, sales agreements.

Product support   This section will cover the resources and costs associated with keeping the product in production, including the cost of updates, providing a help service to customers, and, where relevant, hardware and software maintenance.

Sales   This section will cover the resources and costs associated with ongoing sales activity, including sales staff, commission schemes, attendances at exhibitions and conferences, and consumption of sales support material.

Royalties   This section will cover the payment of royalties to third parties. These will be primarily payments to publishers for the use of copyright material and payment of licence fees for the use of third party software in the product.

Equipment   Where the publisher decides to supply CD-ROM hardware, including CD-ROM players and computer equipment, the product plan will include a section identifying the costs of acquiring and installing hardware.

Revenue items

The breakdown of revenue projections will depend on the sales strategy adopted. The sections summarized here are an example of the sort of headings that should appear in the plan.

Product licence   Projected revenues from an annual licence fee for the basic CD-ROM product, including agreed annual updates, and the right to use proprietory access software delivered with the product. The revenue line will take into account any arrangements made with a third party leasing company to discount the licence revenue.

Hardware leasing   Projected revenues from an agreement to lease or hire necessary equipment, including computers and CD-ROM players. The revenue will include provision for maintenance of the hardware, and, as for the product licence, may be discounted through a third party leasing organization.

Package revenue   Revenue from a 'bundled' service where hardware leasing and product licence are combined in a single annual fee.

Product profit/loss

This section will provide a phased financial plan showing the expected profitability of the product. Depending on the publisher's project funding procedure, this part of the plan will include allocation of company overheads and costs of project finance.

Cash flow

Where appropriate, a phased version of product costs and revenues designed to indicate the projected funding requirements and profit contribution on a cash basis.

Figure 4.1 CD-ROM product — project plan

decision to invest in the development and marketing of the product must be made. As with any investment decision, a proper financial case is needed, and the basis of this is a detailed Project Plan. The Plan will provide the data from which detailed cost and revenue projections can be made.

The main headings for the Project Plan are summarized in *Figure 4.1*, and each of these will be discussed in more detail in following sections of this chapter.

Implementation

The project plan and its associated financial projections will be subject to the internal approval process operated by the publisher or, in the case of a new venture, will be used as the basis for raising venture capital. Once approval is given and development funds are available, the next stage in the cycle is the implementation of the activities set out in the project plan. It is important that a proper project control system is put in place, and procedures established for reviewing and controlling the project.

Preliminary stages

As outlined earlier, before spending significant sums of money on a new CD-ROM product the publisher will undertake a preliminary assessment of the market and prepare an outline product design. These activities will involve largely inhouse resources, and the amount of time and effort expended will depend very much on the level of understanding of CD-ROM markets and products that exists within the publisher's organization. This section identifies some of the key tasks that the publisher must consider and to which resources need to be allocated. No attempt is made to give other than a very rough guide to the amount of resources needed and the likely timescale.

Market assessment

Task: market overview and assessment

DESCRIPTION
This task is concerned with undertaking the preliminary assessment of the market outlined earlier. The objective of the task is to establish the general area into which the product will be sold and thus the terms of reference for the product design.

ACTIONS
- Study competitive products.
- Obtain and study published market surveys.
- Examine known markets, e.g. for equivalent print products.
- Conduct informal market research, e.g. by interviewing a sample of possible users.

- Consider whether to commission formal market research at this stage, based on quality/quantity of preliminary market data available.
- Review data obtained by the market overview activity.
- Prepare outline analysis of product market, including broad estimate of sales volumes and price expectations (small markets/expensive product versus mass market/cheap product).

DELIVERABLE ITEMS
- Market assessment report.

TIMESCALE
This task is a preliminary activity that precedes the formal project plan timescales. The length of time needed to complete the task will vary considerably, depending on the amount of market intelligence already available to the publisher.

RESOURCES
Inhouse resources will be involved in this task, primarily existing marketing staff with an understanding of current markets for equivalent print products. Bought-in resources will include acquisition of published market surveys and possibly purchase of competitive products for assessment. It would also be wise to acquire CD-ROM equipment for assessment of the medium.

BUDGET

Inhouse resources:	up to 3 man-months	
Bought-in resources:	CD-ROM hardware	£1500
	competitive products	£2000
	market surveys	£2500
	Total	£6000

Note: If formal market research is commissioned the budget noted below for market research may be brought forward to this stage.

Outline product design

Task: information assessment

DESCRIPTION
This preliminary task is aimed at producing an initial understanding of the information content of the proposed product, to enable an outline design to be undertaken, based on the initial market assessment.

ACTIONS
- Review market assessment.
- Identify information needs.
- Identify information sources.
- Identify information media.
- Identify information volatility.

DELIVERABLE ITEMS
- Preliminary information analysis.

TIMESCALE
As for the market assessment task, no precise timescale can be given to this preliminary activity, since this will depend very largely on the knowledge of existing sources available to the CD-ROM publisher.

RESOURCES
This task will require inhouse resources.

BUDGET
Inhouse resources: up to 2 man-months.

Task: technical assessment and outline design

DESCRIPTION
This task reviews the basic elements of product design described earlier in the light of the assessment of information content and of the market assesment task. The objective is to produce an outline product design document which will form the basis for further development activity.

ACTION
- Prepare preliminary analysis of information categories.
- Identify basic product structuring.
- Identify basic access procedures.

DELIVERABLE ITEMS
- Outline product design.

TIMESCALE
The same comment applies to this task as to the preceding one.

RESOURCES
While inhouse resources will be primarily responsible for this task, it may well be advisable to employ consultants with some expertise in CD-ROM product design and development to assist in the technical aspects of product design.

BUDGET
Inhouse resources: up to 1 man-month
Bought-in resources: consultancy 20 days at £400 per day   £8000

Market research

As described earlier, the preliminary tasks of market assessment and outline product design may well have provided a sufficient basis for preparing a full project plan and financial assessment for the proposed product. However, the CD-ROM publisher should give serious consideration to the value of commissioning formal market research in order to establish a clear picture of the viability of the product. Market research can also provide valuable input into the process of product design through feedback from potential users exposed to the initial ideas for the product.

The tasks described in this section provide guidance on the activities and resources that could be needed in order to conduct such a piece of research. Budget figures are very tentative since the scope and duration of market research into new information products will vary enormously depending on the publisher's requirements.

Preliminary market research tasks

Task: preparing the briefing document

DESCRIPTION

This task draws on the preliminary work outlined earlier to prepare a statement of the objective for the proposed market research, that will be aimed at looking into areas not fully covered by the preliminary assessments. The brief will itself form the basis for the terms of reference to be agreed with the market research contractor.

ACTION
- Review market assessment report.
- Review outline product design.
- Identify areas where research is needed.
- Define research objectives.

DELIVERABLE ITEMS
- Market research briefing document.

TIMESCALE

This task will require about four elapsed weeks to complete.

RESOURCES

This task will draw on the inhouse resources used for the preliminary tasks described earlier.

BUDGET

Inhouse resources: up to 1 man-month.

Task: establish market research resources

DESCRIPTION

This task will identify the market research organization that will undertake the research, and reach a contractual agreement for the research activity. The invitation to tender should set out the objectives of the research, and identify the depth to which research should be undertaken and whether both qualitative and quantitative analysis will be required. The amount of attention to be given to the product design and the feedback required on the market's perception of the way the product is to be delivered must also be specified. The research may also be required to cover the market's understanding and attitude to computers, competitive products, competitive delivery methods (e.g. on-line), and to CD-ROM. The tender should also indicate whether a demonstration version of the product will be available to assist in the research activity.

A contractor will be chosen in response to the tendering procedure, and following selection detailed terms of reference will be agreed, depending on the contractor's expertise and based on the requirements set out in the tender document.

ACTIONS
- Review market research brief.
- Prepare invitation to tender.
- Identify potential contractors.
- Select market research organization.
- Commission market research.

DELIVERABLE ITEMS
- Invitation to tender.
- Market research agreement.

TIMESCALE
This task should be completed within two months, allowing one month for preparing the tender and one month for selection of a contractor.

RESOURCES
This task will require inhouse resources.

BUDGET
Inhouse resources: up to 1 man-month.

Conduct market research

Task: market research activity

DESCRIPTION
This task is the implementation of the market research contract agreed under the previous task. The extent of the activity will have been established in negotiation with the contractor. The end result of this task will be a detailed market research report which will include (if agreed) a detailed commentary on the market's view of the proposed product design.

The CD-ROM publisher commissioning the report will not be directly involved in the activity, but may usefully attend some of the research interviews to benefit from comments and reactions to the product.

ACTIONS
- Agree research plan.
- Conduct research.
- Produce report.

DELIVERABLE ITEMS
- Market research report.

TIMESCALE
The duration of the research will be variable, depending on the detailed terms of reference, but should be completed over a period not greater than three elapsed months.

RESOURCES
This is essentially a bought-in task, but inhouse resources will be needed to monitor progress and to take part in some of the interview sessions.

BUDGET
Inhouse resources: up to 1 man-month
Bought-in resources: market research fees could range from £20 000
                      to £50 000 or more depending on requirements.

Project plan

This Chapter earlier provided an overview of the contents of the project plan. The following sections expand on this overview and give details of the tasks and actions needed to implement the plan. An example of a typical product development bar chart is given in *Figure 4.2*, and the detailed explanation that follows is based on the development of a typical CD-ROM product. The assumptions are that the product is being developed by a CD-ROM publisher who will be drawing on source material owned by third parties, aimed at a professional marketplace for a relatively high value, low volume product. Timescales are based on the plan in *Figure 4.2*.

Task: produce detailed project plan

DESCRIPTION
This task describes the process of producing a detailed plan. As explained earlier, a detailed plan is needed in order to determine the level of funding required and the projected revenues for the product, and thus whether to proceed with the product.

ACTIONS
- Agree overall timescale and objectives.
- Establish list of activities.
- Prepare resource/timescale/cost estimates.
- Produce detailed plan.
- Obtain approval for product development.

DELIVERABLE ITEMS
- Draft plan.
- Signed off plan with product and funding approval.

Week number

1 2 3 4 5 6 7 8 9 10 11 12 13 14 15 16 17 18 19 20 21 22 23 24 25 26 27 28 29 30 31 32 33 34 35 36 37 38 39 40

Preliminary tasks
Produce detailed project plan
Detailed product design
Establish conversion resources
Establish integrator resources
Agree on access software
Agree use of source material
Agree on hardware provision

Production tasks
Collect source materials
Convert source data
Integrate software and data
Produce CD–ROMs
Produce documentation

Marketing tasks
Launch planning
Produce demonstration
Sales planning
Launch product
Full scale selling starts

Figure 4.2 Product development timescale

TIMESCALE
Start: week 1   Finish: week 4.

RESOURCES
This is an inhouse activity, although contact with third parties will be needed in order to obtain estimates of likely costs and revenues.

BUDGETS
Inhouse resources: up to 2 man-months.

Initial development tasks

Product design

Task: detailed product design

DESCRIPTION
The objective of this task is to produce a detailed description of the product in terms of the source material to be used and the overall structure to be incorporated in the product. Structure design will include identifying the key elements of data to be distinguished by the search software (for example, in a work of reference based on a printed text book, data elements might include title, chapter, section, paragraph, footnote, reference, and the reference element additional structure such as title, publisher, date, author), and cross references between these data elements. The product design will also consider the search strategy to be adopted, for example whether to use full text search with inverted file structuring, hierarchical structures involving menus, use of keywords and so on. Other features of the design activity will be consideration of the need to provide a subject thesaurus. An editorial team should be established with knowledge of the subject matter and of the way the expected market will use the product. This editorial team should, if possible, have members who are independent of the product developer, able to provide unbiased advice and guidance. For professional markets it may well be an important marketing aid to be able to publicize this input from experts in the subject matter of the product.

ACTIONS
● Set up editorial team.
● Agree terms of reference.
● Define source material.
● Define product structure.
● Approve product design.

DELIVERABLE ITEMS
● Terms of reference.
● Initial design report.
● Approved design report.

TIMESCALE
Start: week 1   Finish: week 13

RESOURCES
This task will require both inhouse and bought-in resources. Consultants used for the outline design may well be required to continue their work on detailed product design. Editorial resources in the form of editorial advisers may also be deployed.

BUDGET
Inhouse resources: up to 2 man-months
Bought-in resources: consultancy fees (20 days at £400)   £8000
                      fees to editorial team   £2000

Development resource contracts

This group of tasks is concerned with identifying and securing the resources needed for product development.

Task: establish conversion resources

DESCRIPTION
This task will identify the method and resources to be used for carrying out data conversion. The work on product design will have identified the source material to be used, and this task will assess the amount of data conversion needed, in terms of rekeying or reuse of material already in electronic form. Conversion options will include use of keying bureaux, use of optical character recognition (OCR) equipment, and use of specialist data conversion services. The strategy adopted will depend on a number of factors including the type of source material available, volumes, need for updating, and the output format needed for further processing.

An invitation to tender will be produced, setting out the technical and commercial requirements to be met by contractors. Technical details will include the source formats, volumes, timescales, and the output format required. Commercial details will include the pricing basis for the service (fixed price or time and materials) and the rights of ownership of any special conversion software needed. Final contracts for conversion will need to be placed so that conversion of source materials can begin in time for the CD-ROM production activity.

ACTIONS
- Quantify CD-ROM data conversion workload.
- Review conversion options.
- Agree conversion strategy.
- Identify potential resources.
- Produce invitation to tender.
- Select conversion resources.

DELIVERABLE ITEMS
- CD-ROM data conversion strategy report.
- Invitation to tender for conversion.
- Conversion resources contracted/acquired.

TIMESCALE
Start: week 3   Finish: week 13

RESOURCES
This task will mainly utilize inhouse resources. For a highly complex conversion task, it may be necessary to run a pilot or trial to evaluate alternative strategies, and this would result in some bought-in costs.

BUDGET
Inhouse resources: up to 4 man-weeks
Bought-in resources: for pilot trials, if required   up to £5000

Task: establish integrator resources

DESCRIPTION
This task identifies the organization that will provide integrator services for the product. These are fundamental to the success of the final product, and involve the process of creating the CD-ROM database, integrating this with the chosen access software, and creating the master tape from which CD-ROMs are produced. This task will set out the requirements for integrator services in the form of an invitation to tender, and the selection of an integrator organization in response to the tender document.

The invitation to tender will include an outline description of the product, details of volumes, data formats, database structures and access software to be used, and details of updates and turnround times. Other items to be covered will be whether the integrator is to manage the product through the CD-ROM production phase and the production of demonstration or trial versions of the product.

ACTIONS
● Agree objectives for use of CD-ROM integrator service.
● Prepare invitation to tender.
● Agree short list of integrator service suppliers.
● Issue invitation to tender.
● Review tenders and agree supplier.
● Place integrator services contract.

DELIVERABLE ITEMS
● Invitation to tender.
● Integrator service contract.

TIMESCALE
Start: week 6   Finish: week 13

RESOURCES
This task will mainly require inhouse resources. In some cases the integrator will offer to undertake a paid feasibility study as a preliminary to quoting for the full job. The benefit of this is that a clearer picture of the requirement may be produced resulting in more precise cost estimates.

BUDGET
Inhouse resources: up to 1 man-month
Bought-in resources: optional feasibility study   up to £5000

Task: heads of agreement for access software

DESCRIPTION
This task is related to that of determining the integrator resources, since in many cases the integrator will also supply access software. However, it is important to treat this as a separate invitation to tender, since reaching agreement on provision of software raises different issues.

A functional requirement specification (FRS) for access software will describe the database structure and the way the data will be searched, as set out in the product design document. Among the items to be included will be the type of access (menu-driven, keyword, full text) and the way the access software should appear to the user (the man-machine interface). Other issues will include output (use of printer, interface with word-processor) and security (protection from excessive or unauthorized down-loading). The specification should also define the expected minimum access time for retrieval of different types of information.

The FRS will form the basis of a formal invitation to tender for provision of access software. The contractor may be invited to quote for supply of a standard package, together with special modifications to meet the FRS. The basis on which modifications will be undertaken, and who will own the result should be made clear. If modifications are substantial, the publisher should retain ownership. The tender document will also state the licence terms preferred by the publisher, although the software supplier will normally expect the publisher to accept the licensor's standard contract.

The result of this task will be an agreement with the chosen software supplier for use of the software with the database product.

ACTIONS
● Agree functional specification for CD-ROM access software.
● Prepare short list of possible software products.
● Prepare invitation to tender for software supply.
● Issue invitation to tender.
● Select appropriate software package.
● Sign agreement with supplier.

DELIVERABLE ITEMS
● Software functional requirement specification.
● Invitation to tender.
● Signed agreement.

TIMESCALE
Start: week 8   Finish: week 13

RESOURCES
Resources will be primarily inhouse. Suppliers may offer to undertake a

paid feasibility study before final agreement is reached, and this may be a useful preliminary bought-in activity that will help refine the functional requirement specification.

BUDGET
Inhouse resources: up to 1 man-month
Bought-in resources: optional paid feasibility study   up to £5000

Task: agreement for use of source materials

DESCRIPTION
The objective of this task is to reach formal agreement with the owners of source materials on terms for use of their information in the CD-ROM product. Source materials will have been identified at the product design stage, and copyright owners will need to be identified. In the majority of cases, negotiations will be with the publisher of the print version of the source, since most publishers will have acquired electronic publishing rights from the author. In some cases, negotiation will be directed to the author or agent.

The CD-ROM publishers should prepare an outline of the terms of the agreement being sought. This will include the proposed royalty structure, and any guaranteed or up-front payments. The agreement should also include the medium on which the source material is to be delivered, and any guarantees of quality and consistency to be provided by the source owner. Other items in the agreement will include provisions on exclusivity, and restrictions on copying and downloading to be imposed on the eventual end user. The question of royalty payments is discussed in further detail later.

ACTIONS
● Identify owners of source material.
● Prepare outline heads of agreement.
● Negotiate terms.
● Secure agreements.

DELIVERABLE ITEMS
● Signed agreement.

TIMESCALE
Start: week 6   Finish: week 13

RESOURCES
This task will be undertaken inhouse.

BUDGET
The effort required will depend on the amount of source materials and the number of sources. Up to two man-weeks of effort for each source might be needed to negotiate a satisfactory agreement.

Task: agreement on hardware provision

DESCRIPTION

This task is concerned with setting up the procedures for providing CD-ROM hardware to users. The CD-ROM publisher will have a number of options to consider, including acting as a hardware dealer, purchasing equipment from manufacturers and selling on to users, or arranging for supply through a third party.

This task will consider the various options, select the most appropriate, and secure commercial terms with prospective suppliers (not necessarily exclusively with any one supplier). Arrangements will also be made for delivery, installation and maintenance of hardware supplied to users. At this stage consideration should also be given to financing hardware supply, for example by reaching agreement for hardware leasing through a third party leasing organization.

ACTIONS
- Identify CD-ROM reader suppliers.
- Identify PC suppliers.
- Identify volumes.
- Identify maintenance policy.
- Agree supply terms.
- Agree installation and maintenance terms.
- Agree financing arrangements.

DELIVERABLE ITEMS
- Supplier agreements.
- Financing agreements.

TIMESCALE
Start: week 4   Finish: week 13

RESOURCES
This task will be carried out inhouse.

BUDGET
Inhouse resource: up to 1 man-month.

Product building

The tasks described in this section are all concerned with the detailed production of the CD-ROM product, based on the detailed design described earlier, and deploying the resources identified and commissioned as described earlier.

The budget estimates given are based on services and quoted costs available at the end of 1987, but all cost estimates should be validated by consultation with suppliers at the time product development is planned. Actual costs will vary considerably from the budget figures quoted in this section, depending on the actual requirements of the CD-ROM publisher.

Task: collect source materials

DESCRIPTION

The objective of this task is to arrange for the provision of all source materials in the format agreed with the supplier. In most cases this will be in electronic format, but may include print where no suitable electronic form exists. The task will assemble the material, and validate it against the procedures and formats agreed with the supplier. In some cases, material will be delivered directly to a subcontractor, for example for data conversion processing.

Validation is a key part of this activity, as it is important for the integrity of source material to be reflected in the final product. Points to cover include checking that the complete text of a work has been received (for example, has the typesetter incorporated all final corrections in the electronic form), and that the data is processable (for example, technical details such as leader blocks and recording density conform to agreed standards). Any invalid material must be returned to source for reprocessing.

ACTIONS
- Decide delivery location for material.
- Instruct suppliers to deliver material.
- Initiate validation procedures.
- Confirm valid source data.

DELIVERABLE ITEMS
- Valid source data.

TIMESCALE
Start: week 7   Finish: week 15

RESOURCES

This activity will involve both inhouse resources, acting as liaison with the suppliers of source material, and the bought-in conversion resources contracted to undertake conversion. The estimate given here is based on charges from the conversion contractor for handling the receipt of source material and carrying out basic validation procedures. The actual costs will vary considerably depending on the state of the source material and the need to develop any special validation software.

BUDGET
Inhouse resources: up to 1 man-month
Bought-in resources: from £5000 to £10000

Task: convert source data

DESCRIPTION

This task takes the source material and creates the necessary structures as determined by the product design. This process includes the replacement of any existing typesetting commands with the structure codes required by the database access software, the creation of cross references between data elements, the production of menus defining the product's hierarchical structure (where relevant) and the production of indexes including file inversion where necessary. The final output of this task is the database converted into the format dictated by the requirements of the product design and the chosen access software. This task will also include the production of other elements to be incorporated in the database, such as 'help' pages (i.e. instructions on how to use the product) and any special pages with titles, acknowledgements, copyright data and disclosures.

ACTIONS
- Convert any print material to electronic format.
- Convert source data to CD-ROM database format.
- Carry out file inversion where necessary.
- Create menu pages.
- Create 'help' pages and title pages.

DELIVERABLE ITEMS
- Converted source data in CD-ROM database format.

TIMESCALE
Start: week 15   Finish: week 27

RESOURCES
The data conversion task is primarily a bought-in service supplied by the contractor chosen as described earlier. Inhouse resources will be needed to coordinate activities and check on progress. The budget for conversion costs will depend on many factors, including the extent of manual inter-vention in the editing process, the quality of electronic source data and the need to convert data from print to electronic format. The budget figures given below are a rough guideline based on service costs quoted at the end of 1987. The example assumes source data of 200 megabytes, of which 50 megabytes are in print only.

BUDGET
Inhouse resources: up to 1 man-month
Bought-in costs: editing (cost of manual effort)   £5000 to £10000
                      print conversion (50 megabytes at
                        £0.60 per 1000 characters)   £30000
                      conversion to database format (200
                        megabytes at £30 per megabyte)   £6000
                      file inversion (200 megabytes: fixed
                        charge £4000, £30 per megabyte £6000)   £10000

Task: access software development and product integration

DESCRIPTION
This task is concerned with interfacing the chosen access software with the database. The functional requirement specification for access software will

have described the publisher's requirements. Standard software will usually be satisfactory, but the software supplier may need to carry out adaptions and modifications to meet any special requirements. The activities and resources described further in this task assume some special tailoring of the software. Once the software has been shown to meet the requirements of the FRS, it will be tested against the converted source data, and tests will be carried out to simulate the expected response times from the product once it is released. These simulations will allow the integrator to calculate the optimum layout of the database on the CD-ROM to ensure that performance meets the publisher's criteria. For example, simulation may show that certain menus or indexes are assessed more frequently than others, and these elements may be relocated in several parts of the CD-ROM to minimize access times.

The end result of this task will be the integration of access software and data in a single file whose layout has been mapped onto the CD-ROM and which meets the High Sierra CD-ROM data structure standards.

ACTIONS
- Develop access software modifications.
- Test access software with database.
- Simulate data access.
- Finalize CD-ROM file structuring.
- Integrate software and database.
- Produce integrated file to High Sierra standards.

DELIVERABLE ITEMS
- Complete access software modifications.
- Integrated CD-ROM file.

TIMESCALE
Start: week 15   Finish: week 35

RESOURCES
This activity will be undertaken by the software supplier and the integrator. Normally these will be the same organization, although it is possible that software could be acquired from a different source. Inhouse resources will be needed to monitor progress and formally to accept the product. The budget estimates assume that effort will be spent on modifying the access package, but the figure given will vary in practice according to the extent and complexity of the changes required.

BUDGET
Inhouse resources: up to 2 man-months
Bought-in resources: software modifications   £30000
                      access simulation   £5000
                      software/data integration   £2000
                      High Sierra formatting (200 megabytes at £15
                        per megabyte)   £3000

Task: CD-ROM production

DESCRIPTION

This task is concerned with the physical production of CD-ROMs containing the integrated software and data file created in the previous task. This is essentially a manufacturing process undertaken by a CD replication factory, using exactly the same processing methods as are used for producing audio CDs. Since a CD-ROM, once manufactured, cannot be altered, it is essential that thorough testing is carried out before volume production is begun. The CD-ROM publisher should thus obtain a trial run of CD-ROMs for testing before authorizing full-scale production.

The production process involves creating a pre-master tape. The data is transferred to video tape in a standard format defined by the CD manufacturing process. This pre-master tape is sent to the CD replication factory, and a master disc is produced using laser recording technology. This master is used to produce a trial batch of discs for evaluation. Once validated, the master can be used to 'stamp out' as many production versions of the CD-ROM as required.

ACTIONS
- Create pre-master tape.
- Produce trial batch of CD-ROMs.
- Test trial batch.
- Update pre-master tape with corrections.
- Produce CD-ROMs to volume required.

DELIVERABLE ITEMS
- CD-ROM pre-master tape.
- Trial batch of CD-ROMs.
- Volume production of CD-ROMs.

TIMESCALE
Start: week 36   Finish: week 40

RESOURCES

This task is undertaken by bought-in resources. Inhouse resources will be needed to conduct acceptance tests and authorize the production of CDs in volume. Normally the integrator will be responsible for producing the pre-master tape and coordinating the production facilities provided by the replication facility.

CD-ROM mastering and replication is carried out by an audio CD production facility. At the end of 1987, there were two facilities being set up in the UK, and three in operation in Europe. Production costs will not vary much between plants, but prices will vary considerably according to volume and turnround time.

BUDGET
Inhouse resources: up to 2 man-weeks
Bought-in resources: creation of pre-master tape   £2000

creation of CD-ROM master plus trial discs
(400 megabytes)

7 day turnround	up to £5000
21 day turnround	up to £3000
volume production/packaging	
1–249 copies	£15 each
250–499 copies	£13 each
500–1000 copies	£10 each
1000 plus	negotiable

Task: documentation

DESCRIPTION
A task often overlooked is the need to produce a good user manual for the product. Although the objective is to deliver a CD-ROM that can be used virtually without any training, a helpful, well-written guide to the product will reduce the time spent by the CD-ROM publisher in answering telephone calls from users who get into difficulties. The manual should explain elementary procedures such as how to switch the CD-ROM equipment on, how to insert the CD itself, how to access the first page and so on. Most of the manual will be incorporated in the 'help' pages referred to in the data conversion task, but it is sensible to produce this in printed form as well. A good manual is also a valuable sales aid.

ACTIONS
● Agree outline for manual.
● Design manual.
● Write manual.
● Print manual.

DELIVERABLE ITEMS
● Manual outline.
● Completed manual.

TIMESCALE
Start: week 15   Finish: week 39

RESOURCES
This task can be undertaken inhouse, with assistance from the software supplier, who will provide details of the operation of access software. Design and printing of the manual will be bought-in.

BUDGET
Inhouse resources: 8 man-weeks
Bought-in resources (for 500 copies): £3000

Marketing

Marketing a CD-ROM product is essentially no different from any other marketing activity. The marketing tasks and associated costs outlined in this section will in practice be adapted to meet the approach normally used by the CD-ROM publisher. A CD-ROM will usually be a high-value information product being sold into a sophisticated professional marketplace, and the sales strategies adopted will need to reflect this. The marketing budget should not be skimped: selling CD-ROM products will need as much investment as building the product itself. Marketing tasks are divided into two main categories, launching the product, and full scale selling.

Product launch

Task: launch planning

DESCRIPTION
This task plans the strategy and assembles all the resources needed to launch the product. A key decision in this strategy will be whether to attempt to secure an initial group of customers who will agree to buy the product and to be associated with launch publicity. Another important planning decision will be the need to produce a demonstration version of the product in advance of the final version.

ACTIONS
- Agree product launch objectives and strategy.
- Agree launch budget and resources.
- Agree prelaunch target sales.
- Agree price for prelaunch sales.
- Prepare advanced sales agreement.
- Agree need for demonstration.
- Agree sales literature.
- Produce literature.
- Prepare target customer list.
- Allocate resources.
- Produce product launch plan.

DELIVERABLE ITEMS
- Launch plan.
- Sales literature.
- Sales agreement.

TIMESCALE
Start: week 14   Finish: week 26

RESOURCES
This task involves inhouse resources, with bought-in resources for production of sales literature.

BUDGET
Inhouse resources: up to 2 man-months
Bought-in resources: sales literature   £3000

Task: product demonstration

DESCRIPTION

A demonstration version of the product is a valuable sales aid, particularly in the period leading up to the product launch, while the final version is being developed. This task is concerned with producing a demonstration of the product, that should illustrate the types of information available and the main ways in which information is accessed. The demonstration should use similar hardware to the final product, although the CD-ROM reader can be simulated by magnetic disc. A demonstration script should be developed, acting as a guide for the demonstrator and illustrating a typical user's interaction with the product.

ACTIONS
- Agree scope for demonstration.
- Agree method of demonstration.
- Specify demonstration.
- Acquire demonstration hardware.
- Implement demonstration.

DELIVERABLE ITEMS
- Demonstration script.
- Demonstration hardware.
- Demonstration database/software.

TIMESCALE
Start: week 14   Finish: week 22

RESOURCES

The demonstration will usually be produced by a contractor, probably the integrator or software supplier. Inhouse resources will be needed to specify the demonstration and prepare the script.

BUDGET

Inhouse resources:	up to 1 man-month	
Bought-in costs:	demonstration development	£2000 to £5000
	demonstration hardware	£1000
	(*Note:* hardware may already be available from earlier activity on evaluation of competition)	

Task: product launch

DESCRIPTION

The product launch will be a high profile event, preceded by securing a number of key reference sales that will be announced at the launch itself. The launch could be associated with a major industry exhibition or conference, or could be a special press conference or similar event. Prelaunch sales agreements should include confirmation that the customer will allow publicity. Where possible, these prelaunch customers should be invited to take part in the launch itself, as user endorsement is a powerful sales aid.

ACTIONS
● Close key prospects.
● Sign agreements.
● Agree launch venue.
● Prepare launch demonstration.
● Organize exhibition/press conference.
● Documentation complete.
● Product installed at prelaunch customer sites.
● Prelaunch customers briefed.
● Hold launch event.

DELIVERABLE ITEMS
● Prelaunch sales agreements.
● Launch documentation.

TIMESCALE
Start: month 9   Finish: month 9

RESOURCES
The launch will require inhouse marketing resources, with bought-in
resources to supply materials and the facilities required for the launch
itself. This may involve taking part in an exhibition, and could mean
significant exhibition costs.

BUDGET
Inhouse resources: up to 3 man-months
Bought-in resources: press conference, materials, etc.   £2500
                      exhibition   £10000

Selling

Task: full-scale sales planning

DESCRIPTION
Preparing to sell the CD-ROM product is a critical task. The actions shown
below are those needed to set up a CD-ROM sales organization from
scratch. In practice, a number of these items will already be in place. The
various methods for selling the CD-ROM, and the way the product should
be promoted and are not described in detail, but will require careful
planning.

ACTIONS
● Agree sales strategy.
● Agree product pricing policy.
● Agree hardware policy.
● Agree sales literature.
● Agree sales incentives.
● Evaluate prelaunch sales activity.
● Acquire prospect lists.

- Agree user contracts/terms.
- Agree product order/delivery procedures.
- Produce sales manual.
- Produce product documentation.
- Acquire sales demonstration equipment.
- Agree advertising campaign.
- Approve advertisements.
- Acquire sales resources.
- Train sales resources.

DELIVERABLE ITEMS
- Sales literature.
- Advertisements.
- Prospect lists.
- Sales manual.

TIMESCALE
Start: week 14   Finish: month 9

RESOURCES
This task is almost entirely one for inhouse resources, although bought-in resources will be needed for production of sales materials. A budget will also be required for recruiting sales staff.

BUDGET
Inhouse resources:	up to 3 man-months	
Bought-in resources:	sales materials	£5000
	advertising	£5000
	recruitment	£15 000

Task: commence full-scale sales

DESCRIPTION
This task is the ongoing process of selling the product in accordance with the agreed sales plan. Full-scale sales activity will follow the product launch, and the starting point will be an evaluation of the response to the launch, together with the final agreement of individual sales targets and allocation of prospects or territories to sales staff.

ACTIONS
- Evaluate launch response.
- Set sales targets.
- Sell.

TIMESCALE
Start: month 10   Finish: ongoing

RESOURCES
This activity is entirely inhouse.

BUDGET
Costs will be the salaries, expenses and commissions payable to sales staff.

Support

This group of tasks is concerned with the process of maintaining and up-dating the CD-ROM product, and dealing with the customer base. Product support is not a familiar concept to traditional print publishers, but is an important part of the delivery of a CD-ROM publication, which is much more like the provision of an ongoing service than a once-off publishing event. The size and cost of the support task will depend on many factors. The most important of these is the frequency and volume of changes in the data in the CD-ROM product. CD-ROM is mainly suited to relatively static data, and because the medium is read-only new information cannot be transferred onto an existing disc. Updates mean a complete reprocessing of the product and the manufacturing of new discs containing both unchanged and new material.

Support also includes the need to provide a source of help to customers who will need assistance both in getting their hardware to work and with the use of the access software.

A third category of support is the need to maintain both hardware and access software to ensure continual smooth running of the service provided by the product.

Updates

Task: update product

DESCRIPTION
This task encompasses all the actions needed for producing an updated version of the CD-ROM publication. The stages parallel the stages for producing the initial version of the product, and will involve similar resources. Updated material must be collected from source, edited in the same way as the original material, and converted to database format. Where the CD-ROM database includes an inverted file, the entire data-base (not just the updates) must pass through the inversion process to create an updated index. Editorial material including menu pages may need to be revised to take note of the updates. Finally, the updated data-base must be reintegrated with the access software and then submitted to the process of creation of updated CD-ROMs.

ACTIONS
- Collect updated source material.
- Edit/convert updates.
- Incorporate updates in database.
- File inversion.
- Update editorial pages.
- Integrate with access software.

- Create pre-master tape.
- Commission updated CD-ROMs.
- Test trial batch of updated CD-ROMs.
- Commission production run.

DELIVERABLE ITEMS
- Trial batch of updated CD-ROMs.
- Production of updated CD-ROMs.

TIMESCALE
Variable; normally the timescale needed to complete all the tasks and to produce updated discs (on a 7-day turnround) will be about one month. This could be reduced, but that would incur greater costs.

RESOURCES
Essentially the same resources will be required for creating updates as for the production of the original database.

BUDGET
Updating costs will vary according to the nature and volume of changes, and the frequency of updating. The budget for bought-in services given here assumes that 10% of the material changes for each update.

Collection of updated material	£1000
Editing	£1000
Print conversion	£3000
Conversion to database format	£500
File inversion	£4500
Integration with access software	£2000
CD-ROM formatting	£500
CD-ROM promoting	£2000
CD-ROM master disc creation	£5000
Total	£19500

In addition, volume costs of replication of the CD will apply as for the original production run.

Help

Task: help service

DESCRIPTION
The help service will provide users with a point of contact for resolution of problems encountered with using the product. These problems will be mostly concerned with using the access software, although some problems may also arise from understanding or interpreting the contents of the database, and from using the equipment itself. Each case where help might be needed will need a different problem resolution skill, but the user should be given a single contact point rather than a number of different ones depending on the type of problem. The way the publisher will respond

to help requests and the amount to be invested in establishing and running a help function will depend on the image the publisher wishes to present in the marketplace and on the expectations of the customer. Clearly a high-price product will raise expectations for speedy and experienced help, while a more mass-market product will not be subject to the same pressures. The way help is provided (by telephone, through the mail, etc.) will also be a key factor in assessing the resources to be deployed.

ACTIONS
- Decide on help strategy.
- Decide on help budget (as percentage of revenue).
- Decide on resources (inhouse or bought-in).
- Recruit and train resources.
- Establish help function.
- Operate help function.

TIMESCALE
This is an ongoing function, and planning and establishment should be completed before product launch.

RESOURCES
Planning and setting up the help function will require inhouse resources. Operating the help function could be put out to third parties, in particular help for access software problems could be provided by the access software supplier, and on hardware problems from the organization supplying and installing the equipment. Help on the content of the product will need to be provided by the CD-ROM publisher. It is likely that the CD-ROM publisher will also provide the initial point of contact for the customer, passing on queries to the software and hardware suppliers as appropriate.

BUDGET
No cost estimates are given since the variables are too many to make a sensible estimate. If bought-in resources are deployed, these costs will be part of the negotiation on software royalties and hardware maintenance charges. Inhouse resources will involve at the least manning a telephone during normal office hours, possibly extended beyond these if the product is one used frequently at home.

Maintenance

Task: access software maintenance

DESCRIPTION
Access software will normally be produced by a third party supplier. Part of the agreement with the supplier should be for the maintenance of the product, including correction of errors and a programme of enhancement and modification in the light of user experience. Where (as in most cases) the software is integrated with the database and supplied on the CD-ROM, updates of the software can only be supplied when an updated

CD-ROM is produced, and these will be issued with a convenient product update as described earlier.

ACTIONS
- Agree software maintenance policy.
- Incorporate updates in CD-ROM release.

TIMESCALE
Software updates will be relatively infrequent, and will coincide with a new CD-ROM release as described earlier.

RESOURCES
Software maintenance is the responsibility of the access software supplier.

BUDGET
Maintenance costs will be part of the negotiation for supply of access software, and will be incorporated in the licence fee. Special additional costs may arise if the CD-ROM publisher wishes to develop a major enhancement to the original software.

Task: hardware maintenance

DESCRIPTION
The equipment supporting the product will consist primarily of a standard personal computer and a CD-ROM player. This hardware is relatively robust and does not require a high degree of maintenance. However, the agreement with the hardware supplier should include provision for fixing hardware problems promptly on site. This is one of the normal services provided by the hardware suppliers, and should be readily available.

ACTIONS
- Agree maintenance level.
- Agree maintenance terms.
- Ensure maintenance procedure is established.

TIMESCALE
Maintenance procedure should be established at the time hardware provision is negotiated, and should persist for as long as hardware is at customer sites.

RESOURCES
Hardware maintenance is provided by the hardware supplier.

BUDGET
Annual maintenance fees charged by suppliers vary depending on the level of service provided, and whether or not the service includes replacement parts. A 'rule of thumb' is that annual maintenance charges range from 10% to 15% of the capital cost of the equipment, i.e. from £150 to £250 per annum in the case of a CD-ROM configuration. This amount will be

incorporated in the overall charge for the CD-ROM product and re-imbursed to the hardware supplier.

Royalties

Two important cost items to be considered by the CD-ROM publisher are royalty payments to information owners and to the supplier of access software.

This section describes the factors influencing these costs. Detailed task descriptions and action lists are not provided as these costs are determined largely by negotiation, which will need to be completed at an early stage in the product development programme, before detailed development work begins.

Information royalties

Apart from material directly controlled by the CD-ROM publisher, information going into the CD-ROM product will be acquired from third parties. Although in some cases the CD-ROM publisher may be able to buy information outright, most source material will already be available in another format, and the CD-ROM publisher will be acquiring rights, usually on a non-exclusive basis, to incorporate the material in the product. These rights may be acquired for a single fee, but most negotiations will be for a royalty agreement, where the consideration payable to the information owner will depend at least in part on the success of the CD-ROM product. Factors affecting the level of royalty payment will include:

● Volume of data supplied as a percentage of the total database.
● Technical quality of source material (material that requires little con-version will be more valuable to the CD-ROM publisher and hence attract a higher royalty).
● Frequency and availability of updates.
● Level of exclusivity.
● Duration of licence (note that the CD-ROM publisher should ensure the agreement covers the expected lifespan of the product, and is renewable).

It is difficult to estimate the outcome of negotiations for information rights as these will depend on many variable factors. However, the CD-ROM publisher would expect to have to set aside around 20% to 25% of product revenue to be shared by information owners. In some cases, information owners may require payment of a royalty advance, and this will have cash flow implications when assessing the overall viability of the CD-ROM product.

Software licence

The access software to be provided with the CD-ROM product will normally be supplied under licence from the software owner. The CD-ROM publisher will become a licensee of the product, and in turn will issue a sublicence to each user of the CD-ROM product. The amount paid for a software licence will depend on many factors, including:

- Any product 'tailoring' and ownership of modifications.
- Exclusivity provision.
- Numbers of sublicences to be issued (i.e. number of user licences).

The fees paid to the software provider will vary from supplier to supplier. As an example, one major software provider quotes an annual licence fee for use of access software based on the number of end user licences on the following scale:

1–50 copies	£250 per copy per year
51–100 copies	£200 per copy per year
101–500 copies	£120 per copy per year
500 plus copies	£75 per copy per year

Additional one-off fees may be paid by the CD-ROM publisher for use of special software for tailoring the user interface or for carrying out other system changes. It should be noted that a usage licence only allows the licensee the use of the software and gives no rights over the original computer programs (source code). Additional fees may be payable if the software supplier agrees to offer any special level of help functions to the users of the CD-ROM product. The software licence fee will normally be incorporated within the overall subscription to the CD-ROM product collected by the CD-ROM publisher, and the software licence element will then be remitted on to the software provider.

Hardware

A major strategic decision for the CD-ROM publisher will be how to ensure prospective users of the product have appropriate hardware to read the CD-ROM. It is unlikely that the publisher will find a market already well provided with the necessary personal computer equipment and with CD-ROM players. The choice facing the publisher is whether to supply a 'package deal' including hardware as well as the CD-ROM, or simply to provide information to customers on the equipment needed and expect them to acquire hardware directly. The latter course is the simplest, and since the equipment needed is readily available and simple to install should pose little problem to the user. The CD-ROM publisher should prepare the ground thoroughly, and ensure suppliers are ready and able to serve the marketplace.

The equipment needed in order to use a CD-ROM product consists of a personal computer equipped with a CD-ROM player. Technical details of this equipment have been discussed in some detail elsewhere in this book. A typical personal computer (an IBM PC or equivalent) could cost as little as £500, and a CD-ROM reader another £500, giving a minimum figure for the equipment needed of £1000. This price would exclude useful items such as a printer, and any additional costs for delivery and installation. The CD-ROM publisher who decides to supply equipment as part of a package deal should budget for a cost per user of some £1500 to cover all the costs of acquisition and supply, and will need to recover some £150 to £200 per year for maintenance charges.

Summary and conclusions

Summary

This chapter has attempted to cover the major activities involved in the publication of a CD-ROM product. A prospective CD-ROM publisher will need to consider the various tasks described in this chapter, and make

Table 4.1 Cost summary

Task	Inhouse resources (man-months)	Bought-in costs (£)
Preliminary stages		
Market overview and assessment	3	6000
Information assessment	2	
Outline design	1	8000
Market research		
Briefing document	1	
Establish resources	1	
Market research activity	1	20000 (to 50000)
Project plan		
Produce detailed plan	2	
Initial development tasks		
Product design	2	10000
Establish conversion resources	1	5000
Establish integrator resources	1	5000
Agree terms for access software	1	5000
Agree terms for use of information	2	
Agree hardware provision	1	
Product building		
Collect source material	1	10000
Convert souce data	1	56000
Access software/integration	2	13000
(Software changes, if required)		(up to 30000)
CD-ROM production (500 copies)	2	10000
Documentation	2	3000
Marketing		
Launch planning	2	3000
Demonstration	1	6000
Launch (inc. exhibition)	3	12500
Sales planning (inc. advertising)	3	25000
TOTAL DEVELOPMENT COSTS	36	197500
Ongoing costs		
Cost per update		19500
Hardware maintenance (per user per year)		150
Software licence (per user per year)		120
Information royalties 20%–25% of licence revenue		

his/her own assessment of the costs to be incurred, which will vary considerably from product to product. The main costs noted in the chapter are summarized in *Table 4.1* as an overall indication of the orders of magnitude of costs facing the publisher of a high added-value professional CD-ROM product where most of the source material will come from third parties, and where services will be bought-in wherever available. The example is based on a product drawing on some 200 megabytes of source material, of which 150 megabytes is available in electronic format, and 50 megabytes is in print form and needs to be converted.

Conclusion

Putting a CD-ROM product into the marketplace involves far more than simply transferring information from one medium onto another. The majority of the costs that need to be taken into consideration by the CD-ROM publisher are in non-technical areas such as market research, product design and marketing. On the technical side, the process of creating the CD-ROM is relatively cheap; the main costs lie in collecting and editing the source material — the process of creating electronic added value. The more the CD-ROM publisher insists on getting his market right, and giving this market maximum value the greater his chance of success, and reducing costs in these areas will not necessarily result in higher profits in the long run.

Chapter 5

User interface design of CD-ROM programs

Martin Brooks

Introduction

User interface is probably the most important design attribute of any software program, but of CD-ROM programs especially. Any number of interface designs can handle a small amount of data, such as a single wordprocessing document, a database program with a relatively small number of records, or a single spreadsheet. This is because all of the data can be viewed at one time or with a small amount of scrolling or moving around the screen. And with a small amount of data, various kinds of inputting and control devices such as a keyboard, mouse, joystick or lightpen will all operate with equal efficiency. With a small amount of data, it is also possible for end-users to write programs to access and manipulate the data, since the speed of accessing the data will not be a large factor in the design of the retrieval engine, and therefore standard DOS input/output commands can be used to read files.

Data size

With the tremendous storage capacity of CD-ROM, the picture changes considerably. Many CD-ROM programs contain a half-gigabyte of data, the equivalent of 1300 double-sided floppy discs. There is no point having a half-gigabyte of data if there is no efficient way of retrieving data as well as a powerful and efficient method of describing the subset of information required. Without the retrieval engine and specifically designed user interface, the CD-ROM disc is nothing more than a very efficient storage and distribution medium. Imagine trying to scroll a line or page at a time through megabytes of data. In traditional program design, such as the design of a wordprocessor or database program, each document is located within its own file in the disc operating system and the files are called by name. In CD-ROM applications, this approach is not practical. An encyclopedia of 200 000 entries might result in 200 000 files! Also, in CD-ROM applications, it is frequently necessary to load many diverse files at one time. Therefore, a program will have to allow the merging of these diverse files at one time. Yet when files are merged together, calling a file by name might result in a file too large to deal with. Clearly, a different approach

114

towards interface is necessary. As a first step, most CD-ROM applications build a specifically designed retrieval engine between the user interface and the disc itself.

The user interface is the way that the end-user communicates with any program. The nature of user interfaces has changed considerably as the development of computer hardware has evolved.

Hardware interfaces

In the beginning . . . there were switches. The first generation of computers had to be programmed in the only language that the computer could understand — binary numbers. As this was the lowest level of computer communication, the term 'low-level language' came into use. Binary languages were used to represent machine instructions because a binary number could be represented by the setting of a switch. There are only two different characters in binary notation, a one or a zero. A zero could be represented by a switch in the off position, a one could be represented by a switch in the on position. Programmers sat at a computer console and loaded commands one at a time into a computer by throwing sets of switches (*Figure 5.1*).

Figure 5.1 The position of the switches represents the binary number 1110010, which equals the decimal number 114. In ASCII, this represents a lower case r

Large mainframe computers were, and are, extremely expensive to operate. A method had to be found to input large amounts of programming code and information in a short time. A person inputting data directly at the console of a computer was far too inefficient and expensive. Punch cards were developed. The end user would sit at a key punch machine and type a single command on each card. The key punch machine would cut a small hole in the proper position on the card. Each set of holes would represent an alphanumeric or symbol. The cards would be loaded into the computer through a card reader and loaded into the computer in one batch operation.

While this was a large improvement over the single 'switch thrower', it had many drawbacks. If only one card had an error or improper syntax for a program statement, the program would reject the program and one would have to find the improper statement, correct the card, and begin the loading process once again.

With the advent of lower-priced computers and eventually the personal computer, the interface returned to a device that had been around for almost a hundred years — the typewriter keyboard.

The typewriter keyboard has many advantages that are also the hallmarks of a good user interface. Information can be entered quickly. The keyboard has familiarity and the layout of the keyboard is a standard. One can sit at any Qwerty English language keyboard anywhere in the world and find at least 95% of the keys in the same position. The Qwerty keyboard is so named because of the first six letters in the upper row. The Qwerty layout was designed around the turn of the century with the objective of slowing down typists. This was necessary to keep the keys of early typewriters from jamming. A better keyboard can be designed, and in fact it has been. The Dvorak keyboard (*Figure 5.2*) is a simplified keyboard that allows for much faster typing. But how many people have seen a Dvorak keyboard, in spite of its increased power? The Qwerty keyboard remains the dominant keyboard in use because it is a standard, it is familiar, and more training materials exist for it. Computer program users will opt for familiarity over power every time.

This leads to one of the major tradeoffs in user interface design, power *vs* ease of use. The obvious objective is to design a program that is powerful, easy to learn and easy to use.

Figure 5.2 The layout of the Dvorak (simplified) keyboard showing all unshifted characters

But designers of computer programs seem to take a much more complex approach towards interface design than is necessary. What would have happened if a typical computer designer had designed a television set? Well, we probably would turn the power on as we do now. But instead of immediately broadcasting a particular channel (the last one we watched), the set would display, 'going through memory and colour check'. Then we would be confronted by a prompt that looks something like, 'TV>'. Now we have to remember to type something like LOAD TV SEL, dA. Then we get a new menu that asks us whether we want a cable channel or an over-the-air broadcast. We select 'c' for cable but inadvertently press the 'v' key instead and hear a loud beep. A flashing, ERROR 47, ERROR 47, ERROR 47 message displays but gives no additional information on how to correct the problem. We enter again, this time correctly. After a few moments a numbered menu appears asking us if we would like to watch a television programme, watch a video, adjust the colour or shut the set off. If we pick the option to watch a television programme (#2), nothing happens. Why? Well, we forgot to press the **Enter** key. You might think that the set would be smart enough to know what we meant by pressing #2. Now we have a new menu that asks us which channel we wish to watch. Channel number 2 is item number 1 on the menu, Channel number 3 is item number 2, etc. We select a channel and we are told to place the 'channel loading program' into the drive. Our ten-year-old walks into the room at this time and tells us there is a faster direct command to accomplish all this. It is something like ALT-TV-C-3. We try it but it doesn't work. We attempt to get some help from the 756 page operation manual. We discover that we forgot to hit the **Break** key first. We hear some chatter from the drive and see a display that tells us that we have a 'non-recoverable' error and returns us to 'TV>' and we have to start again.

Luckily, television set designers have long understood how to design a system with the fewest number of controls for people who may not have much practice in reading. And each control performs directly what we want it to do. But in all fairness, they have had a much longer time to design such an interface. The task of most computer programs, which are much more interactive than the passive task of video watching, are much more complex.

Objectives of user-interface design

There are several objectives to user-interface design:

- Satisfy objectives of the application.
- Make it easy to learn.
- Make it easy to use.
- Provide expandability and/or customization.

One of the problems with the four stated objectives is that virtually every software program marketed claims to have achieved all of them. Considering that these very same programs are accompanied by pounds of documentation, one has to wonder.

Objectives

The objective of any software package is not the features that it contains but the benefits it provides. An encyclopedia on CD-ROM provides the benefit of fast access to specific knowledge that is too difficult to locate by thumbing through the book or by using the indexes in the book. Thus the CD-ROM database provides the benefit of providing the capability of access to increased knowledge or more easily accessible knowledge in a shorter time span.

Easy to learn

How do we make programs easy to learn? By making the operation of those programs familiar and intuitive. Users expect space-bars to make spaces, back arrow keys to move backwards, cursor control keys to move cursors. It is amazing how many programs violate even these simple and basic guidelines.

Users also like to do things the way they did before they used computers. That is perhaps why the interface made popular on computers such as the Apple Macintosh is so widely accepted. A metaphor is provided that one can easily relate to because it allows one to work in virtually the same way one operated before using a computer. The desktop metaphor includes documents, file folders, a desktop and a 'trash can'. We do need some minor instructions to inform us how to move and open those documents. But once we learn how to pick up an object using the mouse, we find ourselves in a totally familiar and comfortable environment. We are now seeing this type of interface become a standard as it migrates to many other computer systems such as the new IBM OS/2 Presentation Manager Operating System. These types of interfaces are usually icon based and operate on the principle that it is easier to pick out an object-oriented device than to type a command. But in some instances the use of icons is poorly implemented and it is hard to decide what the icon means. It is generally easier to understand what the word 'volume' on a television receiver means than to try and figure out what a right triangle is trying to represent (providing you can understand the written language). Icon-based systems do have the advantage of being language independent, although they are frequently not culture independent.

Another way to promote familiarity is by the use of standards. If all programs used the exact same set of commands and keys, each new program would be easier to use. But this can also provide drawbacks. Standardization can sometimes lead to stagnation, since better ways of doing things are constantly evolving. One early computer metaphor was that of layered menus. A numbered menu would be viewed at the top level of the program and by selecting a menu option, we would be led deeper into a program where we would find more menus. By making more selections, we would eventually perform the intended task. It seemed a good idea at the time, but what would have happened had we all standardized on layered menus and not evolved to the desktop and icon based metaphor?

Therefore as long as an interface is intuitive, it does not matter that it might be different from the interface of another program. What is important is that the command structure is obvious. Wherever possible, it should also be famliar.

One way of maintaining familiarity is by providing different ways of performing the same functions. One of the mistakes in design made by the designers of the first Apple Macintosh computer, and the early software that supported it, was that it forced the user to use a mouse in all circumstances. In many instances it would have been easier, or preferable to some users, to use cursor keys or command key equivalents for menu functions. Speed was not the only issue; in many cases users were more familiar with keyboard commands. And, as we have seen on the newer Macintosh keyboards and software, it is possible to provide both and react to the user's needs rather than forcing the users to a specific doctrine and methodology of either the hardware or in the case of a CD-ROM application, the retrieval mechanism. In many applications, either a click of the mouse in a highlighted box or pressing the **Enter** key will perform the same action.

Many users have stated that they feel that CD-ROM publishers should get together and provide a single, standard user interface for all CD-ROM applications. But since the nature of the data provided on CD-ROM varies considerably, the nature of the user interface must vary considerably as well. Lotus' *One-Stop* provides financial data that gets loaded into a spreadsheet, the Grolier *Academic Encyclopedia* is a full text database,

Microsoft's *Bookshelf* provide dictionaries and other resources that are used on top of another application, such as a wordprocessor, and Bowker's *Plus Series* databases contain bibliographic data. It is not possible to search all of these databases efficiently using the same interface.

Easy to use

A program that is easy-to-learn is not necessarily easy-to-use. The 'layered menu' program discussed earlier is easy to learn because each of the menus tell us exactly what we can do. But it may not be easy to use because we have to wade through each of those menus. This is time consuming and can also be confusing because we can easily 'lose our way' if we go too deep down the path of menus.

There is at least one successful program that was designed with over 65 menu entries. Each menu entry required an average of five responses before something could be accomplished. Therefore a user had to make over 300 responses to use all of the power of the program. The program was easy to learn because each menu entry told the user exactly what they could accomplish. But it was a horror to use because printing, viewing and editing all took place in different menu options.

A program that is easy to use has an intuitive command structure but also allows us to accomplish our objectives consistently and quickly. Command keys frequently allow us to perform tasks quickly but they are not necessarily intuitive. A program that allows us to print by pressing **Shift-ALT-F6** may allow us to perform that task quickly, but the hundreds of key combinations contained in a complete application such as a word-processor are difficult to remember. Therefore many programs will have built-in redundancy that will allow the user to use either a menu function or a combination of keys to perform the same function. Pehaps the program will also allow the end user to customize the use of command keys. In this way, if one program uses **F4** to print, and another uses **F6**, the user can change the print keys of each to **F5**, which is the way the user learned to use a wordprocessor.

A well-designed program will allow a user to get started and use many of the functions of the program immediately. A good example is a word-processor in which we only have to start typing to use, and the functions to name, save and print a file are obvious. As one gains familiarity with the program, the more powerful functions of the program such as spell-checking, page-layout, indexing, etc. become more obvious.

A well-designed interface will have a minimum of display screens. If there is more than one display, it is frequently useful to overlay the second screen in a window, with the bottom original display still partially visible. In this manner, the user will always know where they are in the program. The 'home' display is always visible and nearby; it is easy to find the path 'home'. Always knowing where home is and how to get there provides much comfort.

The displays themselves should be cleanly designed and simple in structure. The user's eye should always be led to the same place to get the same type of information. This might mean that help messages are always displayed at the bottom of the screen and menu functions always at the top. Important warning messages may be placed just above the help messages in a different colour.

Expandability and customization

The program should adjust to the skill level of the user. One way of accomplishing this is to provide different levels of using the program — perhaps a 'novice' mode and an 'expert' mode. A better method is to anticipate the different types of responses a user may make, plan for them, and enable the program to react to each of them.

An ideal program would allow the user to customize the program. This might include the ability to create new functions, to change the colour of screens, to create new function keys or change already existing ones, to create customized display or output formats and to create program macros. Macros are the ability of the program to memorize a series of keystrokes so that often-repeated procedures can be defined as simple keystrokes.

Speed

Obviously, the program should operate as quickly as possible. Users should get immediate response to their commands or entries. But when it is not possible to respond immediately, there are several design attributes to deal with the situation. It is important to always provide something on the screen for the user to react to. In one computer program, the initial load of the program took about 22 seconds. When the program was tested with potential users, they complained about the 'three minute wait' before they could start using the program. The design of the program was changed so that instead of a blank screen, an animated picture of a bar graph was displayed that showed how much longer it would take to complete the load. When the program was tested again, the complaints about loading time disappeared. While the objective time of loading did not change, the 'subjective time' of loading was reduced considerably.

Good interface design is extremely difficult to describe because good design involves a highly complex combination of different attributes. One can pinpoint all the rules of good filmmaking, but following these rules can result in either a disaster or a masterpiece. And like a good film, a well-designed computer program has a rhythm to the way it reacts to our input; everything in the program feels natural and responsive.

There are a number of factors that affect whether we feel a program is responding to our input. The quickness with which a selected new menu option or button blinks, the smoothness and direction with which a window zoom opens and closes, how fast a character appears on the screen in response to a keypress, how much mouse or cursor movement the program requires us to make, all have a very definite affect on the way a user responds to a program. When all these responses are executed and designed properly, the program seems to flow naturally from our thoughts and fine motor movements. When these are not executed properly, using the program becomes a drudgery.

Terminology

The program should use consistent language and terminology. The user should not have to guess what the program means. Apple Computer Inc. frequently holds developer conferences for publishers and software developers. At one conference, the following story was related about a problem with a question posed in a computer program. The objective of the statement posed to the user was to find out if the user was viewing the program on a colour monitor.

First design

Question   Is the picture above in colour?

Display   A colour graphic is displayed.

Problem   Some users seeing black and white thought the colour might be turned down. Other users working on a monochrome amber display thought the amber meant a colour display was being used.

Failure rate   30%.

Second design

Question   Are you using a colour TV on this computer?

Display   A colour graphic is displayed.

Problem   Users unfamiliar with the equipment did not know whether the monitor was colour or monochrome.

Failure rate   30%.

Third design

Question   Are the words above in colour?

Display   Large-letter words in their own colours: RED GREEN BLUE ORANGE.

Failure rate   Colour TV users: none.
Black and white TV users: none.
Amber or green monitor users: 100% failure.
The amber and green screen users felt that they were looking at a colour.

Fourth design

Question   Are the words above in more than one colour?

Display   Same as above.

Failure rate   Colour TV users: none.
Black and white TV users: 15%.
Amber or green monitor users: 50%.
The amber and green screen users felt that they were looking at two colours: amber and black or green and black. The black and white TV users must have thought that black and white were colours.

Fifth design

Question   Are the words above in several different colours?

Display   Same as above.

Failure rate   Colour TV users: none.
Black and white TV users: 20%.

Amber or green monitor users: 23%.
In this case, it seemed that the users were not really
reading the question, they were trying to outguess it.

Final design
Question   Do the words above appear in several different colours?
Display   Same as above.
Failure rate   None.

The most important factor in developing a good user interface is watching people use the program for the first time. The first time users try to operate a program they will tell you how they expect it to work, and that is probably the way it should be designed.

Natural language interfaces

The difference between a poor and a high-quality intuitive interface is the underlying intelligence beneath the interface. It is how the program reacts to the user. *Figure 5.3* shows examples of the worst and the best interface. Surprisingly, the screens are almost exactly alike.

There is little visual difference between these two interfaces. The first one is the standard MS DOS prompt that exists on millions of computers in existence today. If anything but a standard DOS command is typed, the user will see the infamous:

Bad command or file name

In the second interface I can type anything that I like. I might type:

Please make a list of all French companies with holdings in the United States with more than 400 employees and sort the list with the name of the company first, then the name of the chief executive officer. Print the list in a two-column format.

Writing a program that performs the second task is far from easy. Advances in natural language interface design and intelligent parsers are bringing us closer to such a reality. We find programs that can understand such natural language commands used in adventure games as well as business applications. There are a number of design problems in developing such an interface that have restricted natural language interfaces from more widespread use. The most obvious one is that the nature of the natural language request is often ambiguous. A number of natural language processing techniques have been developed including keywording, pattern matching, knowledge-based approaches and semantic approaches. These various techniques have been developed because the program must take word order into account and understand the roles that different parts of the sentences play. Examine the role of the second word in each of the following sentences:

The library leased the database for $1000 per year.
The database leased for $1000 per year.
$1000 a year will lease the database for the library.
The yearly charge for the library is $1000 a year.

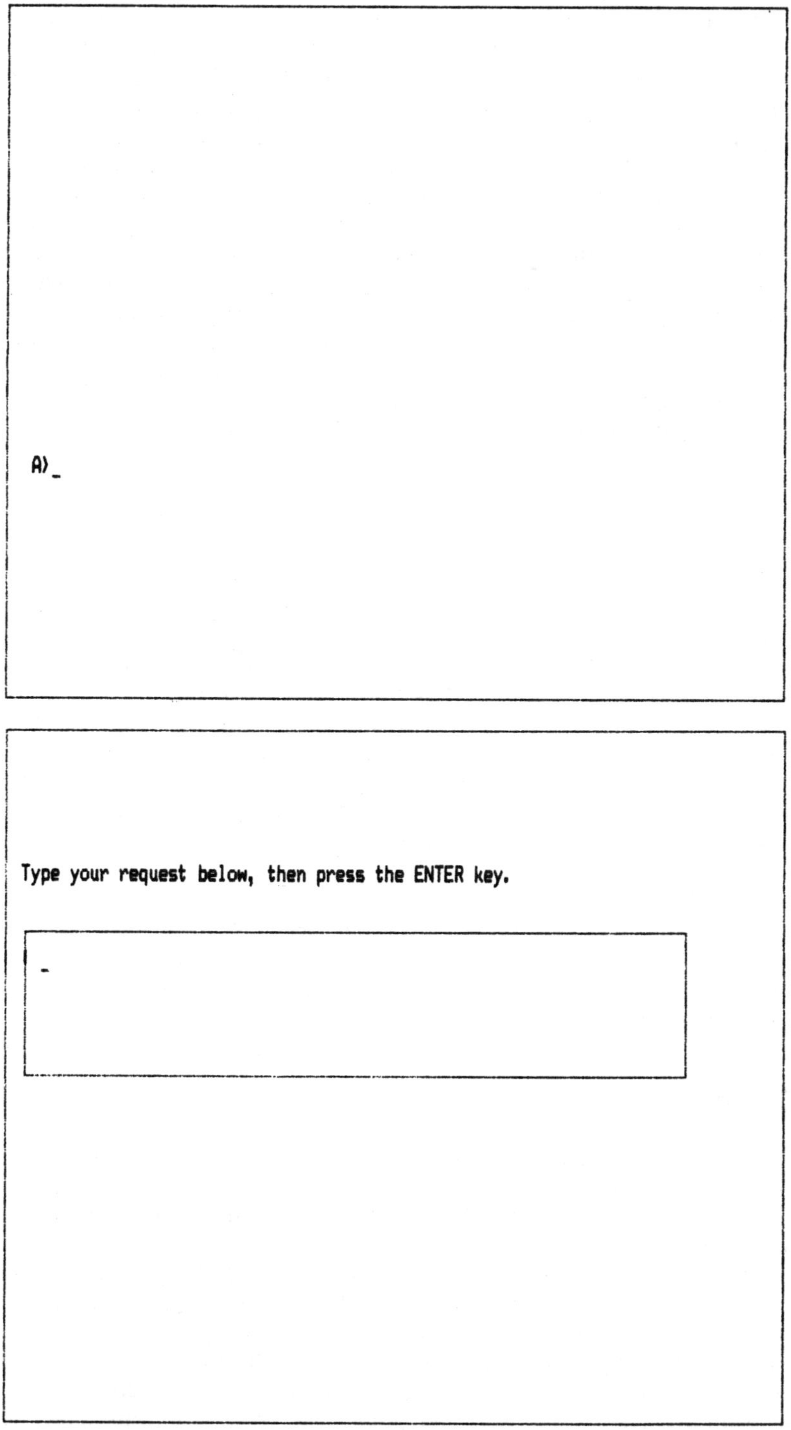

```
A) _
```

```
Type your request below, then press the ENTER key.

    ┌────────────────────────────────────────────────────┐
    │  _                                                 │
    │                                                    │
    └────────────────────────────────────────────────────┘
```

Figure 5.3 (a) An example of a poor interface; (b) an example of a good interface

All natural processing techniques use a system of rules to modify the natural language and rewrite it into language that the computer system can undertstand. Some techniques rely on pattern matching. With this method, sentence fragments of the input language are matched to a list of frequently-used patterns. Grammar-based approaches to natural-language processing break down the word types in a given sentence into a theoretical tree structure that allows them to be rewritten according to a set of fixed rules that take into account word type and order. Knowledge-based approaches rewrite the natural-language request into a simpler script structure based on predefined knowledge of the particular situation. There are also various methods used by the parser to match the input against the rewrite rules. The problem with many such interfaces is that the size of the parser's vocabulary, or the number of structural models it is able to develop, is usually limited enough to cause gross interpretation of the statement or no interpretation at all. Those familiar with natural language adventure games are also familiar with the everpresent, 'I can't do that now' or 'I don't understand what you mean'.

In response to these problems, many natural-language systems let you verify that the interpretation of your request coincides with your true meaning. They will usually let you redefine terms when the program cannot understand your true meaning. However, by the time the user is able to establish proper communication with the program, it would have been quicker, and probably easier, to process the user's requests through more traditional commands and menu functions. This is especially true if there are a limited number of types of requests that the user may make and it is therefore possible to integrate these requests into clearly defined menus.

Until we reach the level of development where computer programs can understand our natural-language vocabulary with all its variations, inter-face designs that use command structures and command keys that are easy to learn (remember) and easy to use (fast and intuitive) will remain prevalent.

Good interface design also provides useful messages to the user that will tell the user what options they have at any given time. These messages will be context sensitive, i.e. they will change depending on what task is being accomplished at any given time.

Hypertext

Ted Nelson coined the term *Hypertext* in 1965. Hypertext is a term used to describe the ability to navigate through text in a non-sequential manner that provides links to associated data through the use of keywords, hot keys, and/or buttons.

For instance, a user might perform a search in a CD-ROM database on the term Shakespeare which results in a list of Shakespeare's plays. High-lighting *Romeo and Juliet* may result in a new display showing the full text of the play. Highlighting *Romeo* in the text of the play and pressing a particular 'hot key' or 'button' may give us a picture of Romeo, an audio track of an actor performing Romeo's lines, or a critic's interpretation of Romeo's actions.

Nelson and other proponents of hypertext have defined a number of models for dealing with data in this freeform manner, such as maps, paths, splices and filters. A map is a graphical view of the structure of the connecting patterns between data. A path is a predefined route through a document, usually the route that you would expect users to follow most of the time. A splice provides the ability to append material from different routes and documents into a single document. A filter provides a way to subset possible links between data. This provides the ability to select material by search category or by type of reference (review, cross reference, forward reference, annotation).

Guide

Guide is a wordprocessor that allows you to create hypertext documents. *Guide* allows the user to create 'hot spots' in a document that are linked to text or graphics in the same or a different document. When the cursor is passed over one of these 'hot spots' the shape of the cursor changes depending on the kind of link that is available. *Guide* provides four kinds of links: a note button, a replacement button, a reference button and an inquiry button. Clicking on a word or picture that contains a note button opens a window that contains additional information about the word or picture highlighted. Clicking on a word or picture that contains a replacement button causes new text or pictures to replace the original ones. Perhaps the new text is written at a lower level than the original text. A reference button links to other text within a document or perhaps a totally different document. Clicking on a brief mention of 'Isaac Newton' could link to a detailed biography of the scientist, then return to the original document. One use of the inquiry button is to customize surveys based on how the user responds to each question.

One of the prime advantages of hypertext documents is that the basic text can be abbreviated and contain only the most important information. Readers that need more detailed information can click on the appropriate text or picture to gain additional insight into the topic desired. Therefore the document can adjust to the needs of each user. Of course hypertext documents can only exist in electronic form.

In the future, we will begin to see the hypertext type of functionality become integrated into application programs and CD-ROM based databases. CD-ROM databases have the advantage of the large disc capacity to hold the many links that a hypertext document may contain. The reason why we do not see more databases make use of hypertext is that the links are generally created manually. Imagine trying to create links on every major noun in an encyclopedia. It would probably take years of work and a very large staff. The indexing process that most databases go through to achieve quick access on a CD-ROM is accomplished automatically with a computer program.

HyperCard and Hypertalk

HyperCard (the application) and *Hypertalk* (the programming language) from Apple Computer is a simple database environment that enables non-programmers to create applications that make use of hypertext techniques. A database of telephone numbers may have a series of buttons on each file card that will lead us to a portrait of each person, a picture of their product, or their personnel record. Clicking on a 'telephone button' may automatically dial their phone number. The strength of systems like *HyperCard* are their ability to link seemingly unrelated sets of information.

In *HyperCard*, information is stored on filecards. Each set of filecards for a given application is called a stack. Many software developers are releasing 'stackware' for use with *HyperCard*. A *HyperCard* session begins at the 'home card' that contains a series of icons representing each application or stack. The demonstration home card provided with *HyperCard* includes an address stack, a calendar stack, a clip art stack, idea stacks and others (*Figure 5.4*). Beneath each icon is an invisible button that links the icon to the related *HyperCard* stack.

HyperCard allows five different levels of access. Browsing allow users to read and navigate through the stacks only. Typing also allows the ability to enter information into data fields on the stackware cards, into the address book stack, for example. The Painting level allows the user to access a MacPaint like toolbox of drawing tools. At the Authoring level, users are given the ability to modify and create fields and buttons. The highest level is Scripting, which allows access to the *Hypertalk* programming language. This also provides the ability to access hardware outside of the Macintosh, including video disc players and CD-ROM readers.

Accessing information in *HyperCard* is largely icon-based. Thus, as long as the icons are well designed and communicate their true intent to the end user, is a truly intuitive, easy to use and easy to learn system. And Authoring and Scripting allows for customization and expansion of the system.

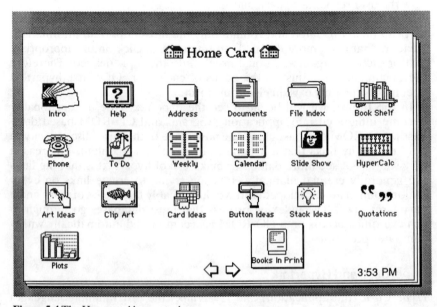

Figure 5.4 The Hypercard home stack

The key to the power of *HyperCard* is the ease with which end-users can create their own links between buttons (functions) and cards. Creating these links is as easy as clicking and pointing. You might imagine these links as a series of strings that tie one card to another. If you want to create a new association between one card and any other, that link can be created regardless whether the link is with a totally new card or an already existing card. Each *Hypercard* stack is made up of cards and each card can contain buttons and text fields as well as graphics and sound. Buttons can be visible and in many styles including an icon, or they can be invisible. One use of an invisible button would be to place it behind the word 'button' in this document. Clicking on the word 'button' would then link to a whole screen filled with different button types or a more detailed text.

HyperCard is different from *Guide* in that information is limited to the space occupied by a card, although scrolling text windows are available. And *HyperCard* only has one type of cursor (a pointing hand), whereas in *Guide* the cursor changes depending on the type of link available. But the power of *HyperCard* is its ability to create complete applications within a hypertext environment.

HyperCard provides much interest because end-users will be able to design and reshape user interface to fit their own needs. If you wish to change the links in an already existing *HyperCard* stack or create new ones, it is possible and relatively easy to do so. Yet, its greatest application may be in the impetus it gives to integrating more flexibility in more traditional applications. An example might be a CD-ROM database of emergency medical data that allows the end users to create links to already existing inhouse data.

A practical example: *Microsoft Bookshelf*

Microsoft Bookshelf is an interesting example of a CD-ROM product that must integrate several different types of databases into a single product. The interface task is difficult because it is necessary to design a single interface that can handle the retrieval of different data types from different sources and operate without conflict with a variety of wordprocessors.

Bookshelf includes the following reference works: *The American Heritage Dictionary, Roget's II Electronic Thesaurus, The World Almanac and Book of Facts, Bartlett's Familiar Quotations, The Chicago Manual of Style, The Houghton-Mifflin Spelling Verifier and Corrector, Forms and Letters, US Zip Code Directory, Houghton-Mifflin Usage Alert,* and *Business Information Sources*.

Bookshelf is loaded on top of another application, usually a word-processor. The *Bookshelf* menu appears when the **ALT-Left Shift** keys are pressed. This menu includes each of the databases, an Options Menu and a Help Menu (*Figure 5.5*). Once a database is selected, a second menu appears (*Figure 5.6*) that is used to retrieve citations by a variety of methods and copy data to a clipboard for pasting into a document.

When *Bookshelf* is active, you can no longer type directly into your wordprocessor. This enables *Bookshelf* to react to a variety of types of entries for quick access. Pressing the first letter of any of the menus reveals the appropriate pull-down menu. Particular entries in a menu can then be selected with the cursor keys and **Enter** key or by pressing the first letter of the entry and the **Enter** key. It is also possible to quickly select the first entry in any pull down menu by pressing the **ALT** key and the first letter of the menu name. For instance the first entry in the Spell Menu is Word. To quickly access the Word entry, you could press **ALT-S**. This might be confusing to some users because **ALT-S** stands for Word. But it makes sense because Spell is visible in the menu bar, not the Word item in the menu.

```
                    Microsoft Bookshelf  (COMMAND LINE)
Thesaurus Dictionary Spell Usage Manual Almanac Quote BIS ZIP Forms Options Help
```

Figure 5.5 The *Bookshelf* main menu

```
              The World Almanac & Book of Facts  (Browse)
Edit    View    Search    Browse    Options    Next    Previous    Help
```

Figure 5.6 *Bookshelf's* main menu is used to access the desired database. The submenu becomes visible once inside a database

```
                    Microsoft Bookshelf  (COMMAND LINE)
Thesaurus Dictionary Spell Usage Manual Almanac Quote BIS ZIP Forms Options Help
                    +-------------------------+
                    | Word            Alt-S   |
                    | Screen                  |
                    | Options                 |
                    | User Dictionary         |
                    +-------------------------+
```

Figure 5.7 Pressing **Alt-S** when the menu is closed will automatically open the word search facility and place the word under the cursor from the wordprocessing document into the window for checking

If the cursor is left on a particular word in the wordprocessing document, pressing **ALT-S** will automatically look up the spelling of the word in question (*Figure 5.7*). This opens a window that displays the word as we have spelled it, tells us whether the word has been spelled incorrectly, and has options to find alternate spellings, do another lookup, add the word to a custom word list, ignore the spelling, replace our word, or cancel all actions. The usual action, Alternates, is highlighted by a double box. Pressing the **Tab** key selects new options. Pressing **Enter** selects the default action. In this case, pressing **Enter** selects Alternates, and displays the properly spelled word (*Figure 5.8*). Pressing **Enter** selects the word and automatically replaces the incorrectly spelled word with the correctly spelled word in our text (*Figure 5.9*).

The *Bookshelf* Thesaurus, Dictionary, Spell Checker and Usage Alert all provide this quick lookup facility and operate with a similar interface.

The more detailed reference works are the *Chicago Manual of Style; The World Almanac and Book of Facts; Barlett's Familiar Quotations; Business Information Sources;* and *Forms and Letters.* These use the *Microsoft Bookshelf* Search interface which allows one to search for several different terms and to match those words to a subset of the particular database.

```
              Microsoft Bookshelf  (COMMAND LINE)
Thesaurus Dictionary Spell Usage Manual Almanac Quote BIS ZIP Forms Options Help
```

```
┌─────────── Spell Check ───────────┐
│                                   │
│  Word:  │concirned            │   │
│                                   │
│       Word is Spelled Incorrectly │
│                                   │
│  ┌Alternates┐ ┌Lookup┐ ┌Add To Word List┐ │
│                                   │
│  ┌Ignore┐    ┌Replace┐  ┌Cancel┐  │
└───────────────────────────────────┘
```

Figure 5.8 The Spell Check window shows that the word is spelt incorrectly. Pressing **Enter** selects **Alternates**, which displays alternate spellings

```
              Microsoft Bookshelf  (COMMAND LINE)
Thesaurus Dictionary Spell Usage Manual Almanac Quote BIS ZIP Forms Options Help
```

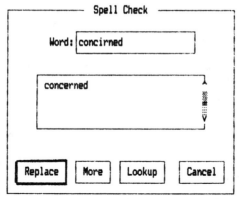

Figure 5.9 Pressing **Enter** selects **Replace**, which replaces the incorrectly spelt word in the document with the alternate chosen

For instance, we might wish to search *The World Almanac and Book of Facts* for information about the population of the country Zambia. In fact, if we left the cursor of the wordprocessor on the term Zambia, the program will automatically place 'Zambia' in the first search box. The terms 'Zambia' and 'population' are typed into separate boxes. There are three boxes that may be used for search terms. Typing an entry into each separate box will 'and' the term with the other boxed term. Typing two terms within a box with a comma in between will 'or' the terms within the box. Typing two terms within a box with a space in between will look for occurrences of both words together, such as 'computer programming'. We move from box to box with the **Tab** key. We can also move the **Tab** key to the 'Match Words' box to select whether we want to match words in the chapter, article, a subsection or paragraph. While the CD-ROM is performing the search (*Figure 5.10*), a blinking cursor tells us to wait, while a bar graph shows us how much of the database has been searched. This is good interface design in that it always lets the user know that an action is taking place and about how much more time the action will take. Once an article is displayed, the words that were searched are highlighted. Pressing **Alt-N** or selecting from the Next Menu selects the next instance of our word; pressing **Alt-P** selects the previous instance of the chosen word.

If there is more than one article, a list of articles appears (*Figure 5.11*) and we are allowed to select an article from the list. Pressing **Enter** displays the appropriate article (*Figure 5.12*). It would be helpful at this point if there was a way to get back to the article list. But there is not, the search has to be performed again. We can 'zoom out' but this brings us to a listing of the first line of each instance of the term we are looking for. Because all information is presented in a single window, there is somewhat of a tendency to become confused as to where one is within the structure of the database. It might have been clearer to use overlapping window and to use the **Escape** key to back up and a function key to return to the wordprocessor. *Bookshelf* uses the **Escape** key to return to the wordprocessor; there is no direct route to backup one step at a time.

The Search window also displays the number of occurrences of the search term and the number of titles. However, the program goes directly to the citation or lists of articles before it displays this information. The only time you see this information is if you return to the Search window to perform another search.

It is also possible to go directly to the table of contents or the index of these reference works. We can make selections from the index that will

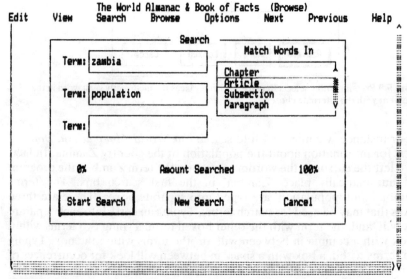

Figure 5.10 Pressing **Enter** will search for occurrences of the words 'Zambia' and 'population' in the same article

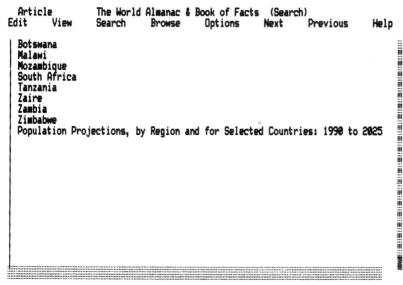

```
Article        The World Almanac & Book of Facts  (Search)
Edit     View      Search    Browse    Options    Next     Previous    Help

Botswana
Malawi
Mozambique
South Africa
Tanzania
Zaire
Zambia
Zimbabwe
Population Projections, by Region and for Selected Countries: 1990 to 2025
```

Figure 5.11 A list of articles available in *The World Almanac* that contain the words 'Zambia' and 'population'

```
               The World Almanac & Book of Facts  (Search)
Edit     View      Search    Browse    Options    Next     Previous    Help

   Region and Country        1990     1995     2000     2025
   Burundi . . . . . . . . . . . . 5.3     6.1      7.0     11.0
    Ethiopia. . . . . . . . . .  42.7    50.1     58.4    112.0
    Kenya . . . . . . . . . . .  25.4    31.4     38.5     82.9
    Madagascar. . . . . . . . .  11.6    13.4     15.6     29.7
    Malawi. . . . . . . . . . . . 8.3     9.8     11.7     23.2
    Mozambique. . . . . . . . .  16.2    18.8     21.8     39.7
    Rwanda. . . . . . . . . . . . 7.3     8.8     10.6     22.2
    Somalia . . . . . . . . . . . 5.9     6.2      7.1     13.2
    Uganda. . . . . . . . . . .  18.8    22.5     26.8     52.3
    Tanzania. . . . . . . . . .  27.0    32.5     39.1     83.8
    Zambia. . . . . . . . . . . . 7.9     9.4     11.2     23.8
    Zimbabwe. . . . . . . . . .  10.5    12.6     15.1     32.7
   Middle Africa(2) . . . . . .  71.9    83.0     96.1    183.5
    Angola. . . . . . . . . . .  10.0    11.5     13.2     24.5
    Cameroon. . . . . . . . . .  11.1    12.6     14.4     25.2
    Cen. African Rep. . . . . . . 2.9     3.3      3.7      6.7
    Chad. . . . . . . . . . . . . 5.7     6.4      7.3     13.1
    Zaire . . . . . . . . . . .  38.4    44.8     52.4    104.4
   Northern Africa(2) . . . . . 143.8   164.3    185.7    295.0
    Algeria . . . . . . . . . .  26.0    30.5     35.2     57.3
```

Figure 5.12 The article displays the population of Zambia. The word 'Zambia' is highlighted. Pressing **Alt-N** will go to the next occurrence, if any exists

bring us directly to the article. However, in this mode, since we have not performed a search on a particular word using the Search interface, the Next and Previous functions do not work.

Bookshelf has other features that increase its flexibility. Using a menu item or function keys it is possible to copy text from any of the databases to a clipboard. Text from the clipboard can then be pasted into a document with the press of a single function key. Once we are within any article, the Search Menu has a 'Find' option that allows us to search for any word. It is also possible to create Bookmarks with additional notes.

While the *Bookshelf* interface is not totally intuitive, it is a bold and worthy attempt to integrate a large number of distinctive databases into what from the user's standpoint appears to be a single interface. Future editions of *Bookshelf* will probably further simplify the interaction process that will further enhance the ability to access a great deal of valuable information quickly during the writing process.

Another approach: the *KRS Interface*

The first CD-ROM application marketed to a consumer audience was the Grolier 20-volume *Academic American Encyclopedia,* which includes retrieval software developed by KnowledgeSet Corporation.

Although the Grolier product is currently under revision, the KRS interface is used in many CD-ROM products. This software interface depends mostly on the use of the ten function keys. These function keys are modal, i.e. their use changes depending on where you are in the system. However, a picture of the keys and their use always appears on the left side of the computer display, making the program easy to learn.

When we first enter the system, the centre of display contains the KRS logo. The left side of the display contains the graphic of the function keys; five of the keys are labelled for current use. **F1** gives us information about the keys, **F2** gives us information about KRS, **F3** gives us a setup program, **F4** lets us select the type of search that we wish to perform, and **F10** lets us exit the program (*Figure 5.13*).

Pressing **F4** changes the function of most of the keys. Pressing **F2** now displays the system status, **F3** chooses Browse Entry as the type of search, **F4** chooses Word Search as the search type, and **F10** backs up one step to the KRS title.

Choosing **F3**, then Title allows you to enter as much of an article title as you know (*Figure 5.14*). This in turn displays a list of article titles that can be selected. Once selected, the full text of the article appears. From this screen, it is also possible to view an outline of the article where specific sections may be selected and viewed.

If **F4** has been selected from the title screen, a word search is performed (*Figure 5.15*). This leads to a screen where search options can be selected. This determines whether a word search will search article titles, bibliographies, fact boxes, tables, the text of the article or all categories. It is also possible to select the proximity relationships between the words selected for the search. This allows the user to indicate that multiple words should be used to cite articles only if they all appear within the same

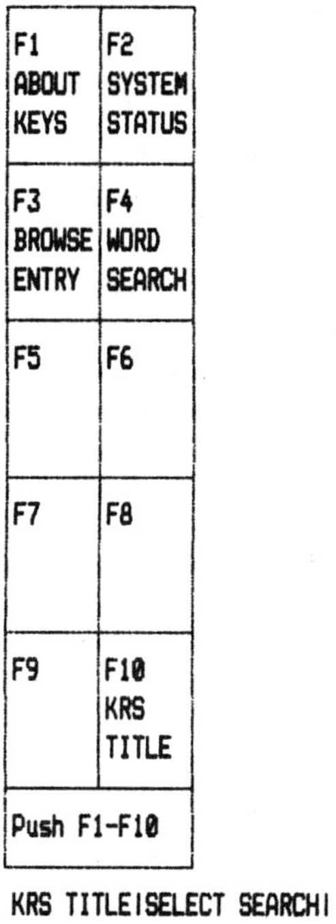

```
F1      F2
ABOUT   SYSTEM
KEYS    STATUS

F3      F4
BROWSE  WORD
ENTRY   SEARCH

F5      F6



F7      F8



F9      F10
        KRS
        TITLE

Push F1-F10
```

KRS TITLE|SELECT SEARCH| **Figure 5.13** The function keys

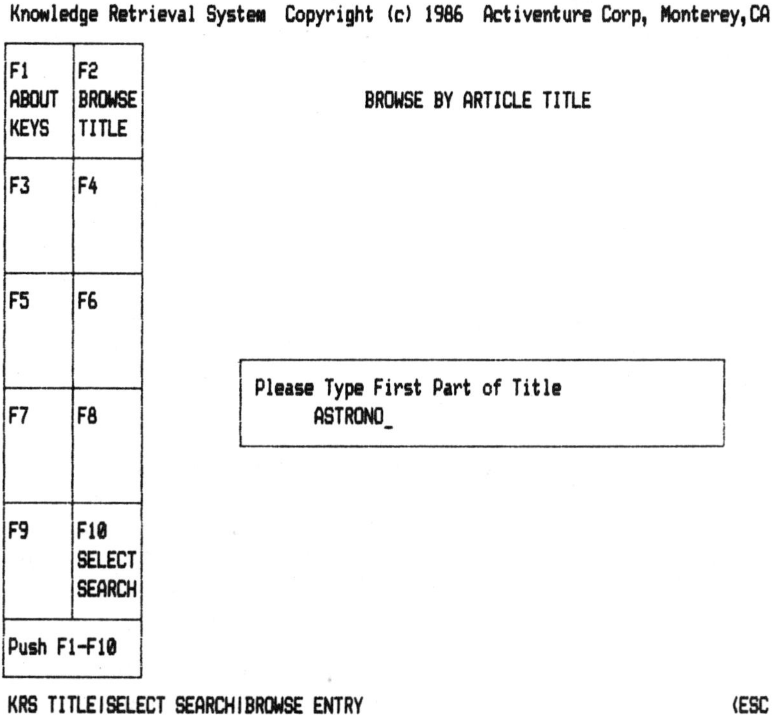

Knowledge Retrieval System Copyright (c) 1986 Activenture Corp, Monterey,CA

```
F1      F2
ABOUT   BROWSE              BROWSE BY ARTICLE TITLE
KEYS    TITLE

F3      F4


F5      F6


                    +-------------------------------------+
F7      F8          | Please Type First Part of Title     |
                    |    ASTRONO_                          |
                    +-------------------------------------+

F9      F10
        SELECT
        SEARCH

Push F1-F10
```

KRS TITLE|SELECT SEARCH|BROWSE ENTRY   (ESC

Figure 5.14 Pressing the **F3, Browse Entry**, key from the opening screen allows the user to enter an article title. Note how the function of all function keys has changed

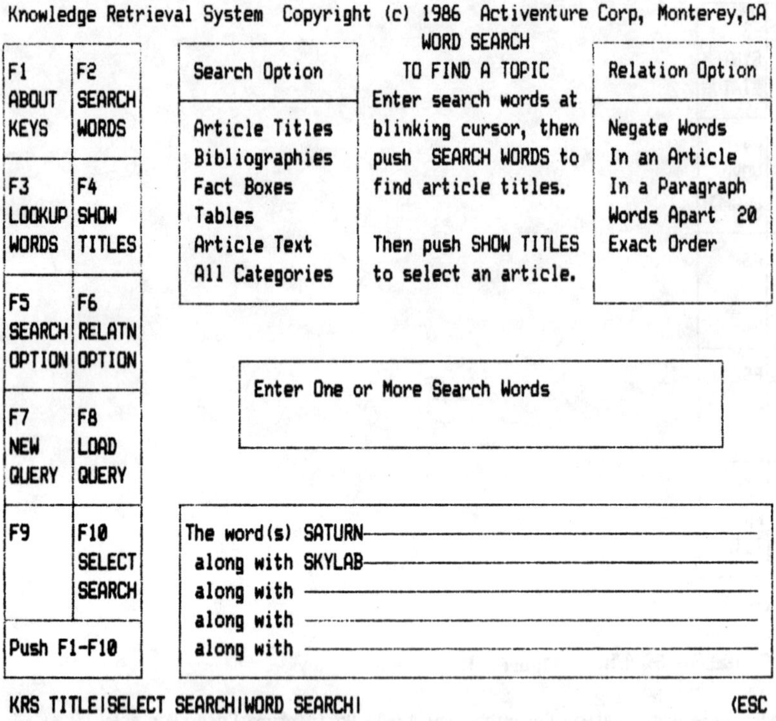

Knowledge Retrieval System Copyright (c) 1986 Activenture Corp, Monterey,CA

F1	F2	Search Option	WORD SEARCH TO FIND A TOPIC	Relation Option
ABOUT	SEARCH		Enter search words at	
KEYS	WORDS	Article Titles	blinking cursor, then	Negate Words
		Bibliographies	push SEARCH WORDS to	In an Article
F3	F4	Fact Boxes	find article titles.	In a Paragraph
LOOKUP	SHOW	Tables		Words Apart 20
WORDS	TITLES	Article Text	Then push SHOW TITLES	Exact Order
		All Categories	to select an article.	

F5   F6
SEARCH RELATN
OPTION OPTION

Enter One or More Search Words

F7   F8
NEW LOAD
QUERY QUERY

F9   F10
     SELECT
     SEARCH

Push F1-F10

The word(s) SATURN————————————————
along with SKYLAB—————————————————
along with ——————————————————————
along with ——————————————————————
along with ——————————————————————

KRS TITLE|SELECT SEARCH|WORD SEARCH| (ESC

Figure 5.15 Selecting **F4, Word Search**, from the opening menu allows the user to select
Search and **Relation Options** and to enter one or more search words. Notice how the status of
the function keys is changed again

paragraph, article, in the exact order indicated or within a certain number
of words from each other. It is also possible to indicate 'Negate Words'.
This is the equivalent of the Boolean term 'andnot'. For instance, one
could find all articles in which the words electronic and display appear but
not the term computers.

The KRS interface does not use overlaid windows. To provide screens
that display the maximum amount of data, each new screen replaces the
one before it, except for the function key graphic, which always displays on
the left of the screen. In many systems of this type, the user might 'get lost'.
In the KRS software, a strip along the bottom of the display always shows
us the 'route' that we took to get to where we are. Pressing the **Escape** key
or the **F10** key always backs up one step.

The KRS interface follows most of the rules of a high-quality interface.
It is easy to learn because all of our options are always displayed on the
screen and all program paths are clearly defined. The screens are well laid
out and easy to read. There is good use of colour. However, many may not
find it easy to use because the function of each command key changes
constantly, depending on your location in the program. While the function
keys still maintain logical sense, it requires most users to constantly look up
and double check the display to make sure that the function key will
operate in the intended manner.

A more ideal approach may have been to keep the function keys non-modal and provide pull down menus for additional functions.

A practical example: the *Plus Series* databases

One of the best selling series of CD-ROM programs are those produced by the R.R. Bowker Company. The interface design of the program was developed by the author in association with Online Systems of Germantown, MD, USA. A very similar interface has been developed for the Library of Congress as well as programs published by the Public Affairs Information Service. Because of the prevalence of this particular interface, we will discuss it here in detail and see how it might be improved even further.

After the initial logos on log-on screen the 'home screen' appears with five submenus listed. There are two ways to move to each menu category. Either one can use the right and left cursor keys or press the first letter of the menu name. This is another important attribute of good user interface design. It is important to provide multiple ways of performing the same operation. In this manner, the program can react to the user's known way of doing things, providing familiarity and comfort.

At this point, the designer does not know if the user wishes to move to another menu, so the user must make the decision to open the menu. This is done by pressing the **Enter** key. Since most of the options within each menu are of equal use, there would not be any point in this program in having a system like *Bookshelf*, where the first item in the menu has the highest priority and a quick means of accessing it.

Pull-down menus are effective because it is possible to view from one screen all of the options available in the program. All menus reside at one level. The number of menus is purposely kept to a minimum so that there is less to remember. The menus are displayed in the order that they will probably be used, with the most frequent at the left. This is so when the program starts operation each day, no selection is needed to move to the first menu.

The first menu is the Search Menu. This is opened by pressing the **Enter** key. In this system, Search means the ability to enter a search statement to find citations from one or a number of indexes. There is also a Browse function, described in detail later, that allows the user to select titles or words from a displayed list. When the Search Menu is opened, all of the searchable indexes are displayed on the left. The Search Workspace (*Figure 5.16*), where searches are entered, is on the right. Instructions are displayed on the bottom of the screen, in green. A search is entered by typing the two character abbreviation for the search category, an operator, such as an equal sign, and a search term. To search on a title, the user would type *ti* = and the name of the title.

Here is where we might begin to think of improvements to this interface. While the search statement seems simple enough, it is not intuitive to someone who has never used the system. A perfect system would use some of the natural language processing described earlier and allow the user to type any term without a search category and would automatically find the correct category and execute the search.

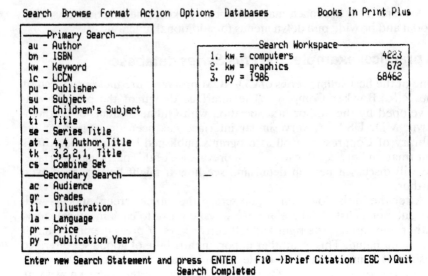

Figure 5.16 Searchable categories are displayed on the left. New searches are entered and displayed in the Search Workspace on the right

Some systems of this type allow the users to type information into a preformatted form. The form would have different areas for each search category. A system of this type is easier to learn, but it is not easier to use once one understands the rules of the system, because it is slower. Because the *Plus Series* databases were designed for users who had familiarity with online searching techniques, the interface was chosen accordingly.

The search is entered and once again, the **Enter** key is used to complete the search statement. In most cases it is not necessary to place the statement in quotes (many systems require this).

Note that after the first search is posted in the search workspace, the bottom line prompts change to inform the user that it is possible to type a *new* search. It is important that prompts to the user respond to the context of the situation.

A second search may be entered. Searches may be complex and include boolean operators. Allowable operators include AND, OR and ANDNOT. If the same operator is used more than once, it need only be entered once. Therefore, the search statement *kw = red and blue* is permissible. The program will automatically parse the statement into *kw = red and kw = blue* for processing. Parenthesized expressions are also allowed to determine order of precedence. A typical search might be *kw = computer and (pu = Holt or McGraw)*. This would find all computer books published by either Holt or McGraw-Hill.

It is also possible to truncate search terms. The '$' symol is used to truncate any groups of letters and the '?' is used to truncate a single letter. Thus *kw = comput$* will find citations for compute, computer, computers, etc.

Depending on the intended audience, it may be desirable to automatically truncate all entered words. This will result in a larger number of 'hits' but in a lower level of preciseness in the resulting citations. Data retrieval can be described in terms of recall (hits) and precision. Recall is how much data you retrieve for a given search. Precision defines how much of what you get is of use. Recall and precision are inversely related. In general, the more generally we interpret the search term, the less precise the results of the search will be.

In the *Plus Series* databases, a decision was made not to provide truncation within a word, but to provide automatic truncation after the first word of each statement for certain predefined search categories. Therefore, a user could enter *pu = Holt* and not have to know that the exact name of the publisher is *Holt, Rinehart and Winston, Incorporated*. The program will automatically retrieve all citations with publishers the name of which begins with the word *Holt*. But a user could enter the complete publisher name if he wanted to. Therefore the level of preciseness is left up to the user.

At this point, it is possible to execute another search or to view our Brief Citations. The prompt at the bottom of the screen informs us that we can view the citations by pressing the **F10** key. This is not necessarily intuitive, although many software packages use the **F10** key to proceed forward in the system. (The Grolier system described earlier uses **F10** to go backwards!) An argument could be made for continuing to use the **Enter** key to move forward. However, since the **Enter** key is used to make multiple selections in the system, a different key is needed to indicate that the selection process is complete and one wishes to move forward once again. The **F10** key is usually located in the bottom row of the keyboard, making it very easy to find without having to move hands off the keyboard or looking down.

The Brief Citations (*Figure 5.17*) appear in a window that overlaps the

```
Search  Browse  Format  Action  Options  Databases          Books In Print Plus

                               ─────Search Workspace─────
                              │   1. su = accounting              1104
                        ─Brief Citations──────────────────────────────
   Author               Title                   Price    Date    ISBN
   ──────               ─────                   ─────    ────    ────
 ) Batty, J.            Designing & Presenting Fin $120.00 04/1988 0566027151
   Agrawal, Surendra    International Guide to Acc  $28.00 01/1987 0910129630
   Batty, J.            Accounting for Research &   $70.00 10/1987 0566027143
   Behrenfeld, Willi    Accountant's Business Manu $119.00 05/1987 0870510002
   Blagrove, Luanna     AMERCE Tribute Account: Ac  $24.59 06/1987 0939776316
   Blagrove, Luanna     AMERCE Tribute Account: An  $24.95 06/1987 0939776286
   Blagrove, Luanna     AMERCE Tribute Account: Bo  $24.95 06/1987 0939776308
   Blagrove, Luanna     AMERCE Tribute Account: Ta  $24.95 06/1987 0939776294
   Bodnar,              Accounting Information Sys  $31.00    1987 0205103081
   Burnet,              Essentials of Accounting    $11.50    1987 0538014903
   Cashin, J. A.        Schaum's Outline of Accoun          02/1987 0070103534 v

                       ENTER ->Select  ESC ->Quit
```

Figure 5.17 The Brief Citation display overlays the original Search Workspace. Additional items found on this search of the subject accounting can be displayed by pressing the **PgDn** key

original 'home' screen. To return to the Search Workspace, the user backs up by pressing the **Escape** key. This is true throughout the system, **F10** always moves forward, **ESC** always moves back one step.

Selections are made on this Brief Citation screen by pressing the **Enter** key. This allows users to further filter the results of a given search, increasing the precision of a search. Selecting an entry highlights it and moves the indicator arrow down one position. An already highlighted entry can be deselected by pressing the **DEL** key. The user can skip an entry by pressing the up or down arrow keys. The user can also move to the next screen (if there are more than 11 entries) by pressing the **PgDn** key. They can go to the top of the list by pressing the **HOME** key or the bottom of the list by pressing the **END** key.

It is also possible to select a large number of entries by pressing the **Ctrl-X** key, the **PgDn** or **END** key, and the **Enter** key. All selected entries may be deselected by pressing **Ctrl-D.** In case the user forgets the **Ctrl-X** or **Ctrl-D** commands, they also appear in the Options Menu. They may be turned on from the Options Menu, but the menu also provides a reminder as to what the quicker key commands are. The choice of **Ctrl-D** for 'delete' is a good mnemonic, though **Ctrl-X** was probably not the best choice. The standard command on a Macintosh for 'cutting' a selection is **Command-X.** Perhaps **Ctrl-S** would have been a better choice. What is most important is that within a single application, all keys are used consistently. If in one part of the application **Ctrl-X** means select and in another it means erase all files, the user will never trust the application again.

Once Brief Citations are selected, they may be viewed as Full citations (*Figure 5.18*) by again pressing the **F10** key. If no citations are selected when the **F10** key is pressed, the user is reminded that they haven't selected anything.

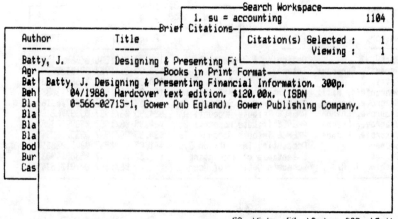

Figure 5.18 The Full Citation display in the standard format. The citation may also be viewed as a catalogue card, order form, or in several fielded formats

On slower computer systems, there may be some time delay in viewing the full citations. In order to reduce subjective time, a prompt is displayed to indicate that the CD-ROM disc is being accessed and a second prompt is displayed to explain that the display is being formatted. The user is never left to guess whether a correct key has been pressed. On most recent computer systems, such as those operating at clock speeds of 6 MHz and above, the prompts are hardly noticeable in most situations.

The Full Citation is displayed in a third window, layered on top of the Brief Citation window. Again, this tells the user where they are in the program. And the user may back-up by pressing the **Esc** key.

Once the full citation is displayed, the following citations may be viewed by pressing the + or − keys. If the citation takes up more than one window, the user may scroll down by use of the down arrow (a line at a time) or the **PgDn** key (a page at a time). A small arrow at the side of the citation indicates that more material exists. The + and − prompts at the bottom of the display only appear if more citations exist for viewing. Again, the prompt is context sensitive.

In one version of this interface, additional linked material may be viewed. Specific information about the publisher of a given citation is available. A specific function key, the **F2** key, is assigned to view this linked data. Because this is not intuitive, the prompt for this key appears at the bottom of the display whenever this information is available for viewing. Redundancy is built in as it is also possible to select this information from the Action Menu (*Figure 5.19*), which once again is what the function key shortcut is. Note however, that the screen display itself is not cluttered with redundant information.

In another version of this interface, a review of a book is also available. In this case, the **F10** function key is used once again to proceed forward to view the linked reviews. If multiple reviews exist, the + and − keys are used to move to each review, just as these keys were used to move to each citation. The **PgUp, PgDn, Home** and **End** keys operate just as they would when a Full Citation is displayed.

As can be seen by these examples, it is important that commands be used consistently throughout an application. In this manner, users have less new information to learn.

It is also possible to change the display format. The Format Menu is accessed by pressing the **ALT-F** keys. (The Action Menu is accessed by **ALT-A,** etc.) A format is selected by using the arrow keys and the **Enter**

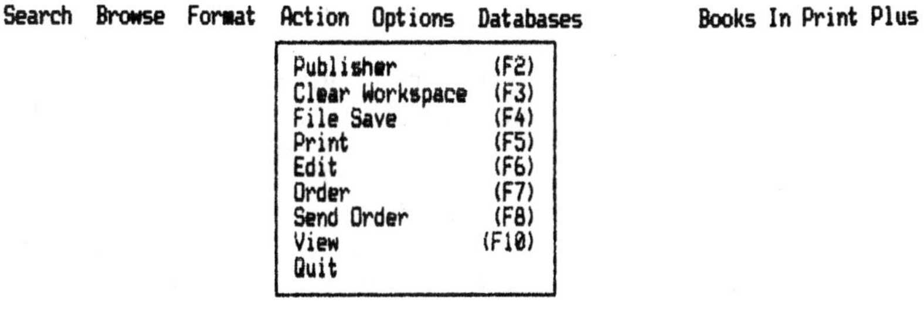

```
Search  Browse  Format  Action  Options  Databases        Books In Print Plus
                        Publisher      (F2)
                        Clear Workspace (F3)
                        File Save       (F4)
                        Print           (F5)
                        Edit            (F6)
                        Order           (F7)
                        Send Order      (F8)
                        View            (F10)
                        Quit
```

Figure 5.19 The Action Menu also displays the respective function keys that perform the same functions

key. It is also possible to select by pressing the first letter of the entry desired. For instance, pressing 'O' will move the highlight to **Order Form**. If there are two entries with the same first letter, pressing the letter the first time moves to the first entry, pressing the letter again moves to the second entry. Note also that the last entry selected has a small box indicating such. This is similar to the checkmark used in the Macintosh interface. The **Home** key will move the highlight to the top of the menu and the **End** key will move the highlight to the bottom. One of the displays is a Custom Format. When the program is installed, the user can select from a list of 35 fields, just the fields that are desired to appear, allowing customization of the program.

In addition to the small box in the menu, a title appears at the top of each window, describing the format that the user has selected. These signposts are useful to let the user know just where they are in the program.

It is also possible to save and print citations. The **F4** key starts a Save procedure and the **F5** key starts a print procedure. Both functions are also accessible from the Action Menu and the user is reminded once again what the shortcut function keys are. If either of these keys are pressed when a Full Citation is displayed, a single citation is saved or printed in the current display format. If either of these keys are pressed when a Brief Citation is the topmost window, the user is first asked whether they wish Brief or Full Citations to be saved or printed. Then all selected citations are saved or printed. If no citations are selected, all in the window are automatically selected for saving or printing. The user may determine the Save path so that citations may be saved to a floppy or hard disc, in any subdirectory.

During the Saving or Printing process, the user is kept informed of the total number of citations and the number that have been saved or printed so far. Again, this is to reduce subjective saving or printing time and to keep the user aware that the computer is still processing data. These windows are placed on top of the current display window and automatically disappear when the process has been completed.

Besides the five display formats, there are three special formats that may be saved to files. These are special orders, electronic orders and purchase orders. Each of these order types contains a header record that is specific to the application as well as ordering quantity information. The type of order is selected from the Format Menu. Information is entered into a form. The **F7** key is used to start an order. A 'binding window' opens where quantities are entered for each binding. The **F8** key is used to complete the order and send the information to a file. If the **F7** key is pressed before a selection is made from the Format Menu, the program automatically opens to the last type selected.

Note however, that regardless of the type of order selected, the process to complete the order is exactly the same. The order type is selected, the **F7** key opens the binding window, quantities are entered and the **F8** key completes the order and the window is closed. After quitting the program, a new menu appears with the name of each order vendor and the number of order records that exist for each. If an order vendor is selected, the vendor's order software is loaded, the file is transferred into the order software, and the user may send the order to the book distributor through a modem.

The system also provides a function so that a small wordprocessor can be loaded into the program so that citations can be edited while the *Plus Series* programs are still in memory. The edited citations can be printed and saved to disc.

The Options Menu has several special features aside from the selection options described earlier. One determines whether the publisher data is automatically appended to the full citation when saving or printing. Another allows a term from a browse index to be posted in the Search Workspace, allowing the term to be further manipulated or combined with another search.

The Database Menu allows users to switch to other CD-ROM programs without having to return to DOS.

One can easily see how this interface can be adopted to many different types of bibliographic databases. It has already been used for several different types of bibliographic databases of books, serials, audio-visual materials and video tapes. With the use of hot-keys, additional links could be developed to associate terms or citations to other types of data. Citations could be linked to additional reviews, cataloguing information, pictures, samples of text, etc.

The future

In the future, interfaces will be defined by the end user, not by the publisher of databases. The structure of database programs will allow end users to link any word or idea with any other. These links will not only operate within a database but between different databases. Users will be able to define their own windows. They will be able to customize Help messages to their own needs. These new interface designs will make the current models, interactive and powerful as they are, seem simply like turning the pages in a book. We will be able to leave function keys and commands behind us and turn totally to the association and development of ideas. And that is the point of providing access to large amounts of data. We must be able to make use of this expanded flow of information in ways that can make us more productive. And I am sure that as we gain more experience in dealing with large databases and understanding the benefits that they provide, new, more powerful interfaces will be developed to help us manage this information.

Chapter 6

Technology and applications of compact disc–interactive

Martin S. White and David Rosen

Introduction

It is interesting how particular locations come to have a special significance. All too often the significance is tinged with sadness, such as Dallas or Sarajevo. Others have a happier connotation. In the world of information science, Cranfield certainly held a position of renown for many years. In the second half of this decade, Seattle has become indelibly associated with CD-ROM and CD-I through the two conferences sponsored by Microsoft. Closely linked with the conferences have been the two definitive books on CD-ROM technology and applications, the *New Papyrus* and *Optical Publishing*. Any author attempting to provide an introduction to the technology and applications of read-only optical memory products must inevitably lean heavily on these books. The aim of this chapter is not to attempt to cover the technology of CD-I in all its complex detail, but to indicate where the technical attributes of the media can either provide an opportunity for new products, or limit the capabilities of these products.

CD-audio has been the most rapidly-adopted consumer product ever created, and because of its widespread availability it is difficult to remember that CD-ROM is only a few years old. The IBM PC was only launched in 1981, and few forecasters then could have foreseen the way in which the PC industry would explode with clones, portables and enhancements. The rise of the PC was a function of the standardization IBM brought to the market, primarily in the software arena. In 1987, IBM changed the rules with their PS/2 PC and its new operating system. CD-ROM, and CD-I, also depend on standards for their success, but we must be very careful in limiting our vision of the capabilities of these products to those based around the existing standards. In five years time we may well look back, as we do on the original IBM PC, and become bemused with its apparent immaturity. The world of new information and communication media is one of continual evolution to meet our demand for access to information, and entertainment, to stretch the mind to new horizons.

In the beginning came the laser, a device of visual simplicity and chemical complexity. NV Philips, with its origins in electric light bulbs, has always been a world leader in optical research and technology. The company has also held a prestigious position in recorded sound, both from the aspects of recording technology and as a record producer. It is therefore not surprising to learn that by the early 1970s Philips were studying the use of laser beams to provide high-density storage on rotating optical discs as an alternative to magnetic media. The recording of video signals and the creation of a replacement for the vinyl LP evolved from this research. Alongside the recording aspects, Philips also had to develop a means of replicating the optical discs if they were to be used for the distribution of information. All these strands started to come together in the late 1970s, and the LaserVision optical disc system was launched in North America.

The compact disc audio player was first announced in 1979, and following agreements between Philips and Sony to create an international standard the first discs became available in 1983. CD-ROM itself followed in 1985, and CD-I was announced in 1986. Compact-Disc Video followed in 1987, and the commercial availability of CD-I is planned for 1988.

CD-I and CD-ROM

Although based on a consumer product, CD-ROM was clearly targeted at the professional user, initially as a peripheral to a PC. The standards for file structure etc. were designed to allow maximum freedom of choice in terms of the hardware and operating software configuration to meet specific applications. The professional user is also an ASCII user, where graphics are used to only a very limited extent. That is not to say that CD-ROM cannot be used as a picture store. Of course, it can be so used, and indeed the use of audio with CD-ROM could have important applications.

The evolution of LaserVision from a linear video programme carrier into an interactive product for training, education and entertainment showed there to be a demand for a multi-media format. At the beginning of 1985, Philips and Sony collaborated in the creation of a new specification, Compact Disc–Interactive, for just such a multi-media product, but based on the physical format of the compact audio disc.

CD-I was announced to the world at the first Microsoft CD-ROM conference in Seattle in February 1986. However, not only were there no samples available, the specification itself, known as the Green Book, was not available. Indeed it was not available until several months after the conference, which did not help the world's press to clarify the differences between CD-I and CD-ROM, and that initial confusion still exists.

D. C. Geest of Philips' Corporate Group Home Interactive Systems has set out the following objectives and criteria for CD-I:

- To create a business opportunity for the publishing industry at large to publish interactive and multi-media software with broad appeal to consumer and institutional markets.
- To generate full compatibility by specifying the parameters for both the medium and playback system.
- To create conditions for an easy-to-use home appliance.

He has also stated that it was not Philip's prime intention to create an electronic publishing medium for the world of computer users.

Philips has also given a set of criteria it felt had to be met for achieving the above objectives. In this context, CD-I must:

(1) Offer very strong capabilities in the all-important application areas of education, 'edutainment' and entertainment.
(2) Provide all the required capabilities for other application areas such as: work at home and when travelling, communication and information, home shopping etc.
(3) Cater to the latest technological developments in the areas of audio and video, and audio and video processing.
(4) Include state-of-the-art capabilities for interactive and real-time use.
(5) Support text and data at a level equal to the requirements of business and professional applications.
(6) Offer a complete, comprehensive and future-proof standard, in order to obtain the full support of the leading hardware and software industries.
(7) Provide the conditions for compatibility, upgradability and extend-ability in hardware so that new players can accept a variety of optical media, ranging from linear discs such as CD Digital Audio, CD-Video and LaserVision, right up to CD-I and its future enhancements.
(8) Allow for improvements and enhancements that can be expected in the future, without obsoleting the investments both of the publishing and software industries in their repertoire, their skills and their know-how.

As far as (7) is concerned, CD-I is not compatible with CD-V and LaserVision. There is a CD-V Combi player that handles compact audio and CD-V, and then can be upgraded to handle CD-I.

To meet these objectives and criteria, there are both similarities and differences between CD-I and CD-ROM. Physically they are identical, based on the 120 mm diameter disc, and the players being developed for the consumer market will be able to play both compact audio and CD-I discs. The digital signals are also encoded on the same spiral track, and mastering and replication are identical. However CD-I is designed to be selfcontained, and a CD-I disc, therefore, has to contain both the information and the application software, without recourse to a floppy disc or other memory device. The player for CD-I discs must also be able to play the audio discs, and to act as a file server for a wide range of current and future consumer output devices, including high-definition television.

The standards developed have had to accommodate:

- varying levels of sound quality,
- varying levels of video quality,
- real time interactivity,
- data integrity.

Compared with the LaserVision specifications and compact audio discs, the CD-I Green Book is several orders of magnitude more complex. Let us now look at some of the features of CD-I.

Audio capabilities

In view of the origins of CD-I, it is convenient to start our conducted tour by looking at the audio specification. There are four levels of audio quality, based around the concept of a 'channel' being some 70 minutes of continuous playing time.

The first level, level DA, provides one channel of stereo sound at CD digitial audio standard, and uses the 16-bit pulse code modulation (PCM) developed for the audio disc. Of course this would occupy the entire CD-I disc, but is in the specification so that the operating system can detect an audio disc and decode the PCM signal.

The second level, level A, described as hifi music mode, is roughly equivalent to a vinyl LP in quality, and using this a CD-I disc can give 2 channels (i.e. roughly 2 hours) of stereo sound or 4 hours of mono sound. To achieve this a technique known as Adaptive Delta Pulse Code Modulation (ADPCM) is used, based on either 8-bit or 4-bit sampling.

The third level, level B, is described as mid-fi music mode, and is intended to be equivalent to a VHF FM broadcast signal. At this level 4 hours of stereo or 8 of mono sound are achieved. Finally there is speech mode, with 8 hours of stereo or 16 hours of mono, designated level C.

At the ISI Annual Lecture in London in September 1987 (given in association with the Institute of Information Scientists), Philips staff demonstrated these audio levels. At the level C, the ear recognizes a reduction in dynamic and frequency range usually associated with a poor recording, yet there are none of the imperfections usually associated with such recordings, and the sound is quite acceptable.

In practice, the audio level will probably be determined by the space left on the disc after everything else is in place. However the audio tracks are the most susceptible to any imperfections in timing or interactivity. Dropping out a couple of video frames a second is scarcely detectable, but delay speech synchronization by 1/12 second, and it is detectable.

Video coding

A key difference between LaserVision and CD-I is that, in the former, the video signal is coded in an analogue format, whereas CD-I uses a digital format. There are three implications of these differences. Firstly, the digital format enables the problems associated with the incompatibility of the PAL and NTSC television signals to be overcome. Secondly, a digital image can be processed by a microprocessor and, finally, a digitized image occupies more storage space than an analogue image. This last fact accounts for the current lack of a moving full-screen video image, other than for a few seconds, since an interlaced video picture occupies 650 kilobytes (uncompressed), which gives room only for 1000 pictures on a 600 megabyte disc, or about 40 seconds. In practice, an interlaced picture is not normally required.

The first issue to address is that of resolution. To achieve the resolution of a current 625-line PAL television set requires each picture to be digitized at 384×280 pixels for the full screen. However, the NTSC standard used in Japan and North America utilizes only 525 lines, so to give a picture fitting an NTSC set requires a 'safe' area of 320×210 pixels. The maximum distortion for a 625-line disc on a 525-line terminal is an almost undetectable 7%, which compares with a 20% distortion when television signals are converted.

A slightly higher level of resolution is given by a standard with twice the horizontal digitization, i.e. 768 × 280 pixels. This gives improved clarity to the Kanji characters used in Japanese script whilst using the same line rate. Finally there is a 768 × 560 pixel (640 × 420 for the safe area) resolution that is of studio quality and is available in advance of the introduction of high-definition television (HDTV) as a consumer product.

Resolution is only one factor. The second is how to encode information on colour into the signal. Natural pictures are encoded using YUV encoding, in which the luminance information (Y) is encoded at full bandwidth, and the chrominance information (U and V) is encoded on alternate lines at half-bandwidth. Even without interlacing a twin-field picture each image occupies 325 kilobytes. This can be reduced to 108 kilobytes using Delta YUV encoding.

As well as this picture mode, there are two graphics modes. The first is called absolute RGB encoding, in which the red, green and blue signals are coded using PCM. At 8-bit PCM each graphics picture occupies 108 kilobytes. An alternative mode is to use the Colour Look-Up Tables (CLUT) widely adopted by the computer industry. RGB graphics can be manipulated by the user, whereas CLUT graphics can only have the colours varied by the user. Animated sequences can either be CLUT encoded or by run-length coding, the latter requiring a highly complex description to do it justice.

Finally there is text information, which can be encoded either using character coding (e.g. ASCII) or by a bit-mapped technique that enables the characters to be manipulated. The resolution of even a 625-line set limits the number of characters to 40 on 20 lines, as used in teletext and video applications.

The final video element is the creation of special effects through the use of video planes. There are three basic configurations. Single-plane effects include scrolling, the updating of part of the image, or colour manipulation through CLUT transformations. The second configuration involves overlays, and the third the use of two planes in conjunction. The CD-I specification allows for four such planes. The first plane, 'nearest' to the viewer, contains the cursor. The second plane is a general image plane, and can be encoded in DYUV, CLUT or run-length techniques. The third plane is also a general image plane, while the fourth is the backdrop plane. Using RGB encoding at the 8-bit level on two adjacent planes (normally the second and third), the wide range of video effects now seen on television can be generated.

Before leaving the video area the question of full-motion video needs to be addressed. There are two aspects to be considered. Firstly, each picture image needs 108 kilobytes, so there is a finite limit to the number of images a CD-I disc can carry given that it needs nearly 2000 picture images a minute for full-motion. The second problem is a data transfer effect. The transfer rate is 175 kilobytes per second, so that it would take around 0.6 second to fill a screen, and this is obviously too slow. However, if only (say) one-ninth of the screen is used, then an image refresh rate close to standard video rates can be achieved, so that (for example) the head of a presenter could be positioned in the corner of the screen, and synchronized with a sound commentary.

Digital Video Interactive

If CD-I was the surprise of the First International Conference on CD-ROM, then Digital Video interactive was the news event of the 1987 conference. DVI has been developed by the David Sarnoff Laboratories of RCA in Princeton, New Jersey. DVI addresses the First Law of Storage: no matter how much storage you have, you always need more. The objective is to provide a much higher degree of video compression than is possible using CD standards.

DVI is based around a set of microchips. The video images are compressed by a factor of nearly 100 during the pre-mastering of a CD-ROM disc. The images are decompressed using two Video Display Processor (VDP) chips involving VLSI architectures. One chip processes the decompression algorithms, and allows for full-motion video, text and graphics to be accommodated in the same video frame. Overlays are emulated on a single video plane. A second chip manages the output in terms of resolution, screen area and computer interfacing.

The demonstrations at Seattle and at the Eikon Conference were impressive, but no comparison with CD-I was possible because of the lack of even demonstration players. However direct comparison would be misleading. DVI uses custom chips on a board in an IBM PC/AT acting as a controller to a CD-ROM drive, and is not a software program resident on the disc. The cost of using DVI is considerable, not just in terms of the custom chip set, but in the processing of the original video compression. The initial market would seem to be in the business/professional market, not the consumer market.

The DVI announcement did have the effect of bringing up again the current lack of full-motion full-screen video on CD-I. Philips argues that this is not necessary for many applications. For others it is, and all that is certain is that, in the not-too-distant future, CD-I and CD-ROM will both have enhanced capabilities in this area, as additional research on video compression proceeds.

Real-time operation

From the foregoing description, the complexity of the task facing the operating system can begin to be grasped. The real-time operation can be considered at two levels, the physical level and the system level. The physical level enables the operating system to cope with sectors containing differently encoded material, such as ASCII text and RGB graphics. The system level copes with multi-tasking and the synchronization of audio and video. This is (in computer jargon) a non-trivial task, since there is no 'physical' link between the video and audio as there is in a film soundtrack. For a given video picture, there could be multiple language sound tracks in support.

The operating system used is OS-9, developed by Microware Systems Corp, Des Moines, Iowa. OS-9 is based around the powerful Motorola 68000 chip family, and was originally developed for real-time process control applications in the chemical industry. The first track on a CD-I disc always contains the Super Table of Contents, and other file description data. The Table of Contents indicates the position of the file directory and the bootstrap. Files can be opened with a single seek. The CD-I player is designed to operate with a mouse, though other control devices, including a full keyboard, could also be accommodated, but are not included in the base-case specification.

The operating system is called CD-RTOS (Compact Disc Real-Time Operating System), and consists of four primary elements. Between the core operating system and the disc programs are some libraries that cope with areas such as synchronization and interleaving. On the peripheral side, there are a set of 'managers' and 'drivers' for the various devices, such as mouse control or an audio amplifier.

There are two sector formats on CD-I. Each sector consists of 2352 sequential bytes. Form 1 has error detection and correction blocks, and is equivalent to Mode 1 CD-ROM except that Forms 1 and 2 can be interleaved. Form 2 replaces the error detection and correction with an auxiliary data field.

	Form 1	Form 2
Synchronization	12B	12B
Header	4B	4B
Subheader	8B	8B
User data	2048B	2324B
EDC	4B	N/A
EEC	278B	N/A
Reserved	N/A	4B

Authoring

The process of creating a CD-I program is known as authoring, and is a highly complex task. For this reason, computer-based authoring systems are essential. To support these programs, the New Media Systems Group of Philips has published a designer's guide, providing basic information on the preparation, encoding, programming and testing of CD-I programs. The costs involved in creating CD-I discs are considerable, and certainly well in excess of the US$100 000 guideline used for LaserVision discs.

CD-Video

CD-Video was announced in March 1987 and became commercially available in September 1987. CD-Video combines analogue video with digital sound, and as such is a development of LaserVision. Three disc sizes are set out in the Blue Book specification, of 12 cm, 20 cm and 30 cm. All three sizes can be played on the Combi player that became available in the UK in 1988.

The use of analogue video means that the PAL/NTSC/SECAM standard problem raises its head again. The 12 cm CDV single has a gold coating to distinguish it from the audio discs. Each disc carries 6 minutes of video and up to 20 minutes of digital audio. In CD-V players, the lead-in tracks identify the CD-V material and raise the motor speed. The 20 cm and 30 cm discs are double-sided and provide 20 minutes and 60 minutes of play per side. Constant angular velocity discs are also provided for in the Blue Book, which reduces the playing time to 36 min for a 30 cm disc, but enables freeze frame and other LaserVision features to be incorporated.

Creating a CD-I industry

Not only is the technology of CD-I complex, but it provides a creative opportunity that existing consumer technology products can not even begin to match. From the point of view of Philips, the company realized that the only way to create a market for CD-I was to develop quality programming, and so create the demand for the players. Since the costs of production are high, the authoring systems complex, and the players have still yet to appear commercially, it was clearly necessary to stimulate programme creation.

Philips has entered into a series of joint venture and cooperation agreements with companies around the world. Firstly it kept the licence fee for the transfer of CD-I technology and know-how low, in order to build up quickly a blue-chip list of partners from both the hardware and program software areas.

The next action was to establish two companies to act as creative and technical expertise centres in North America and in Europe. American Interactive Media (AIM) was set up as a joint venture between Philips and Polygram International in April 1986, based in Los Angeles. Then in September 1986 European Interactive Media was established in London. The aim of both these operations is to act as a catalyst to CD-I development through the establishment of joint ventures, or by providing advice on programme creation, production, marketing and distribution.

As has been outlined above, the process of actually creating the programme is quite difficult. To provide a resource in this area Philips and R.R. Donnelley and Sons have set up OptImage Interactive Services Co. R.R. Donnelley is the largest printing company in the USA, making extensive use of computer-based production techniques. Based in Chicago, the joint venture will provide to CD-I publishers the equivalent range of services a company such as Donnelley would offer to a conventional publisher. Donnelley has an operation in the UK, but it will be some time before a formal decision is made as to the location of a European facility.

To match the services to be provided by OptImage, Philips has set up Denshi Media Services as a joint venture with Toppan Printing Co., a leading Japanese printing company. In Japan, Philips had already created Japan New Media Systems as a joint venture with Kyocera, primarily to develop MSX software products. JNMS began operation in July 1985.

Although not of direct significance to CD-I, it is worth noting the purchase by NV Philips of North American Philips Inc. in mid-1987. The

North American company had been set up as an independent company at the time of World War II, and since then had continued to plough quite an independent route. Philips has now rationalized this situation.

Other Philips companies worth a brief mention are Philips Du Pont Optical (PDO), which has operations in both the Netherlands and in Wilmington, Delaware, to handle the physical production of the CD-I (and other CD format discs). Philips New Media Systems is not a company in its own right but is a division of Philips Home Interactive Systems, which has overall responsibility for the development, launch and marketing of CD-I.

Applications

Right from the initial announcement Philips clearly positioned CD-I as a consumer product. To quote from the press release:

> The new (CD-I) specification will also enhance the capabilities of home and personal computers with easily accessible, high-quality, audio-visual information. Thus Philips and Sony expect that this new medium will create many opportunities for the hardware, software and publishing industries to provide consumers with truly new forms of interactive entertainment and education ranging from songs with text and pictures to talking dictionaries and encyclopedias, as well as other applications which are yet beyond imagination.

There is nothing fundamentally new with CD-I. Other media can give high-quality audio, interactivity, video, text and graphics, etc., but so far only CD-I packages these elements in a flexible manner. From the designer's viewpoint it is rather like going from 2D to 4D, and to accomplish the intellectual and creative leap needs the vision of a Jules Verne or an Arthur C. Clarke!

In the meantime, profits have to be achieved and some of the early application areas are going to be mapped for their relationship to the capabilities of CD-I. In general terms, what will a CD-I programme look like? To UK readers the closest yet to CD-I is the Domesday Project from the BBC.

The Domesday Project commemorates the 900th anniversary of the *Domesday Book*, compiled on the orders of King William I. However, instead of parchment, the 1986 version uses LV-ROM technology, which incorporates digital data on a LaserVision disc. The disc provides an excellent example of the type of programming that could work well on CD-I, especially since LV-ROM has many of the same capabilities CD-I has.

The scale of the Domesday Project is immense, involving a budget of US$5 million and over 22000 man-years effort. The disc's software and file structures were designed from scratch by Logica. The database for the project is contained on two discs, a national and a community disc.

The national disc contains textual and visual material on a wide range of subjects, including detailed statistical information from government organizations, private research groups, and universities, 1500 articles from newspapers and magazines, extracts from Hansard and other specialist sources, and specially commissioned essays. In addition, the disc provides data on local amenities including shops, post offices, banks and pubs.

In all, there are about 9000 sets of data on the national disc. They have been selected with the guidance of an editorial board of professional researchers from major national bodies, including National Data Archive at the University of Essex, the Centre for Urban and Regional Development Studies at Newcastle, the Institute of Terrestrial Ecology, and Birkbeck College, London University.

The main result of the 1981 Population Census are included, together with government surveys such as the General Household Survey, the Family Expenditure Survey, extracts from the annual Social Trends and many others such as the BBC's own 'Daily Life in the 1980s'. In addition, there are data from Ordnance Survey, environmental institutions and key economic and financial sources.

Another major feature of the disc is its ability to calculate areas and distances, and to present a range of user-defined pictorial representations, which can be overlaid on the video display. In addition to 50 000 pictures, the disc uses many video sequences of British events from 1980 to 1986.

The community disc is based on 24 000 Ordnance Survey maps covering the entire United Kingdom at four different scales, along with street plans for major cities and floor plans for specially-selected buildings. The disc also uses 900 aerial photographs and 500 specially taken satellite pictures.

The disc's first display on the screen is a map of the whole of the United Kingdom. By means of a trackerball that moves a pointer over the screen, users can move around the country selecting from the choice of different-scaled Ordnance Survey maps. Information and photographs of each of the quarter of a million place names of the gazetteer can be accessed by simply typing in its name or grid-reference, or any particular topic can be explored by entering keywords, as on the national disc.

The maps are supplemented by photographs and text at all levels. The most original data on the disc consists of material compiled by 14 000 schools and numerous community groups throughout the country in the recently publicized Domesday survey.

The system hardware consists of a front-loading LV-ROM player specially developed by Philips, a BBC Master Series microcomputer with a VideoDisc Filing System (VFS), LV-ROM interface and a trackerball (mouse) control. The complete system retails for under £6000 with the discs themselves priced at around £400 a set.

The BBC is now examining other projects that could utilize the LV-ROM technology, such as an ecology database drawing on its natural history expertize.

In reviewing potential applications for CD-I, it is worth remembering that it is not necessary to use all the features all the time. Only a small section of a disc may be interactive, for example, or only one video plane used. There may be a tendency with the initial products to want to dazzle consumers with the technology. This could well be counterproductive. The launch products must tread a careful line between over-sophistication and over-simplification, and show the unique features of CD-I in a clearly appreciated way.

Potential CD-I applications

Some of the applications which seem to suit the features of CD-I are the following:

- *Entertainment.* This is difficult to define because 'games' and 'entertainment' are often used as synonyms. A high-quality documentary can be as entertaining as a sophisticated arcade game.
- *Education.* The use of CD-I by schoolchildren both at school and at home is an attractive market, especially as parents become increasingly concerned about the quality of education their children are receiving in some communities. Standardization is important here, to overcome the problems experienced in the transfer of computer-based education from a school computer to the one available to the pupil at home.
- *Edutainment.* This word has been coined to describe the action of learning through entertainment. Thus interactive golf programmes might fall into this category. At one level, there is the challenge of beating your partner, but in addition a golfer may learn more about club selection or the optimum approach to the 18th hole at St Andrews.
- *Training.* This rather broad category covers job training and training for non-work activities. In the former comes the type of programme already available on videotape and interactive videodisc, but in a more powerful, and portable, format. The latter could encompass the training of people interested in first-aid, or in the care of babies and young children.
- *In-car navigation.* A well-publicized application is the provision of maps, route information and tourist information in the car using a CD-I player instead of the CD audio player.
- *Reference.* Many of the initial products are likely to take the form of sophisticated electronic encyclopedias and reference books.
- *Home shopping.* An extension of the reference book concept is that of the home shopping catalogue, which could be integrated with an online ordering capability. The players could also be installed in shopping malls.

Current projects

Already a number of projects have been announced for CD-I, and brief details are given below. This section was compiled in September 1987, and it should be remembered that the eventual CD-I disc may vary substantially from the announcements made so far. American Interactive Media claim to have some 60 titles in various stages of production.

Italian cultural archive

SIDAC, a subsidiary of the Italian IRI/STET holding company, has been developing an archive of Italian historical, artistic and architectural artefacts, initially for use on CD-ROM but with an obvious eye to CD-I.

Kyoto guide

Matsushita have demonstrated a CD-I prototype programme that gives a multi-media guide to the Japanese city of Kyoto, covering tourist attractions, hotels, restaurants and transportation.

The Record Group

The Record Group was working on at least four projects, including a guide to London, a history of civilization from 700 BC, a highly sophisticated multiple-route computer game, and an audio-visual encyclopedia of music, but now that the Group has been absorbed into AIM it seems these discs may not be released.

Academic American encyclopedia

Grolier Inc. is planning to add a CD-I version of its encyclopedia to the existing online, videodisc and CD-ROM versions. The design work is being undertaken by New Media Productions, a UK company.

Other companies are less willing to say just what they have planned. If theirs is going to be the catalyst product to develop CD-I, then with a world market at stake silence is the best approach.

CD-I launch schedule

After the initial announcement in 1986 at Seattle, Philips made a provisional CD-I Green Book specification available in May 1986, and received an immense amount of feedback. Some of the key events over the last year or so are:

March 1987	Philips releases the specification agreed with Sony.
March 1987	DVI announcement at Seattle. CD-I Green Book available. Thomson (France) announces endorsement of CD-I.
April 1987	Philips Du Pont Optical issues a draft Information Exchange Protocol for multi-media file management. Microsoft, Olivetti and SEAT form EIKON.
June 1987	Compact Disc-Video launched at the Consumer Electronics Show in Chicago. Philips and Sony hold seminars for CD-I licensees.

The next step, eagerly awaited, is the launch of the commercial CD-I player and initial discs.

Conclusion

CD-I is going to be the most interesting consumer technology product launch this decade. Can Philips and Sony be wrong? It is too early to say. The critical success factors are:

- the extent of the installed base of CD-audio, which will need either adaptation or replacement;
- the price of the CD-I player, which needs to be not significantly more than a CD audio player at the time of launch;
- the availability of quality software, especially for the European market;
- no other major consumer product launch before or near CD-I;
- affordable CD-I discs.

By the time you read this chapter many of these issues may have been resolved.

Further information

Philips have established two information centres for CD-I:

New Media Systems Information Centre, Philips International BV, Building HWD-2, PO Box 218, 5600 Eindhoven, Netherlands.

Philips New Media Systems Information Center, 1111 Northshore Drive, Box 204, Knoxville, Tennessee 37919, USA.

CD-I: A Designer's Overview was published by Kluwer in 1987, and a revised version will be available at the 1988 Microsoft Conference.

CD-I News, a monthly newsletter, has been published monthly since October 1986 by Link Resources, 79 Fifth Avenue, New York, NY 10003, USA.

Note. The views expressed by the authors are not necessarily those of Link Resources Corporation.

Chapter 7

The European Commission role in developing a European market for CD-ROM and related optical media

Franco A. Mastroddi

Over the past three years, CD-ROM has taken an increasingly important role in the European Community's activities in the area of electronic publishing. The EC currently supports nine CD-ROM projects with European publishing concerns and information providers, and has sponsored initiatives taken by private industry to encourage standardization.

CD-ROM is one of the new information technologies that the Commission of the European Communities (CEC), the EC's executive branch, has explored within its programmes for the development of the information market. Other technologies include the videodisc, networking and microcomputing techniques, online information retrieval, digital facsimile, advanced telecommunications and research and development into information technology.

This chapter sets out in brief the main motivations for the CEC's actions in this business, relates some of the experiences and achievements to date, and looks forward to the next five years, up to the CEC's deadline of 1992 for the creation of an internal market of goods and services in Europe.

Firstly, some definitions of the terminology and key phrases used in this paper would be useful.

The recurrent theme of all of the CEC's activities in this area is the application of new information technologies (IT) to the electronic information market (EIM). The word *information* is used in two different senses here: first, it refers loosely to computing, data processing and telecommunications techniques; second, it refers to the bodies of recorded or imparted knowledge that exist within databanks, archives, manuals, reference works, periodicals, books and other literature. These two different spheres are gradually converging, but not as quickly as could be imagined. They are grouped together by the CEC under the general heading of 'information industries'.

The department of the European Commission that is responsible for the Community initiatives in this field is Directorate General XIII 'Telecommunications, Information Industries and Innovation', which was formed in 1986 from different existing services (Directory, 1987).

The Community's interest in the use of optical media for the storage and distribution of information stems back to 1980, when a series of workshops and studies were initiated into technical, economic and organizational aspects of electronic publishing and electronic document delivery (Collier and Burrell, 1982; Norman, 1981; Page, 1981; Gurnsey, 1982; Wells *et al.*, 1983; Birkenshaw, 1984; Maslin *et al.*, 1984; Gurnsey and Henderson, 1984; Martin and Singleton, 1985; Van Slype *et al.*, 1987).

These explorations were motivated by the fact that conventional online information networks, including the CEC-sponsored Euronet DIANE network, did not cater very well for full texts or documents.

The problem that faced potential providers and users of full-text information and primary publications were essentially three-fold.

Firstly, the technological limitations of online information systems meant that data entry of full texts was slow and laborious, storage space on magnetic disc packs was limited for full documents, networking protocols and bandwidths for dial-up customers catered primarily for low-speed data transmission (typically between 300 and 1200 bits per second) and receiving equipment such as modems, terminals and printers could only handle a limited throughput.

The online systems could not cater for page-formatted information, nor different kinds of typefaces or character sets, special symbols, graphics, etc.

Table 7.1 (Wells, *et al.*, 1983) will give an idea of the kind of limitations that these seemingly petty technical constraints have placed on suppliers of online electronic information. It is a detailed analysis of the characteristics of over four hundred documents, periodicals, books, reports, standards and patents. It indicates, in percentage terms, the number of times a particular feature was found in the different categories of documents.

Most of the conventional online systems, still today, can only handle the ASCII (American Standard Code for Information Interchange) character set, thus limiting themselves to straight text, simple tables and columns, and some mathematics or Greek symbols.

This meant in practice that the supply of electronic information was dominated by bibliographic reference databases, directories, inventories and numeric data banks. A paradoxical situation arose where a bibliographic reference could be found in a few minutes during an online search, but the ordering and delivery of the document could take days or weeks.

The second kind of limitation that faced full-text information providers is economic. Electronic publishing is evolving against a background of well-established conventional print media, which have little to fear for their future.

A survey carried out by the European Institute for the Media (Luyken, 1987; Wedell and Luyken, 1985) analysed the print media markets in the twelve EEC member countries, Scandinavia, Austria, Switzerland, USA, Canada, Japan, Australia and Brazil. In the case of daily newspapers, general-interest magazines, and trade and technical periodicals, where electronic publishing is often thought to be a competitor, the existing market base is strong.

Over 8000 different national and regional daily newspapers are published in the 22 surveyed countries, with a total circulation of 250 million copies. The daily press survived a reduction of titles in the 1970s, accompanied by an increase in overall circulation and increased competition.

There are over 12 000 general-interest magazines in the surveyed areas, with a total 300 million circulation. This is an economically healthy sector with good prospects for the next decade. There is, however, a relative shift away from general interest towards specialized leisure magazines such as hobbies, photography and microcomputing.

In the trade and technical magazine market, there are around 80 000 titles with a global circulation of over 200 million. This sector is characterized by a higher number of low-run titles than the other areas, highly specialized and targeted to narrow market audiences. This is an important marketing factor, not least for advertisers, who provide a large proportion of the publication revenues.

In these three sectors, the so-called pre-press technology is making fast inroads, for example for electronic manuscript preparation and for direct author-typesetter-printer links. The main output product is still paper-

Table 7.1 Features found in document types. *Source:* DOCTERM Study, CEC, Luxembourg, 1983, p. 26

Features of documents	Periodicals STM	Periodicals social sciences	Periodicals popular/trade	Reports STM	Reports social sciences	Books STM	Books social sciences	Conferences	Patents	Standards
	%	%	%	%	%	%	%	%	%	%
Straight text	67	56	17	84	85	94	100	80	38	72
Text in columns	67	78	98	20	15	9	0	30	69	39
Running heads/feet	97	94	94	9	15	90	81	30	94	89
Footnote	81	84	38	64	55	76	44	63	6	94
Multiple fonts	100	100	100	56	60	92	100	87	100	72
Display types	11	12	38	4	10	6	0	7	13	0
Dropped initials	3	12	17	2	0	0	0	0	0	0
Superiors/inferiors	99	81	35	76	45	92	31	87	81	94
Unusual characters, e.g. phonetics, accents	87	69	25	51	30	41	13	70	6	11
Mathematics/Greek	91	50	25	38	0	92	25	73	44	78
Chemical notation	45	0	8	7	0	31	0	20	13	0
Regular diagrams	84	53	42	31	20	80	69	73	25	50
Irregular diagrams	97	66	52	60	20	94	56	83	69	67
Regular diagrams with more than one colour	3	6	13	2	0	2	0	0	0	6
Irregular diagrams,, more than one colour	3	6	13	9	0	6	0	0	0	6
Special symbols	83	41	33	42	25	63	25	80	19	17
Tables	97	97	67	73	65	92	88	87	31	89
Halftones, low resolution	35	38	87	51	5	45	6	60	0	6
Halftones, high resolution	60	9	19	18	5	55	0	43	0	6
Colour halftones	1	0	27	4	0	9	0	0	0	0
Total number of documents in each category	150	32	52	45	20	51	16	30	16	18

based, sometimes paralleled by online full-text services like Datasolve, GCAM and GENIOS.

These kind of considerations have led potential producers to look more closely at other, more static, forms of information products, where high interactivity to find specific items is an advantage. This includes inhouse documentation, technical documents, manuals, databases, reference works, directories, encyclopedias, statistics and archives. Some competition may start to emerge in these fields, especially where microform or magnetic tapes are used.

It is estimated that the global revenues for the entire print and electronic information market is in the order of 100 thousand million European Currency Units (ECU) (Michel, 1987). The electronic information market is estimated at between 3 and 5 billion ECU (Michel, 1987; Irwin, 1987).

The disparity between these two markets, one of which is several hundred years old and the other barely 20 years old, is primarily due to the novelty of electronic information systems and to the lack of infrastructure. The production, distribution and retail channels for electronic information are still in their infancy. It will be seen later in this paper how the Community aims to play a role in accelerating the rate of development of production techniques, dissemination and data transmission infra-structure and advanced techniques for information retrieval that should enhance the attractiveness of databanks.

A further constraint is likely to be the unsuitability of new media technology for advertising purposes. The periodicals print media rely heavily on advertisers for income; in some cases this income outweighs revenue for subscriptions.

As optical media have the capability to present high-quality graphics and information, up to and beyond the standards of TV broadcasting, it was felt that they could offer good opportunities as advertising carriers. However, a study carried out by the European Association of Advertising Agencies for the CEC (European Association (1987)) pointed out the drawbacks. An advertisement placed on a CD-ROM or videodisc would always be bypassed by the sophisticated information retrieval software. Its unsolicited appearance would be intrusive and unattractive to the user. The periodicity of CD-ROM publications further reduces their suitability for the 'adformation' type of publicity. The study envisages some potential for CD-ROM as a type of illustrated catalogue at point of sale or exhibitions, but concludes that the medium will not be a competitor to existing advertising media.

The third kind of barrier that faces the development of CD-ROM can be termed loosely as organizational, whereby a synergy is required between CD-ROM and existing products, services and practices.

The success of CD-ROM will be determined to a large extent by its ability to integrate into the normal working environment. Here the product shows very promising signs of its flexibility and adaptability, but at the same time will sound alarm bells for managers who wish to master the arrival of CD-ROMs into their organization.

The facility of CD-ROM to be driven from microcomputers is a point that should encourage its penetration into a broad customer base of several million PC users. This is not as straightforward as could be expected, owing to the need for a separate CD-ROM drive, either internal or as an external peripheral, driver software, a minimum PC hardware configuration, etc.

It is difficult to estimate how quickly this process will occur. A management brief in the United States (DCMA Special Report, 1985) predicts that CD-ROM and other optical digital discs will have a major impact by 1988/89. Its introduction, if ignored, will reenact the introduction of the microcomputer, when organizational anarchy reigned in large organizations, and traditional bounds of responsibility between managers, the data processing staff and users were transgressed.

The report also stresses that managers who delegate CD-ROM matters to their technical staff risk delaying its proper introduction and consequently promulgating the acquisition of products that do not effectively match the organization's business objectives.

It concludes that managerial inertia is 'a high-risk, high-cost, low-yield option'.

Europe's position in the CD-ROM market

Whilst the development of the CD-ROM medium is subject to accelerating and retarding factors, sight should not be lost of the gamut of products and services that are evolving.

The CEC is conscious of the requirement for any information product, whether online, on optical disc or in print form, to match the needs of a particular target audience. This is especially true if the electronic information market is to expand by the orders of magnitude that are suggested by its current rapid growth rate of 20% per year.

Europe has a potential market of 320 million inhabitants, still fragmented by many technical, legal and linguistic barriers. It has an abundance of raw information material and a healthy traditional information industry with some eight to ten thousand commercial publishers, 93000 libraries and several thousand organizations that publish a secondary activity, such as government bodies and research associations. However, the Community produces at present only half as many online databases as the United States and a small percentage of existing CD-ROM products: only three out of the eighty-four products listed in a current directory (Optical Publishing Directory, 1987). Of the total number of listed products, fifty contain bibliographic information, eleven full text, fourteen have reference material, seven contain statistical data and two have images and sound. It seems that the potential of CD-ROM for full text and graphics is not yet fully explored.

A more recent survey carried out by the Commission (Cardoso, J., 1987, unpublished data) has confirmed the imbalance of information products if not manufacturers, systems integrators, etc. (*Table 7.2*).

Table 7.2 reveals that the worldwide base for CD-ROM production is established around a solid core of manufacturers, and of pressing plants. In this latter case, the number includes CD-audio plants. The 1987 CD-ROM production and replication capacity of Europe versus the United States is estimated at a ratio of 1:1.8 (110 million to 180 million units) and will evolve by 1990 to 1:2.2 (250 million to 550 million units), according to

Table 7.2

CD-ROM market	Total number	Europe	USA	Other
Retrieval software packages	32	14	17	1
Data preparation services	20	8	11	1
Pre-mastering services	19	9	8	2
Mastering services	19	10	9	0
Pressing/stamping plants	40	15	25	0
CD-ROM drive models	22	2	4	16
CD-ROM products	137	36	90	11
CD-ROM vendors/suppliers	90	23	59	8

Jean Ledieu, President of Digipress, a major French pressing plant (Ledieu, 1986). Here, European manufacturing capacity is, exceptionally, increasing more rapidly than in the US.

The projected number of shipped CD-ROM drives worldwide varies considerably. *Figure 7.1* is derived from different sources, and serves here only to give an illustration of the expectations of market observers. It is interesting to note that the expectations for 1987 are by no means fulfilled. The predicted penetration by CD-ROM drives of the microcomputer market is minimal, at less than one per cent over the next three years. This slow evolution may be accelerated by the projected rise in the number of professional microcomputers, which in 1988 is some seven million units and in 1989 13.5 million units worldwide.

The very high number of retrieval packages is reminiscent of online systems, where different command languages flourished, but became a perceived barrier to usage. However, in groups like the Optical Disc Forum, customers and providers resisted the *a priori* imposition of a common command language for CD-ROM, partly on the assumption that the expected high level of user friendliness would outweigh the need for standardization.

The estimates of the CD-ROM market size in terms of revenue or turnover are also highly speculative. A brief glance at the current market projections (*Figure 7.2*) reveals a spread of forecasts for 1992, for example, of between US$1.2 billion and US$3.28 billion. All three of the cited projections forecast a steady growth in market turnover. If the predictions are fulfilled, the CD-ROM market will have reached half of the volume of the online market, which is calculated for the USA at US$4.2 billion (Frost and Sullivan, 1986), and for Europe at US$2 billion (Link, 1986). It appears that no estimates of the mutual impact of these two markets, whether competitive or complementary, have yet been offered.

Although these predictions are undoubtedly positive and consistent in their judgements about upwards trends, it is suspected that they are based on the assumption that CD-ROM will:

● automatically address a wide, international market, albeit amongst professionals;
● be considered as a straightforward peripheral to the business microcomputer;
● constitute a low-cost, user-friendly and comprehensive service to the professional end-user.

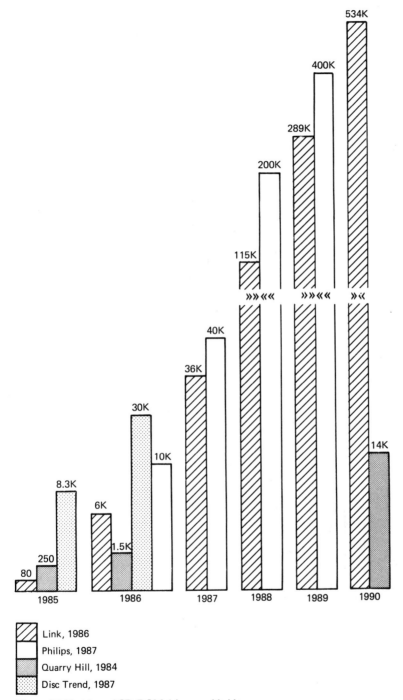

Figure 7.1 Number of CD-ROM drives worldwide

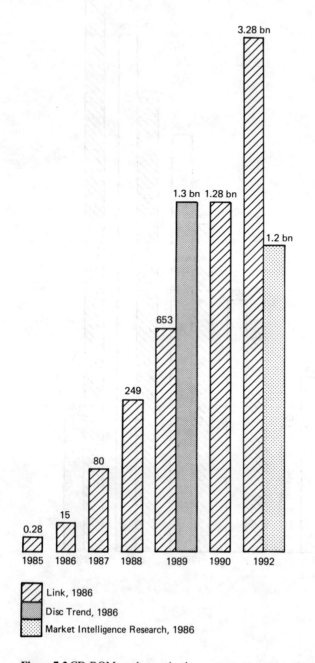

Figure 7.2 CD-ROM market projections

As experienced practitioners (Arnold, 1987) have pointed out, these assumptions and many other similar claims are often exaggerations or simplifications of the true situation. The primary significance of CD-ROM, however, in terms of its impact on the overall development of the electronic information market, is that it presents a wide range of publishers and information providers with an opportunity to enter the optical publishing market at a relatively low cost and to experiment with the cost-benefits of electronic information distribution.

In this respect, the European Commission has encouraged the spread of awareness of CD-ROM's potentials and limitations within the member countries, and the gaining of early practical experience in the development of products, systems and software.

The role and aims of the European Community

The overall aim of the European Commission is to broaden the base of the electronic information market, away from the relatively specialized offerings of today, towards information products and services which are of more direct benefit to trade and industry.

The Commission's programmes that have contributed towards this aim over the past fifteen years can be summarized as follows.

1971   Resolution by European Council of Ministers, to the effect that 'it is important for economic, scientific and technical progress that scientific, technical, economic and social documentation and data be made available, by the most up-to-date methods, as rapidly and as economically as possible' (Official Journal C 122, 10.12.71).

1975   First Community Action Plan for the creation of a European online information network (Euronet) (Official Journal L 100, 21.4.75).

1978   Second Action Plan, for the completion of Euronet (which was opened in 1980) (Official Journal L 311, 4.11.1978).

1981   Third Action Plan: transformation of Euronet to a public network; development of high-quality information services in Europe; marketing and user support; application of new technologies and methodologies, including optical storage media (Official Journal No. L 220, 6.8.81).

1984   Fourth Action Plan concentrating on the one hand on the development of information systems in three 'vertical' subject areas: materials, biotechnology and patents and, on the other hand, on three 'horizontal' priority areas:
   ● improving information towards industry,
   ● reducing regional discrepancies in the European information market,
   ● developing electronic publishing services and image banks, using CD-ROM, videodisc and related technologies (Official Journal L 314 of 4.12.84).

In 1987, an important new initiative was taken by the Commission to prepare the ground for the establishment at Community level of a policy and a plan of priority actions for the development of an information services market (Commission of the EC, 1987).

The rationale behind these programmes is not purely technology-driven, but rather to take advantage of the Community's vast information resources to improve the competitiveness of trade and industry.

These programmes each have a budget ceiling, currently running at some five million ECU per year. This budget is used in the case of pilot projects to provide a part of the cost of developing new products or services. The CEC's share in any venture is typically between 25% and 40%, for example, in the case of the CD-ROM projects.

This kind of role, which avoids a permanent presence of the Community in the operational or commercial aspects of any particular product or service, is in line with the recommendations of trade associations as EURIPA (European Information Industry Association), EUSIDIC (European Association of Information Services), and the recently formed Information Service Providers and Users Groups (ISPG/ISUG).

The public authorities in each member country advise the CEC on a regular basis on the policy framework and priority actions to be undertaken.

Achievements to date

Since 1982, the Commission has issued several calls for proposals for the support of advanced information products and services. These calls resulted in the definition and launching of a number of projects, on digital optical storage media. The projects are all run by private or independent organizations, according to the specifications of shared-cost contracts with the CEC.

Amongst the projects and experiences gained so far, i.e. by mid-1987, one can cite:

Electronic document delivery (1984–1986):
- write-once digital optical disc within the TRANSDOC project,
- as a comparison, vector coding of diagrams in the Electronic Patents project.

Electronic publishing (1986–1988):
- nine CD-ROM projects,
- one videodisc project.

Electronic document delivery: a centralized approach

In 1984, the Commission launched the DOCDEL support programme for experiments in electronic document delivery. Two of the ten selected projects applied the digital optical disc (DOD) as a storage medium for full texts of documents. The DOD was originally conceived by manufacturers such as Philips, Thomson and Hitachi as the basis of an electronic office archiving system. The DOD does not lend itself to mass replication, and the recording of data is carried out at the user's site.

The studies and workshops which preceded the launching of the DOCDEL experiments had identified two major, contrasting techniques for the conversion of printed documents to electronic form and for subsequent storage.

Character coding consists of keyboarding the text with, for example, a microcomputer. Conventions are required for the coding of characters and symbols outside of the ASCII set. Although data entry is slow, the memory requirements of coded character texts are low, and the text can subsequently be retrieved through free text searching.

Digital facsimile scanning, on the other hand, allows rapid conversion of documents which already exist. The disadvantages lie in its much higher storage requirements and lack of searchability. A coded character index is required.

As the CEC did not wish to prejudge the suitability of either approach, both were explored in different projects. The experience gained is directly transferable to CD-ROM operations, as will be seen.

TRANSDOC

The TRANSDOC project (Soulé, 1987) attempted to overcome some of the disadvantages of the conventional document delivery systems by adding electronic storage and retrieval of documents to existing services in the biomedicine, patents and energy fields. The three services are the Scientific and Technical Documentation Centre of CNRS (CDST), a French patent information service (INPI), and the information service of Electricité de France (EDF/GDF).

TRANSDOC is based on the use of a digital optical disc as the electronic storage medium, capable of storing some tens of thousands of pages in facsimile format. It is controlled by a minicomputer system that locates the position of wanted documents, for extraction and printing on a laser printer (*Figure 7.3*).

The optical disc system is centred on a configuration of a scanner, disc drive, laser printer and Image Link Controller, by Integrated Automation, California, and put together by MC2, a Grenoble-based company. The DOD was Alcatel Thomson GD 100.

From the supplier's point of view, the system functioned regularly over the six-month period of routine operations.

The experimental service is coupled with a major French bibliographic host providing information retrieval services (Télésystèmes Questel), so that an automatic document ordering system following a bibliographic search was also tested as part of the experiment.

Another important innovation was an experimental method for levying and collecting royalty payments on behalf of journal publishers, by means of an agreement between CNRS and the French Copyright Centre (CFC) representing the publishers.

The agreement ended in December 1986, but provided an invaluable practical study of the mechanics of a royalty collection system for electronic media.

By January 1986, a total of 50 journals in biomedicine, 17000 patents and 3000 electrical research reports had been stored on the disc system, totalling 105 500 pages. A management decision to change from a prototype to a production disc drive unit in summer 1985 caused delays and extra cost, but marked the project's move from a mere trial towards an operational system. The overall conclusion from TRANSDOC was undoubtedly positive. It is clear that the write-once disc system can play an important role for large centralized document collections. Both INPI and EDF will take over the system for this purpose. INPI will create a centre for the storage of 7 million pages of French patents. The microfiche cabinet will

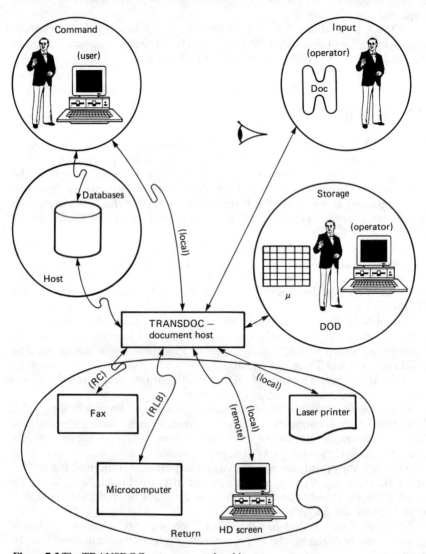

Figure 7.3 The TRANSDOC system: general architecture

form the basis of a commercial information service on trademarks offered by INPI.

A further important industrial spin-off is the creation of an international scanning bureau, which was awarded the European Patent Office's 14.5 million ECU contract to digitize 65 million pages of patent documents for future storage on optical media. The contract would otherwise have gone outside Europe. This spin-off alone practically justifies the whole DOCDEL investment.

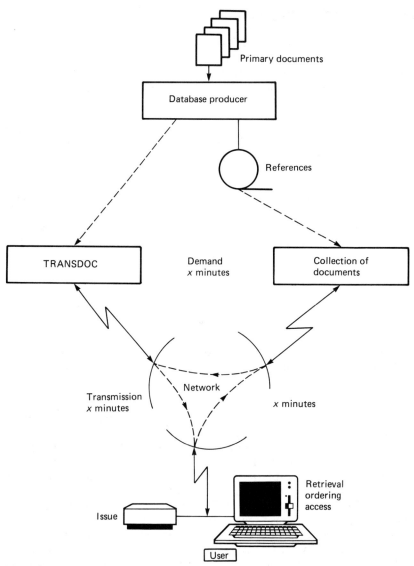

Figure 7.4 TRANSDOC: future situation

The digital scanning technique was also adopted in 1986 by the ADONIS Consortium (see Chapter 8), this time to store periodicals on CD-ROM.

TRANSDOC has also extended the DOD system towards telecommunications (*Figure 7.4*), in order to deliver documents directly from the disc to remote customers either by Group III telefax on a public packet-switched network (with a throughput capacity of 1–2 minutes per page) or through high-speed networks such as the Telecom 1 satellite link, Transdyn or Transcom, where A4 pages can be transmitted in a matter of seconds. These services were tested during 1987.

Electronic publishing of patents

TRANSDOC demonstrates that it is only now practicable to link up optical disc systems with public packet-switched data networks.

It is interesting to contrast their approach with that taken by another DOCDEL experiment, 'Electronic Patents Project'.

This project, run by the Fachinformationszentrum Energie, Physik, Mathemathik (FIZ 4) together with the German Patents Office, Satzrechenzentrum Hartmann and Heenemann and Co. and GID, aimed at creating a combined online full-text and graphics patents databank. It differs from TRANSDOC in several ways:

TRANSDOC	*FIZ 4 — Patents databank*
Existing bibliographic databases used.	New bibliographic database created, called PATDPA.
Full text (including diagrams) scanned at 8 pixels/mm.	Full text elements keyed in. Line diagrams scanned at 16 pixels/mm and converted to vector codes.
Document store on optical disc.	Document store on magnetic disc.
No remote browsing.	Remote browsing possible with PC plus graphics card, using a downloading technique.
Delivery by post, and later PSTN or high-speed data channels.	Delivery of main document elements by existing public data network to IBM PC or compatible.

The technical development work by FIZ 4 concentrated on the development and application of a system, called SCORE, to convert digital facsimile images into vector coded graphics.

The advantages of this process are several. Firstly the system is software-based and can run under an IBM PC AT or equivalent. The vectorization process also yields a highly faithful reproduction of the image. The only limitation on reproduction is the quality of the printer or terminal screen, as SCORE is device-independent. The processing time under mass production conditions was also reasonable, taking approximately 1.5 minutes per page on the PC. Perhaps the most interesting advantage of this technique, especially for CD-ROM products, is the space-saving effect of using vector codes. The system reduced the bit requirement for one A4 page by a factor of eighty, from 2 megabytes of uncompressed data for a page scanned at 16 pixels per millimetre to between 3 and 40 kilobytes (on average 15–25 kilobytes), depending on the complexity of the drawing.

This allows the resultant databank, called PATDPA, to be stored on conventional magnetic disc and to be marketed through STN International, the online information network.

It also has important ramifications for CD-ROM operators, as a compact disc could theoretically hold only three hundred facsimile images at the high resolution, but in the order of 24 000 images, in the vectorized form.

This kind of technique has in fact been adopted by some of the CEC-supported CD-ROM projects, where line drawings are to be included.

In conclusion, a rigid comparison between TRANSDOC and PATDPA, or between digital facsimile and vector coding, would be misleading, as each is suited to different categories of documents.

The decentralized approach: CD-ROM, videodisc

In 1985, the Commission took a strong initiative to encourage the development of commercially viable information products on compact disc (CD-ROM). CD-ROM's read-only memory and mass replication characteristics overcome, perhaps by chance rather than design, some of the publishers' major objections to electronic storage media. One advantage, as seen from the Commission's point of view, is that CD-ROM practically obliges the information provider to seek economies of scale in production and distribution, in particular by selling to a wide, preferably international, audience. New levels of user friendliness would also be required. Full advantage should be taken of the microcomputer's interactivity and flexibility to attract users who are not familiar with handling databases.

In July 1985 the CEC launched a call for proposals for the development of value-added information products and services based on digital optical storage media (Commission, 1985). The aim was explicitly to encourage private and public sector bodies to build potentially economically viable databases that were aimed at a specific target market sector or audience.

Out of 40 proposals received by the Commission for CD-ROM projects, it was evident that: some were over-ambitious within the two-year development time-frame. Their lack of detailed technical knowledge inevitably led to an underestimation of the problems involved. Others realized the need to get further expertise by means of research and development. The most promising came from the large organizations that had been able to inform themselves well enough to plan out a project.

Nine proposals were selected for funding from the forty. The total estimated cost of the proposed projects is in the order of ten million ECU. The Commission's estimated share, assuming that all of the projects get underway, is approximately 2 500 000 ECU, representing an average support figure of 25% per project. The CD-ROM projects are shown in *Table 7.3*. Twenty-four publishers participate in these projects, together with a number of software and system houses and, of course, Philips or their licensees.

Whilst several of these projects have opted to use keyboarded text and

Table 7.3 CD-ROM projects funded by the CEC

	Scanned	Mode of storage coded character	Vector
Full text of standards	x	x	x
Updates of 3 bibliographic databases in biomedicine		x	
European company directory		x	
Chemistry monographs		x	x
Biotechnology periodicals	x	x	
Full-text of scientific journals (ADONIS)	x	x	
Abstracts in civil engineering		x	
General interest encyclopedia		x	
Multilingual lexicography for office automation market		x	

data (i.e. coded character), some aim to scan documents, thus reducing the number of pages of text and graphics on any one disc.

The cofunding programme was accompanied by a broader initiative by a joint group of publishers, public bodies and manufacturers to learn about the various standards issues surrounding CD-ROM. The Commission took the opportunity to support this initiative. An optical disc forum was created and managed by Learned Information. Although it only met twice, it resulted in a comprehensive report on international initiatives on CD-ROM standards (Schwerin, 1986) and in some feedback to the High Sierra *ad hoc* standards group in the United States, to the European Norms Committee (CEN/CENELEC), to the European Computer Manufacturers Association (ECMA) and eventually to the International Organization for Standardization (ISO).

Another CEC workshop (Stanford-Smith, *et al.*, 1987) held in early 1987 gave an update of progress in the industry.

A closer analysis of the nine CD-ROM projects reveals that there are essentially five different categories of products that are envisaged: merged bibliographic files; bibliographic files plus graphics or diagrams; full text in digital facsimile form, with accompanying coded character indexes; full text in coded character form, notably directories or reference works; and an integrated office tool, acting as a back-up to wordprocessors. The projects therefore are reasonably representative of the spread of CD-ROM products currently available on the market.

Merging bibliographic databases

The motivation for merging existing online bibliographic databases in specific sectors, namely biomedicine and technical standards, is relatively straightforward.

In the case of both MEDATA-ROM and the AFNOR/BSI/DIN standards projects, a user of biomedical literature or respectively of standards documents would need to consult three different online hosts, and be confronted with different retrieval languages, thesauri, database structures, document ordering and delivery procedures, passwords and invoices.

The implementation of a joint bibliographic product, merging the different databases under one disc and a single retrieval system certainly seems attractive, and allows the information provider to repackage or to tailor existing products better to the users' needs. This idea comes close to the Commission's concept of 'adding value' to information in order to increase its usefulness.

In the first case, MEDATA-ROM associates INSERM (Medline database), ELSEVIER (EMBASE) and CNRS (PASCAL), three of the best-known biomedical information suppliers. As the databases are all very large, totalling several million records, it was decided to limit the coverage to 8000 publications and to produce only updates on CD-ROM, at two-monthly intervals and to issue a cumulative disc every year, should interest be strong enough.

A preliminary market study will determine the precise shape and size of the product, and will give indications on the user requirements in terms of the common formatting of records from each database. MEDLINE carries title, heading and catalogue information only, PASCAL includes a short abstract, often in two languages, and EMBASE records often comprise quite long, informative abstracts in English.

The standards project is similar in scope. The three existing bibliographic files, NORIANE, BSI Standardline and DITR-Databank are also on three different online systems. These files are not bibliographic in the classic sense, but contain instead a set of data elements: document identifier, document status, dates of issue or withdrawal of the standard, validation data and a description of the contents of the standard.

Preliminary investigations on a CD-ROM product indicate that although a definite interest in computer-readable standards exists, there is some uncertainty about the application and advantages of CD-ROM over, for example, microfiche. Since most standards contain tables, drawings and formulae, they would have to be scanned. This however would lead to a capacity problem as the complete collection of standards is more than 300000 pages. Users also think that something better than CD-ROM will appear in the near future.

In general, the user would have to decide whether to keep a complete but unwieldy set, at a relatively high subscription cost, or to remain with the present on-demand services.

The problem of making an attractive product for an existing professional niche market is amplified by the lack of penetration of suitable equipment in the envisaged customer base.

Further non-trivial problems are the harmonization of the different indexes and thesauri, the creation of a master database from which relevant segments are stripped for loading on to a CD-ROM, and the optimal placing of inverted files for rapid searching.

Adding graphics to bibliographic files

A particular document can be said to have three types of image: text, line drawings and halftones, such as photographs or graphics with filled areas.

The DOCDEL experiments demonstrated that a business microcomputer of the AT range could satisfactorily reproduce images on screen, providing that a graphics card (Hercules, CGA or EGA) ensured adequate screen resolution, that a proper driver software for retrieving, buffering and displaying bit-map images was installed and an elegant solution was found for the problem of dimensioning the image on screen, manipulating it, making it searchable etc. There are only a few standards in this area such as the Graphics Kernel System (GKS), which creates a metafile of codes for vectorized images, and the CCITT Recommendations for the dot-density of raster scanned images, as with digital facsimile scanning techniques.

The issue of using vector codes for line drawings and facsimile for half-tones arises again, as do compression techniques, and optical character reading (OCR) for data entry.

As with the DOCDEL experiments, it is interesting here to compare briefly two CD-ROM projects that have opted respectively for vector coding and for digital facsimile scanning of graphics, in order to enhance the value of a bibliographic file on CD-ROM.

The object of the Comprehensive Compact Chemistry Project, run by Pergamon Infoline, is to provide a CD-ROM of core literature on hetero-cyclic chemistry that will improve on the limitations of printed reference works in this area. Chemical compounds can only be indexed by name or molecular formula, but chemists think of compounds in terms of their structure and would like to search accordingly. Also, the formal structures of the printed subject indexes can be supplemented by full text searching and browsing facilities.

The first chemical reference work to be published in this project is called *Comprehensive Heterocyclic Chemistry* (CHC). It covers the synthesis, properties and reactions of known substances and is designed for researchers of different levels. In print, CHC extends to over 8000 pages (equivalent to 40 megabytes of digital data) and includes 70000 chemical structures, equivalent to over 100 megabytes of digital data in vector coded form. A menu-driven retrieval system is envisaged. Its most innovative feature is the capability to carry out chemical structure and substructure searches, including browsing, panning and zooming, and access to cross-references.

Features such as the simultaneous display of text and graphics under the GEM environment and the Graphics Knowledge Retrieval System (GKRS) will be explored.

The approach taken by the BIOROM project of Derwent Publications and Télésystèmes is to develop a hybrid database from the Biotechnology Abstracts Journal. Whilst the text will be searchable, the images may be stored in either bit-map or vector form, and will be available for display only, as an integral part of the textual record.

Key development work to be undertaken in this respect includes the image compression and decompression software and the coordinated display of a particular textual record and its associated image.

Full text in facsimile

A third and starkly contrasting approach is taken by the ADONIS project, which is described in Chapter 8.

It is relevant here to recall that the ADONIS consortium's objectives are to provide document supply centres with a pictorial representation in electronic form of printed periodicals. The advantages of this approach are that the integrity of the document's format is preserved, and the whole management and operation process of on-demand document delivery can be reviewed. The copyright issue for document delivery is re-examined from the publishers' angle.

The project is a highly collaborative venture and will involve the digital scanning of some 200 biomedical journals from a consortium of publishers, the creation of a weekly CD-ROM with accompanying cumulative indexes and the delivery of the disc to output centres around the world, typically large libraries or document delivery services.

The particular requirements imposed by the choice of digital facsimile scanning can be resumed as:

- Need for a scanning service. Two or three bureaus opened in Europe during 1987, from the momentum provided by TRANSDOC and the European Patents Office projects.
- Need to decide a sufficient level of resolution, in this case 12 pixels/mm, and highly efficient data compression and decompression techniques to fit as many images as possible on the disc.
- Need for a system of document identifiers that can be made universal. Here, the ADONIS will serve as a test-bed for the implementation of a unique document identifier within a related CEC project called DOCMATCH (Ayres *et al.*, 1986).
- Need for an advanced workstation in the £15000–20000 range which can display and print A4-format images, provide statistical and accounting facilities, and, at a later stage, drive a CD-ROM jukebox, incorporate high-speed links to data networks etc. Such a workstation is being developed in a companion project to ADONIS, by the British Library Document Supply Centre.

Full text in coded character form

The use of computer-generated typesetting tapes for the generation of printed works and online databases is a current feature, especially for the parallel production of full-text directories, catalogues, press wire services and newsletters.

The adaptation of this technique to the production of CD-ROM databases has the advantage of avoiding to rekey data, but entails an often complex initial conversion task.

The European Kompass-On-Disc (EKOD) project, for example, intends to place on CD-ROM a five-language directory containing commercial and industrial information on 320000 enterprises in Europe. The input tapes are already processed for the online database EKOL and are obtained from the different publishers of the twelve national Kompass directories.

This kind of cooperative information product, as is generally the case, entails the harmonization of different physical and logical characteristics of the input tapes. In the case of EKOD, the different interpretations given to the international company and product classification scheme, translated versions of text and prompts, and the requirement for a new CD-ROM specific, full-text retrieval system all needed to be harmonized.

A general problem is that the contents of photocomposition tapes usually need to be cleaned of printers' control sequences and unwanted text or data fields. The restructuring of the contents, perhaps through an online master database or with a CD-ROM simulation tool, is necessary to make logical links between different elements of records (text, graphics, indexes), which could be scattered throughout tapes.

At the same time, however, the opportunity occurs to improve upon the basic product. EKOD, for example, will aim to extend its five-digit classification scheme to seven-digits, permitting an increase from 1200 to 90000 classifications.

The parallels between the print and CD-ROM versions of this category of product are likely to be felt more acutely than, say, with online. Full-text products that form part of a multi-media approach need especially to define marketing and pricing strategies that reflect the particular characteristics and added-value features of CD-ROM.

Integrated office tools

The emergence of integrated office computer packages like Microsoft *Bookshelf* and Lotus *One Source* is a sign that CD-ROM could develop potential as a large data source that is always on tap to back up word-processing, spreadsheet or micro-database applications. The CD-ROM could contain spellcheckers, grammars, thesauri, reference works, dictionaries, general statistics etc. that can be imported directly into the application in hand.

The aim of Eurolexic is to develop a multilingual dictionary-based tool for professional commercial and administrative correspondence. A major aspect of the development work would include the lexicographical analysis and control software.

The next phase: electronic image banks

As mentioned earlier, CD-ROM is only one, early example of a series of optical storage and distribution media.

It is important because of its potential for holding whole databases or segments, full text, graphics and even sound on a highly interactive medium. However, as previously discussed, CD-ROM is unlikely to cater for all of the growing number of niche applications in the area of electronic text/sound/image banks.

On the one hand, the characteristic requirements of image banks such as storage space for large numbers (several thousand) of high-resolution stills, moving images, often in colour, and accompanying sound tracks call for higher interactive storage capacity than CD-ROM can offer at present.

On the other hand, manufacturers such as Philips are developing a range of products which cater, to some extent, for mutually exclusive potential applications and target audiences:

- analogue videodiscs such as Philips LaserVision or JVC VHD (54000 video frames, little data, per disc side),
- hybrid analogue/digital videodisc such as LaserVision ROM (324 megabytes of data plus 54000 images per disc side) for the professional market,
- compact disc, including CD-ROM (adequate data content for professional market), CD-I (some text and data, but strong audio and visual orientation for 'edutainment' consumer market), and CD-V (strong emphasis on moving video and sound for music industry and home consumer),
- write-once discs for either images (e.g. facsimile) or numeric data,
- magneto-optic discs that can be reused,
- laser card, e.g. Drexler Laser card or DAINIPPON,
- holographic memory.

With these actual and projected product categories are many further subdivisions, different formats and competing features. For example, a new compression chip by RCA is reputed to enable images on CD-ROM thereby threatening CD-I; CD-V will replace the consumer version of LaserVision; new multi-standard players such as Philips COMBI are on the horizon; personal information systems based on optical storage media are being postulated, etc.

Despite this state of technological flux, the European Commission is anxious to explore the potential of image banks as a possible important new sector of the electronic information market. Image banks represent in some respects a logical progression from the previous two major 'waves' of information products, bibliographic data and full text.

For this reason, a survey of image banks (DOCMIX, 1987) was commissioned in early 1987 with the CNR, Italy, and at the time of writing is in mid-course.

It covers the technological state of the art of storage, dissemination and retrieval methods, accelerating and retarding factors with regard to supply and demand, and an overview of present and planned applications.

Some of its preliminary analyses and industrial enquiries point to a series of constraints on the development of image banks, whatever the medium:

- Currently commercially available data storage and transmission facilities are inadequate in terms of costs and performance for some image applications.
- User requirements seem very heterogeneous, making it difficult to set generally acceptable aims for product development.
- The continuous announcements of advanced products and the lack of established standards are creating technological uncertainty and stagnation.
- The construction and maintenance of an image bank can be very difficult and time consuming.

- There are no general software tools (languages, operating systems, pattern recognition algorithms) suitable for developing application packages in image banks.
- Query and retrieval methods are often too complex.
- Commercial relations between producers and end-users are not well established or transparent to the market.

The overall market shape and size in Europe can only be guessed at the moment. The United States market for image processing, a closely associated business, varies for 1986 between US$580 million (Frost and Sullivan, 1987) and US$996 million (Yencharis Consulting Group, 1987). This, however, includes artificial vision products, graphic art and prepress systems.

Products like CD-I are expected (Frost and Sullivan, 1987) to boost the overall electronic information market in Europe up to US$2.6 billion range by 1991.

The number and type of applications or projects in Europe are better known. Over 50 organizations in France, 25 in the United Kingdom, 35 in the Federal Republic of Germany and 40 in Italy are engaged in major projects (Pelletier, 1986; Jovine, 1987; Cardoso (internal communication), 1987). These range between do-it-yourself training lessons, museum art treasure banks, health and safety prevention etc.

Some of the main application areas, with examples of projects, are given below:

- Remote-sensing images and data from satellites, such as SPOT and Earthnet, are sold for environmental planning, commercial purposes, or as in the European Commission's Statistical Office, for improving the statistical base on crop usage etc.
- Medical images are produced in thousands by the various hospital radiographic machines such as scanners, X-ray, and echographs. The CEC-sponsored MEDIMAG project will collate several thousand groups of text and images on a videodisc for the training of hospital staff in pathology diagnosis.
- The BBC Domesday disc, which gives a contemporary view of life in the United Kingdom via 50000 photographs, 250000 pages of facts, figures, texts and 25000 maps, is providing a major general educational tool for schools and universities.
- The Italian government has launched a 600 billion lire operation to salvage a sizeable part of its national cultural heritage (books, images, archives, folklore etc.) for the general public, within 39 different projects.
- Major German car manufacturers plan to equip their dealer networks with product presentation discs for both staff and customers.
- The public authorities of La Villette in France will produce some 300 videodisc sides for public consultation via 180 display stations. A 10000 disc capacity 'robot' jukebox will sit at the heart of the system.
- Lloyds Bank in the UK has a corporate training scheme via videodisc for cashiers and other staff.

In conclusion, the development of image banks in certain niches, whether for the general public or for corporate professional purposes, seems assured, if slow. The trend towards the replacement of large discs and dedicated drives with compact discs and players with a more open architecture can be seen as an effort to bring down the price and to increase the customer base.

The increasing number of bi- and tri-literal agreements on technical standards between European, American and Japanese firms — as exemplified by the Philips-Sony accord on CD-audio and now CD-I — should reinforce these efforts, at least on a product-per-product basis.

Leapfrogging into the next technological generation

Today's electronic information market, whether for CD-ROM or other optical storage media, relies on hardware, software and techniques that were only in part developed for information products and services. Information providers and users often take the path of least resistance in choosing equipment and systems, to the detriment often of European suppliers.

The European Community has initiated a series of collaborative research and development ventures into information technology, including optical processing and storage media, within the ESPRIT programme (ESPRIT, 1986). These are designed to leapfrog the current technology and re-establish European IT sourcing. ESPRIT, which is run by the European Commission's DG XIII-A in Brussels, totals over 200 projects, run by 420 organizations from industry, universities and research. Over thirty of the projects concern image processing. With the EUREKA and ALVEY programmes, the total number of European projects is nearer one hundred (SDCE database, 1987).

In the office systems field, several projects are either testing the use of video channels and optical fibres for networking or developing advanced workstations, e.g. for graphics picture editing.

The HERODE project concerns the handling of mixed text/image/voice documents, based on the Office Document Architecture standards, and another project, Multos, is developing a multi-media filing system for optical and magnetic storage. On a broader front, a consortium of AEG, Olivetti, Philips and Plessey has developed a graphics coder to improve the efficient data compression of graphical data. A five-country consortium including British Telecom, CCETT, Nixdorf, KTAS and CSELT is evaluating several options for transmitting highly-compressed photographs via videotex.

Some of the most spectacular long-term leads in ESPRIT and other programmes like ALVEY and EUREKA deal with image and sound-based interfaces for interaction between computer and the real world. Such projects concern the processing of the content of: two-dimensional images, such as X-rays; three-dimensional scenes, with techniques such as stereo-vision and expert systems for occlusion analysis, i.e. working out what is behind an object; three-dimensional moving sequences, where a study of processing algorithms and applications in robotics has started.

The work on pattern recognition may well find applications for example for the interpretation of remote sensing data, for non-destructive test simulations in the construction industry, or in cases where the direct study of physical phenomenae is expensive, dangerous, damaging or simply impossible.

Conclusion: calls for new projects

The European Community's electronic publishing and information technology programmes are taking increasing account of optical storage media, image processing, visual information retrieval methods and of the advanced hardware and communications infrastructures that are required to house and transport them.

There is however still a major discrepancy between today's humble optical disc and CD-ROM projects and the fruits of the long-lead research and development like ESPRIT and ALVEY.

The gap is expected to be reduced with two major new programmes launched in the second half of 1987.

The ESPRIT II programme will enable R&D projects with a total cost in excess of three billion ECU to be carried out. Although it retains the same basic aims as the first phase, there is now some emphasis on IT application technologies, one of the subareas being integrated information systems. The role of the user of information technology is stressed, particularly the requirements of less skilled operators of computers or terminals. The accent is also on the integration of IT components into systems rather than developing more components, on generic telecommunications and on low-cost technologies and large-scale applicability rather than purely pre-competitive research and development (ESPRIT, 1987).

On the other hand, the Commission's programme for the development of the information services market has evolved during 1987, broadening its scope on policy issues and launching a call for interest in pilot/demonstration projects.

The priority initiatives for the Commission to explore have been boiled down to some key issues for the market:

- eliminating technical, administrative and legal barriers which presently fragment the market, such as lack of standardization, different fiscal regulations and disparate intellectual property rules,
- increasing synergy between the public and private sectors, to avoid direct competition in the operation of information services,
- improving user access to existing information products and services, through reference tools, awareness, training, multilingual tools,
- stimulating advances into a new generation of information products and services, through pilot projects. Such projects should aim to break the mould of existing services, by taking greater account of the linguistic diversity of Europe and tailoring information more closely to the needs of the end user in business and industry (Commission, 1987).

On this last point, a 'Call for Declarations of Interest for Pilot Demonstration Projects aiming at the development of a Community Information Services Market' was published in July 1987 (Commission,

1987). The response to this call from the actors in the information industry will determine its precise shape and size. It is intended to promote the maximum of cooperation between the different proposers in order to identify large-scale projects that will have a significant, catalytic impact on the market as a whole. The first signs at the time of writing are that this approach has broad support, and some projects, strongly oriented towards optical storage media, are already under consideration.

The continuation of the European Community's role in the CD-ROM market and in optical publishing for the next four to five years therefore seems assured.

References

ARNOLD, S.E. (1987) A baker's dozen of CD-ROM myths, *Electronic and Optical Publishing Review*, **7**, no. 2, Learned Information, Oxford and New Jersey

AYRES, F.H., ELLIS, D., HUGGILL, J.A.W., LINE, M.B., LONG, A.B., MILLSON, D.R., RUSSON, D. and YANNAKOUDAKIS, E.J. (1986) *The linkage between bibliographic and full text databases — a feasibility study (DOCMATCH 2)*, CEC DG XIII-B-2, Luxembourg

BIRKENSHAW, J. (1984) Computer composition for scientific, technical and medical publishing, *Electronic Document Delivery V*, Learned Information, Oxford and New Jersey

COLLIER, H. and BORRELL, J. (1982) Calls for proposals on electronic document delivery and electronic publishing, *Electronic Publishing Review*, **2**, Supp. No. 1, Learned Information, Oxford and New Jersey

Commission of the European Communities (1985) Call for proposals for the development of advanced information services in specialized areas, *Official Journal of the EC, C 190, July 7*, OPOCE, Luxembourg

Commission of the European Communities (1987a) *Communication from the Commission on the establishment at Community level of a policy and a plan of priority actions for the development of an information services market, COM (87) 360 final*, CEC, Luxembourg

Commission of the European Communities (1987b) Call for declarations of interest for pilot/demonstration projects aiming at the development of a Community information services market, *Official Journal of the EC, C188, July 17*, CEC DG XIII-B and OPOCE, Luxembourg

DCM Association (1985) *Special report: CD-ROM print/publish/file breakthrough for organizations: the vice-president's advance brief and action plan outline*, DCMA, San Francisco

Directory of the Commission of the European Communities (CEC) (1987) office for Official Publications of the European Communities, Luxembourg

ESPRIT (1986) European strategic programme for research and development in information technology: the first phase and results, *Communication from the Commission to Council (COM (86) 687 final)*, CEC DG XIII-A, Brussels

ESPRIT (1987) *Advance notice of 1987 call for proposals*, CEC DG XIII-A, Brussels

European Association of Advertising Agencies (1987) *Electronic publishing and advertising*, CEC, DG XIII-B-I, EUR 11029

FROST and SULLIVAN (1986) Report 1517, Infotecture 101, December

FROST and SULLIVAN (1987) *The new electronic publishing market in western Europe*,

GURNSEY, J. (1982) Electronic publishing trends in the United States and Europe, *Electronic Document Delivery III*, Learned Information, Oxford and New Jersey

GURNSEY, J. and HENDERSON, H. (1984) electronic publishing trends in the United States, Europe and Japan, *Electronic Document Delivery VII*, Learned Information, Oxford and New Jersey

IRWIN, F. (1987) Electronic publishing for business and finance: present situation and future developments, in *Proc. Electronic Publishing: The New Way to Communicate, Luxembourg 1986*, Kogan Page, London

JOVINE, U. (1987) *Government initiative means a promising future on online in Italy*, Gruppo Machiavelli, Rome

LEDIEU, J. (1986) Techniques de mastering des compact-discs, in *Actes du Premier Colloque Français sur le CD-ROM et ses Applications, Versailles 1986*, Agence de l'Informatique or GFFIL, Paris

Link Resources Corp. (1986) *The European electronic information industry 1986–1990*, Link, London

LUYKEN, G.M. (1987) Electronic publishing: a real competitor to conventional media?, in *Proc. Electronic Publishing: The New Way to Communicate, Luxembourg 1986*, Kogan Page, London

MARTYN, J. and SINGLETON, A. (1985) Final report on Docosys: document identification, ordering and location systems, *Electronic Document Delivery VIII*, Learned Information, Oxford and New Jersey

MASLIN, J.M., CAMERON, C.A., THOMPSON, M. and GATES, Y. (1984) A study of character sets and coding, *Electronic Document Delivery VI*, Learned Information, Oxford and New Jersey

MICHEL, J. (1987) The European Community's role in electronic publishing: summing up and recommendations, in *Proc. Electronic Publishing: The New Way to Communicate, Luxembourg 1986*, Kogan Page, London

NORMAN, A. (1981) The ARTEMIS concept for document digitalization and teletransmission, *Electronic Document Delivery I*, Learned Information, Oxford and New Jersey

Optical Publishing Directory (1987), on *Infotools CD-ROM demonstration disc for Optica 87, Amsterdam 1987*, Infotech, Pittsfield, and Learned Information, Oxford and New Jersey

PAGE, J.R.U. (1981) Proc. Workshop on the DG information market and innovation, December 1980, *Electronic Document Delivery II*, Learned Information, Oxford and New Jersey

PELLETIER, F. (1986) 'Les applications du videodisque en Europe', *L'image laser '86, actes du salon international du videodisque, Paris 1986*, Le Carrefour International de la Communication, Paris-La-Défense

SCHWERIN, J. and HENDLEY, A. (1986) *International initiatives for CD-ROM standards*, Learned Information, Oxford and New Jersey

SDCE database (1987) ECHO Host Service, Luxembourg

SOULÉ, J. (1987) TRANSDOC electronic delivery programme, *Electronic publishing — European opportunities*, Pergamon Infotech, Maidenhead, and CEC, DG XIII-B-2, Luxembourg

STANFORD-SMITH, B., HENDLEY, A. and WALSH, R. (1987) *Report on the intensive workshop on CD-ROM, February 12, 1987*, CEC DG XIII-B-2, Luxembourg

VAN SLYPE, G., PAGE, J.R.U. and VAN HALM, J. (1987) *Evaluation of experiments in electronic document delivery and electronic publishing (DOCEVA 2)*, CEC DG XIII-B-2, L-2920 Luxembourg or OPOCE, EUR 11208, Luxembourg

WEDELL, G. and LUYKEN, G.M. (1985) *Media in competition: the future of print and electronic media in 22 countries*, European Institute for the Media, Manchester

WELLS, J., PATERSON, A., THOMSON, M., MASLIN, J. and GATES, Y. (1983) User requirements and product availability of terminals for use in electronic document delivery, *Electronic Document Delivery*, Learned Information, Oxford and New Jersey

Chapter 8

ADONIS: the story so far

Barrie T. Stern and Robert Campbell

Introduction

ADONIS is a trial document delivery service that supplies 219 biomedical journals published in 1987 and 1988 on CD-ROM. The approximately weekly discs are delivered to major document centres in Europe, USA, Mexico, Australia and Japan and are used to fulfil requests for individual articles received by centres in the course of their normal activities. ADONIS is a Registered Trade Mark.

Throughout the 1970s there had been a heated debate between some of the major journal publishers and libraries over the widespread development of photocopying in libraries without any copyright revenue to the publishers. The publishers felt that photocopying had reached such a scale that it was leading to libraries cancelling subscriptions as they could easily obtain photocopies.

The ADONIS project dates from 1979 but at last is now testing the original idea — that publishers can gain copyright revenue by supplying their journals in machine-readable form for document delivery centres to print out individual journal articles on demand at lower cost than photocopying from back runs stored on shelves. From the beginning it was thought that using newer technology based on optical storage might lead to cost saving.

A further objective was to enhance the relationship between commercial and other publishers and librarians, who are partners in delivering information to the scientific research community.

The project is currently run by four individual publishers of major scientific, technical and medical (STM) journals, but they have been helped along the way by other companies and libraries. Indeed, one of the features of the project has been the collaboration between rival publishers and the cooperation between the publishers and libraries despite their long-running dispute over the photocopying of copyright material.

Biomedicine was chosen as the subject area to be used for the trial as the results of market studies and three major document delivery surveys showed that the highest number of requests per printed page are in this area. Within biomedicine most requests are for articles less than three years old. Many of these articles have a relatively high number of halftones.

This chapter outlines the early history of the project and, after describing the technological constraints which prevented its earlier launch, goes on to describe how the technology 'caught up' sufficiently to jusify a feasibility trial. The difficulties of implementation and the current technological constraints are discussed. The characteristics of the publishers' journals in terms of variability of image areas of pages and the various estimates of the amount to be published per year for each of the 219 journals in the trial are considered in the context of the limited capacity of CD-ROMs in relation to the aims of the ADONIS project.

The trial itself is fully described, and the different nature of the centres and their motives for participation are considered.

The increasing demand in the marketplace for document delivery services (see Figure 9.4) can now be monitored by the introduction of continuous surveys of demand and provide for the first time a basis for the carefully planned expansion of services in terms of speed of delivery, number of subjects and cost.

Finally, the future shape of such document delivery services based on CD-ROM is discussed, and a possible combination of hardware and software is described.

The copyright conundrum

During the last twenty years there has been a growing demand for the supply of individual articles. This has been accompanied by increased interlibrary lending, and provision in many of the various national copyright laws of 'fair use' clauses permitting the supply of a single article copy to a private researcher. This has had the effect of providing for unlimited use of the journal, to the detriment of the individual article reprint business of the publisher and, arguably, erosion of full subscriptions.

In the 1970s, therefore, journal publishers sought changes in the copyright legislation to control photocopying. They were hampered, however, by the lack of quantitative evidence that photocopying does indeed conflict with the normal exploitation of their copyright material.

The lack of such evidence eventually decided the most famous photocopying case: the 1973 action of the US publishers Williams and Wilkins against the US Government for copyright infringements allegedly committed by the Department of Health, Education and Welfare, through the National Library of Medicine and the National Institutes of Health. The basis of the judgement of the US Supreme Court was the opinion that the photocopying practices were a fair use of copyright material and that the plaintiff could not prove detrimental economic effect from photocopying.

Discussions between publishers and librarians were inconclusive in the absence of quantitative data; librarians struggled with declining budgets and ever-increasing numbers of research journals at steadily increasing prices, and publishers were faced with declining circulation. Publishers saw the development of interlibrary services as a major threat. They had more success in the courts in controlling photocopying in educational establishments but the making of single copies for research purposes, the basis of document delivery, remained largely untouched by their legal forays.

Market studies

During the planning and implementation of the Euronet project in the mid-1970s it became clear that there would be considerable frustration if librarians could identify the existence of suitable references by on-line searching, only to have to wait days or weeks before obtaining a copy of the article for the requester.

Against the background of expanding document delivery services and the frustration of both publishers and librarians in not having quantitative data, a major survey was undertaken at the British Library.

The British Library survey (1980)

To find out exactly what was being copied most, the British Library Lending Division (now known as the British Library Document Supply Centre or BLDSC) and Elsevier Science Publishers jointly undertook a two-week survey in May 1980.

All requests for copies of articles (or other types of published material) were logged and details of the number of requests received per journal title were arranged in ranked order. The two-week survey, in itself a statistically significant sample of 3.84%, showed that biomedical journal article requests ranked highest as a subject group and that most requests were for articles less than three years old (Clarke, 1981).

Although the BLDSC delivers more copies of articles than any other library (with an annual volume now more than three million — see Figure 9.4), the results of one survey at one centre were insufficient to justify launching a trial. Consequently other document supply centres were approached to determine if similar request characteristics existed.

Centre de Documentation Scientifique et Technologique (CDST)

It was suspected that a French centre's requests would contain a proportionately higher volume of French-language articles. Although statistics of usage were compiled in 1980, these were not such that they could be compared directly with those of the BLDSC survey; that comparison had to wait until the International Council of Scientific and Technical Information (ICSTI) 1985 study.

One early conclusion in 1980–81 was that the operation of such services varied widely (with different methods of cost allocation, proportion charged for overheads, etc.), which made it very difficult to calculate the possible cost savings that were an assumption of the original hypothesis.

From these first two surveys and knowledge of other centres it was clear that the high level of photocopying of the major journal publishers' titles had a considerable impact on those publishers. It was apparent also that the journals from many publishers would need to be included if the service was to have any value to document delivery centres. Approaches were made to various publishers to determine their level of interest in being involved in a consortium. As a result Academic Press, Blackwell Scientific Publications, Pergamon Press, Springer Verlag and John Wiley and Sons joined Elsevier Science Publishers to carry out further studies.

The consortium achieved an understanding of the document delivery market quite quickly, but their lack of knowledge of information technology and their naivety in the area of the rapidly developing computer and transmission systems was to cost them dear; in 1981 they had little idea of what they were really attempting to do.

Further studies

Staff from the publishers in the consortium, with the assistance of Cuadra Associates and King Research in the US, surveyed the known volume of requests for STM articles at libraries and other document supply centres in fourteen countries. Using computer simulation techniques the existing demand, together with the latent demand that would be fulfilled if services existed that did not suffer the delays of postal delivery, amounted to 11 million STM requests per year in Europe with a similar figure for the US.

Table 8.1 Prices charged per 10-page article copy

Europe

Country/centre	Price	US $
UK, BLDSC	UK only: £1.75	3.04
	Other countries: £2.20	3.82
Finland (average)	FM10	2.11
Sweden, Karolinska	SKr17.5	2.86
West Germany	DM2–DM15	0.81–6.08
Switzerland	SF4	1.91
Austria	ASch15	0.87
France	FF19	2.74
Belgium	BF100	2.12
Netherlands	DFL4	1.48

US

Type	Organization	Charge US $
Learned societies	Center for Research Libraries	Annual fee
	Chemical Abstracts Service	10.00
	Engineering Science Library	8.00
Commercial	Find/SVP	7.50
	Information on Demand	7.75
	Information Store	7.50
	Institute for Scientific Information	6.25* (1982–80 pub.)
		9.00* (1979–78 pub.)
	University Microfilms	15.00*
Subsidized	National Agricultural Library	2.00
	National Library of Medicine	4.00
	New York State Interlibrary Loans	1.00
	Wisconsin Interlibrary Loan Service	3.50 (average)

Only services marked * charged copyright fees

The survey gave a good insight into the different document delivery practices in different countries (e.g. centralized versus scattered, government-funded versus commercial, etc.).

To give some idea of the value of such a volume of business, the prices then charged by different document delivery services were surveyed. *Table 8.1* shows the 1982 prices being charged in some centres in Europe and the US. It is interesting to note that the US figures are rather higher than those in Europe (which are mainly subsidized) but were lower than the $12.00 average reported by King Research in their study for the Register of Copyrights. A fuller discussion of these aspects can be found in the Report of a Workshop 'Scholarly communication in transition' (Meadows, 1983).

The results were sufficiently encouraging for the publishers in the consortium to invite discussion with other publishers. By this time the consortium had taken the name ADONIS, following the custom in European documentation projects of using the names of Greek and Roman gods.

The British Library 1983 survey

A second survey was undertaken at the BLDSC, with joint funding from ADONIS, to find out if there was any difference since the earlier 1980 survey in the pattern of requests given the increased volume and the relative maturity of on-line searching. The same two-week period was chosen in May (when there was an approximate midpoint between the highest and lowest monthly volumes).

Table 8.2 shows the rankings of the top journals in 1983 compared with the rankings in 1980. In general, requests for biochemistry and engineering (particularly broad subject scope titles) had increased. Again biomedical article requests ranked highly, although the actual ranking of titles had altered and there was a surprisingly high ranking of non-STM journals such as *Country Life*. Requests for *Brain Research* and *Biochimica et Biophysica Acta* were fewer than in the 1980 survey, but overall the same conclusions were found as had been reached after the first survey (British Library, 1983).

Table 8.2 Rankings of the ten most frequently requested journals

1983 survey			1980 survey
Journal of Chromatography	1	1	Brain Research
Annals New York Academy of Sciences	2	2	Journal of Chromatography
Papers — Society of Automotive Engineers	2	3	Biochimica et Biophysica Acta
Biochimica et Biophysica Acta	4	4	Annals New York Academy of Sciences
Science	5	5	Science
ASTM Special Technical Publication	6	6	Medical Journal of Australia
Papers — American Society of Mechanical Engineers	6	7	Papers — Society of Automotive Engineers
Lancet	8	8	Papers — American Society of Mechanical Engineers
Progress in Clinical and Biological Research	8	9	Journal of Biological Chemistry
Journal of Biological Chemistry	10	10	New England Journal of Medicine

A striking feature of the studies was that a well-established major STM journal does not appear as high up the document request rankings as might have been expected, especially after considering the requests per page as opposed to the requests per title. The explanation is that a journal might be frequently requested because it is not readily available in local libraries; such a journal might be a title from South Africa that could be discriminated against for political reasons, or a recently launched title that has still to gain circulation but is publishing papers of wide interest. A journal such as *Nature* or *Science* scores fewer requests than at first expected as they are to be found in nearly every library; requests in these cases might be more often for older articles no longer kept in local libraries.

The International Council of Scientific and Technical Information (ICSTI) study

The programme of technical activities of ICSTI includes document delivery and electronic publishing. The difficulties of comparing the statistics of different document supply centres, given the very large volumes of data

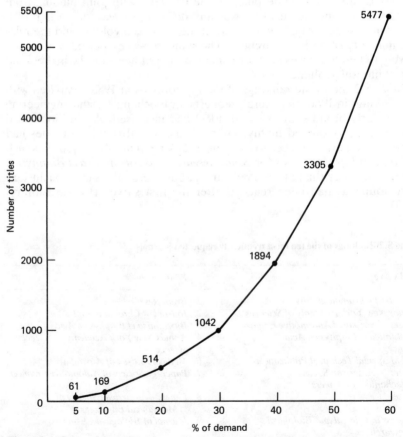

Figure 8.1 'Composite' document supply centre: number of titles required to meet $n\%$ of demand

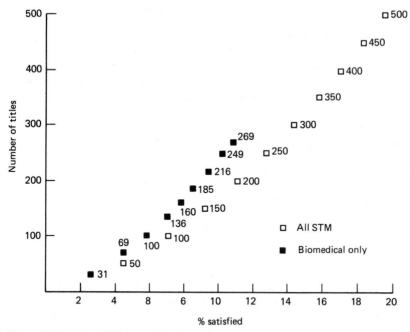

Figure 8.2 Number of titles to satisfy demand

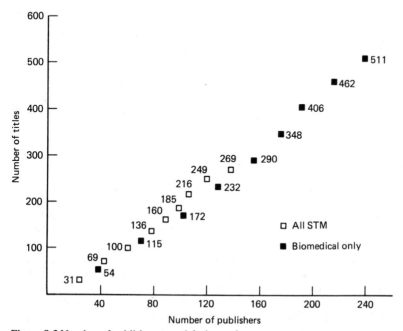

Figure 8.3 Number of publishers to satisfy demand

requiring computer analysis, led to a proposal to develop a single methodology and to provide the basis for future comparative studies.

In 1985, with part funding from the US Council on Library Resouces and the British Library, ICSTI developed such a microcomputer-based methodology. It then compared the 1983 statistics for article requests received at BLDSC, Centre de Documentation Scientifique et Technologique (CDST), Paris, and the services of *Chemical Abstracts* (Columbus, Ohio), the US National Library of Medicine and the Online Computer Library Center (OCLC) (ICSTI, 1987).

The subject coverage of the five services differs in nature between single disciplines (*Chemical Abstracts* and the National Library of Medicine) and multidisciplinary (BLDSC, CDST and OCLC). Nevertheless it is possible from the ranked lists to determine a notional list of journal titles that are common to two, three, four or all five services that between them satisfy a significantly high proportion of requests for articles. This in turn leads to the concept of a core collection of titles that a library might wish to retain to satisfy a major proportion of requests.

Twenty per cent of all demand at the five centres can be satisfied by 514 titles, 30% by 1041 titles and 60% by 5477 titles. This is reflected by *Figure 8.1*, which covers all subject areas. A similar result is seen in *Figure 8.2* from an earlier ADONIS study, which shows the number of titles needed for all STM subjects and for biomedicine alone. When this is translated into the number of publishers involved in offering an ADONIS-type service, whereas only 40 publishers between them offer 54 highly demanded biomedical titles, the number rises to 240 different publishers for 511 titles (*Figure 8.3*).

Having developed the methodology and associated microcomputer software it is hoped to repeat and extend the survey in the future. The justification for such activities lies in the market opportunities offered by the worldwide volume of STM articles, estimated as worth tens of millions of dollars per annum. This in turn motivated the publishers, normally strong rivals, to participate in a collaborative research project to develop new methods of delivering STM information to the international research community.

Early history of the technical aspects

Character-coded and bit-mapped information representation

The emergence of high-capacity optical disc technology provided a possible option for the delivery of journal articles to libraries in machine-readable form.

Most machine-readable products represent the text as characters using the American Standard Code for Information Interchange (ASCII) where the character is coded by a series of '0's and '1's. For example the letter 'A' is represented in ASCII by the code '1000000'. To 'write' the letter 'A' on an optical disc a high-intensity laser beam is focused on the surface of the disc and a series of pits or holes is burned, each measuring about 5 μm (5×10^{-3} mm) in diameter. To read the information from an optical disc a finely-focused laser beam, of lower intensity than that used to write the information, is passed across the disc surface as it spins. The reflected beam is sensed to create a series of electrical impulses corresponding to the '0's (no impulse) and '1's (impulse) to recreate the original ASCII code, which can then be used to drive a suitable printer to recreate the required text.

However, much of the STM literature contains special mathematical and chemical symbols, complex graphs and tables, and above all halftone illustrations. Handling such material via ASCII codes is difficult, and is impossible for halftone photographs. To accommodate these it is necessary for optical disc systems to 'bit-map' the page. In this system a fine-focus laser beam scans the printed symbol or part of a picture many times, each time moving very slightly down the page. For example, if the image is the letter 'A' (*Figure 8.4*), the beam can be moved from left to right and register a miss or a hit each time it encounters white space or the black printed image.

0 0 0 0 1 0 0 0 0
0 0 0 1 0 1 0 0 0
0 0 1 1 1 1 1 0 0
0 1 0 0 0 0 0 1 0
1 0 0 0 0 0 0 0 1

Figure 8.4 Bit map for the letter 'A'

Clearly, the finer the laser beam focus the more often it can scan from left to right and the greater detail it can pick up. This brings us to the question of resolution. Each time the laser scans a page from left to right it produces a bit stream of '0's and '1's; the finer the detail needed, the more times it must scan across the page.

An additional advantage of bit-mapping is that the character representation of text is a replica of the typeface used in the original printing whereas, in general, ASCII-based systems can only reproduce a limited number of printed characters according to the sophistication (and cost) of the printer equipment.

Scanning resolutions are expressed as either 'lines per mm' or 'pel'. The first refers to the number of times the beam scans a character theoretically 1 mm high, and the pel is the number of 'picture elements' per square inch, which is equivalent to the number of misses and hits that would occur in scanning a page area of 1 inch breadth and 1 inch height. For our purposes we can assume that 8 lines/mm equals 200 pel and 12 lines/mm equals 300 pel.

From the beginning of the ADONIS project it was intended to use bit-mapping for the information representation because of the high proportion of halftones. In the document delivery model the ADONIS system competes with photocopies. The aim, therefore, was to produce a facsimile of the original article which would compare favourably with a photocopy.

The early systems

In the early 1980s there was considerable research into the development of systems using 30 cm discs covered with a thin film of rare earth compounds (such as tellurium suboxide) which were capable of recording pits on the surface burned by a laser beam. One of the problems was to ensure a long life of the information so that it was not lost in future years. There was the possibility of a gradual migration of the film material from the walls into the pits, which if filled would cause the information to be lost. Accelerated aging tests showed a likely life of not less than 10 years. Although this is still not the archival quality achieved by silver halide microfilm, it was sufficiently encouraging for system developers to plan archival office systems where large numbers of documents could be stored compactly.

ADONIS picked up the idea of using this technology as the basis of a document delivery system for supplying discs to libraries. The Philips 'Megadoc' system, as it came to be known, was still in a research phase. Although the basic laser recording and laser reading facilities were in place and a 'jukebox' to load discs into the reader and replace them in a storage rack was at the prototype stage, the scanner in use (not of Philips manufacture) was inadequate in terms of speed and resolution.

The American company, Addressograph Multigraph International (AMI), had developed a suitable scanner based on an Eastman Kodak piece of equipment. ADONIS arranged for collaboration between Philips and AMI and the signing of mutual non-disclosure agreements so that the necessary specifications could be drawn up and appropriate software written.

At the end of the principal research phase Philips had not taken a decision as to when 'Megadoc' would be available as a commercial product. At about the same time AMI filed under Chapter 11 of the US bankruptcy laws to permit reorganization of the Company. These two factors caused ADONIS to look for alternative hardware/software solutions. It identified two American organizations that were working with applications of image systems. Each was commissioned to give a design specification for a hardware/software combination that would meet the ADONIS requirements.

The proposal envisaged the establishment of a scanning factory where copies of the printed journal issues would be received from the publishers, the articles indexed and the pages scanned, and both index and scanned images 'written' to a master disc from which copies would be made and sent to libraries. Basically 3500 STM journals were to be included in the service, which would scan 100 000 pages per week and write the contents to one disc (Thomson-CSF double-sided 2 gigabyte capacity per disc) every four weeks.

The system proposed by Xerox Electro Optical Systems was based on the use of twin minicomputers back-to-back, whereas the suggestion of Teknekron Controls Inc. (now known as Integrated Automation) used somewhat simpler configurations.

Tests were carried out in 1982 on sample pages from journals for minimum typeface size, paper weights used (to determine scanning problems of 'see-through' of print on the reverse side of a printed page), presence of colour, paper dust and the tolerance of variation in the accuracy of pages cut from a journal issue into separate sheets.

It is interesting to note that the smallest typeface encountered in the journals sampled had a minimum character size of 1.0 mm high and

0.1 mm wide (the corresponding maximum character height and width in the smallest typeface used was double these sizes). This implied the need to scan at the higher resolution of 12 lines/mm (300 pel) rather than the then generally accepted 8 lines/mm. This higher resolution became a recommendation to the industry and was published by ICSTI in 1986. It is the resolution now used in many other optical storage systems for patents, reports, etc. installed by Integrated Automation.

Satellite transmission

A possible extension to the ADONIS document delivery service was the use of satellites during 'off-peak' night hours to transmit to remote laser printers. An expensive study was carried out for ADONIS by an ex-Xerox consultant who had been associated with the US company Satellite Business Systems (SBS). SBS had invested heavily in establishing a satellite-based data transmission system for electronic mail and was looking for applications to absorb some of the unused capacity. Ironically the hardware system design was contracted by SBS to AM International. The concept involved the establishment of wide-band, high-capacity terrestrial networks located in major US conurbations that were interlinked by satellite for high-volume electronic mail delivery.

In 1985, three years later, such use of satellites for document delivery had not matured and the European Commission was also trying to absorb spare capacity on the satellite facilities rented from the European Orbiting Satellite as part of the Apollo Project. The speed of such broad-band transmission can be seen when it is realized that the whole document delivery request traffic from BLDSC *in a year* could be transmitted within 10 working days.

Although technically feasible (test transmissions have been carried out successfully for Apollo at BLDSC), the sheer speed of transmission capability exceeds the known market needs and there are continuing attempts to find other applications on the back of which document delivery services can ride with lower tariff prices.

Disc copying limitations

Unlike the copy pressing of long-play audio records, in order to produce the copies from the 30 cm master disc it was necessary to rewrite the discs by reading the pits burned in the master and use the resulting signal to burn corresponding series of pits on other blank discs. The state of the art did not permit pressing of the copies from the master, and this rewriting process took between two and three hours for the content of one disc. Even writing copies in parallel was a cumbersome process.

The capacity of one of these double-sided discs was estimated at about 20 000 printed pages, and 12 master discs per year would be created for a database of 5 million pages from 3500 journals. For each disc perhaps 10 copies would need to be made, and so to create a service based on the 5 million pages per year a minimum of 700 hours per year would be needed for scanning and 500 hours for copying. To provide some spare working capacity to allow for equipment breakdown and publishers' underestimating of the volume to be published, required the installation of multiple laser copying units.

Financial constraints

Factory costs

The cost of the basic scanning equipment (suitably modified to have a hopper capable of holding separated journal pages of varying size) and the multiple copying units was of the order of $1 million. There would be a minicomputer installation, and the indexing workstations (for preparation of bibliographic information) together with journal accession information for logging the receipt of issues, alerting for missing issues, the number of articles and pages contained in an issue, etc. required the development of a specialized subsystem. This subsystem would have cost about $250 000.

When the costs of staff, buildings, courier service (to give rapid delivery to the libraries who would need the discs as soon after publication of the printed journals as was possible), etc. were added to the hardware/software costs, the total cost of the factory required for ADONIS was of the order of $2 million capital cost and $750 000 annual running costs.

Efforts were made to find other applications for the technology to increase the revenue flow to support the costs of the ADONIS bureau, and although the consultants Mackintosh International showed many potential applications in banking, insurance, technical engineering manuals and structural and civil engineering, this took the project further away from the main aims and interests of the ADONIS publishers.

As the service was still to be tested it was decided to restrict the number of titles by reducing from 3500 to 1000. With a collection of 1000 titles it was clear that ADONIS would have to specialize in one subject area rather than all of science and technology; it was logical to choose the subject area that had the greatest demand, namely biomedicine. This also suited the ADONIS partners, who were all strong in biomedicine.

The exact savings could not be determined until it was known which journals would be included in the service; this in turn meant being able to predict the volume of copies that might be sold through the document delivery services.

There was, therefore, detailed analysis of requests per page of each title (as opposed to requests per title) as this relates more accurately to the costs of scanning and storing on disc. Thinking in terms of a more limited service, i.e. about 1000 titles, produced more attractive estimated revenues per page stored. But the total revenues from document delivery would be considerably less than for the 3500 titles, yet the factory costs would not drop by the same amount; many of the costs were fixed.

The possibility of scanning and producing the discs in the United States was considered, but the facilities were limited and they were unwilling to take on a major contract at a price acceptable to the ADONIS group.

Also the danger existed that, in making the trial smaller to reduce costs, insufficient operating data would be available for valid conclusions and decisions.

Workstation costs

Each of the participating libraries would need at least one workstation that contained a laser reader, perhaps a jukebox and a subsystem that handled the index information but was directly linked to the disc library.

The cost of each workstation was of the order of $250000, and only the very large libraries or document delivery services could justify such an expenditure. Even then such expenditure could be considered only if the proportion of requests that could be satisfied by the service was a significant part of the total volume handled by each of the participating libraries.

Participating publishers and libraries

Throughout the early years of the project it was assumed that the ADONIS concept would be so attractive to other publishers that it would be relatively easy to gain their cooperation when required. About thirty were approached in December 1982 and their varying response brought home the problem of bringing in enough publishers to give 3500 frequently requested titles on the discs. Understandably the publishers wanted to know what income they would receive in return for subscribing to the cost of their titles; they were surprised and often put off by the small number of requests per page that the ADONIS staff predicted on the basis of their survey data. A typical response would be to offer to try one of their titles as a gesture of support for a project tackling the photocopying problem, rather than offering their whole list.

Another problem was the lack of knowledge of information technology amongst most academic publishers and the suspicion that some of the major publishers, i.e. the ADONIS group, were using their position of strength to get further ahead of them. As with other technology-based projects, people can prove as difficult or even more difficult than the technology.

The comparison with the response from the librarians is worth noting. The British Library's early interest and encouragement, together with that from the European Commission, was soon joined by other major European libraries: notably the CDST service in Paris, the Medical Library in Cologne and the Royal Academy for Science in Amsterdam. These four centres were all in the business of offering document delivery services and were all funded from taxpayers' money. The four services formed a nucleus of 'core libraries' indicating that they would give serious consideration to participation in the trial, especially in obtaining continuous and consolidated usage statistics that would help them rationalize their holdings in the light of ever-constricting public-funded budgets.

The initial announcement of the ADONIS concept generated widespread interest in the library community. The ADONIS publishers were embarrassed by the flood of requests for more information, especially as libraries in countries where there was inadequate access to telecommunications networks for on-line searches saw the project as a 'stand-alone' collection of biomedical research literature that could be used to enhance their existing holdings. Later on it was the support from the four major European libraries that enabled ADONIS to enter into a trial.

The Logica study

With these cost estimates emerging it was decided that the operating costs of a document delivery service should be examined and compared with the cost of operating an ADONIS service based on the use of 30 cm discs. The potential saving was, after all, one of the original motivations for considering the introduction of an ADONIS service.

Consultants from Logica Ltd were commissioned to make an independent comparison between the costs at the British Library Lending Division and the proposed ADONIS service.

The results showed that in the early years of service, until there was a sufficient reservoir from which to draw articles up to 3 years old (which either meant creating a backfile at the beginning or waiting for the service to mature), the savings were at best marginal. Even with the volume of demand from the British Library Lending Division, which was then approaching 3 million requests per year, the economics of setting up a workstation and printing from the discs did not establish a clear advantage over the economics of the existing method of collecting by hand the printed journals from the shelves and making photocopies.

The study had to make a number of assumptions relating to the titles to be included and other factors. The validity of these assumptions could not easily be proven. Nevertheless, it was concluded that although the cost of establishing a service based on a scanning factory was not justified at that stage, the original concept was worth further development.

The need for a bureau service

The publishers felt that one of their inherent difficulties was the pricing policy of the major document delivery centres. Estimates of the real cost of interlibrary lending suggested that a charge of $12 to $15 would be appropriate even without a copyright fee (see *Table 8.1*), but because of the strong competition between the subsidized agencies the actual charges were perhaps half of this figure. Production costs of articles printed from the ADONIS discs would be subject to rigorous financial scrutiny, yet the ADONIS disc system had to compete in price against non-commercial subsidized services.

The original concept of 3500 scientific and technical journals had already been abbreviated to one of 1000 biomedical journals. Even then the cost of starting with a full-scale service based on a scanning factory was prohibitive as outlined above. Given the high cost of creating such a factory, it was decided to seek the services of a scanning bureau in Europe as otherwise it was rather like a group of publishers planning to build a printing press to produce just one book. This sounds an obvious strategy, but surprisingly it took the publishers a long time to come to it. The idea of keeping the publishing side of the project and sub-contracting the scanning and disc production gave the project fresh hope.

The emergence of CD-ROM technology

In 1985 this new 'editorial policy', linked with lower computing costs, the development of CD-ROM and the announcement of relatively inexpensive laser printers, enabled the ADONIS group to come up with a revised project that attracted the support of several major European libraries and the European Commission. This would result in the 1984 cost of $250000 for the workstation used for the large discs being reduced to a figure for handling CD-ROM that is currently about $20000 but expected to fall.

Another factor was that the publishers no longer had to be concerned with providing the funds to create a scanning bureau. As a result of the tripartite agreement between the European Patent Office, the US Patent Office and the Japanese Patent Office (whereby each would create an optical store of all patent documents), plans were announced for the establishment of three separate scanning bureaux in Europe to capture the content of the European patents with an estimated total volume of more than 60 million pages. ADONIS was able to secure the services of one of the three bureaux at a competitive price.

After five years, then, a technical solution was at last appearing to be viable and the ADONIS publishers agreed in July 1986 to set up a trial.

Capacity questions

The libraries in the trial had indicated that they would be unhappy to have to handle more than about 50 CD-ROM discs per publication year, given the absence of suitable automatic jukebox equipment. It was known that the available capacity of a CD-ROM is 550 megabytes. The index information and a safety margin would use 50 megabytes, which left 500 megabytes for storing the scanned pages.

It was known also, from theoretical considerations of compression ratios (see below), how much storage space on average a page would require. This enabled us to assume that 500 megabytes, i.e. each disc, could store 5000 pages (including halftones). The service could, therefore, offer weekly discs complete with index that would contain the equivalent of about 250000 pages per year.

A list of candidate journal titles was produced, working from the number of pages published in a given biomedical journal together with the ranking of that title in the demand tables produced by the various surveys.

Once we had a list of candidate titles we could approach some of those publishers whose biomedical journals showed strongly in the document delivery surveys. Generally the response was positive, and six 'participating publishers' agreed to include their titles in a trial that would contain about 250000 pages per year.

The main publishers in the project were Blackwell Scientific Publications, Elsevier Science Publishers, Pergamon Journals and Springer Verlag, i.e. the partners of the ADONIS consortium. These four publishers had biomedical journals that together generated over 300000 pages per year, so some pruning was necessary. When other publishers expressed interest in joining the project to get the detailed market statistics as to usage of their material, further selection of the lists of the four main publishers was needed to make room for the additional journals.

Based on the estimates of the publishers as to the number of pages to be published per year, it was necessary to reduce the number of journals from about 300 to the final figure of 219. These journal titles, together with the number of issues, articles and pages to be produced in 1987, are shown in the Appendix to this chapter.

Compression ratios

A technique exists to suppress the white non-printed space on a page which does not carry any 'useful' information. By compressing the useful information, disc storage space is optimized, as is the transmission of such data whether within a computer system or to a remote printer.

The legibility of laser prints of English, French and Japanese (Kanji) journal pages was tested, and the minimum acceptable resolution and the compression ratio implications were studied in yet another expensive consultant's report. The publishers were learning the hard way that being first can be very expensive!

The letter 'A' in *Figure 8.4* consists of 45 discrete picture elements, of which only 11 carry 'useful' information. The degree of compression achieved is usually expressed as a ratio. The various compression techniques need not concern us here — suffice it to say that the finer the resolution used for scanning (i.e. the greater the number of lines per mm), the larger the amount of data that is generated and needs to be stored. The total number of bits in the uncompressed scanned image can be represented as:

Total bits = (image width × horizontal resolution) ×
$$(image\ height \times vertical\ resolution)$$

(It should be noted that scanning resolutions can differ in the horizontal and vertical directions.) Scanning at 12 lines/mm generates a bit stream 50% greater than that at 8 lines/mm, so there is a greater need to employ effective compression ratios. For pure textual material with no halftones a ratio of 8–12:1 is achievable, with higher ratios where there are tables or graphs and thus greater area of white unprinted page. The corollary is that the 'denser' the information on a printed page, the lower the achievable compression ratio as there is less scope for squeezing the greater volume of data.

Halftone content

The amount of information in a halftone photograph is considerably more than with printed text (there is less white space between the dots than between letters) and consequently more storage space is needed on a disc. The limited amount of storage on a CD-ROM coupled with the need to store as many pages as possible — including halftones — means that a rather accurate estimate of the number of halftones to be published in the journals is needed.

Sampling the 219 journals revealed that halftones occurred on about 20% of all pages. However, these did not always occupy the full printed page area and an estimate of the full-page halftone equivalents indicated that 10% was a usable figure.

Scanning tests

In order to convert the physical printed image into the equivalent disc storage needed, a series of tests was carried out in February 1987 and reported later that year (Stern, 1987; Campbell and Stern, 1987). This was the first opportunity to verify the theoretical calculations of storage needed and, therefore, the number of pages of text and halftone that can be stored on a CD-ROM. The results of scanning are shown in *Table 8.3*.

Table 8.3 Results of scanning tests and storage requirement

No. of pages per year	Average storage/page (kilobyte)	Scan resolution (pel)	Storage needed (gigabyte)	No. of discs
255 000 text	100	300 × 300	25.59	46.4
255 000 text	67	300 × 150	17.1	31.1
30 000 halftones	500	300 × 300	15.0	27.3

The effect of scanning text at 300 pel horizontally and 150 pel vertically saves approximately 30% in the volume of disc storage space needed. When the stored page images were laser printed the resulting quality was acceptable to sophisticated medical research staff who were asked to compare the two qualities. Although this was a subjective test, it is valid as the purpose of the ADONIS service is to provide scientific readers with acceptable copies of articles. It is not surprising that the lower vertical scan resolution is acceptable as the amount of useful information 'between' the printed lines is less than that along the line. Subscripts and superscripts were perfectly legible, even down to a 6 point typeface size (the smallest typeface normally used in scientific journals).

Page image area

The tests reported above were carried out on a journal with a printed page area of 25.0 × 16.0 cm. Other journals have a different page area and it was necessary to measure the image area of the 219 journals in the trial. However, in order to determine the average page image area it was also necessary to take into account the number of pages each journal publishes in a year. The number of pages was known (details are given in the Appendix), so it was possible to calculate the overall statistically-weighted average image area per page (by adding together the total image area published in a journal each year — i.e. the individual page area multiplied by the number of pages for that journal — and dividing the total image area by the total number of pages published in the 219 journals).

From the 'weighted average page area' it was possible to adjust the

Table 8.4 Storage requirement adjusted for 'weighted average page areas'

No. of pages per year	Scan resolution (pel)	No. of discs	
		Old	New
255 000 text	300 × 300	46.4	39.4
255 000 text	300 × 150	31.1	26.4
30 000 halftones	300 × 300	27.3	23.2

storage requirements and hence recalculate the number of discs needed. *Table 8.4* shows the corresponding results. From these it appears that the number of discs required for a database of 285 000 pages per year containing about 10% full-page halftones will be 49.6 if the text is scanned at 300 × 150 pel and the halftones at the full 300 × 300 pel, compared with 62.6 discs for scanning everything at 300 × 300 pel.

Indexing requirements

Although the emphasis was on the storage of facsimile images in a bit-mapped mode for subsequent printing, the location of the appropriate images and their retrieval required some form of indexing. Such indexing conceptually could be of three types, which in the ADONIS environment are distinguished as levels 1, 2 and 3 respectively.

Level 1 indexing is a mere physical location indicator which states that a particular range of images is to be found at a certain address or sector on a given disc. Such indexes are uninformative as to the content of the articles and cannot be linked readily to other library services without further intellectual effort.

Level 2 indexing provides details of the bibliographic citation (article title, authors, journal title, year of publication, volume and issue numbers and pagination range) as well as the physical location information of level 1 indexing.

Level 3 indexing is the information contained in levels 1 and 2 with the addition of subject indexing. This could be based on the content of the abstracts or summaries but is much better based on the complete text of an article. Minor points in the text of the article, such as the analytical methods used, can be of interest but are less likely to be mentioned in the abstract. Subject indexing may use controlled language terms derived from either an authority list or a fully-structured thesaurus.

Article identifiers

For a document delivery service, there is a great advantage in having a unique and unambiguous code which can be used for online or paper-based ordering. Such a system is easier to key-in as it is shorter than the full bibliographic citation, but it does not easily provide a meaningful content representation such as a journal name or an article title.

There were in existence two document identification systems: the Bibliographic Identifier (BIBLID), which can be computer- or manually-generated from the bibliographic citation, and the Serials Industry Systems Application Committee (SISAC) identifier (now known as Serial Article and Issue Identifier — SAID) developed by the Faxon Company as an aid to library journal ordering and issue receipt, particularly in connection with their business as journal subscription agents. BIBLID is now an International Standard (ISO 9115) and the SISAC/SAID system is a draft US National Information Standards Organization (NISO) Standard.

Both BIBLID and SISAC were intended primarily as library tools, and neither is suitable for allocation by the publisher at the time of publishing — clearly desirable if a single unambiguous system is to result.

The International Standard Serial Number (ISSN) is well established in the publishing and library environment, and it was decided to devise an identifier for use in the ADONIS system that was based on the ISSN. The year of publication rather than the volume number was felt to be more important (including both would lead to a longer code) as both are unique in combination with the ISSN (which is an accurate representation of the full journal title). To represent the article a simple consecutive number, beginning at the start of each calendar year of publication, is allocated. The resulting ADONIS identification number consists therefore of:

1234-5678	87	99999	X
ISSN	Yr	Art.	Check
		no.	digit

where the ISSN is standard, the year is represented as the last two digits of the year of publication as shown on the cover (i.e. ignoring late publication from a previous year or publication years that are not complete calendar years) and the page range has a maximum of nearly 100 000 pages per year (one of the largest scientific journals is *Biochimica et Biophysica Acta* with 17 997 pages published per year). The check digit at the end is in addition to any ISSN check digit (which is retained as the ISSN itself is a complete recognizable code which would be distorted if any character were to be omitted). The resulting 16-character code (the hyphen and the spaces in the example above are omitted) is considerably shorter than the BIBLID or SISAC code (which can be 38 characters long), thereby helping to minimize keying errors at the time of online document ordering.

Whatever system of article numbering is adopted, it is a clear advantage if it is allocated at the time of publication by the journal publisher. However, until it has proved itself capable of use in field trials it should not be adopted by the publisher/library community. For this reason the ADONIS identification number is being allocated at the time of level 2 indexing. During the two-year trial it is planned that field tests will be carried out by the British Library comparing the performance of the ADONIS number with the BIBLID and SISAC systems.

The trial

Having described the preparatory investigations and the thinking about the design of the trial, we can now describe the actual operations. These are summarized in *Figure 8.5.*

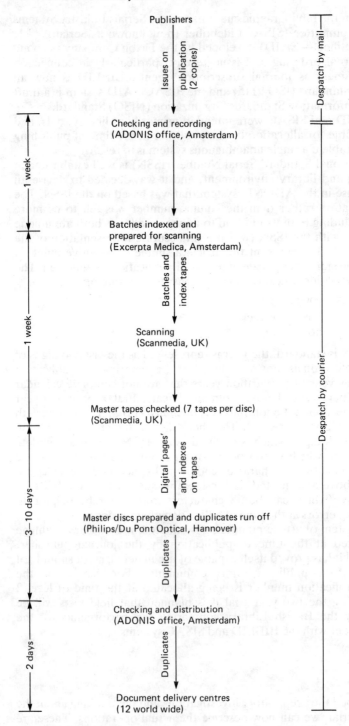

Figure 8.5 ADONIS disc production schedule

Production

The journals are sent (two copies of each issue published in 1987 and 1988) from the publishers to the ADONIS office in Amsterdam, where the details (number of issue, number of items to be indexed, number of pages, etc.) are entered into a database which has an automatic alerting system for missing issues. One copy of the journal issue is sent for indexing (a batch of issues for indexing is assembled twice daily), the other copy being retained as a back-up.

Each week the contents of the 219 journals are indexed by Excerpta Medica in Amsterdam (level 2 indexing) and an ADONIS article number is allocated. All editorial matter is indexed including editorials, letters, book reviews (but not software reviews) and reports of conferences (including abstracts of papers presented) as well as formal articles. Advertisements, announcements and patents abstracts, contents pages and author and subject indexes are not included. A separate ADONIS number is allocated for all items included.

After indexing, the details are sent as an ASCII file to the scanning bureau in England together with the corresponding journal pages already cut into separate sheets for loading into the hopper of the scanning machine.

A special program checks that the number of pages to be scanned corresponds to the page range of the citation in the level 2 indexing.

A French scanning bureau was originally appointed as a subcontractor in 1986. After several months no software had been developed and it became clear that an alternative had to be found. Therefore a new scanning bureau was appointed (Scanmedia), which immediately began a crash programme to write the necessary software. A pilot disc using 10% of the disc capacity was prepared in April 1987 and was used to carry out preliminary testing of the workstation. The first two full discs were prepared in July; these were used to ensure that the index on each disc could be successfully added to the cumulated index on the workstation hard disc. These two sets of tests between them took several weeks and led to some frustration at the centres, some of which had equipment installed but no software or a regular supply of discs.

In order to conform to the wishes of the participating libraries not to have more than about one new disc per week, it was decided to scan text pages at 300×150 pel and pages containing halftones at 300×300 pel (see *Table 8.3*).

After scanning, the Scanmedia bureau merges the bit-mapped data stream and the ASCII index information into a preformatted set of tapes (some seven full tapes per week) and sends them to the disc facility of Philips and Du Pont Optical at Hannover, in Germany. A copy of the tapes is retained by Scanmedia until after acceptance tests of each disc are completed both at Hannover and at Quasa, the software development company in England.

Each disc carries a label that identifies the weekly batch, as well as the index information written in ASCII relating to the scanned page images on that particular disc.

The throughput time from receipt of the printed journal to delivery of discs at the centres should be about four weeks (one week each for indexing and scanning and 10 days for disc production). It is essential for discs to be at the centres before the content of the journals generates requests to the centres via current awareness or other sources of alerting.

On receipt of the discs the participating centre reads the content of the ASCII index into a cumulating index with which to match incoming requests for copies of articles.

Typically requests for items are sorted into ADONIS and non-ADONIS journals, and the latter processed conventionally. The ADONIS requests are sorted into disc order by using the cumulated ADONIS (ASCII-based) index and are retrieved and printed after loading each appropriate disc. By 1989 it is expected that jukeboxes capable of handling more than 100 discs will be available commercially at a price of about $15 000.

The centres

From early in the development of the project as a whole, and not just the trial itself, BLDSC gave support and has continued to play an active role in helping to develop the system. In 1986 it was joined by CDST, the Medical Library in Cologne and the Royal Academy of Sciences in Amsterdam. These four 'core' libraries have since been joined by a number of other document delivery services. The locations of the 12 test sites are given in *Table 8.5*.

Table 8.5 List of participating centres

Europe	BLDSC, Boston Spa, UK
	CDST, Paris, France
	Instituto Ciencia y Tecnologia, Madrid, Spain
	Karolinska Institute, Stockholm, Sweden
	Medical Library, Cologne, West Germany
	Royal Academy of Science, Amsterdam, Netherlands
	Technical Information Library, Hannover, West Germany
USA	Information on Demand, Berkeley, California
	University Microfilms International, Ann Arbor, Michigan
Mexico	Universidad Autonoma de Nuevo Leon, Monterrey
Australia	National Library of Australia, Canberra
Japan	Kinokuniya, Tokyo

Each centre has installed one or more of the specially designed ADONIS workstations which are used for retrieving and printing requested articles.

Every three months the collected statistics of which articles have been printed out (as recorded by the software on the basis of the ADONIS article identifier) are sent on floppy disc to the British Library, which then presents a consolidated report to ADONIS.

From the list of centres it can be seen that they vary in nature from those that are supported by public funds to those that are commercially oriented; some are multidisciplinary in their subject coverage, others are single-subject specialist services; some are part of a library service, others are dedicated to document supply only.

The centres themselves often compete in the same marketplace. Thus BLDSC, the Royal Academy in Amsterdam and University Microfilms all sell in Japan, where Kinokuniya is based. Another feature is that some of the libraries act as a focal point for delivery of copies on behalf of a number of other document supply centres. Into this category falls the Royal Academy in Amsterdam, which acts on behalf of SALINFO (Samenwerkingsverband voor de Nationale Literatuur en Informatievoorzienung in de Beta-sector) and the Faculty of Medicine in the Universidad Autonoma de Nuevo Leon. Indeed the Mexican library is collecting requests from other libraries in Mexico, and previously would send a member of staff by air to the University of Texas library in Houston, USA, to make copies.

Financial support for ICYT in Madrid, the Instituto de Informacion y Documentacion en Ciencia y Tecnologia, is provided by the Centro de Traitemento de la Documentacion, a commercial organization with interests in microfilming and digital optical storage.

Kinokuniya is a subscription agent that has developed special services for libraries and sees the project as providing additional services to its customers. Similarly University Microfilms and Information on Demand see the project as developing new or more efficient ways of delivering information to fee-paying customers.

The case of Karolinska is interesting. The average patient stay in the associated clinics is only five days, after which the patient is discharged. Heavy use is made of the journals by readers in the library, which made it difficult to make copies of articles unless duplicate journal copies were available. Limited budgets made this impossible and the ADONIS discs give an opportunity for copies to be made and delivered to the clinics' physicians before the patient is discharged.

All centres have an interest in determining how newer technology can be used to improve the effectiveness of their operations. Thus all are making a contribution to the project, both financial (made up of a token subscription of 62 500 guilders, about $30 000, as well as the investment in the workstation) and in staff and other resources. Funding comes from a number of sources, ranging from government or university budgets to commercial sponsorship from technical companies or normal commercial sources.

In addition to the subscription fee, a royalty is payable for copies made in excess of 10 000 during the course of the two-year project. It is interesting to note that the licence to copy, provided by the copyright holders (the publishers), is not subject to the normal 'fair use' clauses found in copyright legislation. The publishers in effect are granting permission to the centres to make as many copies (prints) as required, provided a fee is paid on the number of copies made — even of a single article. Even the subscription fee payable by the centres for the first 10 000 copies can be thought of as a fee per copy with a minimum of 10 000; this fee is set at a level that takes into account the royalties paid to the Copyright Clearance Centre, which are paid anyway by the commercial services. The only major restrictions laid down by the contracts is that the copies must be made via the workstation and that subscriptions to the printed versions of the journals (if these are taken normally by the centre) may not be cancelled during the term of the trial.

Workstation design and development

Hardware
The British Library was awarded a contract to develop a workstation, not only for use with the ADONIS discs but also suitable for general library purposes. A Request for Proposal was issued and a contract was awarded to the French Company MC2 of Meylan, France. The configuration is shown in *Figure 8.9.*

The workstation is based on the LaserData workstation Laserview, consisting of an IBM PC (XT or preferably AT) or compatible (with a 30 megabyte hard disc and 640 kilobyte memory), a CD-ROM player (Hitachi, etc.), a laser printer with a resolution of 300 pel (e.g. Ricoh LP 4081) and an optional Laserview LV-700 high-resolution monitor capable of displaying a full A4 size page at 300 × 150 pel. Three proprietary interface cards (sandwiched so as to occupy only two expansion slots in the PC) link the monitor (LV-610 card), disc player and printer (LV-620 card) to the central processor and provide the compression/decompression module (LV-630 card). All the centres chose to use the high-resolution monitor seen in *Figure 8.6,* which shows the full workstation configuration.

Figure 8.6 ADONIS workstation

Software
The software consists of two groups: image retrieval management and image printing based on Laserview LV-915 Application Interface Software

and Unify Industry Standard database management system; and ADONIS software specially developed by the British Library and MC2. This latter package also provides the facilities for generating the statistics of usage as well as generating front sheets to documents (including the mailing address for the document), copyright notices, etc.

Retrieval and display characteristics

On starting the system the entry screen offers the following options:

1. Document search
2. Batch printing
3. System maintenance

To search a document a preformatted frame is presented for ADONIS number, ISSN, journal details, article title, author(s) etc. to be entered as described below.

The cumulated index can be searched by the following fields: journal title, year of publication, volume number, issue number, part/supplement number, ISSN, article title, author(s), page number or ADONIS number. A search in the journal title field is limited to a 50-character string maximum that occurs within the title entry. The character string may contain 'wild cards': a '?' for any single character or an '*' matches any string of any length including zero-length strings. The year of publication can be specified precisely or within a range and is defined by two fields: the lower boundary or exact year (four digits) or the upper boundary (four digits). If both fields are entered then the system searches for all records that lie within the two specified years. The article field can be searched with a minimum of six characters, but searching this field alone is slow: the longer the character string, the faster the search. Authors (up to four) can be searched with a maximum of 20 characters each; the wild card option is available. Page numbers can be searched as a range if not exactly specified. The ADONIS number can be the only search field entered, but all 16 characters must be entered exactly.

If multiple documents are retrieved as a result of searching, the truncated titles are displayed in a list for selection. Selecting a document from the index displays the complete citation and other details. The system indicates which CD-ROM should be mounted in the player for retrieval of the document images for display and/or printing. If the selection is not what is required, the searcher can be returned to the index display.

After searching, the document (including halftones) can be displayed on the screen, with page browsing forward and backward. Priority printing or entry of the order into a batch print queue requires the completion of details in a form displayed on the screen using the following information: request form number, requestor code, name and address of requestor and organization name as well as a delivery address. A batch of print orders can be resorted into disc number order.

Every three months the content of the statistics file is downloaded on to a floppy disc. The current file on the hard disc is closed, moved to the floppy and a new one opened. The file also contains the opening and closing dates. The data is coded so that it is not possible to remove records from the file without altering the code.

The first version of the software to search the index and to retrieve images from the discs and display them or print them, is far too slow. The index itself is larger than anticipated because of the unexpected inclusion of thousands of abstracts. The CD-ROM disc access speed is known to be relatively slow, and this is accentuated when handling the large volume of data in halftones. These disadvantages can be improved within the limits of the design of the architecture of present personal computers, but for large indexes it may be desirable to store them in a minicomputer linked to a series of personal computer-based workstations.

Duration of the trial

The original intention was to run the trial over a two-year period with delivery of discs covering the issues published in 1987 and 1988, and for the centres to use them until the end of June 1989. However, the software development took longer than expected/promised and the first discs did not appear until July 1987. This was three months later than planned, but even then delays occurred in amending the software (both the production software used to merge the ASCII index information and the scanned images, and the workstation retrieval software).

By the end of October 1987 the initial teething problems were overcome and the first 16 production discs were distributed. These had a total of 21 453 items indexed and a page count of over 100 000. Because of the delays and the need for a certain familiarization period for the centres to adjust their operating procedures, it was decided to extend the trial a further six months until the end of 1989 so that adequate use could be made of the discs representing the 1987 and 1988 material and for sufficient statistics to be generated.

Statistics

One of the main objectives of the trial is the opportunity to gather detailed information on document requests. This is of considerable interest to publishers and libraries alike, and the trial envisages continuous statistics gathering over a two-year period as opposed to the previous 'snapshots in time' offered by two-week surveys.

Every three months the centres will download the statistics from their workstations and send them to the British Library for analysis on behalf of ADONIS. Most of these statistics are automatically collected each time a print is generated and show:

Automatic by workstation
The ISSN
The issue of the journal requested
The ADONIS item identification number
The centre generating the report
The date of usage

Indicative by proportion
The proportion of requests arising from the type of user making the request (categorized as academic, governmental, industrial or other) and country of origin.

Publisher's journals — characteristics and storage implications

The method of calculation of the kilobyte requirement for a page of text scanned at 300 pel horizontally and either 300 or 150 pel vertically has already been discussed, as has the importance of knowing the actual image area for the text in the 219 journals in the trial.

Figure 8.7 shows the percentage deviation from the overall average page image area; of the ten publishers, six have average page image areas that differ by more than 10% from the overall average. There is no problem with larger or smaller page areas, merely that for purposes of calculating the number of new discs to be mastered in the trial, it is important to have the details of this variability and not rely on the overall average.

Similarly, it is necessary for budget purposes to have an indication of deviation from the publisher's expected number of pages to be published and of the number of items to be indexed. *Figures 8.8* and *8.9* show these deviations, although it must be emphasized that late receipt of journals will give a lower figure when calculating the number of pages and items expected by a given date. From *Figure 8.8* it can be seen that there is no great excess over the expected number of pages. However, when looking at *Figure 8.9* it can be seen that of the items to be indexed four of the ten publishers are considerably above the expected limit. The explanation is

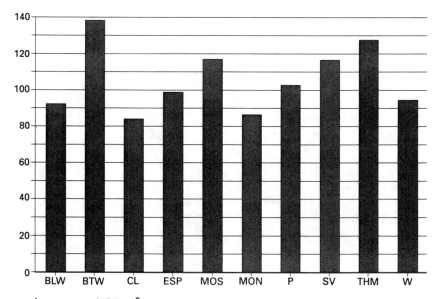

Average area 343.5 cm^2

Figure 8.7 Percentage deviation from average page area

that publishers tend to give details of articles in their budget and not the other items that are all to be separately indexed such as abstracts of papers presented at conferences, book reviews, letters to the editor, etc.

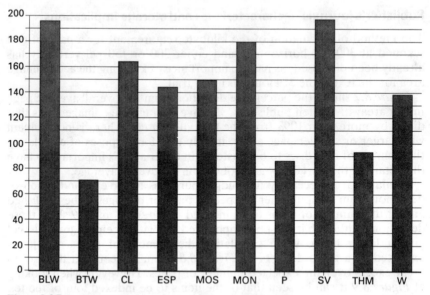

Figure 8.8 Percentage deviation from budget: pages published

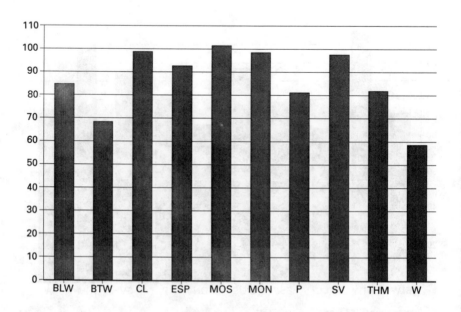

Figure 8.9 Percentage deviation from budget: articles published

European Commission involvement

The Commission has for a long time been encouraging the ADONIS concept. Indeed in some respects it had its origins in the early 1970s when one of the authors was acting in an advisory capacity on the establishment of the European online network, then known as Euronet. It was realized that the list of references obtained from online searching in a matter of minutes would lead to great frustration if the articles were not readily available in a local library. The researcher might have to wait weeks before the article was available. From that time interest in document delivery services grew, and a number of Commission-funded studies provided the necessary stimulus for plans to be laid.

A Call for Proposals in the early 1980s brought forward a number of schemes based on extensive discussions that had been taking place under the guidance of the Commission. These proposals all had certain character-istics in common: consortia or joint ventures; participation amongst organizations from different European countries; and market-driven projects to meet defined needs of specific user groups. The level of funding was always such that the projects themselves needed to finance the bulk of the costs.

A further Call for Proposals was made in 1985, this time with the focus on optical storage/publishing and the use of CD-ROM. Again a number of projects were selected for support including ADONIS, which included the document delivery aspects of the earlier Call as well as using CD-ROM technology. The grant from the Commission has enabled ADONIS to set up the trial, which was originally based on the support from the four core libraries but which had aroused interest in other parts of Europe as well as having export potential outside Europe.

Financial support has been provided by the European Commission in three different areas: direct support for the ADONIS trial, funding to support the design of the workstation, and indirectly a study contract to the British Library for field trials to compare the performance of different article identifiers (Docmatch 2).

Legal aspects

Altogether a total of 27 contracts were involved in establishing the trial. Separate contracts were needed for each of the ten publishers, the twelve centres and the three subcontractors, plus the statistics analysis manage-ment contract with the British Library and the contract for support from the European Commission. In addition there were the two contracts between the European Commission and the British Library (for the design of the workstation and for Docmatch 2).

A complex arrangement for licences for the use of copyright material by ADONIS on behalf of the publishers, who either own the copyrights or who act as agents on behalf of the societies for whom they publish, necessitated different versions of contracts.

Similarly the centres needed assurance not only that there was per-mission to reproduce copies of the copyrighted material, but also that they were protected from any third-party claims against them in product liability suits. As ADONIS is a joint venture operation with a budget sufficient only for the trial, it was necessary to obtain indemnity from the publishers for whom ADONIS was acting, so as to be able to transfer that indemnity to the centres.

A further consideration is to ensure that the usage fees or royalties are set by the publishers themselves so that ADONIS is merely acting on their behalf. Any future service operating under commercial terms must ensure that these usage fees are controlled by the publishers/copyright holders and that there is total freedom for publishers to set their own usage fees independently and not in concert.

It is worth stressing that the publishers are relying on a legal relationship with the library and the users based on a contract rather than general copyright law.

Evaluation of results

The ADONIS office records the number of items to be indexed and pages to be scanned for each of the journals included in the database, and gives feedback to the publishers as to the deviation from their budgeted figure. Reference has been made already to the quarterly analysis of the statistics received from the centres. This will give the publishers an insight into which journals are most heavily used and also other factors such as age of article, geographic demand and type of user (industrial, academic researcher, etc.). These statistics are of considerable interest to the libraries, whose limited budgets may not support the systematic collection of usage statistics for their own organization, as well as a basis for comparison with other centres using precisely the same format.

At the end of the trial a comparison will be made of the costs using the ADONIS system and the conventional document supply servicing using photocopies. In addition, there will be user evaluation of the acceptability of the quality of prints and the ease of use of the system.

Key considerations

An objective of the trial is to learn about the impact of such a service on end users (i.e. the customers of libraries ordering copies of articles), which will contribute to knowledge about information (re)packaging. The trial explores aspects of the implementation of digital technology to effect savings that can be shared with publishers, thereby providing a solution to the conflict between publishers and document delivery services over the interpretation of copyright legislation. Also of interest will be the reception given by the libraries to the ADONIS system, and whether the system will influence the way they work.

From the viewpoint of the libraries the project should provide a service with improved economics to benefit all parties, and/or improve the service to library users (which will enhance the publisher/library relationship). The trial is limited to certain aspects of information awareness and delivery. In order to demonstrate potential savings it is necessary to participate in actual operations on a sufficiently large scale to be credible while keeping costs as low as possible for what is essentially a research experiment.

An experiment that addresses a particular problem worldwide must be capable of local evaluation. Copies of the ADONIS discs will be used in Europe, North America, Central America, Japan and Australasia. It is regrettable that negotiations over the use of the system in Africa, India and South-East Asia have not been successful within the time limits of the trial. Nevertheless, the trial will involve state-funded, academic and purely commercial services — all with very different budgetary and operational constraints.

The present economics of the publishing/library environment are already finely balanced. The widespread cuts in library budgets are coming at a time when publishers are required to invest more in editorial, production and distribution services. For example, editors are demanding more assistance and help with their expenses, authors look for higher standards of production, and subscribers expect quicker despatch which now usually involves airfreight. A revenue from document delivery could enable publishers to keep their more specialized titles going. If the ADONIS concept can be proved to work, it will play an important role in maintaining the present diversity of research journals.

The principle of the ADONIS project can only be tested in an experiment involving real operations and with deliverable products. The experience gained by commercial and public-funded document supply centres will validate or reject this particular technological approach, which in any case is likely to evolve into more cost-effective variants as the technology develops.

Even though the trial is far from complete, ideas for its extension are under discussion. The complexity of establishing a service requires a considerable lead time. After all, the idea was born in 1979 and only came to life in a tangible form in 1987.

It is clear already that given the storage inadequacies of CD-ROM, which translates to a mere 5000 pages of journal articles in facsimile, a different approach is desirable. Further, the slowness of existing alerting services in providing details of articles of possible relevance to the scientist weeks after actual publication of the article may point to areas for improved services.

Future products and services

Alerting

Interest has been expressed already in an earlier and more comprehensive alerting service as to the existence of, or the future existence of, articles in the journal literature. Current systems depend on the existence of the printed journal or contents pages and, therefore, necessarily run some weeks later than the delivery of the journals.

In principle it may be possible to create awareness services by publishers at the time of final proof *even before page number allocation,* as the ADONIS identifier is page independent. This could give an alerting service

publishing details of new articles about seven weeks ahead of existing
services. The page range of an article can be supplied later as a simple
look-up table in machine-readable form.

Indexing

Clearly the addition of subject indexing is desirable and in principle could
be allocated at the time of final proof. This could be done by matching the
machine-readable photocomposition tapes against the machine-readable
authority list or thesaurus so as to obtain a list of candidate subject index
terms that can be post-edited.

  Such an index could be delivered in either machine-readable/electronic
form or in print, and could be combined with the early alerting service
referred to above. This would also enable the electronic matching of
subject interest profiles against new subject indexes of forthcoming or just
published articles (thus returning to the Selective Dissemination of
Information concepts of the 1960s). For example, if a researcher asked his
library to supply all articles on the immunology of frogs, such a service
could supply automatically a list every month of new papers on this topic
and, if required, copies of the articles from the discs.

Mixed mode

The limited 5000-page capacity of CD-ROM suggests an extension of the
hybrid storage system of ASCII and bit-mapped data, whereby the text is
represented in ASCII and only graphics/halftones are bit-mapped. Page
make-up can be on the basis of vectors as already demonstrated in the
European Commission supported project for document storage. Some
typeface characteristics can be simulated at the time of laser printing using
typeface codes embedded in the ASCII text. Such systems (e.g. Palantir,
Omnifont) are beginning to become commerically available.

Disc capacity

Calculations based on the above mixed-mode approach suggest a
CD-ROM capacity in excess of 30 000 pages including halftones and using
compression ratios similar to those of the current ADONIS trial. This
implies an annual file of one million pages based on a weekly CD-ROM
which can be readily handled by use of jukeboxes with a capacity of 100+
discs (without caddies or other containers) such as are being developed in
Europe.

Subject areas

Delivery of files of one million pages annual capacity enables the publishing
of individual subject clusters on CD-ROM. The choice of subject areas is a
subject where considerable work still needs to be done, not least in terms
of identifying the appropriate journals that make up a 'critical mass' of
information to satisfy the needs of particular user groups.

Conclusions

General conclusions

Although the technology itself is not new, what is novel is the blending of different aspects of the technology to give a new type of service. Certain characteristics of such a test can be identified that are common to other new applications of existing technology:

● The lead time needed is often much greater than might be expected, and slippage is almost inevitable when working with subcontractors, particularly if they operate sequentially and in different countries.

● The investigation phase is often underestimated as far as costs are concerned, yet is very necessary to determine realistic costs that must be built into a business plan.

● Where cooperation between different players is essential for the design of hardware, software or services, the overall development speed is limited to the slowest of any critical parts (as identified by techniques like critical path analysis) and must be identified at the planning stage.

● The size of the potential market is difficult to estimate in the early stages before there is a tangible product to demonstrate, by which time the planning phase may be over. Therefore, an element of 'graceful expansion' should be included for subsequent phases.

Specific conclusions

From the experience gained so far it is already possible to draw certain conclusions:

● Document delivery services will need far more journal titles than 200 to offer a broad subject coverage.

● The number of publishers involved in a broader coverage will be considerably larger than ten.

● The existing capacity of CD-ROM as used in its present largely facsimile mode is inadequate, and more pages need to be stored per disc.

● The development of networks will encourage shared resources between libraries, and future services based on optical disc storage should accommodate sharing of resources as well as providing stand-alone applications.

● Fees paid per article copied, including a royalty to the copyright owner, as part of a contractual licence will avoid the ambiguities of copyright legislation interpretation.

● The application software for displaying and printing articles must be improved to provide a service an order of magnitude faster.

● Considerably more automation (e.g. use of jukeboxes for automatically loading and unloading discs) is essential to minimize costly human intervention.

● The introduction of subject indexing, available at a far earlier stage than present services allow, will stimulate the demand for articles from libraries. Such expansion of the librarian's facilities will give bigger opportunities for justification of the costs incurred when introducing newer technology.

References

British Library (1983) The use of serials at the British Library Lending Division. *Interlending and Document Supply* **11**, 163–164

CAMPBELL, R.M. and STERN, B.T. (1987) ADONIS — a new approach to document delivery. *Microcomputers for Information Management*, **4**, 87–107

CLARKE, A. (1981) The use of serials at the British Library Lending Division. *Interlending Review*, **9**, 111–117

KENT, A.K., MERRY, K. and RUSSON, D. (1987) *The Use of Serials in Document Delivery Systems.* Paris: ICSTI (International Council for Scientific and Technical Information)

MEADOWS, J. (1983) Scholarly communication in transition. *Journal of Information Science*, **7**, 81–97 (in particular the contribution by R.M. Campbell on pages 93–97)

STERN, B.T. (1987) The status and future of ADONIS. *Proc. Optica 87,* **1**, 211–218

Appendix: List of biomedical journals

The three figures at the end of each line are, from left to right, the total number of issues, articles and pages published each year as notified by the publisher. The codes used for each publisher are:

BLW   Blackwell
BTW   Butterworth
CL   Churchill Livingstone
ESP   Elsevier
MOS   Mosby
MUNK   Munksgaard
P   Pergamon
SV   Springer
THM   Thieme
W   Wiley

In the database there are distinctions made between journals published in other locations, e.g. ESPSH is published in Shannon and SVNY in New York.

Title	Pub.	Iss.	Art.	Pag.
Acta Anaesthesiologica Scandinavica	MUNK	8	153	710
Acta Neurologica Scandinavica	MUNK	12	162	1140
Acta Orthopaedica Scandinavica	MUNK	6	114	704
Acta Pathologica, Microbiologica et Immunologica Scandinavica: Section A	MUNK	6	55	396
Acta Pathologica, Microbiologica et Immunologica Scandinavica: Section B	MUNK	6	62	419
Acta Pathologica, Microbiologica et Immunologica Scandinavica: Section C	MUNK	6	39	270
Addictive Behaviors	P	4	50	400
Alcohol and Alcoholism	P	4	40	450
Alimentary Pharmacology and Therapeutics	BLW	6	70	600

Title	Pub.	Iss.	Art.	Pag.
American Heart Journal	MOS	12	400	2500
American Journal of Obstetrics and Gynecology	MOS	12	600	2840
Anesthesia and Analgesia	ESP	13	144	1156
Annals of Biomedical Engineering	P	6	60	600
Annals of Occupational Hygiene	P	4	56	650
Applied Microbiology and Biotechnology	SV	12	144	1200
Archives of Dermatological Research	SV	8	100	520
Archives of Emergency Medicine	BLW	4	38	240
Archives of Environmental Contamination and Toxicology	SVNY	6	88	772
Archives of Gerontology and Geriatrics	ESP	4	144	1156
Archives of Gynecology	SV	12	30	768
Archives of Microbiology	SV	12	225	1248
Archives of Oral Biology	P	12	168	1100
Archives of Toxicology	SV	6	90	480
Atherosclerosis	ESPSH	15	220	1320
Australian and New Zealand Journal of Surgery	BLW	12	117	600
Australian Paediatric Journal	BLW	4	84	360
Behavioral Ecology and Sociobiology	SV	12	100	912
Behaviour Research and Therapy	P	6	90	700
Biochemical Pharmacology	P	24	960	4200
Biochimica et Biophysica Acta	ESP	123	2571	17997
Biomaterials	BTW	6	98	504
Biopharmaceutics and Drug Disposition	WUK	6	48	624
Biorheology	P	6	120	900
Blood Cells	SVNY	3	37	520
Blut	SV	12	108	912
Bone	P	6	60	400
Brain Research	ESP	81	1490	10430
Brain Research Bulletin	P	12	130	1600
British Journal of Clinical Pharmacology	BLW	12	152	1728
British Journal of Dermatology	BLW	12	300	1500
British Journal of Experimental Pathology	BLW	6	80	768
British Journal of Haematology	BLW	12	250	2300
British Journal of Obstetrics and Gynaecology	BLW	12	285	1300
British Journal of Surgery (The)	BTW	12	895	1336
British Journal of Urology	CL	6	161	840
British Medical Bulletin	CL	4	74	478
Bulletin of Environmental Contamination and Toxicology	SVNY	12	210	1482
Calcified Tissue International	SVNY	12	104	730
Cancer Chemotherapy and Pharmacology	SV	8	120	720
Cancer Genetics and Cytogenetics	ESPNY	12	220	1920
Cancer Immunology Immunotherapy	SV	6	105	576
Cancer Letters	ESPSH	12	240	1440
Cell and Tissue Kinetics	BLW	6	80	700
Cellular and Molecular Biology	P	6	72	750
Chemico-Biological Interactions	ESPSH	12	300	1800
Child Abuse and Neglect	P	4	44	540
Child: Care, Health and Development	BLW	6	30	432
Child's Nervous System	SV	6	66	384
Chromosoma	SV	12	121	960

Title	Pub.	Iss.	Art.	Pag.
Clinica Chimica Acta	ESP	24	600	3600
Clinical Allergy	BLW	6	70	600
Clinical and Experimental Dermatology	BLW	12	121	680
Clinical and Experimental Immunology	BLW	12	307	3072
Clinical and Experimental Pharmacology and * Physiology*	BLW	12	76	600
Clinical Endocrinology	BLW	12	93	1500
Clinical Otolaryngology and Allied Sciences	BLW	6	63	480
Clinical Physiology	BLW	6	57	600
Clinical Psychology Review	P	6	42	650
Clinical Radiology	BLW	6	190	660
Clinical Vision Sciences	P	4	56	400
Comparative Biochemistry and Physiology * Part A: Comparative Physiology*	P	12	600	2500
Comparative Biochemistry and Physiology * Part B: Comparative Biochemistry*	P	12	600	2500
Comparative Biochemistry and Physiology * Part C: Comparative Pharmacology and* * Toxicology*	P	6	240	1300
Computerized Radiology	P	6	60	450
Computers in Biology and Medicine	P	6	50	420
Contact Dermatitis	MUNK	10	94	704
Developmental and Comparative Immunology	P	4	60	800
Developmental Brain Research	ESP	12	400	2800
Diabetic Medicine	WUK	6	90	576
Diabetologia	SV	12	190	1000
Differentiation	SV	9	104	864
Disease Markers	WUK	4	24	256
Early Human Development	ESPSH	6	133	798
Electroencephalography and Clinical * Neurophysiology: Evoked Potentials*	ESPSH	6	324	1944
Enzyme and Microbial Technology	BTW	12	180	800
European Archives of Psychiatry and * Neurological Sciences*	SV	6	32	384
European Biophysics Journal	SV	8	50	640
European Journal of Anaesthesiology	BLW	6	37	400
European Journal of Applied Physiology and * Occupational Physiology*	SV	6	102	621
European Journal of Biochemistry	SV	24	720	5200
European Journal of Cancer and Clinical * Oncology*	P	12	300	1700
European Journal of Clinical Investigation	BLW	6	88	550
European Journal of Clinical Pharmacology	SV	12	320	1584
European Journal of Haematology	MUNK	10	170	960
European Journal of Obstetrics, Gynecology * and Reproductive Biology*	ESP	12	133	798
European Journal of Pediatrics	SV	6	192	618
European Journal of Pharmacology	ESP	42	800	4800
European Journal of Respiratory Diseases	MUNK	10	113	764
Experimental Brain Research	SV	12	240	2700
Experimental Gerontology	P	6	50	500
Experimental Hematology	SVNY	11	111	1014
FEBS Letters	ESP	30	1000	6000

Title	Pub.	Iss.	Art.	Pag.
FEMS Microbiology Ecology	ESP	6	94	605
FEMS Microbiology Letters	ESP	15	236	1512
FEMS Microbiology Reviews	ESP	4	63	405
Forensia	SV	4	25	248
Gastroenterology	ESPNY	13	393	2750
Gene	ESP	33	332	1992
General Pharmacology	P	6	80	650
Graefe's Archive for Clinical and Experimental Ophthalmology	SV	6	55	290
Health Physics	P	12	300	2400
Hematological Oncology	WUK	4	32	384
Hepato-Gastroenterology	THM	6	75	304
Histopathology	BLW	12	170	1344
Holistic Medicine	WUK	4	28	256
Hormone and Metabolic Research	THM	12	220	700
Human Genetics	SV	12	280	1410
Human Psychopharmacology: Clinical and Experimental	WUK	4	32	256
Immunogenetics	SV	12	132	1262
Immunologial Reviews	MUNK	6	45	1000
Immunology	BLW	12	293	2500
Immunology Letters	ESP	12	120	720
Intensive Care Medicine	SV	6	70	448
International Journal of Biochemistry	P	12	480	1750
International Journal of Cardiology	ESP	12	250	1500
International Journal of Eating Disorders	WNY	6	84	720
International Journal of Geriatric Psychiatry	WUK	4	40	256
International Journal of Health Planning and Management	WUK	4	20	400
International Journal of Immunopharmacology	P	8	120	1000
International Journal of Nursing Studies	P	4	80	320
International Journal of Pharmaceutics	ESP	21	420	2520
International Journal of Radiation Oncology–Biology–Physics	P	12	300	2500
JMCI — The Journal of Molecular and Cellular Immunology	SVNY	6	49	380
Journal of Applied Bacteriology	BLW	12	129	1152
Journal of Applied Toxicology	WUK	6	72	480
Journal of Behavior Therapy and Experimental Psychiatry	P	4	100	400
Journal of Biotechnology	ESP	12	43	258
Journal of Cancer Research and Clinical Oncology	SV	6	90	612
Journal of Child Psychology and Psychiatry	P	6	66	920
Journal of Chronic Diseases	P	12	300	1000
Journal of Clinical Pharmacy and Therapeutics	BLW	6	46	432
Journal of Clinical Ultrasound	WNY	9	135	752
Journal of Comparative Physiology A: Sensory, Neural, and Behavioral Physiology	SV	12	168	1750
Journal of Comparative Physiology B: Biochemical, Systemic, and Environmental Physiology	SV	6	100	900
Journal of Cutaneous Pathology	MUNK	6	65	384

Title	Pub.	Iss.	Art.	Pag.
Journal of Emergency Medicine	P	6	84	400
Journal of Hepatology	ESP	7	90	800
Journal of Immunological Methods	ESP	20	551	3306
Journal of Labelled Compounds and *Radiopharmaceuticals*	WUK	12	132	1440
Journal of Medical Microbiology	CL	8	104	768
Journal of Membrane Biology	SVNY	18	154	1724
Journal of Mental Deficiency Research	BLW	4	40	432
Journal of Neural Transmission	SVVNY	12	72	916
Journal of Neurobiology	WNY	6	36	674
Journal of Neurology	SV	6	84	384
Journal of Pathology	WUK	12	120	1152
Journal of Pharmacological Methods	ESPNY	8	60	768
Journal of Psychiatric Research	P	4	120	400
Journal of Psychosomatic Research	P	6	150	600
Journal of Steroid Biochemistry	P	12	480	2800
Journal of Substance Abuse Treatment	P	4	50	320
Journal of the American College of Cardiology	ESPNY	13	400	3200
Journal of the Neurological Sciences	ESP	15	350	2250
Journal of Tropical Medicine and Hygiene	BLW	6	40	350
Kidney International	SVNY	12	201	1906
Klinische Wochenschrift	SV	24	181	1184
Leukemia Research	P	12	300	1500
Life Sciences	P	52	676	6000
Magnetic Resonance Imaging	P	6	80	600
Medicine and Law	SV	6	40	576
MGG — Molecular and General Genetics	SV	12	450	2766
Micron and Microscopica Acta	P	4	80	400
Molecular and Cellular Endocrinology	ESPSH	15	218	1308
Molecular Immunology	P	12	240	1400
Muscle and Nerve	WNY	9	140	1098
Mutation Research	ESP	54	673	4038
Naunyn-Schmiedeberg's Archives of Pharmacology	SV	12	238	1339
Neurobiology of Aging	P	6	66	600
Neurochemistry International	P	8	200	1100
Neurochirurgia	THM	6	60	250
Neuropathology and Applied Neurobiology	BLW	6	44	504
Neuropharmacology	P	12	240	1500
Neuropsychologia	P	6	120	950
Neuroscience	P	12	480	4000
Neuroscience Letters	ESPSH	30	757	4542
Neurotoxicology and Teratology	P	6	90	700
Nuclear Medicine and Biology	P	6	120	600
Nutrition Research	P	12	180	1200
Obstetrics and Gynecology	ESPNY	14	240	1920
Oecologia	SV	12	286	2000
Ophthalmic and Physiological Optics	P	4	120	400
Pain	ESP	12	200	1600
Parasitology Research	SV	6	80	701
Pediatric and Perinatal Epidemiology	BLW	2	15	150
Pediatric Cardiology	SV	4	65	364
Peptides	P	6	160	1200
Pflugers Archiv: European Journal of Physiology	SV	12	204	1382

Title	Pub.	Iss.	Art.	Pag.
Pharmacology, Biochemistry and Behavior	P	12	290	2500
Physiology and Behavior	P	12	480	2400
Prenatal Diagnosis	WUK	9	63	560
Prostaglandins, Leukotrienes and Medicine	CL	15	160	1800
Psychoneuroendocrinology	P	4	80	500
Psychopharmacology	SV	12	240	1632
Radiation and Environmental Biophysics	SV	4	40	320
Research in Developmental Disabilities	P	4	32	500
Research in Experimental Medicine	SV	6	50	480
Rheumatology International	SV	6	40	246
Scandinavian Journal of Clinical and Laboratory Investigation	BLW	8	123	800
Scandinavian Journal of Immunology	BLW	12	143	1200
Social Science and Medicine	P	24	720	2600
Springer Seminars in Immunopathology	SV	4	36	438
TAG — Theoretical and Applied Genetics	SV	12	190	1278
Thrombosis Research	P	24	720	3600
Toxicology	ESPSH	15	120	720
Toxicology Letters	ESP	15	229	1374
Ultrasound in Medicine and Biology	P	12	150	1000
Urological Research	SV	6	65	304
Vaccine	BTW	4	61	250
Vision Research	P	12	204	2200

Totals   Issues: 2357   Articles: 43 285   Pages: 285 755

Chapter 9

Publishing on CD-ROM: some financial principles and market considerations

Robert Campbell and Barrie T. Stern

Before considering publication on compact disc, it is worth looking at how libraries, as the main market for information, have changed their acquisition pattern. It is likely that further changes might create a strong market for CD-ROM and similar optical media. To exploit this market, its requirements and the basic principles of publishing on these new media need to be understood. Some understanding of the financial aspects can be gained by a comparative approach, and this will be discussed and illustrated in some detail.

The shifting market

Books to journals

The largest producers of copyright information in science, technology and medicine, the so-called STM sector of publishing, are the journal publishers. Over the last 30 years, a relatively small group of STM publishers have launched and developed international journals for the publication of research papers. These publishers have also produced large numbers of high-level books which mainly sell to libraries. The changes in the library market have resulted in these publishers generally giving less emphasis to book publishing and more to journal publishing, thus creating more pressure on an already over-crowded market. The situation is well demonstrated in *Figure 9.1*, which shows the relative expenditure on books and journals by the library of Iowa State University. The story is typical of academic libraries throughout the world; to maintain the periodical holdings the budget for the acquisition of new books has been sacrificed.

The growth in the journal business is thought to have reached its peak and there are indications that the market has weakened over the last two or three years. A 1984/85 survey of 85 research libraries in the United States found that the number of current serials held decreased by 2% over the last five years. *Figure 9.2* shows the 68.5% growth in sales over 1981 to 1986 reported by the British journal publishers; as can be seen, the drop in export sales since 1985 is bringing down the total figure. Predictions for 1988 suggest a further drop as North American libraries struggle with the declining exchange value of the dollar; the subscriptions of many of the leading research journals are charged in strong European currencies.

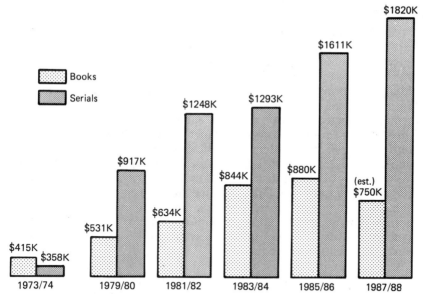

Figure 9.1 Expenditure on books and journals by the library of Iowa State University.
Reproduced by permission of the library of Iowa State University

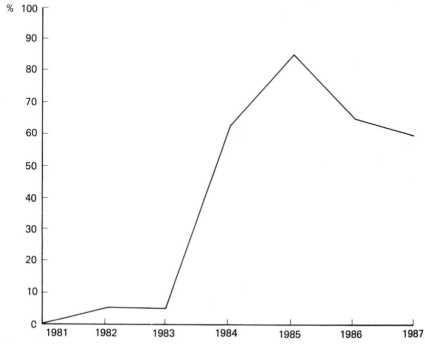

Figure 9.2 Sales volume of journals from British publishers from 1981 to 1987. The percentage
changes are grossed up at constant (retail price index) prices. Source: The Publishers'
Association

Journals to documents

As the STM journal publishers see the circulations of their journals begin to drop, they become more anxious about the growth in the use of online services and inter-library lending, basically document delivery. Where libraries have a teaching function they are tending to maintain their holdings of primary journals, including considerable back-runs, but libraries servicing research workers, such as in a pharmaceutical company, are making increasing use of online databases and document delivery. *Figure 9.3*, for example, shows the expenditure on different categories of materials in 1985 by ICI Pharmaceuticals Division. The expenditure on document delivery (British Library Document Supply Centre, BLDSC) includes copies of older articles as well as recently published material; like other similar libraries, ICI has adopted the concept of the steady-state library whereby the volume of stock discarded matches the volume acquired. This policy should maintain a demand for older material from document delivery services, unless a new means, i.e. preferable to micro-forms, is found for storing back-runs.

The cutbacks in library holdings and the improved awareness of the literature through the use of alerting services and online databases has driven up the demand for individual documents. The growth in the volume of documents supplied by the BLDSC (see *Figure 9.4*) clearly demonstrates this. Other national centres report a similar pattern of demand with current expectations of annual growth ranging from 4 to 8%. It is almost certain that the graph for the number of documents supplied by the BLDSC will

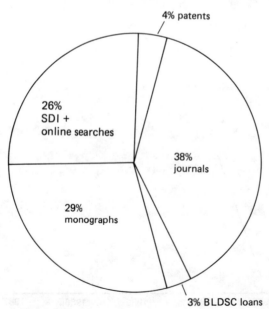

Figure 9.3 Percentage expenditure on different categories of materials in 1985 by ICI Pharmaceuticals Division. Reproduced by permission of Aslib, from *ASLIB Proceedings*, **39**, 3, 75–86

continue upwards in marked contrast to the volume of journal subscriptions, as shown in *Figure 9.2*.

Faced with this situation, the interest in document delivery amongst journal publishers would appear to be obvious, yet it is surprising how few publishers outside the major international organizations are aware of the situation. The prediction of this situation in the late 1970s and the photocopying/copyright problem led to the formation of the ADONIS group; their story is told in chapter 8.

Publishers of secondary information services, such as abstracts and bibliographies of the primary literature, are also reporting a decline in subscriptions for the hard copy edition, but an increase in revenues from other sources such as online vendors. One of the major abstracting services has revealed that revenues from 'electronic publishing' could exceed the

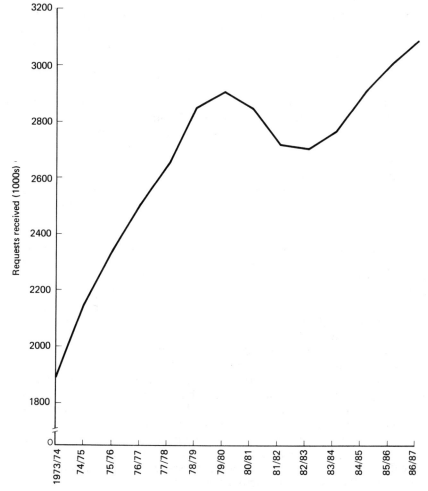

Figure 9.4 The increasing demand for interlibrary loans, mainly photocopies of articles, from the British Library Document Supply Centre (BLDSC)

revenues from hard copy subscriptions by the early 1990s. Successful development of compact discs as a medium for the major secondary services could bring forward this crossover point.

To CD-ROM?

Another consideration is the current concern over the relatively small proportion of library budgets that is actually spent on acquiring publications. For example, in Britain there are around 43000 employed in libraries and information departments. The total spent on staff and stock was around £600 million in 1985. Out of this £82 million was spent on publications from Britain, about 10% of the industry's output. In the area of journal publishing, libraries spent about £18 million on British publications and £42 million on publications from abroad. It is estimated that around £8 million was spent on online services.

Senior library administrators have suggested that if publishers can come up with products that can be used more efficiently within the library, the proportion of library budgets devoted to overheads should drop. The more cynical doubt that any such savings would actually be switched to purchasing more of the publishers' output. Perhaps CD-ROM will succeed where an earlier optical storage medium, microforms, failed. It does appear to give libraries fast access to large amounts of information without requiring hundreds of feet of shelving and elaborate cataloguing. And with the low cost of computing and high storage capacity, compact discs offer lower duplication costs and easier access than microforms for the same amount of information.

Analysis of the current online market shows the domination by credit and financial information services, followed by services on market/products, then law. Some primary research in science, technology and medicine is available online, but these ventures do not appear to have been particularly successful. The CD-ROM market is too small at this stage to give a comparable breakdown of any real meaning, but predictions suggest that the market will be dominated by databases on markets and products, with the STM and library sectors becoming as significant as credit, financial and legal. An important consideration in the application of CD-ROM in STM publishing is the facility to deliver a high-quality image, including photographs and halftones, at a relatively low cost. The bulk of the requests handled by the BLDSC (*Figure 9.4*) are for articles from STM publications, the significance of which has not been lost on some STM publishers looking at the potential of CD-ROM in the library environment.

One of the problems with optical storage media, however, in the context of publishing primary research is their high storage capacity. The time taken to fill one disc could delay the availability of the new information. Distributing the equivalent of 200 research journals is less expensive in theory on compact discs than in hard copy form, but no library wants the same 200 titles. For distributing one title, or even a small group of titles, optical storage media are too expensive if discs are to be sent out frequently as virtually all the storage capacity would be wasted.

Possibly as computing costs continue to drop it will eventually be possible for a library's selection of titles from a large publisher, or group of publishers, to be distributed to that library as 'tailor-made' discs. This would require universal standardization of equipment and software, publishers holding their journals in machine-readable form and lower disc production costs. Providing tailor-made discs for libraries could be the role of an agent acting between the publishers and the libraries, a role similar to that of subscription agents who handle around 85% of library subscriptions for hard copy.

Another possibility would be for more technically sophisticated libraries to record their own discs by downloading at night, when communication costs are lower, from the publishers or some central agency acting on behalf of the publishers. This would make the latest issue of a research journal available to users locally with perhaps simple indexing to title and author ahead of when the hard copy can be despatched after printing and binding. Such a system would introduce new questions on how to charge users, but perhaps group initiatives such as the ADONIS project will answer some of these.

Some financial principles and comparisons

Books, microforms and discs

The potential of CD-ROM and other high capacity optical storage media is appreciated by many in publishing, but the economics of optical publishing are not widely understood. The problem was similar when microfiche was first seriously proposed as a publishing medium in the late 1960s. The early view was that publishing standards would drop as it was so inexpensive to produce large amounts of material on microfiche. Publishers who had struggled with trying to sell out print-runs of conventionally-produced books were fascinated by the idea of on-demand publishing apparently made possible by microfiche. A comparison between conventional hard-copy publishing, microfiche publishing (in a sense a forerunner of optical publishing) and optical publishing can be a helpful exercise.

Anyone with experience of book publishing will know how the unit production cost relates to the length of the print-run (see *Figure 9.5*). The unit cost of a reprint is much less, but it is still high for small quantities, such as below 750 copies, although the situation is improving as more suppliers offer standardized 'budget plans' for short-run printing and binding. Microforms with very much smaller production runs give a reasonable unit cost. Indeed, it is rare to duplicate more than 50 copies at most, as the savings for larger quantities are minimal. The story for CD-ROM is similar (see *Figure 9.6*) although more confused as suppliers can be persuaded to come up with special deals to gain market position in this young industry. Most publishers are looking at projects that will require a single disc, and probably special attention from the manufacturer. With the ADONIS project, where suppliers are producing a master a week to a standard specification, it has been possible to negotiate appropriate terms.

A more useful comparison between book, microform and compact disc publishing can be drawn by considering all the costs (*Figures 9.7, 9.8* and *9.9*) and setting these against the revenue. Typically, books are priced to give a net profit towards the end of the first print-run which in academic

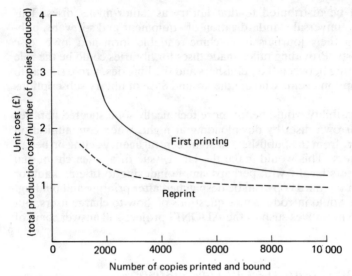

Figure 9.5 The relation of the unit cost of a book to the print run. The graph is based on a cloth-bound volume of 256 pages (an 'even working', i.e. eight signatures of 32 pages) produced on modern equipment designed to give relatively low unit costs with short print runs. Source: Michael Bodinham

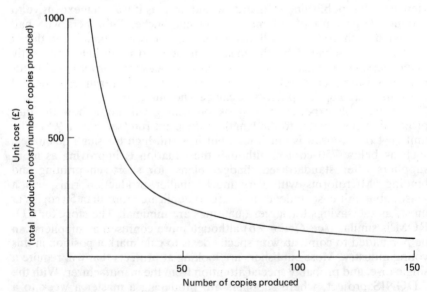

Figure 9.6 The relation of the unit production cost of a CD-ROM, which could carry 400 megabytes plus index, to the production run. Assuming that such a project might sell for £1200, the production cost becomes a relatively small proportion of the selling price within a run of 100 copies, unlike conventional book production. As the industry is at a very young stage, prices charged by suppliers vary greatly. The costs of organizing the database, producing the master disc and duplication are included in these figures

publishing might number 1500 copies, in trade or general publishing 3000 to 20000 copies, and in mass market paperback publishing 20000 to 50000 copies. With the latter, the initial production costs are often relatively small when compared with the marketing costs, i.e. a situation not unlike microform publishing. Provided that the first printing is not underpriced the reprint of a book, if there is sufficient continued demand, quickly gives a net profit.

The graphs in *Figures 9.7, 9.8* and *9.9* suggest a clear break-even point followed by an eventual net profit, but the idea of a break-even point can be detrimental to sound publishing. In economic terms, any publication that does not achieve an acceptable level of profit, i.e. return on investment, is a failure. The concept of breaking-even is also misleading as the effect of inflation and capital tied up in the project is often not properly taken into account as it is so variable.

With a typical microform publication, a sale of 50 copies might be the target for the first year. It could take on average 90 days to collect payment from customers, while filming and editorial fees will have been paid in the year before publication, and sometimes earlier. Adding an interest charge to the original investment will delay the actual break-even point. If the value of the masters is considered as an asset to add to the revenue, the accounts for the project could suggest a much better result. Giving the masters an asset value, however, will not help the cash flow as discussed later in this chapter.

With microforms the project may still be showing a loss when the initial production run has been sold (*Figure 9.8*). A similar situation is only generally seen in book publishing when a textbook publisher is trying to penetrate a substantial course market and may cost the textbook on the basis of sales projections over, say, three years calculating to make a profit during later printings. Such publishers, who are used to long development periods, complex production and to having to hold their nerve as they slowly gain a market position that could then give returns for many years, could have the right background for optical publishing. *Figure 9.8* shows how the apparent economies in small-scale production of microforms can be misleading. The initial investment in aspects of the project other than filming and duplication necessitates a sale of at least 50 copies to achieve any reasonable return on the original investment, unless the market can take a high price, i.e. a high gross profit to the publisher.

In microform publishing 'reprint' projects have usually been priced lower than the more creative projects that require greater editorial effort and, therefore, greater investment from the publisher. This idea of 'added value' making the project more attractive to the customer and, therefore, justifying a larger margin to the publisher is important in optical publishing. It is a feature of the difference in pricing strategy between conventional hard copy publishing and microform or optical publishing.

In book publishing, the production costs are usually the basis for calculating the selling price as they are the dominant cost of sales. Overheads are often taken into account as a fixed percentage of the costs or revenue, a percentage usually based on the trading figures of the previous year. Some overheads may be included as standard discrete items in the determination of the selling price; for example, a few publishing companies allocate some

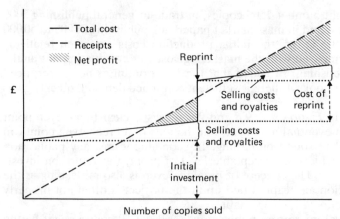

Figure 9.7 How a book is usually priced to make a profit towards the end of its first printing. This profit will be sunk into a reprint if orders justify it. The initial investment covers the editorial, production and promotion costs plus any fixed overheads. Those overheads that increase with sales, such as accounting and distribution, are included under selling costs. Reproduced from *Microform Publishing*, by P. Ashby and R. Campbell, Butterworths, 1979

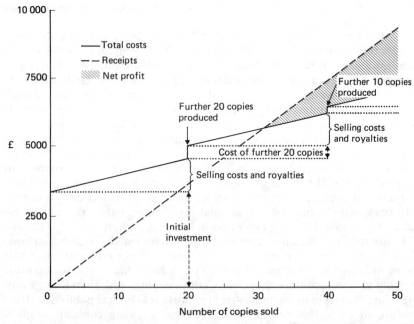

Figure 9.8 How the increase in costs is less abruptly affected by 'reprinting' in the production of microforms than in the production of books, because the investment in actual copies is a much lower proportion of the selling price. The graph is based on a package consisting of 25 microfiches with silver halide duplicates. With a package that includes conventionally printed elements, such as an introduction, list of contents and index, the initial investment will be larger as it is the usual practice to print enough copies of the eye-readable material so that there is little or no chance of having to reprint. Reproduced from *Microform Publishing*, by P. Ashby and R. Campbell, Butterworths, 1979

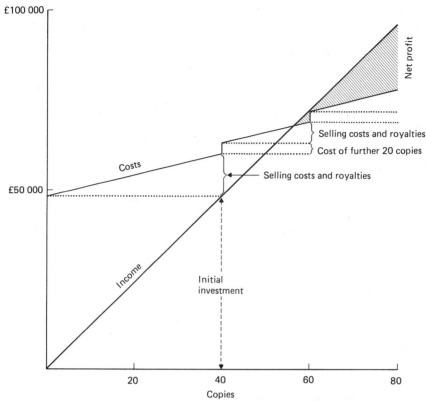

Figure 9.9 How the increase in costs is less affected by producing another batch of duplicate compact discs than in the production of conventionally produced books. The graph is based on a database carried on one disc. Prices vary widely, but here it is assumed that the final manipulation of the data and preparation of the master disc cost £10 000

of their overheads as a fixed sum applied to every book whatever its size. As can be seen from the graphs, after the preparation of the master, whether film or disc, has been paid off the charge for printing or duplication is not a large part of the selling price.

Factors in pricing a disc

The major investment with an optical project will be the collection and processing of the data, often more than the cost of the master, and the marketing and after sales service; the latter will be a new problem for most publishers and one that they should bear in mind when planning a compact disc project and cost in accordingly. At this early stage of CD-ROM publishing, for example, it is common to supply a disc player along with the disc. The selling price of the disc will need to be high enough to cover this; indeed the publisher will probably need the expectation of continuing subscription sales for updates to the database to get back the cost. Again there are implications for the cash flow.

Another factor in the overheads will be the high cost of technical staff whose average salaries are much higher than many authors and most book subeditors. In practice, publishers of optical media tend not to employ such staff but go to an outside agency for technical assistance on a consultancy basis. In some cases a specialist agency will make part of its charge by taking a royalty on sales, thus reducing the initial investment for the publisher and giving the agency an incentive to produce a successful publication. This dual charging might also apply for the licence to use 'off the shelf' software to structure the database and create the index, i.e. part of the charge might be a royalty on sales or a fee per duplicate (whether sold or not) which will drop in relation to the number of duplicates.

At this early stage of CD-ROM publishing, there is no set pattern on which to base a financial model; *Figure 9.9* is very much a first attempt. The revenue is calculated on the assumption that the duplicated discs are sold at full price and the customer can then 'read' the disc without further charge. With some projects, such as ADONIS, there may be an initial subscription price then a usage charge as laid down by the contract between the vendor/ publisher and the customer, i.e. use is controlled by contract rather than the copyright. The advantage of this pricing policy is that for the amount of information on a disc that might initially be required by the user the single price could seem too high. Once, however, the disc is installed in the library usage fees should build up as people learn how to get the most out of the disc. It is possible that publishers will offer alternative prices: a low initial price plus a usage fee, or a very much higher price allowing for unlimited use.

Some cashflow comparisons

The graphs in *Figure 9.10* are representations of the different patterns of cash flow from books, journals, online services and compact discs. The pattern of cash flow is a major difference between the traditional means of publishing research information, the journal, and an online service; indeed, this is one of the reasons why it does not appear possible for the electronic journal to be financially viable on its own as opposed to a spin-off from a hard copy journal. With a conventional research journal, the publisher will collect much of the subscription revenue well ahead of meeting any supplier's invoices. The issues are bought on trust before publication; they are pushed out and might, or might not, be read. *Figure 9.10(a)* illustrates this pattern of cash flow.

With a book, the cash flow is not so easy, but at least the publisher expects to meet most of the costs near to publication and will collect much of the revenue within a year; see *Figure 9.10(b)*.

The real cash problems come with an electronic publication. Much expensive research might be involved in setting up the project; by their

Figure 9.10 Cashflow patterns showing the relationship between the timing of expenditure and receipt of revenues for (a) a journal sold on subscription, (b) a book, (c) an online project with customers charged on usage, and (d) a CD-ROM publication sold on subscription without usage fees. It is assumed that new editions of the disc are issued at a low or 'continuation' price to existing subscribers. These new editions may attract new subscribers

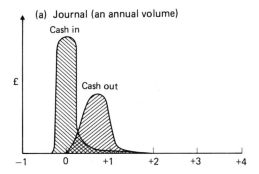

(a) Journal (an annual volume)

Cash in

Cash out

£

−1   0   +1   +2   +3   +4

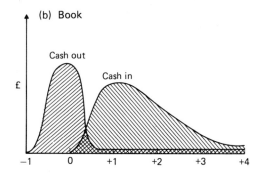

(b) Book

Cash out

Cash in

£

−1   0   +1   +2   +3   +4

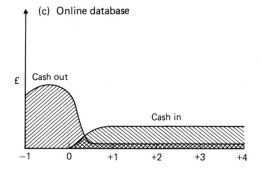

(c) Online database

£   Cash out

Cash in

−1   0   +1   +2   +3   +4

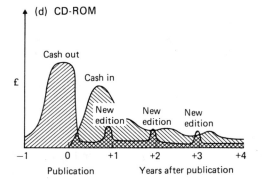

(d) CD-ROM

Cash out

Cash in

£

New edition

New edition

New edition

−1   0   +1   +2   +3   +4

Publication   Years after publication

nature they usually require the collection and processing of huge amounts of data, which must then be organized for fast access. When it is eventually published, development costs may have built up over several years; then there are marketing costs, demonstrations and user support services. Revenues will only grow steadily as users learn to access the publication, and such revenues depend on the user actually seeking some information that they require; the pattern of cash flow of this 'pulling' system is illustrated in *Figure 9.10(c)* and does not compare favourably with conventional publication.

In practice, much of the information made available online has already earned revenue through conventional publication, but there may be keyboarding, text processing and data manipulation required, all of which will add to costs. Increasingly, publishers are trying to spread the initial investment in keyboarding by coding the machine-readable form in a standard way so that it can be used both for driving a typesetter and serving as a searchable database. There are various committees looking at how a standard mark-up language might be put into practice, but as authors have never managed to submit simple typescript in any standard form the chances of a standard mark-up language succeeding look remote. It is more likely that publishers will rely on a specialist bureau to process the different formats peculiar to each publication when in machine-readable form to put them into a standard format suitable for a searchable database.

Revenue from conventional publication can improve the pattern of cash flow for a project made available through a range of media, but electronic publishers are looking to subscriptions or 'up-front' fees; this can be done more easily if the database is sold as a package on a compact disc or a copy of the database on tape is available on lease. It should also be borne in mind that running an online service is such a complex and expensive business that the industry has concentrated in the hands of a few large database 'supermarkets'. Their high charges, telecommunication costs and the common requirement to learn sophisticated search procedures have limited their appeal and should enable small companies to get involved in electronic publishing through compact discs. One of the weaknesses of online services is the lack of illustrations; as mentioned above, these can be included on compact discs along with a generally higher standard of presentation with no difficulty and could well be used as a feature in the competition against online publications.

An important factor for publishers, however, is the chance to operate within a more favourable cash flow pattern, as illustrated in *Figure 9.10(d)*. It is not as favourable as the conventional research journal (*Figure 9.10(a)*), but it can be similar to the pattern for books (*Figure 9.10(b)*). If it is used in conjunction with the hard-copy edition, such as in the ADONIS project, much of the origination cost will have been met by subscription revenue; the discs, through document delivery, will then give usage revenue. Editorial fees, software, data conversion and advances on royalties, as well as disc mastering and duplication, can amount to a major prepublication investment.

In some cases, it may also be necessary to purchase a number of disc drives to supply along with the disc. To limit tying up cash in hardware, it should be possible to make an arrangement with a disc manufacturer or distributor to offer their equipment at a special price alongside the disc. The advantage of this is that the responsibility for after sales service then lies with the supplier. UMI, for example, are offering a 22% discount on Philips compact disc drives to new subscribers to *Dissertation Abstracts Ondisc.*

The evolution from online publication to disc publication and the development of a range of sources of revenue is demonstrated in the Grolier Inc. case study described below.

Hard copy to online to disc

Grolier Inc., a major North American reference book publisher, took on the exploitation of the machine-readable form of the Academic American Encyclopedia (AAE). It started by stripping out the typesetting codes to produce a database version for searching through a computer. This version was converted to run on most of the major online host services. The database was updated quarterly, but there were no illustrations. Without the restrictions of the printed volume, the machine-readable form has longer articles giving a more comprehensive coverage.

In this form, the AAE was made available to at least 650000 subscribers through online vendors. Yet revenue has been insufficient, apparently, and Grolier estimates that the vendors would need 3–10 million subscribers to make the venture profitable. One of the main findings was that around 90% of the users ask questions that are answerable from the database but remain unanswerable through limitations of the search methodology; this is now under further research and Grolier believed that improved searching capability could be achieved by packaging the database on compact disc.

Other problems with online publication include the users' dislike of communication charges and the limitations on revenue through the non-negotiable royalty terms from online hosts. Publishers do not like finding themselves in the situation of the royalty dependent author.

As a result, Grolier moved towards offline products: database leasing, 12 inch optical discs and CD-ROM. By leasing copies of the AAE on magnetic media to local school area networks, Grolier have gained all the revenue for themselves and in advance of usage.

With 400000 videodisc players in homes in the United States, there seemed potential for a version on 12 inch optical disc; the text was recorded in analogue form to fit these players. Users access individual frames using the 'freeze frame' function. The disc and player together were priced at less than the hard copy edition, yet sales were disappointing. The analogue format on a videodisc used on a simple domestic player gave limited searching capabilities.

CD-ROM gave greater potential as a low-cost peripheral to a home computer with more powerful indexing and access. Search time for a word or group of words in the 9 million word database is less than five seconds thanks to an electronic index almost as large as the encyclopedia itself. The price for the disc (there are annual updates) is well below that of the hardcopy, but the full set of equipment including retrieval software is well above; yet it is looking like a commercial success.

Other optical media

The emphasis has been on CD-ROM as this medium appears to offer the most potential to publishers, certainly in STM. As already mentioned, CD-ROM has too great a capacity for some applications, but smaller capacity media such as the Drexler 'lasercard', which has 2 megabytes of memory, are relatively expensive to produce and duplicate for the amount of information they can carry. Where machine-readable form is not needed, a book offers lower costs for the same amount of text. One application for these types of cards could be in loose-leaf publishing. Here, commonly, information is distributed regularly to subscribers in a form that gives quick access. Much will depend on the availability and cost of the reader units. These are expected to sell for around £300 in Britain, but this does not compare favourably with, for example, the new Atari CD drive at £400, which will run on Atari's new and extremely powerful ST microcomputer of much the same price.

It is more likely that some CD-ROM projects will migrate to larger discs as they grow. The advantage of the larger discs is that they offer much faster access to large stores of data. Should a major CD-ROM compilation involve the accumulation of a number of discs, users may prefer larger discs for the 'back-run' with new information coming in on the smaller discs. The publisher can transfer the digital information from CD-ROM to a larger optical disc for around £200 per compact disc.

Taking a long-term view of a project

One problem when viewing the commercial viability of projects on new media is the reluctance to take a long-term view through uncertainty over the medium. When Elsevier launched their first international research journal, they had to wait five years before they made an annual profit.

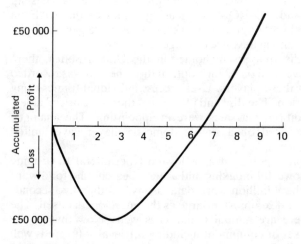

Figure 9.11 The launch of a new research journal can involve heavy losses initially and a wait of eight or nine years before accumulated losses are won back

Although the idea was relatively novel, they knew that the physical form was widely accepted. Now that this type of publication is well established, publishers are prepared to wait even longer for a new title to reach profitability (*Figure 9.11*). If publishers were confident in the future of compact discs, they might be prepared to take the same long-term view. Perhaps by using the budget on a CD-ROM venture that they might have otherwise devoted to launching a new journal, they could establish the same position in a new market that Elsevier now occupies in journal publishing.

Chapter 10

Pergamon and CD-ROM: a case study

Christine Baldwin

Introduction

Role of the publisher

The publisher's role is to identify information needs, create information products to fill those needs and distribute those products to the waiting market. Authors provide the raw data, and the publisher transforms it into an information product. Editorial panels and referees ensure that the information is accurate, and internal editorial staff impose organization, editing and indexing. Designers and production staff create a visually appealing product, and marketing/distribution staff get the product to the users who wanted the information in the first place.

Part of the process is selecting the right delivery method, one that is right for both the information and its users. The publisher's role is now more complex than in the days when print was the only medium available. Now there is a choice between print, online, microform, magnetic and optical media. The publisher must therefore be aware of their characteristics and limitations in order to select the right one when designing his information product.

Pergamon Press

Pergamon Press is one of the largest publishing groups in the world. Its main business is the publication of books and journals for use by the international scientific community. Pergamon Press was founded jointly in London by Butterworth and Company (Publishers) Ltd and Springer-Verlag of Heidelberg and Berlin. When it was acquired in 1951 by Mr Robert Maxwell, it published 5 journals and 2 books. Today Pergamon has over 6000 book titles in print and publishes 390 international research and educational journals and serials.

Over the years, the Pergamon Group has expanded rapidly to encompass publishing on all media, including print, microform, online, magnetic and optical media. Over 100 databases are available online through Pergamon Orbit Infoline. Through Maxwell Communications Corporation and Mirror Group Newspapers, Pergamon now provides national newspapers, popular magazines, cable television, entertainment films and computer software.

New media

Pergamon's policy as a publishing and information group has been to expand into new markets and adapt as existing markets change. The basic information that Pergamon publishes for the international scientific community has not changed greatly over the years. However, two other trends have had an enormous impact. Firstly the scientific community, both in universities and industry, has become computer literate. Secondly there are new media such as CD-ROM that allow publishers to develop new ranges of information products.

Whenever a new medium is developed, there are always a number of zealous individuals who refer to its development as a 'revolution' and who are sure the information industry will be magically transformed, as will be the libraries that have traditionally stored much of the world's information. This was true for microforms in the 1960s, online in the 1970s and will probably be the case for CD-ROM in the 1980s. Each is, in fact, simply a new medium for distributing information and has characteristics that should be diligently explored by all concerned with information, before deciding which medium is appropriate for a particular application.

In the history of publishing, online was certainly important as the first medium that allowed publishers to create interactive information products. It allowed individuals rapid random access to thousands of megabytes of data; they could select and pay for precisely the information that they wanted. Online databases could be updated regularly and an online search of recent abstracts represented a considerable time savings over a manual search of the print equivalent.

Online as a medium had certain limitations. It was based on mainframe database technology of the 1960s and was great for well-structured files containing many short records. It was not so great for full text, and no good at all for illustrations. Online search software was not easy to use or to learn to use (it was developed for programmers, not scientists or librarians). Online was not practical for occasional searches or for browsing. And of course it needs access to a modem and reliable telecommunications.

From a publisher's point of view, online was good for distributing well-structured documents such as abstracts to a well-defined group of regular users. Pergamon was often approached by academic, industrial and scientific organizations who had databases they wanted to make available to the scientific or business community. In many cases online was not the right medium, just as square pegs do not fit into round holes. Editorial staff who had to turn down these projects knew there was a need for a new medium, and were eager to take a look at CD-ROM when it came along.

CD-ROM

CD-ROM was launched at just the right time, in 1984 at the peak of the microcomputer revolution. By 1985 several products had been developed. They were not innovative products by today's standards, but they were worth looking at because they illustrated the characteristics of the medium. With a little creative thought it was possible for publishers to speculate about the potential of the medium.

Pergamon was first interested in CD-ROM because of its most publicized characteristic, its large storage capacity, the mysterious 500 megabytes that could be distributed in such a compact form. This capacity would accommodate the databases offered previously that were not suitable for online. Alternatively, it would hold several smaller works such as several encyclopedias or a document collection on a single subject.

Secondly it was noted that CD-ROM was a publishing medium. Once the discs were manufactured, they could not be copied and the data on them could not be altered. This was of great interest to a publisher concerned with copyright and safeguarding its intellectual property. CD-ROM was also of interest because it could handle graphics as well as text. Again it might allow publication of databases containing graphics, which are not suitable for online.

Lastly Pergamon was interested in CD-ROM because it was used with a PC. Over the past five years the market was becoming increasingly computer literate. Authors had wordprocessors and wanted to submit manuscripts on floppy disc. Many had computer software they wanted to publish along with their book. Librarians who bought our books and journals were using computers for backroom applications such as cataloguing, as well as online searching. Pergamon perceived a demand for PC-compatible products, and CD-ROM had distinct physical advantages over magnetic media as a distribution medium.

At this stage Pergamon was already familiar with the market for PC-compatible products. Pergamon Press had developed the successful range of Manuscript Manager™ wordprocessing software for journal authors and editors. It was felt that CD-ROM would not only extend the range of PC-based products for this same audience, but also allow concentration on delivering information rather than applications.

Pergamon therefore approached CD-ROM with considerable enthusiasm. In some respects there was too much initial enthusiasm. The hype associated with the launch of CD-ROM and the market expectation generated by industry analysts was enormous. Some enthusiastic editoral staff were bound to be disappointed when they found out about the realities of publishing on this new medium compared with initial promises that paper would now be obsolete.

Purpose of this chapter

This chapter describes how Pergamon became interested in CD-ROM and has explored its potential both as a publisher and a system integrator. In this respect, Pergamon's experience is unique. It is both supplier and consumer of CD-ROM services, and views the product development process from both perspectives. This chapter focuses on the product development process rather than the more technical aspects of production. This encompasses the creative aspects of identifying information problems and user needs, and translating this into a functional and marketable CD-ROM product.

It is hoped that this experience will be of interest to the information industry in general, but in particular publishers and information managers. Publishers are in a position to create CD-ROM products. However, it is information managers who are most intimately involved with using published information and are therefore in the best position to identify the important problems CD-ROM has the potential to solve. It is hoped that greater familiarity with the product development process on both sides will initiate a dialogue between publishers and information managers, and in the end lead to more creative and successful products.

Planning a CD-ROM project

Decision to experiment

The initiative to conduct an experiment with CD-ROM technology came in 1985 from Kevin Maxwell, Chief Executive of Pergamon Press and a Director of Maxwell Communications. He felt CD-ROM was a medium to be explored. In addition he reasoned that Pergamon had a wealth of intellectual property in its books, journals and databases, and the right combinations of these on CD-ROM could create new markets for scientific information.

In the summer of 1985, he invited representatives of all Group companies involved in new technology to submit proposals outlining how they would identify and exploit the potential of CD-ROM. After evaluating the proposals, he decided to conduct a technology experiment to evaluate the potential of CD-ROM and selected a project team to implement the experiment. A small research and development sum was allocated to initiate the project, but it was recognized that further funding would be required.

Goals of the project

Whenever a new publishing technology is launched, some publishers will invest and some will watch from the sidelines. Those who watch and wait may breathe a sigh of relief if the technology does not live up to expectation. But if the technology is successful, those who invested may have a market edge, and may even be able to exclude late-comers from the market. Therefore a publisher has to weigh the risk of investment against the price of being left behind.

Pergamon's original goals for conducting a technology experiment were to learn about CD-ROM technology by experience, to identify the problems involved in publishing for/with this new medium, to assess market response to new products, and to allow others in the Group to benefit from their experience.

Learning by experience
Having examined CD-ROM on paper, it was felt the only way to evaluate it further was to get 'hands on' experience. When experimentation is left to your competitors, it is of course possible to read the papers they publish (if they choose to publish) and examine their products. You will probably only learn of their success, but little about their failures, their mistakes and what they learned along the way. Pergamon felt the only real way to learn how to 'do it right' was to 'do it'.

Identifying the problems

Pergamon reasoned that a technology experiment would at least identify the problems involved in publishing with this new technology. Creating a CD-ROM product, even if it was not a best-seller, would at least identify how the editorial, production and marketing requirements were different from those of traditional publishing. By identifying what went wrong in creating the first product, by reverse engineering it could be decided how to do it right the next time.

Assessing market response

Though much had been written about CD-ROM technology, in 1985 there were few if any commercially available CD-ROM products. There was nothing to show to scientists or information managers to assess their interest in the medium generally, or to find out what products they would like to have and what features these products should have. In order to test market reaction to the kind of products Pergamon might ultimately publish on CD-ROM, they needed their own product to demonstrate. And in order to find out if a product would sell, they really needed to create one for sale.

Sharing knowledge

Pergamon felt CD-ROM was a medium that could be used to deliver many different types of information and therefore could be ultimately exploited by many of the Group companies, both printing and publishing. By focusing research and development on one project and selecting a team from several Group companies, it was hoped to avoid duplication of effort and maximize direct participation in the project. Reports would be prepared at regular intervals to keep other individuals and companies not directly involved informed of progress.

Project organization

It was decided that the project would be planned, managed and implemented by Pergamon InfoLine Ltd (now Pergamon Orbit InfoLine Ltd). InfoLine was a logical choice because of its technical resources, expertise in electronic publishing and previous track record in research and development. There were over 40 technical staff experienced in database creation, information retrieval and structuring information for output in various forms (online, magnetic tape, print and microform). Computing resources were available, both in terms of hardware (VAXs and micro-computers) and support systems. Management had conducted large scale and challenging projects before, both to external contract and for Group companies. InfoLine was not only a logical 'home' for the project of investigating CD-ROM, but CD-ROM would be a logical complement to its existing output media.

The project team included representatives from Pergamon Orbit Info-Line, Pergamon Press, BPCC Graphics (Information Services Division) and BPCC Product Development. BPCC Graphics, like Pergamon InfoLine, structures information for multimedia output. The participation of these key companies was supported by others in the group: Mirrorsoft, a consumer software publisher just launching a range of desktop publishing software; Pergamon Technical Services International, a group specializing in technical documentation and computer services; Pergamon Infotech (part of PTSI), a company expanding from conferences and computer services into development of online documentation systems; and Microforms International Marketing Corporation, which was examining the potential of CD-ROM to enhance access to information about microforms.

It was a conscious decision to ask current members of staff to contribute their time as necessary and as other commitments allowed. This meant that the project might take longer to implement. But a major goal of the project was to learn and to apply what had been learned within the respective companies. Profiting from experience was considered to be more important than conducting the experiment quickly. It was therefore decided against hiring a person specifically for the duration of the project or alternatively subcontracting out the work to another company.

Choosing a product to put on CD-ROM

The first decision the project team had to make was about what kind of information to put on a CD-ROM and the kind of product that would be created. Pergamon Orbit InfoLine's experience in the online industry indicated that users now wanted information, not merely access to information. They were well served electronically with access tools like abstracts and indexes. There were also already indications that other publishers were putting abstracts and online database on CD-ROM. It was therefore decided to put source documents rather than abstracts on CD-ROM, because it was what users wanted, and this would teach more than transferring an online file to another medium.

It was decided to publish a multivolume reference work on CD-ROM because of Pergamon's excellent reputation in this area and experience with this market. Having decided on a reference work generally, our criteria for selecting one in particular were quality and editorial standard of the work, market interest in the subject area, Pergamon's reputation in the subject area, potential to add value to the information with CD-ROM, and availability of the information in machine-readable form.

It would be desirable if the text (and if possible graphics) were available in machine-readable form. It would also be less complex to select a major work that had already been published in printed form, i.e. one for which the text had been finalized by the authors and editors. However, this would mean that the information might age considerably during the course of the project. This might be acceptable for a prototype, but not for future CD-ROM products.

The major work selected for the project was *Comprehensive Heterocyclic Chemistry* (CHC) because Pergamon could add considerable value by adding chemical structure search software; the software could be 'reused' for other chemistry major works; Pergamon has an excellent reputation for chemistry publications, and considerable editorial and marketing expertise in chemistry.

A limitation of printed chemical reference works is that generally it is only possible to search for chemical compounds by name (not by structure). If it was possible to solve the problems of presenting graphics adequately on screen, and searching for graphics (a chemical compound structure searching system), then significant value could be added to the information. Having invested in the search software, it could be used to develop a new range of products on CD-ROM.

Project funding

In autumn 1985 the Commission of the European Communities (DG XIII) made a call for proposals in the area of CD-ROM products and services. They wished to assist the development of profitable information ventures in Europe that used CD-ROM technology, by providing up to 25% funding. Criteria for selection included the following:

- commecial viability,
- market need,
- resources and expertise,
- use of new technology,
- user friendliness,
- technical flexibility,
- standards,
- European Community-wide relevance.

Until this stage, Pergamon was only conducting a technology experiment, one that might succeed gloriously, but on the other hand could be allowed to sink quietly without trace if it failed. A decision to seek funding from the CEC or other external source would make their goals, objectives, products and success or failure very public. On the other hand, having outlined an amibitious project, Pergamon certainly did need external funding.

It was decided therefore to submit a proposal, and to change the emphasis of the project somewhat. Instead of creating a single chemical reference work on CD-ROM, Pergamon would create a series of CD-ROM products for the same audience. Though the first product might not be profitable, future products would be. In addition there would be potential revenue streams from product updates and from licensing the CD-ROM chemical retrieval software.

The proposal was submitted in November 1985 and predictably it was some time before a decision was reached. In February 1986, DG XIII interviewed a short list of applicants, but it was not until June 1986 that Pergamon received a draft contract and was asked to submit a formal work programme. The final contract and work programme were signed in December 1986, a full year after the proposal was submitted. During this year Pergamon was optimistic about the chances for funding but had no assurances. Work therefore began on developing a requirements speci-fication and looking for partners (subcontractors) in this venture.

Developing a requirements specification

A requirements specification serves two purposes. Firstly it can serve as a tender document to give to outside contractors, and secondly it can assist to clarify in your own mind and on paper precisely what you want to achieve. It should cover the product itself and the relationship you are looking for.

It was necessary to rely to a large extent on intuition, conjecture and personal experience in defining what was wanted. The features required for a CD-ROM product depend on how users will want to interact with the information. Pergamon had seen a few CD-ROM products, but knew nothing about how they were designed/structured or what was possible. Surprisingly little useful information had been written on how people use information in general or printed reference works in particular.

The requirements specification covered the following areas:

- product description: purpose and general characteristics,
- hardware and software environment,
- standards,
- relationships sought with a supplier,
- design parameters
- software features.

Pergamon wanted it to be specific enough to describe precisely what was wanted, yet generic enough to cover a range of information products.

In terms of software features they were looking for the following:

Search features
- full-text search,
- chemical structure and substructure search,
- Boolean logic,
- proximity operators,
- truncation,
- indexes, e.g. author and subject.

Browsing features
- browse table of contents and headings,
- thesaurus, e.g. chemical names,
- browse text and graphics,
- follow cross references.

Display features
- WIMP (Windows, Icons, Mice, Pointers),
- split screen display for text/graphics,
- display related material at a keystroke,
- highlight search terms in text,
- scroll and page text.

Special features
- notepad facility to make 'margin notes',
- compatibility with databases for downloading bibliographic references,
- bookmark facility to tag pages to return to,
- ability to download and reformat portions of text.

This was the preliminary wish list. It was not complete or final, but designed to locate the right partners in this project.

In retrospect it was felt that more detailed knowledge of CD-ROM or familiarity with particular CD-ROM products or retrieval systems would not have helped. As system integrators today, Pergamon meets many potential clients who have studied CD-ROM of today so carefully they find it difficult to imagine CD-ROM of tomorrow. They collect together the features of several different products rather than focusing on the particular problem they wish to solve and identifying features that will contribute to the solution.

Identification of partners

Having put together a detailed requirements specification, there were four options on how to proceed:

- develop a chemical retrieval system for CD-ROM from scratch,
- identify good CD-ROM retrieval software and ask the developer to write chemical structure search modules,
- identify good chemical structure search retrieval software and ask the developer to redesign it for CD-ROM,
- identify good CD-ROM software and chemical structure handling software, and integrate the two.

The first option was rejected fairly easily: Pergamon's expertise was in publishing and disseminating information, not in writing software. Pergamon could learn more by working with experts on CD-ROM and chemical structure search than itself attempting to become expert over-night. It was also known that good CD-ROM software and good chemical retrieval software were specialist products; an expert on one would not be an expert on the other; and a company that had successfully written one type of software could not necessarily be expected to write the other. It seemed more sensible to approach experts in each area and see first whether they could work together and secondly whether their software could be integrated in some way.

CD-ROM retrieval software

In terms of CD-ROM retrieval software, there were two main types available: standard information retrieval (IR) software designed for searching mainframe databases; and retrieval software developed specifically for CD-ROM applications. Many of the first CD-ROM products were online databases published on CD-ROM with PC versions of their mainframe retrieval software. As Pergamon did not intend to publish an online database, there seemed little reason to use a scaled-down version of mainframe software.

On the other hand, it was felt there was every reason to use software designed specifically for CD-ROM. Software written for CD-ROM applications would suit our purposes better because it was:

- developed for CD-ROM and optimized for the characteristics of that

medium,
- designed for use with PCs to their display and graphics standards,
- written in a modern high-level programming language,
- more suitable for text-based applications.

Though predisposed in favour of software developed specifically for CD-ROM, Pergamon sent its specification to all known developers whose software had been used with a CD-ROM product so far. At that time, early in 1986, there was no such thing as a 'system integrator'. It was a matter of getting in touch with all the CD-ROM developers and discussing in technical terms whether their software would work for the intended product.

At this stage the problem was selecting a company to work with as much as selecting software for the product. Pergamon was looking for a developer that had good software already, could customize it to the specification, integrate chemical search modules, and allow them to participate fully in product development.

Of the half dozen possible companies Activenture (subsequently re-named KnowledgeSet) of Monterey, California, rose to the top of the list. Their software had both search and browse features, handled graphics as well as text, allowed cross referencing and navigation, and was easy to use. They were both willing and able to customize their product. In short, they met all the criteria. In addition they seemed interested in licensing their CD-ROM technology, both the retrieval software itself and the data preparation software used to invert files for CD-ROM.

It might be useful to mention why some of the other companies approached fell further down the list. In most cases it was because their software did not have the features required, or would not without considerable redesigning. Another important reason was their approach to product development. Encyclopedias, directories, online databases and parts manuals are all different products that need different retrieval features and user interfaces. It was essential that a software supplier recognize these differences and work with Pergamon to develop different products for different markets. Lastly, Pergamon wished to avoid a black box approach to product development, for example just sending off a tape and getting a product back. They wanted to participate fully in the design and creation phases. For some suppliers this was not an option.

KnowledgeSet Corporation was selected as a supplier in June 1986. About this time it formed a joint venture company with Sony called Publishers Data Service Corporation (PDSC). This allowed KnowledgeSet to concentrate on developing its CD-ROM retrieval software, the Knowledge Retrieval System (KRS), and CD-ROM products for different markets. PDSC concentrated on production-related aspects of product creation such as data preparation, premastering, mastering and replication.

A similar process was used to select chemical retrieval software and a partner to work with. In terms of software a chemical structure input and registry system was looked for, with structure and substructure search, a visually appealing display, and one that was easy to use. A developer was sought that could customize its software to our requirements, and could integrate its search and display modules within KRS. In addition, if the developer could take on the work and administration of inputting the

70 000 chemical structures, there would be no need to hire staff to do this on short-term contract.

As with the CD-ROM retrieval software there were many options, both mainframe and PC-based, varying in terms of ease of use and aesthetic appeal. In the end the PSIDOM range of chemical structure management software developed by Hampden Data Services was selected. PSIDOM stands for Professional Structure Image Database on Microcomputers. Both the product and the developer met the list of requirements, and William G. Town, Managing Director, had worked as a chemical consultant with Pergamon Orbit InfoLine over a period of years.

The next three sections of this chapter cover the decision to become a system integrator and the experience in developing two distinctly different CD-ROM products, the chemical information system and Pergamon's *International Encyclopedia of Education*. For convenience these three activities are described separately, but the work took place concurrently.

Pergamon as a system integrator

Decision to become a system integrator

As described in previous sections, Pergamon was originally looking for retrieval software with the right features to allow the creation of a CD-ROM product. In addition it was looking for the right company to assist in the process: to undertake software development and product creation work, but to allow Pergamon to participate fully in the process. Early in 1986 there were CD-ROM products and developers of CD-ROM software, but very few companies dedicated to offering CD-ROM services, and the term 'system integrator' was unknown. Pergamon did not therefore at the time make a conscious decision to become one. It was probably only later when several companies were offering similar services in CD-ROM product development that someone felt it necessary or useful to apply a name to this activity.

Pergamon had wanted to establish a close relationship with Knowledge-Set so that it could learn as much as possible. Certainly Pergamon Orbit InfoLine had large data processing resources, considerable experience in database creation and in structuring information for electronic publishing generally. It was reasoned that much of the work on the planned products could be done inhouse, certainly any preprocessing required to get machine-readable data into a suitable form for CD-ROM data preparation, and perhaps the database creation itself.

Initial discussions with KnowledgeSet were along these lines. During negotiations, the opportunity arose to license both their retrieval software, the Knowledge Retrieval System (KRS), and their proprietary CD-ROM data preparation software. By licensing the data preparation software, Pergamon could do much more of the work inhouse, in fact all data preparation steps up through creating a pre-mastering tape. This would give much greater participation in the process and make Pergamon less dependent on KnowledgeSet.

On the other hand, such a licensing arrangement offered quite another opportunity. If Pergamon could create its own CD-ROM products inhouse, it could also create CD-ROM products for other publishers inhouse. It could, in fact, offer a complete CD-ROM service to other publishers, by subcontracting out the work which could only be done externally, such as mastering and replication. The prospect seemed quite attractive but there were many factors to consider.

At the time there was much publicity about CD-ROM technology, but few if any serious applications. Many people were experimenting with CD-ROM, but few stated publicly that they were actually making a profit using it. There were few CD-ROM drives on the market, though there had been astonishing forecasts about the number of drives that *would* be sold. In sum, there was much speculation but very little collective experience.

It also had to be considered how CD-ROM would fit into the Pergamon/ MCC publishing and printing group. The technology had been considered carefully, but not in the context of offering a new service. In the end it was decided this would be precisely the right approach to take. Adding CD-ROM to Pergamon Orbit InfoLine's electronic publishing services would extend its range of media, then already encompassing online, print, microform and magnetic media. It would be a logical resource for other group companies to draw on, both in terms of services and general advice and consultation. It would allow both InfoLine and other group companies to offer a more extensive service to information providers.

The last major consideration was technical, and this was more straightforward. KnowledgeSet's data preparation software ran on VAX VMS, which was precisely the hardware environment already installed at Pergamon Orbit InfoLine for online and electronic publishing services. There was a large staff already employed there supporting these services. The system was in place for loading, maintaining and updating databases, many on a weekly basis. Technically the situation was ideal.

There was no guarantee that CD-ROM would live up to the hype, but it was felt that licensing CD-ROM software and launching a CD-ROM service were the right decisions, whether it did or not. Philosophical and technical considerations were put aside and the serious business and financial decisions began. The one most relevant to this discussion is that of exclusivity.

In order to establish the service quickly in Europe with a competitive edge, it was decided that an exclusive license on the Knowledge Retrieval System was essential. An agreement was concluded with KnowledgeSet granting exclusive rights for Europe, including the right to sublicense. This meant Pergamon would be the only company in Europe with the right to create CD-ROM products that use the KRS software, whether these products were for Pergamon or another company.

A similar agreement was concluded for the data preparation software with the newly established Publishers Data Service Corporation, a joint venture of KnowledgeSet and Sony, dedicated to CD-ROM production services. The rights covered using the software inhouse for Pergamon products, using it inhouse to create products for others, and sublicensing it to other organizations.

Typical product scenarios might be as follows:

● Pergamon would create and publish its own CD-ROM products, each accompanied by a copy of KRS.

- Pergamon would create a CD-ROM product for any other publisher in the same way.
- A publisher or other organization who wished to create many CD-ROM products might prefer to license the data preparation software and KRS from us and create their own products inhouse.
- A CD-ROM service in a particular European country might wish to license the data preparation software and KRS for his particular market.

The only other comment on the negotiation and licensing process is that it all took much longer to complete than anyone anticipated. This had less to do with the parties involved than the state-of-the-art of software contract. High-technology contract law was at the time a growth industry, particularly in the USA. Though Pergamon, KnowledgeSet and PDSC concluded heads of agreement easily and painlessly, it was months before everyone could agree on the precise wording of legal clauses. Since that time both the industry and associated law have matured. Publishers are nevertheless advised to delegate high-technology contracts to lawyers skilled in the art.

Pergamon announced the agreements with KnowledgeSet and PDSC and launched Pergamon Compact Solution at the Electronic Publishing Conference in London (30 September to 2 October 1986) and the Frankfurt Book Fair (1–6 October 1986). This was greeted with enthusiasm, not least because it was the first publishing group to launch such a service.

Knowledge Retrieval System

Before describing the service offered in more detail, it might be useful to describe some features of the Knowledge Retrieval System. Pergamon's approach had been to identify a CD-ROM product, look at CD-ROM retrieval software and select the right system for the product. KRS was found to be more an approach to handling information than merely CD-ROM retrieval software. The Knowledge Retrieval System:

- is intuitive and easy to use,
- makes full use of relationships between information,
- offers several complementary methods of access,
- includes productivity features, and
- gives the publisher greater control over his product.

The following section therefore describes KRS in terms of the value it adds to information rather than how it works in detail.

Ease of use

The Knowledge Retrieval System was designed for CD-ROM. It was not designed first for another medium (mainframe, online, PC, etc.) and then adapted to work with CD-ROM. Mainframe and online retrieval systems have always been difficult to use. As KRS was developed from scratch for CD-ROM, none of the old ways of handling information in a mainframe environment were retained. KRS is easy to use because this was one criterion of design. This is an important distinction between KRS and other

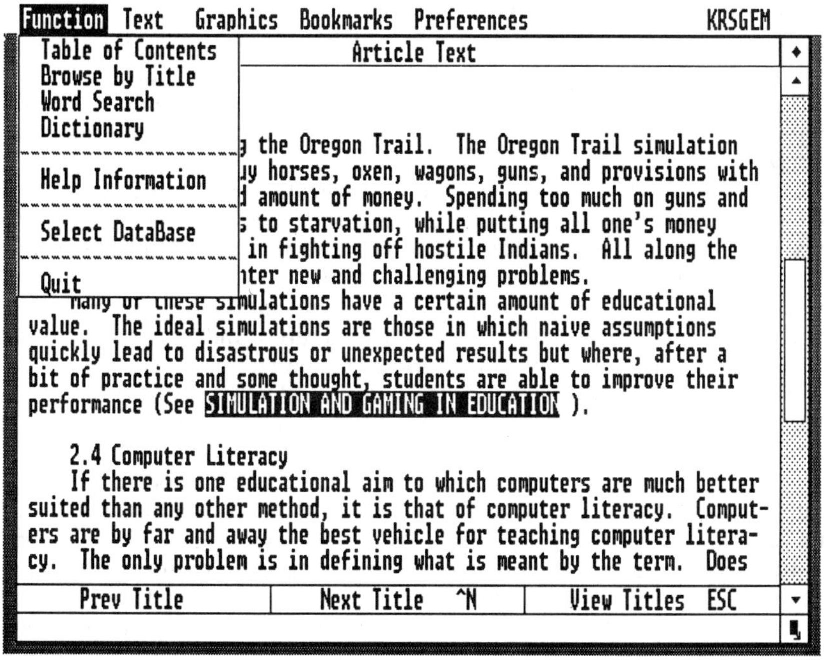

```
┌──────────────────────────────────────────────────────────────┐
│ Function  Text  Graphics  Bookmarks  Preferences       KRSGEM  │
├────────────────────┬───────────────────────────────────────┬──┤
│ Table of Contents  │            Article Text               │♦ │
│ Browse by Title    │                                       │▲ │
│ Word Search        │                                       │  │
│ Dictionary         │ g the Oregon Trail.  The Oregon Trail simulation
│ ─────────────────  │ uy horses, oxen, wagons, guns, and provisions with
│ Help Information   │ d amount of money.  Spending too much on guns and
│ ─────────────────  │ s to starvation, while putting all one's money
│ Select DataBase    │ in fighting off hostile Indians.  All along the
│ ─────────────────  │ ter new and challenging problems.
│ Quit               │
```

Many of these simulations have a certain amount of educational value. The ideal simulations are those in which naive assumptions quickly lead to disastrous or unexpected results but where, after a bit of practice and some thought, students are able to improve their performance (See SIMULATION AND GAMING IN EDUCATION).

2.4 Computer Literacy
If there is one educational aim to which computers are much better suited than any other method, it is that of computer literacy. Computers are by far and away the best vehicle for teaching computer literacy. The only problem is in defining what is meant by the term. Does

```
│ Prev Title  │  Next Title   ^N  │  View Titles  ESC │ ▼
```

Figure 10.1 Graphic Knowledge Retrieval system

Knowledge Retrieval System   Copyright (c) 1987   KnowledgeSet Corp, Monterey,
                                    WORD SEARCH

F1 HELP	F2 SEARCH WORDS
F3 LOOKUP WORDS	F4 SHOW TITLES
F5	F6
F7 NEW QUERY	F8 LOAD QUERY
F9	F10 SELECT SEARCH

Company Name   _____

Address   _____
                 _____

Key Personnel   _____

Parent Group   _____

Company Name   _____

Other Information _____

Enter One or More Search Words Above

KRS TITLE│SELECT SEARCH│WORD SEARCH│   ◄E

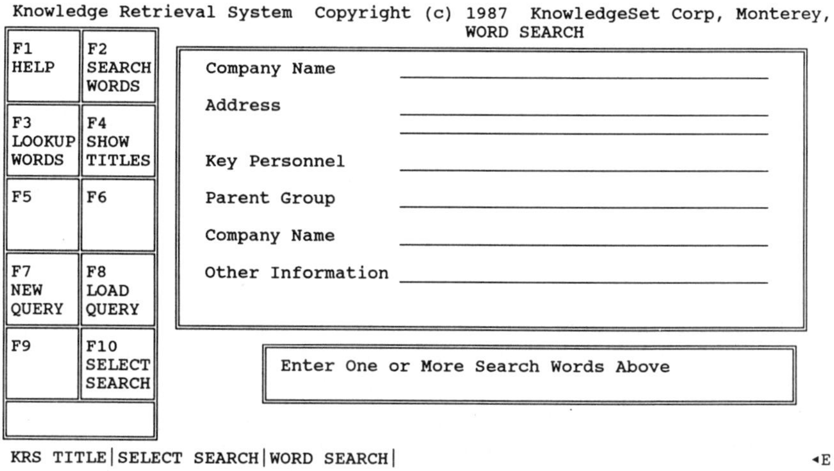

Figure 10.2 Text Knowledge Retrieval system

CD-ROM retrieval systems that started out difficult to use and were subsequently improved by adding 'user-friendly' front ends.

There are two versions of the Knowledge Retrieval System: Text KRS and Graphic KRS. Each is distinctively different in appearance but equally intuitive and easy to use. Graphic KRS is suitable for products that contain both text and graphics, and runs on PC/AT-compatibles with 640K RAM and graphics card/monitor. Text KRS is suitable for text-only CD-ROM applications and runs on a less expensive equipment configuration, a PC-compatible with only 256K RAM.

Graphics KRS (*Figure 10.1*) runs as an application under GEM (Graphics Environment Manager) from Digital Research. There are no commands to type in or complex protocols to learn. The user interacts with KRS using a mouse to manipulate various screen display features such as icons, windows, and pull-down menus. The user selects activities from those available on screen by 'pointing' at one of interest and 'clicking' with the mouse. It is ideal for applications for first-time computer users who feel daunted by the complexity of a keyboard, as well as applications for senior management who have little or no time to learn how to use a new application.

Text KRS (*Figure 10.2*) has the same basic functionality as Graphic KRS but does not need a graphics environment. Activities are selected by pressing function keys; options available at any time are indicated on a keypad at the left of the screen or a menu bar across the bottom. Browsing, searching and other KRS features are just as easy to use in Text KRS and generally involve only a keystroke to implement. The choice between Graphic KRS and Text KRS depends on whether graphics are essential to either the product content (the product contains images as well as text) or presentation requirements. Text KRS is ideal for products that contain text only and are targeted at the low-end PC market.

Hypertext and cross references

Printed products are based on a sequential approach to information. Textual information is written down, edited, typeset and printed as a serial progression of words. Though people may read novels in this serial way from beginning to end, most other publications are read selectively. Publishers generally impose a structure on the information (this book is organized by chapters, headings, etc.) and enhance access by adding a table of contents and indexes to help the user find the information he wants.

The sequential approach to information leads to two-dimensional information products: imagine a horizontal stream of text and a vertical matrix of access points provided by indexes. References to related material tend to interrupt the narrative; users often find that bibliographic references and footnotes, for example, are collected at the end of an article where they do not interfere. Figures or tables cited on one page may be printed on another for convenience of layout. Two-dimensional products are designed around the needs of the publishers but not necessarily the user.

Hypertext is a non-sequential approach to presenting and using information. KRS uses hypertext to allow the user to identify relationships between information and to display related information on screen. This related material may be a figure, a table, another document, a bibliographic reference, the full text of a cited article, biographical information, a 'digression', etc. The hypertext concept involves building links between related material. In KRS these links are referred to as 'hot links'.

KRS takes full advantage of the hypertext approach to information. In KRS hot links are displayed in reverse video. In Graphic KRS, the user 'clicks' on the cross reference; in Text KRS, he presses the function key for HYPERTEXT or HOT LINK. Hot links allow the user to display a selected graphic on the same screen as the text, as illustrated in *Figure 10.3*. Hot links also allow the user to browse through full text or structured databases in an open-ended manner taking advantage of the links between different types of information.

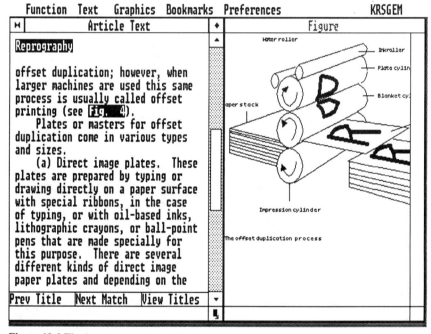

Figure 10.3 The hypertext feature of KRS allows users to display related information, such as a diagram or table

In this context, hypertext can be described as a 'navigational' feature as well as a retrieval feature. It allows the user to create his own branching path through the information following the links he sees as relevant. He will not however become 'lost', as the PATH TO DOCUMENT feature is like leaving a trail of breadcrumbs behind. It will display at a keystroke the documents browsed through, allowing the user to retrace his steps and select a previously viewed document or to return to the beginning. As we move into the new information age, KRS allows publishers to develop three-dimensional CD-ROM products.

Retrieval and access

In KRS, retrieval features are complementary to the hypertext feature allowing more structured access. Printed publications normally have tables of contents and indexes for access, and structured databases have inverted index files. KRS was developed for CD-ROM, so its retrieval features do not attempt to recreate the printed or database approach. In combination they are far more powerful. KRS offers:

● full-text search,
● field specific search,
● hierarchical access,
● browseable indexes.

Full-text search

WORD SEARCH is the full-text search feature of KRS. The Word Search screen is illustrated in *Figure 10.4*. It allows the user to find every occurrence of any word, combination of words or phrase in the CD-ROM database. Each word is individually indexed so that only two access commands to the CD-ROM drive are issued by KRS: one to find the word in the directory and the other to locate it on the disc. This design makes the search and retrieval access speed very fast. Speed is important when searching through millions of words. The full-text search feature is very powerful as it allows the user to take into consideration the following characteristics of each word being searched:

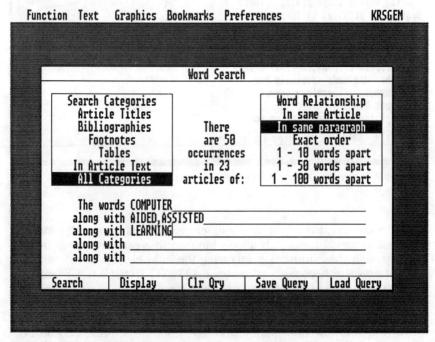

Figure 10.4 The Word Search screen of the Knowledge Retrieval System

- *Context.* Traditional Boolean AND, OR, NOT includes or excludes specific words and their synonyms.
- *Proximity.* Specifies that the words should occur in the same document, in the same paragraph, next to one another, within two words of each other, etc.
- *Type of information.* Restricts the search to certain types of information, e.g. document titles, text, bibliographies, etc.
- *Word stem.* Truncation locates the word root and searches for it with various suffixes.

If a user is unsure of what word to use or how it is spelled, he can look it up in the word index by selecting the DICTIONARY feature.

It has sometimes been argued that full-text search is of limited value as different authors use different terminology, and full-text search focuses on terminology, rather than concepts. This is more often the fault of the data than the search feature itself. On the other hand, it allows the user to look for words he thinks are important in context, not what an indexer thought should be indexed. Publishers should consider the requirements of full-text search in preparing text for CD-ROM. The use of spelling checkers for accuracy and the use of controlled vocabularies for consistency and precision are recommended.

Field-specific search
For files of highly structured records such as databases and bibliographic files, KRS offers a custom-designed screen for field-specific search. Such a screen would list all the searchable fields in a fill-in-the-blank format, allowing the user to type in his search criteria. In the case of a directory database of companies, he might search by company type, size and location; in a bibliographic file, he might search by author, title and publication year.

Hierarchical access
Hierarchical access is access to information through the structure of the information hierarchy. For an encyclopedia, the information hierarchy is alphabetical, and the hierarchical access screen for the *International Encyclopedia of Education* is shown in *Figure 10.5*. For a Yellow Pages directory, the organization is by subject heading and subheading. For any database where documents can be arranged in a hierarchical way, KRS can provide structured access. This like the hypertext feature allows browsing through databases, but in a more structured way. In a database of company information, for example, the user could browse through the classification hierarchy to find 'Software Companies' and within that to find 'Desktop Publishing Systems' for a list of relevant companies.

If the user is familiar with the information hierarchy, he may use the HEADING FINDER feature to save time. Instead of browsing through sets of nested headings and subheadings, it allows him to type in a heading for direct access to that part of the information hierarchy. Hierarchical access is possible right down to the headings and subheadings of the document itself. When a document is displayed on screen the DOCUMENT

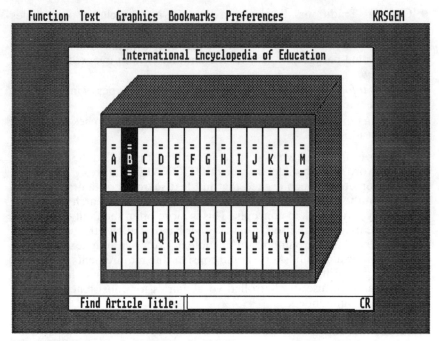

Figure 10.5 Hierarchical access is alphabetical for an encyclopedia such as Pergamon's *International Encyclopedia of Education*

OUTLINE feature displays the various nested headings/subheadings in a highly structured article or the types of data available in a directory listing.

Browseable indexes
Taking advantage of the hypertext feature, it is possible to construct a single hierarchical index, or several indexes, to the information content. These are browseable, in that the user can browse up and down within the hierarchy of index terms and select the most relevant one. Where printed indexes are filled with 'see' references to guide users to the term used by indexers, CD-ROM indexes can allow him to select the terms of his choice by building in appropriate links between related headings.

Every CD-ROM product is different and therefore so will be the access points required. One product may lend itself to full-text search and another to field-specific search; one to browseable contents and another to browseable indexes. KRS offers the flexibility of having all these methods of access along with hypertext browsing. Pergamon has found this to be a unique and flexible combination of search and retrieval features suitable for the requirements of most CD-ROM products.

Graphics

One of the most important features of KRS is its ability to handle graphics, not only to include them as content in a database but to manipulate them on screen and output to disc or printer. Graphic KRS can handle both raster graphics (bit-mapped images) and vector graphics. All the major standard graphics formats are supported by KRS including CCITT Group IV (raster) and IGES, CGM, CGI, GKS and GEM VDI metafile (vector). In layman's language, raster graphics are scanned, stored and displayed as arrays of dots, and vector graphics in terms of straight lines and curves. The type of image and the functionality it is wished to achieve are major factors.

Zoom

Graphic KRS can zoom in and out of vector images. This provides the display versatility required for highly complex images such as CAD/CAM technical drawings and schematics. it is not necessary, however, to use a CAD/CAM system to create vector graphics. A software package as simple and easy to use as GemDraw may be all that is necessary.

Pan

Image panning allows the user to move the image horizontally and vertically within the window of view, whether this is the full-size screen, or a split-screen window allowing him to view both the graphic and the related text. Panning is available for both vector and raster graphics.

For large or complex drawings the zoom feature is very useful. However, for smaller simple graphics that fit easily on the full screen, panning may be adequate. Another factor is the number of graphics the database will contain. A typical raster graphic scanned at 300 dpi might take up 200–300 kilobytes where the equivalent vector graphic might take up 10–60 kilobytes. If a large number of images must be stored, vector graphics are a better solution. The important thing to remember is that KRS gives the publisher the option.

Research features

The research features are a group of productivity tools that make the process of using a CD-ROM database easier and add value to the information. The BOOKMARK feature in Graphic KRS allows the user to put 'electronic' place holders at various points in the CD-ROM database. KRS will 'remember' the exact location of each bookmark and keep a running tally of marks during a search session. The user can call up the bookmark screen for a listing and return to any marked place. At the end of the session the marks can be saved to disc. The AUTOMARK feature will automatically insert a bookmark at every document displayed during a search.

The REFERENCE feature displays a report of all documents in the database that are referred to by the one the user is viewing. This is an important feature where hypertext links are used extensively and enhances the browsing capability. The reverse of the REFERENCE feature, the CITATION feature displays a report of all documents in the database that cite the one the user is now viewing. This is an example of the kind of value-added feature that does not exist for print or online. The REFERENCE and CITATION features allow the user to take advantage of 'citation analysis' techniques and develop clusters of related documents.

Developer options

The features mentioned earlier are some of the most important features of
KRS and illustrate its advanced functionality. Pergamon has found that
one of its most important other features is its flexibility and adaptability to
a range of different forms of information. Where other system integrators
have licensed several different CD-ROM retrieval systems to cater for the
requirements of different products, Pergamon has found KRS flexible and
adaptable enough to be used successfully in the context of most products.
The combination of search and browsing features, hypertext hot links,
graphics and research features provides a range of features suitable for
most types of information.

Pergamon Compact Solution works with publishers to identify the right
features for their CD-ROM products and tailors each feature to their
requirements.

Pergamon Compact Solution

Pergamon Compact Solution offers a complete range of services for CD-
ROM product creation. These are described more fully below and include:
include:

- product design,
- data capture and conversion,
- CD-ROM data preparation,
- retrieval software,
- production,
- packaging,
- user manuals and customer support services.

The more technical stages of product creation have been well described
in the literature and are therefore covered only briefly here.

Product design
This is probably the most important service offered by a system integrator.
It is the process that translates user needs into a CD-ROM product with
the right content and features, performs a useful function, and fits easily
into his work environment. The design process therefore begins with a
study of who the 'users' actually are and how they currently use the
information proposed for the CD-ROM product. CD-ROM is a solution
for various information problems, so a prime objective is to determine
what problems are associated with the information itself, its access,
organization, presentation or present medium. Most of the design work is
done on paper and might include a functional specification (description of
features), sample screens, and sample search scenarios.

Data capture
The first technical stage in creating a CD-ROM is to get all the data in
machine-readable form, both text and graphics. There are several ways to
proceed depending on the data started with, the type of product wanted
and the way the retrieval software and data preparation software will inter-

act with the data. The following are the main techniques used, and more than one may be used on any particular product:

- keyboarding,
- optical character recognition,
- digital scanning,
- vectorization.

Data capture is generally done by bureau services. It is often advantageous for the system integrator to arrange for data capture so that any generic or structural coding is done at the time of capture.

Data conversion

Once the raw data is in machine-readable form it is converted to a standard record format so that the data preparation process may begin. The data conversion process for text generally involves developing software to format each record in a standard way, identify the types of information in each record using generic or structured coding, and strip out or replace typesetting or other unnecessary codes. Pergamon Compact Solution recommends the use of codes based on SGML (Standard Generic Markup Language).

For graphics, conversion may involve conversion between different graphics standards. Pergamon Compact Solution performs the necessary conversion from any other graphics format to the ones suitable for KRS. In the case of both text and graphics, this stage involves both software development to accomplish the conversion and the conversion itself.

Data preparation

Data preparation is a multistep process designed to structure the data for storage, manipulation and retrieval from the CD-ROM. The process must necessarily take into consideration the retrieval software that will interact with the data. Pergamon Compact Solution uses the proprietary data preparation software of Publishers Data Service Corporation (PDSC). This was developed to prepare CD-ROM databases for use with KRS retrieval software.

Data preparation itself involves structuring, indexing and inverting the database. Separate indexes and tables with location pointers are created for titles, descriptors, document outlines, word directories, etc., which list pointers to every unique occurrence of every word. Proprietary tables speed up access times, correct certain kinds of database errors and reformat the database to CD-ROM media specifications.

A highly recommended part of this phase involves running the inverted index through a spelling checker. This not only improves accuracy but minimizes false drops during full-text search. Finally, the database is cross referenced and encrypted if necessary. When database testing is complete, a pre-mastering tape is prepared.

Database testing and prototype creation

These are of course part of the data preparation phase but a separate quality assurance exercise. There are two approaches. Either a small fragment of data can be prepared and downloaded to the PC for testing, or the entire data file can be prepared and previewed directly on the VAX. There are of course checking and control programs run at various stages of the data preparation, but there is no substitute for actually testing the fully prepared file before manufacturing begins.

Retrieval software customization
As mentioned previously, there are two generic versions of the Knowledge Retrieval System: Text KRS and Graphic KRS. As every CD-ROM product is different, either one of the generic versions will probably require a bit of tailoring in terms of its features to suit both the data and how users will interact with it. The user interface (what the user sees on the screen in terms of information, menu options and prompts, for example) will require similar adjustments. Help screens must be rewritten for the level of the target audience as well as for the data displayed.

Production
When all testing is completed, the data preparation phase concludes with creation of a pre-mastering tape. This is sent to a suitable manufacturing facility where the CD-ROM is mastered and the required number of copies are made (replication). The CD-ROM discs contain the structured data, indexes, supporting directories and files all to agreed standards (High Sierra, for example). The CD-ROM may also contain the retrieval software, or alternatively this may be delivered on a separate floppy disc.

Packaging
The CD-ROMs (and retrieval software) are delivered to the client according to his requirements. He may, for example, have requested a special label design and asked for the discs to be packaged in jewel boxes. Jewel box presentation can be further enhanced with artwork and descriptive information about the product. The client can, of course, arrange for more extensive packaging.

User manuals and customer support services
The nature of the CD-ROM product and its audience will generally determine the type of support it will require. In most cases, the better the design and execution of the product, the less documentation and support it will require. For most CD-ROM products, some sort of user manual will be required. However, a product with a well-designed user interface that clearly indicates all options, together with well written help screens, can considerably reduce its size. Pergamon Compact Solution can custom write manuals to a client's requirements, or prepare more than one, for example one for users and one for their managers. Training, customer support and user 'hot line' services are all available, as are other customer services such as product distribution.

Phases of development

The activities listed above are all part of the development process. This process has three main phases: initial consultation, feasibility study and product simulation, and CD-ROM product design and development.

Initial consultation

During the initial 'information gathering' stage, the client will learn about Pergamon Compact Solution, the services and pricing, and how to develop CD-ROM products. Pergamon will learn about the client's CD-ROM project — in particular the source data, who uses it and in what way, and what he has in mind for a CD-ROM product. It is often useful to bring along some samples of the various data types.

Feasibility study and product simulation

During this phase, samples of all data types in all formats that will be included in the final product are examined. The work required to create a CD-ROM product from the data is analysed in detail and a report prepared covering:

- assessment of the product's suitability for CD-ROM,
- list of the proposed product's features,
- note of any features likely to require particular care and effort,
- analysis of the key differences between the simulation and the final product,
- product design and software development programme,
- budget estimate for development programme.

A unique feature of the feasibility phase is the creation of a product simulation on floppy disc. The product simulation will contain a small amount of data (0.5–1.0 megabytes) and will illustrate the main features of the final CD-ROM product, without the expense of major software development. The simulation is useful both for preliminary market research and to further refine the product specification.

Though the source data is examined in detail and data conversion requirements are assessed, no data conversion software is written at this stage. For the purposes of simulation it is generally more cost effective to rekey than to convert.

CD-ROM product design and development

The product design phase concentrates on identifying user needs and requirements and translating them into a product specification. This generally includes a detailed description of the product, its features, how data can be searched and manipulated, displayed and output. Sample screens will be provided to illustrate typical search scenarios. The product specification is agreed before development work begins.

Technical development and production phases include:

- data capture (if required),
- software development for data conversion,
- data conversion,
- CD-ROM database creation and data preparation,
- retrieval software customization,
- user interface development,
- database testing and prototype creation,
- mastering and replication.

All work is done according to quotation agreed in advance. Timetables and quotes obviously depend on the work required and the complexity of the project.

Product 1: CD-ROM chemical information retrieval system

The goals and objectives of Pergamon's chemistry CD-ROM project and the proposal to the Commission of the European Communities are covered earlier. As soon as contract terms were agreed with the CEC, planning and development work began on this challenging project. First a detailed work programme was agreed with the CEC, dividing the work into four phases:

Phase I   Product design and system development; creation of a product simulation.
Phase II Data capture and conversion of text and chemical structures.
Phase III CD-ROM data preparation: database creation, inversion and testing.
Phase IV CD-ROM production: pre-mastering, mastering and replication.

It should be kept in mind that the goal was to create both a retrieval system and a series of CD-ROM products. This meant that the initial design phase was the most important as well as the most difficult. The design for the system would have to take into consideration both the specific requirements of Pergamon's *Comprehensive Heterocyclic Chemistry* and the more general features of Pergamon's other comprehensive works, and yet be flexible enough to handle the chemical reference works of other publishers and corporate chemical databases. However, before embarking on any product design and development, it was necessary to evaluate user requirements and therefore conduct some market research.

Preliminary market research

For any novel or complex enterprise, market research is a continuing aspect of the product development cycle. Different types of research can be done at different stages.

● Preliminary market research provides data on how the information contained in the product will be used, and allows designers to specify the product and its features.
● Intermediate market research gives feedback on the product prototype, and will determine whether we have designed a useful product with the right features.
● The final market research will determine the success of the ultimate product and provide feedback to the design of future products.

Having identified a new product concept, it was felt that it would be essential to consult potential users. Panels of chemists were convened to find out how they use printed chemical reference works. The following summarizes some of the results of these meetings:

● The chemists were receptive to the concept of chemical reference works on CD-ROM. They viewed CD-ROM as complementary to printed works. Their libraries would continue to purchase printed works and the chemists would buy the CD-ROM version for personal reference.

● Structure and substructure search would be the most important feature. Without this there would be no point in creating a CD-ROM product.

● Good graphics would be essential as chemists put a high value on the aesthetic visual appeal of chemical structures.

● Some reference works age more gracefully than others. Pergamon's series of 'comprehensive' works, which give an overview of a subject area at introductory research level, tend to date less rapidly than more time-sensitive works aimed at more advanced and specialist researchers.

● There are several distinct user groups of the printed work, and each uses it in a different way. For example, specialists (heterocyclic chemists) vs general users (organic chemists), researchers vs students, and academic vs industrial users all differ in the type of information they want and how they find it. A detailed study of use by type of user might allow Pergamon to structure and even author future major works for different audiences.

In addition they emphasized that no chemical reference work is used on its own. It is normally used in the context of other reference works and of course the primary work cited. Suggestions such as 'can you include all the journal articles as well as *CHC*?', though unfeasible, are reflections of how information is used and must be considered seriously.

In the context of using one type of information with another, it was also noted that they wanted the capability to manipulate the information delivered on CD-ROM in a personal way. They wanted, for example, to download data to their PC and use it with other software (wordprocessor, database, etc.) to print out structures and schemes. This suggested we should not only take a look at the use of PCs and software in their offices and labs, but keep up with new products that might alter their perception/expectation of what a computer can do.

Phase I: product design and system development

The following sections describe the Phase I work in greater detail, because this is the most critical work of the project. At the time of writing this article, Pergamon has progressed to Phase II. It is anticipated that Phase IV will be complete by the end of 1988. Though Phases II–IV are not specifically described here, they are generic stages of any CD-ROM project, and as such are described elsewhere in this chapter.

The specific objectives of Phase I were to:

● specify and design the retrieval system and first CD-ROM product,
● integrate the CD-ROM and chemical software components,
● create a system simulation illustrating basic features,
● assess development work necessary to convert typesetting tapes to a usable form.

The first task was to write specifications for the retrieval system, the first product and the simulation that were detailed enough to begin development work, yet generic enough to accommodate design changes later. At this early stage not all the answers could be known.

Functional specification

Before initiating the project a requirements specification had been prepared. In the end, this served as a functional specification with very little modification. It might be useful to clarify the difference between the two. The requirements specification was our 'wish list' for the system/ product and served as a tender document to identify partners in the development work. It was therefore written in terms of what would be ideal and desirable, not necessarily what would be feasible or possible.

A functional specification, on the other hand, should specify precisely what a system or product is, what it can do, what features it has, and what a user can do to it or with it. It is very much written in terms of the possible and the achievable. The content will vary considerably depending on the type of product described. Headings included in the functional specification included the following:

- target audience,
- information content,
- retrieval features,
- browsing features,
- graphics features,
- navigational features,
- user interface,
- display features,
- output options,
- hardware configuration,
- retrieval times expected.

Information in each category was descriptive, in plain English, indicating what each feature would do and would look like, how it would be used and what the end result would be. No attempt was made to specify how each feature would work technically, how it would be developed or implemented.

As a system integrator with considerably more experience in both writing and evaluating functional specifications, Pergamon is still pleased with this approach. It is the only sound basis from which to proceed to creating a design specification. And in the end, it is the yardstick against which the final product can be measured.

Design specification

The purpose of a design specification is to plan out on paper all the technical work that must be performed to achieve a system/product with the features described in the functional specification. The CD-ROM chemical retrieval system was not started from scratch. Hampden's PSIDOM software and KnowledgeSet's Knowledge Retrieval System are both self-contained and functional retrieval systems.

In order to create the design specification the following points were considered:

- features described in the functional specification,
- generic characteristics of the chemical data to be input, stored, retrieved

and output,

- specific characteristics of the data contained in *Comprehensive Heterocyclic Chemistry*, the first work to be published on CD-ROM using the new retrieval system,
- chemical structure handling characteristics of the PSIDOM software,
- text and graphics handling characteristics of the KRS software working in a GEM environment,
- modifications required to both PSIDOM and KRS to achieve desired system features,
- system architecture required to integrate PSIDOM and KRS to achieve the desired links between text and chemical structures.

The above points were considered independently by the three parties (Pergamon, Hampden Data Services, KnowledgeSet) and jointly at several working meetings. In the end a design was agreed, as was a work programme and timetable.

System product simulation

Having decided on the work involved in creating the final fully functional system, the next step was to build in appropriate tests along the way. The first test would be a small magnetic media simulation to test the basic design assumptions. It would demonstrate essential system features, such as chemical structure search and display. Hopefully it would allow Pergamon to make preliminary assessments of system performance against expectation and to obtain feedback from potential users.

A list of all features wanted in the ultimate system was drawn up, and those features that could be included in the first simulation were ticked off. This list included the existing features of Graphic KRS applied to a chemical reference work, such as full-text search, hypertext hot links to chemical structures and bibliographic references, text manipulation features such as 'bookmarking' and graphic manipulation features such as 'zooming' in on structures and schemes.

A limit on what could be realistically accomplished for the first simulation was set. In retrospect, it seems the exercise of setting achievable goals for the first simulation was a good one. First, it allowed concentration on the most essential features in the initial stages, rather than getting bogged down in how to handle refinements too soon. Secondly, it set aside a group of features to concentrate on in the next development phase. It made the task of selecting a representative data fragment fairly straightforward, as it was known what was to be demonstrated. Lastly, the benchmarks against which the simulation could be judged were set.

Criteria were established for selecting the text and graphics to be contained in the first simulation. There had to be enough text and graphics on one subject in order to conduct meaningful text and structure searches. Material selected had to be representative of *CHC* and organic chemistry in general, yet include a range of variations and complexities to test the system. A total of 100 pages of text, plus 1550 single structures and 2250 schemes, were included.

A second simulation would be created at the end of the second phase that would demonstrate all system features. By then there would be a much larger data fragment on which to test these features. If work proceeded according to plan, the entire content of *CHC* would be available in machine-readable form and it would be possible to test retrieval times and system efficiency as well as functionality.

Software development

The design specification outlined the technical work to be done. This involved a series of enhancements and modifications to both the PSIDOM software and the KRS software, followed by a further phase of integration. Pergamon supervised the actual development work. This was carried out by Hampden Data Services and KSC at their premises. Data fragments were exchanged by VAX link and data post. All parties were posted of progress by phone and VAX mail.

It will not surprise readers to learn that the software development process took longer than expected. This was partly because of the physical distance between the parties: Pergamon in London, Hampden Data Services near Oxford and KnowledgeSet in California. The distance had an impact on communication; when it was 5p.m. in London/Oxford, it was 9a.m. in California. Telephone sessions at regular intervals were necessary as it was easy to get out of touch.

The development process also took longer because all those involved had numerous other projects under way, each with their own schedules and priorities. It was difficult to keep the project on a schedule so that each person received data fragments and software modules from the others when it was most convenient in the context of other work.

Text capture and conversion

One of the reasons that *CHC* was selected as Pergamon's first CD-ROM product was that the text existed in machine-readable form, that of type-setting tapes held by the typesetter of the original printed work. Though it would have been preferable to start with a well-structured 'neutral' file or database, Pergamon was quite prepared to have a go at using a typesetting tape. By 'reverse engineering' they hoped to determine how *CHC* should have been structured, and therefore how future major works should be structured.

Analysis of the typesetting tapes was done by Pergamon Orbit InfoLine in conjunction with BPCC Graphics (Information Services Division). The latter company is not only expert in typesetting but in more advanced methods of electronic publishing, the use of SGML, and the creation of well-structured databases from typesetting files or ones created for different original purposes. The *CHC* typesetting tapes were analysed to determine the following:

● whether the tapes corresponded to the printed work word-for-word, and in the correct order,
● what coding was used, e.g. for fonts, formatting, special characters, tables etc.,

- presence of tags for cross reference, e.g. to/from index entries, biblio-graphic references, chemical structures and schemes, related text etc.,
- approximate cost to convert to a well-structured data file, e.g. using SGML.

The results were somewhat depressing.

Equivalence
The tapes and the printed work were judged to be non-equivalent. This is largely because corrected material was added to the tapes; the original computer file was not changed. This means that some pages appeared twice, some appeared to be missing and there were entire sections of 'author corrections'. In addition, the basic elements of the text (headings, paragraphs, tables etc.) were grouped according to element, and within groupings in apparently random order.

Coding
The typesetter was unable to supply a definitive list of codes used, as the job had been completed some time ago. If such a list was wanted, it should have been asked for while the job was in progress. This meant reconstruct-ing a table from scratch. This was possible, although time consuming. It was rather a surprise to learn that once a typesetting job is complete, there may be no archival record of the codes used. There may be a generic set of codes used, but individuals may use their own variations. When they have gone on to the next job or left the company, a translation table of codes may be very difficult for the typesetter to construct.

Tags from text to related material
There were no tags in the text linking it with related text, graphics or index information. Cross references to chemical structures, schemes and biblio-graphic references could be built fairly easily, but cross references to related text, such as 'see p. 572', would present a problem. Only the indexer knew where on page 572 the cross reference referred. There were also no links between the text and index terms, so again these would have to be constructed manually.

Cost to restructure
A quote was obtained to convert the typesetting tapes into a well-structured database, and interestingly it was about the same as the quote received to rekey the entire text. On the basis of equivalent quotes it would actually be better to rekey as this would include verification to 99.95% accuracy. If typesetting tapes were converted, it would leave the task of proofreading against the printed page to ensure that all corrections had been made. Either case would need the assistance of a trained chemical indexer to identify links between index terms and the text (to paragraph level), and between citations in the text and the text referred to.

Data capture for simulation

Considering the small amount of text to be included in the simulation and the complexity of working from the typesetting tapes, it was decided to rekey the two chapters rather than write conversion programs. The text was captured by Saztec Europe Ltd by rekeying according to agreed guidelines.

Independent tests were performed comparing optical character recognition (OCR) with rekeying for *CHC*. Bureau services are available that use OCR, so this was obviously a method to consider if the data capture work was contracted out. But as high-quality OCR equipment is also now fairly inexpensive to purchase, doing the data capture inhouse was also an option. The Kurzweil 4000 Intelligent Scanner, which recognizes character shapes instead of fonts, and had the potential to be more versatile for a variety of rekeying jobs, was impressive.

Tests were devised to compare OCR with rekeying considering accuracy, speed, manual intervention required, flexibility of output and overall cost. In the end it was decided that though top-rated scanners like the 4000 were excellent for straightforward text, they were not suitable for complex chemistry text containing many special characters, subscripts and superscripts. Too much manual supervision and intervention was required to give us the accuracy needed, whether a bureau did the work or it was done inhouse. And in either case proofreading would be essential.

Hampden Data Services captured the chemical structures as connection tables, each with a unique registry number, allowing a link to be made to the relevant text. A different option for capturing the structures would have been simply to scan the original artwork, creating a digitized image (bit map) of each structure or scheme, exactly as it appears on the printed page. The disadvantage of this method is of course that scanning 'loses' the chemical information; the end product is an array of dots that can be displayed but not searched. In order to retrieve the graphics in an intelligent way, it would be necessary to create an indexing system with chemical tags for each graphic. This was felt to involve too much manual intervention and would not achieve the chemical structure and substructure search that chemists wanted.

Lessons learned

The chemical information retrieval system was Pergamon's first CD-ROM project. Even though the project is not complete, both Pergamon Press, the publisher, and Pergamon Compact Solution, the system integrator, have learned a great deal, most importantly in the area of project organization and management.

Project management

From the beginning it was felt that a 'team' approach to the project would be best: a team to pool their ideas and develop the project concept, several companies to share the development work (Pergamon, KnowledgeSet and Hampden Data Services), and the Pergamon Group to benefit from the experience. The most important 'lesson' learned is that the more individuals and companies are involved in a project, the more important project management becomes, and in particular the importance of designating one person as Project Manager.

By appointing a Project Manager the 'team' approach need not be lost.

His role is to manage the resources of those involved in the project, not to do all the work himself. In order to manage, he will need not only the social and organizational skills necessary to motivate the individuals involved and encourage them to work well together, but the authority to set priorities, assign schedules, take decisions and ensure that all involved perform to expectation.

The second lesson learned is also associated with project discipline: the importance of setting goals and objectives in advance and developing from these an effective project plan and work programme. Without this approach, and indeed a good project planning software package, it would not have been possible to put together the proposal for the CEC. By dividing larger tasks into smaller ones we were always dealing with manageable units of work, and at the end of the day could account for all work done and by specific individuals.

Structuring information

The insights into effective project management were perhaps more valuable to Pergamon Compact Solution than to Pergamon Press. Both did benefit directly from the study of typesetting tapes for this and other projects. It was found that a typesetting tape was not the ideal starting point for creating a well-structured CD-ROM database. Indeed the process of converting typesetting tapes to an accurate and usable data file can be the same cost as starting from scratch.

It was now possible to tell Pergamon Press what would be preferable in future: a neutral text file containing information about document structure (SGML codes) but no information about formatting or typography. The file should contain embedded links to all related material, e.g. index entries, text cross references, bibliographic references, etc. Links should be specific and to a relevant structural unit, e.g. article, section, paragraph, etc., not to a 'page', which does not exist in a CD-ROM document.

During the course of the chemical information retrieval system project and others, Pergamon Compact Solution was able to put together a list of 'dos and don'ts' for structuring information for CD-ROM. It is not surprising to find that it was very similar to Pergamon Press's own approach for structuring full-text reference works or BPCC Graphics' (Information Services Division) approach to structuring technical documentation. All were structuring information for electronic publishing, allowing maximum flexibility for creating more than one information product or outputting the information on more than one medium.

It was not, however, suggested that Pergamon Press adopt this electronic publishing approach for all of its books and journals. As a publisher, Pergamon Press is expert in determining what information is right for a particular market, at what price and on what medium (print, online, microform, CD-ROM, etc.). After assessment of the market requirements for each information product, often only one medium will be found appropriate. It may be more cost effective to structure the information for the one relevant output medium.

On the other hand, where a publisher forsees that the information might be delivered in more than one way, to perhaps two different audiences, the investment in structuring information for multimedia output can be justified. Pergamon has used this approach for creating complementary products (print and CD-ROM, print and online, etc.), new editions of reference works, and supplements and subsets of larger reference works.

Product 2: *International Encyclopedia of Education*

Goals and objectives

Pergamon had initially decided to conduct a CD-ROM 'experiment' with technology, which would identify the problems involved in creating a successful product and allow them to develop solutions. The first project initiated was the chemical information retrieval system, an ambitious project that would take two years to complete. Both Pergamon Compact Solution and Pergamon Press wanted to get 'hands on' experience within a shorter time frame. It was also clear that certain aspects of *Comprehensive Heterocyclic Chemistry* would be quite complex, for example display and printing of tables, data conversion from typesetting tapes, cross referencing and indexing. A less complex reference work was needed to tackle first.

There was a discrete group of technical, editorial and marketing issues to address in the short term. Technical issues included data conversion, graphics and the CD-ROM data preparation process itself. Editorial and marketing issues were interrelated. A CD-ROM product is designed for a specific group of users. The product content, its features and user interface should be designed for that audience. Once created, the product must be marketed and promoted using the most effective techniques and distributed through the right channels. The sooner a demonstration product was available to show authors, editors and potential users, the sooner they could get feedback on product features and commission future reference works with CD-ROM in mind.

Pergamon's *International Encyclopedia of Education* was selected for the following reasons:

- it had been recently published,
- it had received rave reviews and won the prestigious Dartmouth Medal,
- most of the content was nontechnical text,
- illustrations and tables were not too complex,
- it was large enough to illustrate the capabilities of CD-ROM (10 volumes, over 5600 pages),
- the text was available in machine-readable form.

The objective was to create an interactive encyclopedia on CD-ROM using the entire content of *IEE* and the Knowledge Retrieval System. KRS is ideally suited to full-text files such as encyclopedias, and the graphic version of KRS allows users to display text or graphics, or both at once on the same screen. KRS features such as full-text search, open-ended browsing via cross references, and the research features would not only add value to the information in terms of convenience, but would allow users to manipulate the information in ways that are impossible with print.

The following sections describe some of the issues dealt with, problems faced and decisions made in creating the CD-ROM version of the encyclopedia. Because space is limited, the following sections concentrate on the relationship between functionality and the way data is structured. An electronic information product is normally judged by whether it gives users the functionality they want; whether they can find the information they are looking for and display it in a meaningful way. Retrieval, display and overall functionality depend on how the information is structured.

Creation of the printed encyclopedia

Pergamon Press had long been in the business of publishing academic reference works. The *International Encyclopedia of Education* had been an ambitious project including 1448 articles, totalling some 5 million words, submitted by 1300 contributors. The printed version was published in 10 volumes, nine volumes of articles (A–Z) and a separate volume of indexes. A project of such proportions led Pergamon to develop a sophisticated system for manuscript control, markup and coding, indexing and editing.

The system allowed Pergamon Press to input each article as it came in and link to it related information such as author and subject index terms, contributors' names and addresses, and cross references to other articles. Indexes and the list of contributor names and addresses could be generated automatically from the central file of articles. Changes could be made to the entire file, such as altering an article title along with all cross references to it. Decisions on format and typography could be made at any stage up to final pagination.

In terms of flexibility and editorial control, the system was certainly an advance over previous manual systems. It was hoped to reap the benefits in terms of deriving a well-structured CD-ROM file from a well-structured text file. To a large extent this succeeded. Pergamon Press, however, saw the system as an editorial 'front end' to a more complete encyclopedia production system.

Just as work was beginning on the CD-ROM version of *IEE*, Pergamon Press and BPCC Graphics (Information Services Division) completed the new production system that uses generic coding throughout. One might say that the original system had an intelligent front end, but the new system is entirely intelligent! It not only captures text intelligently, but allows it to be stored and updated easily; subsets of a larger work can be extracted and supplement volumes produced.

Typesetting tapes

When work began on creating a CD-ROM version of *IEE,* this new intelligent production system was not available. A set of typesetting tapes derived from the original text file was used. The macros, mnemonics and command codes inserted during the editorial input process had been replaced with typesetting codes. BPCC Graphics undertook the task of examining the tapes in detail, to see how much work would be involved to create a neutral well-structured file of articles. From this new file, printed and electronic products could be produced.

Format

A typesetting tape is used to drive a particular typesetting machine. It is not therefore compatible with most computers (PCs, minis or mainframes) without reformatting. Utilities had to be written so that Pergamon could read the tapes on the VAX, insert block headings and trailers, and impose a record structure.

Content

The tapes contained all the text and tables, but not illustrations (line drawings and halftones) or display maths. The entire content of each article was accurate and corresponded directly to the printed version, and all articles were held in alphabetical sequence on the tapes.

Coding

As with *CHC,* BPCC Graphics would have to develop a translation table for the typesetter's codes. Some of the problems later in data conversion went back to this reverse engineering process. Though the tables were simple, the coding was complex.

Cross references

Cross references ('see' and 'see also' references) had been constructed using article numbers. There were no 'see p. 572' cross references to unscramble. It was, therefore, possible to use existing cross references in the file without problem.

Indexes

Author and subject indexes entries were listed as part of each article. The coding was complex, partly because the subject index itself was complex, with a three-level hierarchy and 'see' references that catered for alternative terminology. Nevertheless, indexing, like cross references, was precise, with index terms referring to individual paragraphs. Unfortunately it was found that the indexes on tape did not correspond precisely to those in the printed product. Corrections had been made at page proof stage and the terms associated with individual articles had not been updated in the file.

Once the tapes were examined, Pergamon Compact Solution decided to create the CD-ROM version of *IEE* directly from the tapes. The system of coding would require care and attention to unravel, but the entire text file (with the exception of index terms) was accurate and corresponded to the printed product. It would therefore not be necessary to proofread the file for accuracy.

Putting the text on CD-ROM

One of the best features of the Knowledge Retrieval System is that it allows a developer to create a CD-ROM product in which every word or phrase is searchable. The *International Encyclopedia of Education* is by no means the largest of encyclopedias ever published, but even so the ability to search all five million words would be remarkable. The text was captured accurately in machine-readable form and the team embarked on the data conversion and CD-ROM data preparation of the text file.

Pergamon decided to concentrate on the text file, and put this on CD-ROM. During the phase of technology transfer from KnowledgeSet to Pergamon Compact Solution several projects were worked on jointly, and *IEE* was the first. From the typesetting tapes and a preliminary list of codes they developed data conversion software (an 'input filter') for the file, performed the CD-ROM data preparation, and created a CD-ROM. This CD-ROM was available at the Frankfurt Book Fair in October 1986. Staff of Pergamon Compact Solution and KnowledgeSet/PDSC were on hand to answer questions about the product creation process itself, the KRS retrieval software and Pergamon's new service.

Pergamon Compact Solution examined in detail the first CD-ROM, the original text file and the input filter. They identified a small but well-defined set of problems to resolve before production of the next CD-ROM. All subsequent work on the *Encyclopedia* was done by Pergamon Compact Solution.

Missing articles

The first surprise was that some 40 articles were missing from the first CD-ROM! The typesetter said that all articles were on the tapes sent to BPCC Graphics, and BPCC Graphics said that all articles were on the reformatted tapes sent to KnowledgeSet and Pergamon Orbit InfoLine. They were not, however, on the tapes received. This was a small problem to correct, and a tape containing the missing articles was soon supplied. It is mentioned here as a problem that all publishers and system integrators should be aware of in order to build in appropriate quality control measures at all stages of product development. Once a tape has left a company, a printout may indicate what is (or should be) on it, but manual checking on receipt is necessary.

Missing text

A more complex problem to solve was the fact that sentences and paragraphs were missing from individual articles on the first CD-ROM. This went back to the original coding used and the fact that there was not a complete translation table to start with. When the conversion software met a code it did not understand, it could not 'handle' the text following it, until it met a code it did understand. Again, this was a simple problem to correct, through further conversations with the typesetter and building a more complete table of codes. But it is again a problem publishers should be aware of, as the disappearance of individual sentences and paragraphs is difficult to detect in a text file of several hundred megabytes! Strict quality control procedures are essential.

Cross references

KRS uses hypertext hot links to allow the user access to other parts of the database referred to in the main text file. Cross references in the text to figures, tables, and other articles are displayed on screen in reverse video. The user can 'point' at them with the mouse and 'click' to display the related material, such as a figure. The data conversion process identifies in the text what constitutes a cross reference, and the links themselves are built in during the data preparation process.

In building a systematic network of cross references, it was necessary to accommodate the fact that individual authors had written their articles in a nonsystematic way. Where one author referred to 'Fig. 1' another referred to 'Figure 1'. There were cross references to several figures at once, for example 'see Figs. 1 and 2' or 'see Figs. 1–4' and, of course, all permutations of capitalization and punctuation.

Inconsistencies like 'Figure' and 'Fig.' are easily identified by examining the inverted index. Either a uniform cross reference system can be implemented or the various permutations can be catered for in the input filter. A worse problem was the absence of a complete cross reference ('in the following Figure') or where figures or tables were not mentioned in the text at all. In the case of incomplete or nonexistent cross references, all occurrences had to be identified and the text file edited.

Special characters

Almost all of the text file comprised standard English character text, numbers and the symbols found on any typewriter keyboard. They could, therefore, be handled by the standard ASCII character set of upper and lower case letters, numbers and symbols. Most of the remaining symbols were handled using the IBM extended character set, again an international standard that includes Greek characters and international currency symbols.

There were a few outstanding characters not included in the above 256 IBM-compatible sets. For these, a display font was created, and substituted for one of the 256 characters that did not occur in the *Encyclopedia*. When a word or equation containing the special character was displayed on screen, the user would see the character just as in the text and would be unaware from the presentation that the font was specially created. The character, however, is not searchable, and should it occur in the middle of a word or otherwise searchable character string, the word would not be searchable.

In context, it is unlikely that users would wish to search for these strings, so this was felt to be a fair tradeoff against accurate display. The other alternative would have been to spell out special characters (perhaps in brackets), in order to make them searchable. Experiments showed that display was not only adversely affected, but users would need guidance on how to 'spell out' the special characters.

Figures

The text file contained references to the figures but did not contain the illustrations themselves. The illustrations were available on the printed pages of the *Encyclopedia* itself and as original artwork at Pergamon Press. The problem was to decide how to incorporate the illustrations into the CD-ROM product, providing users with the greatest functionality and Pergamon with as little manual intervention as possible.

Our first decision was to take advantage of the KRS hypertext feature. KRS indicates the existence of related material when a citation in the text ('see Figure 1') is displayed in reverse video. Users can point to the cross reference in the text and call up the related material. This allows the user to focus on the unbroken text narrative, the choice of viewing an illustration or not, and the ease of 'clicking' once with the mouse to do so. This feature also allows developers to deal with text and graphics as different files with different display requirements.

The next decision was how to capture the graphics in machine-readable form: the options were to digitize the images using a scanner or to create vector representations using a drawing program. The most important factor was functionality from the user's point of view. The user had to be able to see the entire picture accurately on a standard PC monitor with low or medium resolution graphics (CGA or EGA). He had to be able to print it out using a standard dot matrix printer. We could not assume that he owned a high-resolution monitor or a laser printer. After considerable experimentation, it was decided that creating a file of vector graphics using a drawing program was the best option.

Raster vs vector graphics
As previously mentioned, raster graphics are scanned, stored and displayed as arrays of dots, and vector graphics in terms of straight lines and curves. A few more sweeping generalizations can be made. Raster graphics, on the whole, take up more space than vector graphics. Illustrations with grey scales, like halftones, lend themselves to raster scanning, and illustrations like line drawings and graphs lend themselves to vector treatment. Lastly, vector graphics look better than raster graphics on a low-resolution screen. Even if you capture a graphic at high resolution, enough of the information may be 'lost' on a low-resolution screen so that details and fine print are unreadable.

KRS and graphics manipulation
KRS allows developers the choice of storing and displaying either raster or vector graphics, or some of each within the same database. The user is able to manipulate vector graphics on screen using the GRAPHICS function menu. He can ZOOM IN and take a closer look, ZOOM OUT, or return to a FULL PAGE view. For a particular database, the number of levels of zoom can be set according to the size of illustrations, but 3–5 are normal. Text associated with the graphic can be 'filtered out' at overview zoom levels. The user can also pan around the illustration to move it horizontally or vertically on screen. With a raster graphic, panning is normally the only way to manipulate the scanned image. For large illustrations or complex illustrations, it would be a disadvantage not to be able to view both detail and overview.

Considering functionality, target hardware configuration and that most of the original illustrations were line drawings, it was decided to store them as vectors.

Vector input
The options were to create vectors using a drawing program or to input raster images and convert these to vectors. Drawing options ranged from GemDraw to sophisticated CAD/CAM packages. In the end, an artist was

commissioned to recreate the drawings using GemDraw, a very simple package but ideally suited to the straightforward line art contained in *IEE*. CAD/CAM would have been using a sledgehammer to crack a walnut in this case, and very expensive. The raster-to-vector option was preferred, but the state-of-the-art technology available, or rather not available, at the time meant that this too would have been an expensive sledgehammer.

GemGraw was a good technical solution, but it did leave the task of editing the final artwork. Artists are not experts in the area of education and can only draw what they see, not what the author necessarily intended. Therefore the artwork had to be corrected for some 'artistic licence' as well as straightforward typos. Very complex illustrations were the most difficult to draw as the GemDraw grid does not allow the artist to see all parts of the drawing at once.

There was one other unforeseen and surprising complication. The fonts supplied with GemDraw in the UK were different from those supplied with GemDraw and handled by KRS in the USA. This resulted in a mild case of panic when the first set of illustrations went through the data preparation process and was displayed on our screens. Words and numbers which looked fine on the original GemDraw drawings looked oversize in KRS. Even worse, column headings and rows of numbers were displaced giving inaccurate graphs and charts. KRS was promptly altered to accommodate the new fonts, but the lesson was learnt that fonts are not internationally interchangeable.

Tables

Tables were held on the text file derived from the typesetting tape, but the coding was so complex that the coded tables could not be used. A further complication was that most tables, though small and simple on the printed page, contained more than 80 characters horizontally. This meant that they could not be displayed as is on a typical 80-character monitor: a column or more of information would be 'cut off', which was unacceptable. Our options were to reformat the tables and hold them as text or to hold them as graphics.

The text/graphics decision was complex. On the one hand, if the tables were stored as text, each word and number contained in a table would be searchable. However, a table wider than 80 characters could not be displayed on the screen. Splitting up a slightly wider table gave an unsatisfactory screen display and made horizontal comparison of data difficult. Long tables were difficult to scroll and intruded in text sequences.

On the other hand, using a graphics program like GemDraw to input tables would allow display of tables of any width on screen. The user would simply view a table through a window 80 characters wide, panning left and right for comparison as the eye would do on the printed page. Handling tables as graphics would also give us more control over presentation and style. Tables would not be searchable, however. Potential users did not feel it essential that tabular data be searchable, and holding the tables separately (like the figures) preserved the unbroken continuity of the text narrative. Users in fact felt it would be illogical to treat the reference 'see Table 1' differently from 'see Figure 1'.

It was therefore decided to treat tables in the same way as illustrations and the artist who input the illustrations was asked to input the tables.

Retrieval

The first and most obvious retrieval method is by article title. From the Function menu of retrieval features, the user can select the Encyclopedia Bookshelf and find any article by title. This can be done either by 'picking' a volume off the shelf, 'opening' it, and browsing through the article titles. Alternatively, the article may be found by keying in the first word or two of the article title directly. The user may continue in the browsing mode by perusing the Document Outline and selecting a heading or subheading of interest. This direct browse feature is most effective for short articles with up to three levels of heading.

One of the most important features of KRS is the capability of full text search. This feature would not only allow users to search for each word and phrase of the *Encyclopedia*, but would allow constraints according to type of information and word proximity. As discussed above, KRS allows words to be linked using Boolean operators (AND, OR, NOT) and the user to develop complex search strategies. The Dictionary of words in the database may be consulted and one or more terms selected or a word stem truncated. The search may be constrained by its context, for example restricted to words occurring in article titles, bibliographies or text. It may also be constrained by word proximity, for example that two words occur in the same article, same paragraph, next to one another, or with one intermediate word.

This type of searching is unique to electronic publications and is particularly useful for multiauthor works. Experiments with the full-text search feature showed that for an encyclopedia with short articles (1–3 pages long), full-text search was almost as precise in determining relevance as the hierarchical index, and considerably more flexible when search depended on context. Considering this and that the hierarchical subject index required correction, it was decided to implement only the full-text search feature.

Full-text search in combination with the hypertext cross reference system and the other research features have proved to be a remarkably powerful combination. Users can identify a core collection of related articles and through the Reference and Citation features generate a wider or narrower collection of relevant articles. This is a new approach to finding information, and one which it is hoped will be explored by other publishers.

Lessons learned

Retrieval
Firstly it was learned that even in transferring the content of a printed publication to CD-ROM the same retrieval methods need not necessarily be recreated on screen. The *IEE* retained the ability to browse articles by title just as in the printed A–Z arrangement. On the other hand, full-text search and hypertext browse was chosen as an alternative to the hierarchical subject index.

New approaches to access and retrieval should be taken into consideration at the authoring and editing stage for future reference works. In future, greater use will be made of spelling checkers and controlled vocabularies to ensure that full-text search and other computer generated indexes are even more effective.

Graphics
The *IEE* provided the opportunity to experiment with different graphic formats. For *IEE,* and other publications Pergamon Compact Solution has handled, vector representations have proved far more effective from the user's point of view. They allow much greater flexibility for manipulation on screen, the ability to zoom and pan, and to view both detail and overview perspectives. Vector graphics also take up much less space and therefore allow more to be included on disc without expensive compression/decompression hardware or software.

Structuring information
As with *CHC,* even more was learned about how to structure files correctly. Potentially the most expensive step of creating a CD-ROM is the conversion of a file designed for another purpose (print, online, etc.) to one suitable for CD-ROM. This includes interpretation and conversion of codes as well as restructuring the data itself. SGML (Standard Generic Markup Language) is an approach to coding documents based on their component structural elements. Pergamon now uses the SGML approach inhouse, for coding information for multi-media output generally and for CD-ROM in particular.

Summary and conclusions
Pergamon's original goals in exploring CD-ROM were to learn by experience, to identify the problems in publishing with this new medium, to assess market response, and to allow all companies in the group to benefit from our experience. These goals have been achieved, though work on market response will continue as new product types are launched for different markets.

Pergamon's experience with two projects has been related, and this experience speaks for itself. The problems encountered are not necessarily those other publishers will face, but they illustrate the range of new issues that arise and new decisions that have to be taken when exploiting new technology. This experience is offered to publishers, information managers and other members of the information community as a case study in exploring new technology.

CD-ROM is an opportunity

The launch of CD-ROM was accompanied by much unnecessary hype. The expectation of publishers and information managers was raised, and many are still waiting for CD-ROM to prove it really will change the world. Some publishers are waiting for CD-ROM to prove it is a technology to invest in, and some information managers are waiting for CD-ROM to bring them the same information at greatly reduced cost.

CD-ROM is an opportunity for publishers, an opportunity to create new information products that have never existed before. Few publishers have taken advantage of this opportunity, though they are in the best position to do so. Publishers are in the information industry: they understand the market, its needs and how to deliver a product. They are, therefore, in the best position to identify information problems and unfilled information needs. CD-ROM allows them to create multimedia information products and products for new markets. For those who have not yet taken up the challenge the following comments are offered.

Solve a problem

Information in itself has value, and the delivery medium selected can add more value. CD-ROM can add value in terms of providing the user with faster or better access, greater efficiency, more flexibility, convenience, etc. The product should allow the user to do something new, better or faster. Publishers should look at the information problems in their market: getting the right data to the right users in a form that is convenient and easy to use.

Be creative

The first CD-ROM products were media transfer exercises: a product that existed in print or online was recreated on CD-ROM. The same content, indexing/retrieval features and presentation were preserved. Preserving online search protocols that are difficult to learn does not take advantage of the fact that CD-ROM retrieval systems can be very easy to use. Preserving the format of the A4 printed page by scanning does not allow users to take advantage of full-text search. By concentrating on an information problem rather than an existing published product, publishers can overcome the limitations of print, online and microform rather than be restricted by them.

Design is essential

The most important step in creating a CD-ROM product is not technical, it is design. Design involves identifying what a CD-ROM product will be, what it will do, how it will be used, and the role it will have in the user's world. Design must take into consideration content, functionality and presentation. The publisher will want to take an active role in the design phase as he probably knows the most about who the target audience is and how they use information currently. A system integrator is probably in a better position to design the product, because he is experienced in design work, knows the universe of options available, and can integrate performance with functionality in the product design. Publishers should concentrate more on what they want users to be able to do rather than the technicalities of executing a design.

Structure information

Any information product contains different types of information, and each type is used in a different way. Headings and subheadings are used in a different way from a table; a company address is used differently from a paragraph of text. Coding the document according to its structure allows the publisher to retain this information. The art and science of structuring information is available to publishers. Many publishers structure information inhouse using SGML (Standard Generic Markup Language), an international approach to structural coding.

How to structure information is often a less difficult problem than when to structure it. There will always be some publications that are suitable for one medium only, for example print will probably always be the right medium for novels. Research level and high-value information needs more thought as to the precise requirements of the target audience and perhaps two or more formats are the right solution: to deliver the same information to two audiences, or different formats to the same audience. If two or more formats are justifiable, then it is probably better to structure the information for delivery in two formats than to try to derive one from another.

Keep standards at hardware level
From the beginning there has been a market perception that there are standards associated with CD-ROM, and this is a good thing. The Philips/ Sony Yellow Book specifies standards for the physical medium, and the High Sierra standard (ISO 9660) specifies file structure and directories. This is good because it means any CD-ROM can be played on any CD-ROM drive.

Some would go further and suggest that standards should be extended into more complex areas such as the application itself, retrieval software and the user interface. It would indeed be a step backwards if the industry took this direction. In the PC industry there are standards at operating system level, but the industry does not dictate what applications should exist (spreadsheet, database, wordprocessor, etc.) or how they should work. So also in the CD-ROM industry, standards should ensure maximum compatibility at hardware level, but not functionality or 'look and feel'.

New skills are required
CD-ROM is an opportunity and involves new ways of thinking about information, new concepts about what an information product is and new ways of delivering information. This means that new skills will be required in publishing: in authoring information, editing it, product design, production, marketing, customer service and customer support. CD-ROM is used in a PC environment, so many of the new skills will involve knowledge of the PC environment itself and the factors that contribute to success in the PC market. Just as creativity will be required to develop innovative CD-ROM products, creativity will be involved in marketing and supporting them.

Pergamon has benefited enormously from its experience in the new CD-ROM industry. Other publishers should be encouraged to take up the challenge and to create new products for new markets. Information managers should greet these new products with enthusiasm. Every successful new CD-ROM product should solve an information problem. This should be a step forward for all information users.

Chapter 11

How and why should publishers use CD-ROM?

G. Priestley

Introduction

CD-ROM has been hailed as the greatest breakthrough in publishing media since Gutenberg, or even (if the title of one well-known publication on the subject is to be believed) since the time of the Egyptians. There is no doubt that CD-ROM, if exploited intelligently, offers publishers an exciting medium. The purpose of this chapter is to evaluate which publishers should be taking advantage of CD-ROM, and how.

The key to the appropriateness of CD-ROM for a specific type of publication is the type of access required to the data. Traditional publications were intended for serial or limited random access. As an extreme case, a novel is intended for pure serial access; the reader is expected to start at the beginning and continue to the end. Subsequent random access may be required in order to reread parts of specific interest or notoriety, but such a need will be limited. Modern computer technology has made possible the indexing of every word in even the largest body of text, together with the integration of digitized images.

The most complex or obscure enquiry can be resolved immediately by referring to the computer-generated indexes, with incorporation of the appropriate image as required. The major breakthrough of CD-ROM is to provide the storage capacity cheaply, as a peripheral to an inexpensive personal computer.

Types of publisher

In order to examine why publishers should use CD-ROM, it is necessary to consider briefly the different elements of the publishing community.

Traditional publishers

Traditional publishers exist to disseminate information for financial gain. The act of publishing is their sole reason for existence; to fulfil this, they internally create, externally commission, or are solicited to consider, copy for distribution. They cover most market sectors, with products ranging from novels to textbooks to newspapers and magazines. Traditional publishers generally use paper as the medium for information dissemination, although, depending upon the market addressed, microform and online information services are also deployed. The trend towards phototypesetting of printed publications means that traditional publishers now have large amounts of information available in machine-readable form.

Information providers

Unlike traditional publishers, information providers are not dependent upon publishing for their existence. Publishing is used to disseminate information derived from some more fundamental task with which they are charged. Examples include:

- *Government bodies* and government-supported organizations, generate immense quantities of data each year. In the UK, many are published by Her Majesty's Stationery Office (HMSO); many are not. The non-HMSO material (the so-called 'grey literature') is produced by many sources, and not distributed widely.
- *Research organizations* are normally devoted to a relatively narrow subject, in which they publish technical reports and data. Often they support their own libraries or information departments, which gather relevant third-party published material from worldwide sources and consolidate it into internal databases, which may or may not be mechanized. Typical published products include abstracts journals. Where the internal databases are machine-readable, they are often made available to the wider community by online vendors.
- *Patents and standards bodies:* the primary role of a patent organization is to protect intellectual property; the primary role of a standards body is to define standards that will guarantee product interchangeability. Neither type of organization is a publisher in the traditional sense, but without full dissemination of their information and activities to all interested parties each type of organization would be worthless. As before, such organizations will distribute their material on paper, on microfilm, and via online vendors.

Publication types

An attempt is made in *Table 11.1* to summarize the various types of available publication, related to current publisher type, anticipated end user, preferred means of access, data type and current media on which the publication is available. The list is not intended to be exhaustive, but to indicate the breadth of material to be considered for CD-ROM publishing.

Terms used in the table are defined as follows:

(1) Publisher type
    As defined earlier.

(2) Circulation

- *Open circulation:* freely available for purchase or subscriptions.
- *Closed circulation:* available only to the publisher.
- *Limited circulation:* potentially open circulation, but limited by rarity.

Table 11.1 Types of available CD-ROM publications

Publication type	Publisher type	Circulation	Anticipated end user	Preferred access	Data type	Current availability	CD-ROM applications
Leisure literature	Traditional	Open	Consumer	Serial	Static	Hard copy	No
Textbook	Traditional	Open	Professional/educational	Random	Static	Hard copy	Possibly
Rare book/document	Traditional	Limited	Educational	Serial	Static	Hard copy/microform	Yes
Learned journal	Traditional	Open	Professional/educational	Random	Serially dynamic	Hard copy/online	Yes
Abstracts journal/technical database	Information provider	Open	Professional/educational	Random	Serially dynamic	Hard copy/online	Yes
Patents/standards	Information provider	Open	Professional	Random	Serially dynamic	Hard copy/online/microform	Yes
Encyclopedia/dictionary	Traditional	Open	Consumer/educational/professional	Random	Static	Hard copy/online	Yes
Newspaper/magazine	Traditional	Open	Consumer/educational/professional	Random	Serially dynamic	Hard copy/online	Yes
Maps	Traditional	Open	Consumer/educational/professional	Random	Static	Hard copy/microform	Yes
Business/corporate information	Venture	Open	Professional	Random	Dynamic	Hard copy/online	Yes
Directories/handbooks	Traditional	Open	Professional	Random	Dynamic	Hard copy/online	Yes
Legal corpus	Information provider	Open	Professional	Random	Serially dynamic	Hard copy/online	Yes
Technical documentation	Internal	Closed	Professional	Random	Serially dynamic	Hard copy/microform	Yes
Internal documentation	Internal	Closed	Professional	Random	Serially dynamic	Hard copy/microform	Yes

(3) Anticipated end user

- *Consumer:* available to the domestic market.
- *Professional:* available in the appropriate workplace.
- *Educational:* available to trainees, students etc.

(4) Preferred access type
An indication of how the user will need to access the data.

(5) Data type

- *Static data:* data that are predominantly archival. There may be new editions, but the basic content is unchanged.
- *Dynamic data:* data that change often, both in terms of modifications to the basic corpus and additions to it.
- *Serially dynamic data:* data in which the basic corpus is static, but subject to additions that affect the interpretation of the static data.

(6) Current availability

- *Hard copy:* printed matter.
- *Online:* available from some central data host, either a database vendor, viewdata or teletext.
- *Microform:* available as microfiche or microfilm.
- *Venture publishers:* venture publishers are entrepreneurial, integrating data from various sources in order to create a product to serve a niche market, generally consolidating the data of the diverse information providers. Microform publishers, and to a lesser extent online hosts, are examples.
- *Internal publishers:* normally large organizations producing reports, technical documentation, minutes etc. for use solely within the organization or its affiliates. Data are not published for commercial gain.

CD-ROM as a medium

There has been much media hype about CD-ROM, as noted in the introduction to this chapter. It is worthwhile summarizing, at this stage, the advantages and disadvantages of the medium.

Advantages

- *Standards.* Unlike videodisc or WORM, for which no agreed standards exist, CD-ROM was conceived as a standard medium. When its parent, CD audio, was developed, manufacturers cooperated to ensure that any compact disc could be played on any drive, i.e. the digitization standard was fully defined. The promulgation, and subsequent adoption by major drive manufacturers, of the so-called High Sierra Group (HSG) standard means that any disc so laid out can be used on any CD-ROM drive.

Microsoft, with its MS-DOS CD-ROM Extensions (MSCDEX), has done an immense service to the industry by adopting HSG standards. A CD-ROM user can now buy a disc knowing that, once the appropriate retrieval software has been installed, it can be used within minutes. The only reason not to use HSG standards are for purposes of data security.

- *High capacity.* The capacity of a CD-ROM is now 660 megabytes. There are many mind-boggling analogies: over 200000 typed A4 pages, almost 2000 double-sided double density floppy discs, or 20 kg of closely-printed lightweight paper. Alternatively, a CD-ROM can hold over 60000 suitably compressed images or in excess of 70 minutes of high-fidelity audio. It has been suggested that a typist possessing a typewriter without a carriage return, and presumably a suitably wide piece of paper, would have to type a line extending from Los Angeles to Chicago in order to generate enough characters to fill a CD-ROM. More to the point, it would take her over 10 years of continuous typing to do it.

- *Software controlled.* Data on the disc can be accessed randomly; every word on the disc is potentially addressable. Retrieved data can be integrated into other applications *ad libitum,* especially if the retrieval software is memory resident.

- *Low unit costs.* Because CD-ROM is a spin-off from consumer industry (CD audio), the technology and quality assurance for both the discs and drives is already in place. This proven technology, harnessed to the ever-increasing sophistication and performance/price ratio of personal computers, means that the consumer has to pay a low entry price to use the medium.

- *Mixed media capability.* Because CD-ROM is a digital medium, it can carry any data which can be encoded. Text, images and sound can be mixed on the same disc. As more efficient image compression algorithms or hardware become available, and if lower fidelity sound is acceptable, the capacity of a CD-ROM in terms of the number of image frames and minutes of audio will further increase. It is accepted that textual data, images and audio cannot be accessed simultaneously, but this can be accommodated by suitable buffering within the retrieval software.

- *Small size/light weight.* A CD-ROM is 12 cm (4.72 inches) in diameter, and approximately 1.2 mm (0.047 inches) thick, weighing 25 grams. Storage and mailing costs are minimized.

- *Robustness.* Although discs should be treated with respect, they are physically almost indestructible, with an estimated life over ten years. Data are thus not easily corrupted, and are immune to magnetic fields.

Disadvantages

- *Relatively slow access times.* A CD-ROM, unlike a magnetic disc, is not a sectored device; data are recorded spirally from the centre, at constant linear velocity. Thus, as the read head moves across the surface of the disc, the angular velocity of the disc must be adjusted by a servo-mechanism so that data passes under the head at constant linear velocity. Average seek times are therefore of the order of 1 second (compared with 18–40 milliseconds for a PC Winchester disc). Although improvements in access times are being made, it is unlikely that they will fall much below 300–400 milliseconds.

The limits of the hardware can be accommodated to some extent by appropriate disc geography, and by data cacheing within the accessing software. Nevertheless, a common criticism of CD-ROM is that response times are slow. While this may be a valid complaint in absolute terms (compared, say, to a Winchester disc), it is suggested that the response of a CD-ROM to a data retrieval request should be considered in terms of the overall time required to adequately complete the task for which the CD-ROM is used, as opposed to the absolute retrieval times of the discrete steps required to fulfil it. This is especially true when the retrieval software is capable of further manipulating the retrieved data or is integrated with other software packages.

● *Write-once medium.* Data held on a CD-ROM is obviously impossible to update, at least on the disc itself, although the technology has already been developed to embrace CD-PROM and CD-EPROM.

In many ways the read-only property of CD-ROM should be considered an advantage: it was conceived as a medium for the large-scale distribution of information, with concomitant data integrity, not as another means of local dynamic mass storage.

To summarize, the intrinsic properties of CD-ROM together with its low unit and entry-level costs, and its flexibility of use, render it a secure and cost effective medium for the publisher. CD-ROM publishing costs are considered in more detail in the next section.

The CD-ROM publishing process

The prospective CD-ROM publisher will have data available in some form. This may be hard copy, as typesetting tapes, or in some other machine-readable format. This is especially true of the venture publisher, who will have identified a niche market and assembled the data from various sources in order to create a product to fulfil the perceived need. It is normally the role of the system integrator to take the data and from it create the CD-ROM product.

The role of the system integrator is discussed elsewhere in this book, but it is worthwhile to briefly summarize the steps involved.

● *Database design.* The data must be structured to make it retrievable by the software supplied by the integrator. A document structure, or a series of structures, must be conceived in order that the final database can be searched efficiently. Significant data elements must be delimited in some way, and appropriate indexing criteria selected for each data element. If the CD-ROM product is to be mixed media, e.g. text and graphics, or text, graphics and audio, the appropriate linkages between these data types must be determined and constructed.

Database structure must be conceived in parallel with the interface through which the user will access the data. This is often the most difficult process unless the publisher is sure of the market and how the users will wish to use the product.

● *Data take-on.* Depending on the sources of the data, several different activities may be involved. Hard copy must be converted to machine-readable form, either by scanning to generate ASCII text, or, if for any reason the data cannot be scanned, rekeyed. Images will require digitization, and any audio component rendered into an appropriate digital format. At the end of the take-on process, the data should be in a format suitable for loading into the database structure.

● *Database loading.* Inverting the data normally imposes heavy demands on computer resources, depending on the efficiency of the software used. The software must also be efficient in the storage overhead imposed by the creation of the indexes (the so-called 'inversion overhead').

● *Pre-mastering.* Following database loading, the data must be laid out in the appropriate format for subsequent retrieval from the CD-ROM. This involves the creation of the appropriate headers and directory structure according to High Sierra Group format. The magnetic tape or tapes created in this step are then despatched to the CD-ROM manufacturing facility for mastering and replication.

● *Mastering.* The pre-mastered data are now used to produce a stamper disc, using exactly the same technology as used for CD audio with the addition of extra error-checking and correction codes.

● *Replication.* The stamper created in the mastering process is used to create plastic replicas, with appropriate labels.

● *Packaging/distribution.* Perhaps the packaging of CD-ROM products is one of their most attractive features, and there are certainly many imaginative options available. Some products are offered in a package designed to look like a book. Others are offered in the more familiar jewel box, together with insert cards etc. Also some manufacturers will undertake distribution of the discs on behalf of the publisher.

Evidently, it is unwise for the publisher to commit himself to mass replication immediately. Although the risk of data corruption has now been almost totally eliminated from the CD-ROM production process, at least by some manufacturers, there is a risk. It is also necessary to ensure that the retrieval software and user interface function correctly with the disc, particularly that response times are acceptable.

There are two methods by which such checking can be effected:

● *Development discs.* Some CD-ROM manufacturers offer a development disc service, producing a few unlabelled discs before the mass replication is authorized. Provided that the discs perform as expected, there is no need to re-master before mass replication.

● *CD-ROM simulation devices.* Equipment such as the CD Publisher and CD Simulator can simulate the performance of a CD-ROM without the need to cut a disc. In fact, CD-ROM simulators are fully-integrated CD-ROM production workstations, offering over one gigabyte of online storage and pre-mastering software in addition to their simulation capabilities. When attached by an appropriate computer (generally an 80386-based PC), such workstations can be used for data conversion and loading and eventual creation of a pre-mastering tape after the performance of the retrieval software has been checked in simulation mode.

Owing to their high capital cost the use of these devices is generally limited to the system integrators, although a publisher committed to CD-ROM publishing may well regard the investment in a CD-ROM simulator worthwhile.

Storage and retrieval software considerations

Probably the most important choice to be made by a prospective CD-ROM publisher after commitment to a product is the selection of the storage and retrieval software.

There are no standards, and probably never will be. The publisher must therefore select the storage and retrieval software on the basis of its perceived performance for the particular application. The software package has yet to be written that is all things to all men, although extravagant claims are sometimes made.

The publisher must therefore ask several questions of the software supplier:

● How efficient is the indexing for the particular application? Can it address mixed mode data, e.g. text and graphics?
● Is it flexible in use? Can it be tailored to the publisher's requirements relatively easily, and if so by whom?
● In how many applications is it in use? What is the installed user base?
● What are the software licensing arrangements?

The choice of software will generally be intimately related to the choice of system integrators, who will offer a specific product or products. The publisher must therefore ask of the integrator:

● What is their track record? How many disc titles have been produced?
● What is their commitment to CD-ROM?
● What are their relationships with the data preparation companies? With the CD-ROM production companies? With the suppliers of CD-ROM hardware? With their existing clients?

In other words, does the integrator have a good reputation?

The role of the system integrator has been summarized earlier. However, as the provider of the storage and retrieval software the integrator has an additional crucial role to play: the design, with the publisher, of the so-called 'human interface' to the CD-ROM, and its implementation.

It is undoubtedly true that the interface to the data will help to sell the product. It is therefore necessary to render it attractive and simple to use, yet free from irritating gimmicks that will infuriate the user once their novelty has evaporated. The interface, as noted earlier, is data driven, and is determined by the type of product for which it is used. An interface used for accessing business information, for example, will be substantially different from that used for interrogating a database of full-text legal data.

Where necessary the interface can be multilevel and multilanguage, i.e. offer the user alternative paths to the data, and provide a range of languages in which the paths are signposted. The interface may also include access to a multilingual thesaurus.

The interface design will also be driven by the perceived needs of the prospective users, which may well be largely subjective.

Publishers are strongly advised to arrange field trials before the formal release of their product in order to incorporate user reaction into the interface.

The cost of CD-ROM production

This topic is discussed in more detail elsewhere in the book.

Some of the costs involved in developing and producing a CD-ROM are easy to quantify, others are not. For example, the costs of data capture will depend upon the format in which the data are currently held. Similarly the costs of market research and product marketing are variable, and will be intrinsic to the approach of the publisher.

Since these costs will be similar whatever the selected medium of publication, whether it be hard copy, fiche, online or CD-ROM, they are not considered here. The publisher will generally have a good feel for them. The purpose of this discussion is to give the publisher a similar appreciation of the start-up and recurring costs of CD-ROM production from data inversion to replication, and to indicate the major influencing factors.

Table 11.2 Typical CD-ROM project costs. Based on: 200 megabyte of initial data, with 10% annual modifications and 20 megabyte additions (50 megabyte total annual changes); data already in machine-readable form but requiring conversion to load format; CD-ROM product price £1000 p.a. with an installed user base of 500.

1. *Startup costs*

User interface		£15000
Initial data conversion + loading		£10000
CD-ROM production		
Pre-mastering	£1500	
Mastering	£2300	
Replication	£1900	
	£5700	
		£30700

2. *Recurring costs* (£)

Update frequency	Updating	Pre-mastering	Mastering	Replication (500)	Software licensing	Total annual cost
Annual	4750	1500	2300	1900	50000	60450
Quarterly	7750	6000	9200	7600	50000	80550
Monthly	15750	18000	27600	22800	50000	134150

Table 11.3 Typical CD-ROM replication costs as a function of replication quantity and product update frequency

	Total annual cost (£)				
			Number of replicates		
	50	100	250	500	1000+
Annual updates	500	600	1050	1900	3300
Quarterly updates	2000	2400	4200	7600	13200
Monthly updates	6000	7200	12600	22800	39600

A summary is presented in *Table 11.2* of the main cost elements involved. It should be noted that:

- User interface development will naturally depend on the type of interface required. A figure of £15000 is quoted here as a typical value, but actual costs may exceed or be less than this.
- For initial database conversion and loading the assumption has been made that the data already exist in machine-readable form, but require pre-processing in order to delimit data elements in a way appropriate to the design of the interface and database structure. Conversion and loading costs are a function of data volume.
- The cost of CD-ROM mastering is generally virtually independent of data volume. The cost of replication is naturally dependent on the number of replicates, as shown in *Table 11.3*.
- Software licensing will depend on the policy of the software vendor. Such policies vary; the vendor may make a single, up-front charge; charge for each CD-ROM sold; or levy a royalty on the basis of a negotiated percentage of the total revenues accruing to the publisher from the sale of the product. Of the options available, and there are no doubt other policies than those stated here, the royalty arrangements may be most appealing to the publisher in that the software vendor shares the risk of publication; if the product does not penetrate the market, the software vendor is not rewarded.

So why use CD-ROM?

Referring again to *Table 11.1*, five main publishing areas can be identified which can be exploited using CD-ROM: database, reference, education, technical documentation, and internal publications.

Evidently there is some overlap, particularly between database and reference, but these sectors are sufficiently distinct to merit separate discussion.

Database publishing

The first commercially available CD-ROM products were those for which the data already existed in machine-readable form, and were offered as bibliographic databases. They did not exploit the capability of the PC to promote high bandwidth access by offering graphical or pictorial information. CD-ROM simulation of online services undoubtedly has a future, particularly if online hosts offer specific subsets or 'cuts' of databases for niche markets. CD-ROM distribution of online databases is also of value if the perceived market embraces geographical areas in which the telecommunications infrastructure is poor, rendering online access unreliable or impossible. It is, however, unlikely that CD-ROM products based on bibliographic databases will dominate the CD-ROM market, owing to their low added value.

Reference

This sector is likely to dominate CD-ROM publishing in the foreseeable future: it covers a wide range of publication types, in which there is tremendous scope for adding value. This is a sector ripe for exploitation by the venture publisher. Referring again to *Table 11.1,* three main data types were identified: static, dynamic, and serially dynamic.

Several types of potential end user were also shown: consumer, professional, and educational.

It is suggested that, at least in the medium term, the professional end user is the main target for reference CD-ROM products. The consumer market can be ruled out until there is a much higher installed consumer base of appropriate PCs and CD-ROM players. The educational user can probably not be brought into play until suitable educational products are conceived. This latter problem is discussed later.

Encyclopedias, dictionaries, thesauri and the like are all examples of static data as defined earlier. It is interesting that Microsoft selected products of this type as ingredients of their first CD-ROM product, the Microsoft *Bookshelf.* The reasons are clear: it is useful, looks good, has high added value, and is easy to use. In other words, a model CD-ROM product. Its disadvantage, inevitably, is that it is targeted at the US market.

Dynamic, or serially dynamic, data pose greater problems. CD-ROM has been criticized as a medium for distributing dynamic data, owing to its read-only capability. Data on a CD-ROM can never be as current as that available online, which can be updated daily or even hourly. While it is now possible to offer weekly CD-ROM updates the cost is high, as can be

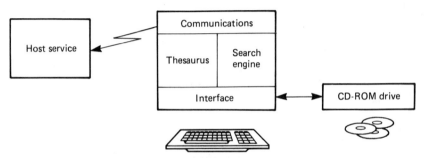

Figure 11.1 Online access. Hybrid online and CD-ROM access

interpreted from *Table 11.3*. Because business information databases are high-value they can generally be sold at a high subscription, and therefore accommodate weekly updates, but even this update frequency may be insufficient.

One possibility is to offer a 'hybrid' system, in which the user can access both an online service and a local CD-ROM using the same interface, either sequentially or simultaneously. The advantages of this technique, illustrated in *Figure 11.1*, are manifold: the bulk of the data are locally available on the CD-ROM, therefore minimizing online connection charges, yet the most recent updates can still be accessed. Moreover, since the same interface is used, the changeover can be seamless. Such an interface could include a locally resident thesaurus for interrogating both the local and remote databases, and would also exploit benefits of the PC display such as windowing.

Evidently such a technique would not overcome the bandwidth limitations of online access, precluding the retrieval of non-textual data, at least from the remote host. Such problems can be at least partially overcome by distributing document images on CD-ROM while maintaining the index to the images on the remote host. This technique, schematically illustrated in *Figure 11.2*, is best applied to documents such as patents or standards that comprise static data with a graphic element.

Legal data, and to a lesser extent patents and standards data, impose the requirement on the retrieval software of connectivity. A user of a legal database, for example, may find a particular case reference, and wish to retrieve all chronologically subsequent documents in which this case is cited. The retrieval software can do this on the fly by formulating a search strategy based on a block of text highlighted by the user. This adds immense value to the data. More efficient techniques may elaborate this capability even further, for example hypertext, with its intrinsic cross-referencing and user linkage properties.

Product types discussed so far have been traditionally published in hard copy. The advantages of CD-ROM are quite clear. In addition to the added value that publishing on CD-ROM potentially confers, they should

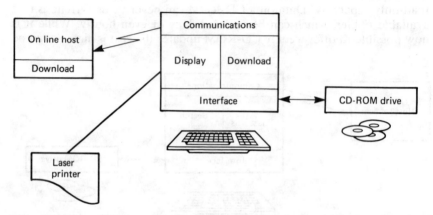

Figure 11.2 Document image management. Local CD-ROM used for retrieving digitized images by downloading frame references from an online host

be cheaper to produce, to store and to deliver. CD-ROM does not have the same advantage over microform, at least if the latter is computer-generated. The production of computer output on microfiche (COM) has reached a high level of efficiency, and is extremely cheap. It has been maintained that CD-ROM would quickly take over the traditional microform publishing markets, but there are as yet few signs of this happening. This may well be related to the satisfaction of existing microform users with existing products, a high installed base of cheap microform readers, and no perceived requirement for sophisticated indexing of the data.

It is, however, interesting to note that an adventurous microform publisher can see the need to adopt CD-ROM. J. Whitaker and Sons are a traditional English publisher, producing (in addition to the famous almanack) *British Books in Print.* Although still available in hard copy, Whitaker's adopted, in 1978, the then revolutionary strategy of introducing a microfiche version. Whitaker's are now the largest consumers of microfiche in the UK, yet, almost exactly 10 years after the introduction of microfiche product, the Whitaker Bookbank was launched on CD-ROM. The reasons for this development follow the new emerging pattern: immensely improved retrieval capability, ease of use, a professional market (librarians and booksellers), and great added value (for example the ability to download data for remote book ordering, or incorporation into stock control systems). By adopting a monthly update service (up to 100000 changed records per month), Whitaker's have not sacrificed the relative currency of the microfiche product.

It is in the reference sector that the venture publisher will be most active. By drawing on data from diverse sources and integrating them into a niche market product, the venture publisher may well catalyse the development of CD-ROM products from the more traditional publishers.

Educational

Education and training is probably a mixed-mode application, in which at least text, images and voice will be combined. There is no sign yet of a commercial product; possibly they will materialise first in the internal publishing sector (see below).

Technical documentation

The adoption of CD-ROM for the storage of technical drawings, computer products and vehicle parts lists is a potentially exciting application of CD-ROM. Digital Equipment Co. (DEC), Ford and General Motors are known to have a strong interest. Vehicle parts lists, in particular, are a strong area for development, replacing existing microfiche products.

The recent announcement by Ford of an integrated vehicle diagnostics CD-ROM product, using a hypertext interface, is especially interesting; no doubt this technology will be exploited in the aerospace industry, amongst others.

Internal publications

There is immense scope for CD-ROM in internal publishing, especially in the corporate environment. Possible applications include the archiving of data from internal databases in order to liberate computer space, data distribution between branches of multinational companies, logging of engineering data, internal training, and many more. CD-ROM will face competition from document management systems using WORM technology. The rationale for selection of the medium will probably be the precision with which the data to be archived are required to be indexed.

Conclusions

- CD-ROM is a viable publishing medium using proven technology.
- The key to the use of CD-ROM is the efficiency and ease of use of the storage and retrieval software.
- The products that will most fully exploit the medium are reference publications aimed at the professional end user, and offering high added value.
- The venture publisher will become more active in identifying valuable latent information that can be integrated into a value-added product aimed at a niche market.

Chapter 12

Sources of information, and keeping up to date

Charles Oppenheim

In such a fast-moving area as CD-ROM and CD-I technologies, it is inevitable that a book such as this quickly becomes out of date. It becomes out of date in several respects. Firstly, the technology itself develops; new hardware and software are launched, and new standards are agreed. Old hardware and software may be withdrawn or superseded. Secondly, the marketplace — the CD-ROM/CD-I industry — changes rapidly over time. New CD-ROM and CD-I publications appear; old ones are withdrawn. New publishers enter the optical publishing arena for the first time. New types of material are put onto the media for the first time. New system integrators and software houses enter the fray.

Anyone with an active interest in optical publishing cannot rely alone on a volume such as this for the most up-to-date information. He (or she) needs to become conversant with, and keep up-to-date with, the latest developments.

There are broadly three methods of keeping oneself up-to-date in this fast-moving area: attending conferences; scanning journals, newsletters and so on for the most recent developments; and corporate brochures.

A number of publishers, including Meckler Publishing, Alan Armstrong and Associates and Learned Information, have published directories of CD-ROM products. It is certainly possible that these directories will become established in this marketplace in the same way as Cuadra's Directory has done for online databases. However, since they are as a rule (so far) only published annually, they cannot provide a totally up-to-date overview of what is currently available.

The listings that follow are not claimed to be comprehensive. Rather, they represent a personal view of the best sources for keeping up-to-date. Comments from readers (and publishers, conference organizers, etc.) would be welcome!

Overall, it will be clear that there is no difficulty in keeping oneself up-to-date. The major difficulty is the wealth of information coming out and separating the facts from the hype.

Conferences

The major conferences organizers in this field are Microsoft, Eikon, Meckler Publishing, The Institute for Graphic Communication, and Learned Information.

The annual Microsoft International CD-ROM conference takes place every March in Seattle. It is by far the most prestigious and important of the CD-ROM conferences, and is used for major launches of new products. It is therefore strongly recommended as an ideal source for the latest news. More than 1300 delegates attend each year. An attempt to create a European equivalent to the Microsoft conference can be found in the Eikon CD-ROM conference that was held in Rome at the end of October, 1987.

Meckler Publishing are responsible for a series of optical information conferences entitled Optical Information Systems. There appear to be three such conferences each year, two in the USA and one in London. The exhibition is open to non-delegates, and provides an inexpensive method of seeing the latest products.

The Institute of Graphic Communication and the Information Workstation Group jointly organize a series of intensive seminars and conferences in the field of optical publishing. These are in-depth and high-priced meetings for industry leaders and are not intended for people with a casual interest. The conferences take place every few months and are at a variety of locations. IGC is at 375 Commonwealth Avenue, Boston, MA 02115, USA. Simply scanning the contents of their meetings in their brochures gives one a good feel for the latest developments.

Learned Information organizes optical publishing conferences both in the USA and in Europe. These follow the well-established pattern of papers, exhibition and product reviews running simultaneously. The Learned Information conferences are not as prestigious as Microsoft's, but still attract many exhibitors. The exhibition is open to nondelegates.

Numerous other conferences, sponsored by organizations such as Online Limited, TOC, Rothchild Consultants and Online Inc., cover the field as well, but someone with an interest in database and information provision applications of optical media will not need to move beyond visiting each year one or at most two out of the five conferences — or their exhibitions — that have been highlighted.

The major journals

There is a large number of journals and newsletters that specialize in covering the optical publishing area. There are many others that happen to cover the area, but that are devoted to a broader subject field, e.g. publishing as a whole, or information retrieval systems generally. This listing combines the best of both types.

CD-ROM Directions is a free newsletter published by Hitachi New Media Products, Box 7138, 17207 Sundbyberg, Sweden. It appears approximately quarterly and provides a useful overview of CD-ROM developments. Although inevitably biased towards Hitachi and its products, the newsletter provides good coverage of new publications and of organizations active in the data preparation and CD-ROM publishing fields. It is highly recommended.

CD-I News is published monthly by Link Resources Crop., 79 Fifth Avenue, New York, NY 10003, USA. Although nominally carrying a cover price of $20 per issue, this newsletter appears in practice to be generally distributed free of charge. The newsletter is subsidized by Philips and other companies active in CD-I technology. It specializes in interviews with key industry figures, but also includes news items, conference reports, etc. It provides a useful listing of forthcoming conferences around the world. A reasonably useful source of up-to-date information, and the only publication (so far) to concentrate wholly on CD-I. It assumes some technical knowledge, a problem for readers new to the field.

CD-ROM Librarian, formerly known as *Optical Information Systems Update Library and Information Centre Applications,* is one of three important Meckler Publishing (11 Ferry Lane, West, Westport, CT 06880, USA) journals in the field. It includes articles on library and information applications, and news items on personnel, conferences, surveys and products. It is published bimonthly and costs $65 per year. It is heavily biased towards US developments, but is a useful source.

Optical Data Systems is a more expensive (£115 per year) monthly newsletter published by MicroInfo Limited (PO Box 3, Newman Lane, Alton, Hants GU34 2PG, UK). It comprises short news items on all aspects of optical publishing and is edited by Tony Hendley. It also covers video-disc, videotex and interactive video systems, but its primary thrust is in optical publishing. A useful publication, with critical evaluations of products, services and conferences. Recommended.

Electronic and Optical Publishing Review is the major Learned Information (Woodside, Hinksey Hill, Oxford OX1 9AU, UK) journal in the field. It is edited by one of the industry's major personalities, Julie Schwerin, and includes articles, interviews, book reviews, a regular directory of CD-ROM databases, bibliographies and industry news. The journal costs £45 per year and is issued quarterly. There are useful CD-ROM product reviews. Recommended.

Optical Information Systems is the second Meckler journal. This is issued bimonthly and costs $95 per year. It is a larger journal than Meckler's *Update* and includes more lengthy articles, and detailed information mainly on videodisc projects. With its US bias and emphasis on videodiscs, this journal is less likely to be needed by an organization primarily interested in CD-ROM and CD-I.

CD-ROM Review, published by CW Communications, is a US glossy magazine intended for the bookstall rather than on subscription. It includes sophisticated graphics and much advertising. The articles are fairly general, but are very clearly written and laid out. The magazine has a North American bias.

Mémoires Optiques is published by ARCA Editions (PO Box 303, 56007 Vannes Cedex, France) and appears in two languages (French and English). It appears monthly, and is an excellent critical publication for keeping up-to-date on hardware and software launches.

CD Publisher News is a free newsletter issued by MeridianData Inc., 4450 Capitola Road, Suite 101, Capitola, CA 95010, USA. Although giving heavy emphasis to Meridians' products and services, it also contains useful news snippets and interviews.

Optical Times is a similar free newsletter from Optical Storage Limited, Rye House, Brook Way, Leatherhead, Surrey KT22 7NA, UK, but has very little material other than that promoting OSL.

Optical Information Systems Update is the final Meckler journal. It is published biweekly, it includes brief news items of new videodisc and optical disc products. Again, it is very US biased and costs $189.50 per year.

Information Media and Technology is the bimonthly journal for CIMTECH members. It features news and product reviews in the areas of microform, facsimile etc. and has been providing increasing emphasis on optical media. CIMTECH (PO Box 109, College Lane, Hatfield, Herts AL0 9AB, UK) also invite subscriptions at £50 per year. Recommended for those interested in hardware evaluations. CIMTECH also publishes very useful technical reports on CD-ROM technology from time to time.

Communication Technology Impact (CTI) published by Elsevier Newsletters, 256 Banbury Road, Oxford OX2 7DH, UK, is a monthly newsletter covering all aspects of electronic publishing. It includes short news items and critical articles on new developments. Recommended if your interests are broader than just CD.

Data Storage Report is another Elsevier monthly newsletter, costing $250 per year. It provides an emphasis on CD-ROM and WORM but also covers floppy discs and other media. Similar in style to the older establishing and better known CTI, it is a promising newcomer to the field.

A Jour, the French publisher of *Infotecture*, also publishes newsletters in the field of optical media. The monthly *CD ROM . . .* (in French) started publication in September 1987. It costs 1200 FFr per year. An English language equivalent started publication late in 1987. Both versions include product news, commentary and interviews of the European CD-ROM industry. They are obtainable from A Jour at 10 rue Danielle Casanova, 75002 Paris, France.

Information World Review (IWR) is a monthly newspaper published by Learned Information Limited. It costs £18 per year, and provides very useful coverage of the entire information industry, including optical publishing. It has a European bias. It has published useful optical publishing supplements from time to time, e.g. March 1987 issue.

Information Today is Learned Information Inc's (143 Old Marlton Place, Medford, NJ 08055, USA) US equivalent to IWR. Like IWR, it includes news items and lengthier in-depth interviews and articles. Monthly, it costs $22 per year.

Information Times is another US-biased newspaper, for members of the Information Industry Association. Only IIA members can obtain the publication, which includes useful trade news and conference reports, including CD-ROM. Similar trade bulletins include *Information Industry Bulletin, IDP Report and Database Update.*

Publishing and New Media Newsletter is a biweekly newsletter published by Pergamon Journals (Headington Hill Hall, Oxford OX3 0BW, UK) costing £115 per year. It covers company news, market trends and news products in all areas of electronic publishing. CD-ROM is given relatively little space.

The *Financial Times,* London, UK provides good coverage of the compact disc industry, but with an inevitable bias towards the audio side.

Database and *Online* are two bimonthly journals published by Online Inc. (11 Tannery Lane, Weston, CT 06883 USA). They cost $85 per year. Each has a regular column entitled 'The Silver Disk', with informed commentary on CD-ROM developments. In addition, *Database* has produced a useful directory of databases on CD-ROM.

Library and Information News, the very personal and quirky commentary newsletter on the UK and US library scene, covers CD-ROM from time to time.

Library Hi Tech News, a monthly newsletter published by Pierian Press, PO Box 1808, Anne Arbor, MU 48106, USA, is one of the best sources of news on CD-ROM developments. It gives news of product and services and includes a very useful current awareness bulletin covering a wide range of other journals. The monthly newsletter costs $65 per year.

Information Retrieval and Library Automation, a monthly newsletter costing $48 per year, mainly covers library automation but also has a useful coverage of CD-ROM developments. It can be ordered from PO Box 88, Mt Airy, MD 21771, USA.

Optical Publishing Report was a newsletter from Headland Press, well known for its business information journals. The monthly newsletter cost £99 per year and was full of useful commentary and news items on CD-ROM developments. It ceased publication in May 1987, perhaps the first publication devoted to CD to do so!

Inform is the new name for a well established journal, *Journal of Information and Image Management.* This journal, not to be confused with the better known and long-established Institute of Information Scientists' newsletter, covers micrographics, videodiscs, optical discs and related topics. It is a glossy monthly with many advertisements, and includes articles, interviews, book reviews, notices of forthcoming meetings and commentary. It has a pronounced US bias. It costs $70 per year from 1100 Wayne Avenue, silver Spring, MD 20910, USA.

Other CD-ROM journal titles of interest include:

CD Data Report. Nov. 1984. McLean, VA: Langley Publications. Monthly. $225.00/yr. ISSN 8755-5727. Covers new products, standards, etc.
Digital Audio and Compact Disc Review. Peterborough, NH: WGE Pub. Monthly. ISSN 0891-9046.
Digital Recording Report. Stamford, CT: Technical Systems Group. Monthly. $45.00/yr. ISSN 0748-6871.
Information Technology and Libraries. Chicago, IL: LITA. Quarterly. ISSN 0730-9295.
Micrographics and Optical Storage Equipment Review. Westport, CT: Meckler Corporation. Annual. Library rates vary. ISSN 0882-3294.
Optical Memory News, San Francisco, CA: Rothchild Consultants Inc. Bimonthly. $295.00/yr. ISSN 0741-5869. Covers CD-ROM industry developments, standards and industry trends.

The Optical Memory Report, San Francisco, CA: Rothchild Consultants
Inc. Annual, $1995.00. ISSN 8755-1195.

CD-ROM Business Information. This is a new Headland Press (1 Henry
Smith Terrace, Cleveland TS24 0PD, UK) monthly publication with
in-depth tests of major business databases on CD-ROM, plus general
news. It represents the second attempt by Headland Press to enter the
CD-ROM periodical publishing business.

CD-ROM Newsletter, a free irregular newsletter from Microinfo (PO Box 3,
Alton, Hants GU34 2PG, UK), is a combination of short news items and
Microinfo CD product sales pitch. A sort of poor man's *Optical Data
Systems.*

Other library and information journals to cover CD-ROM developments
in articles (or news stories) from time to time include *Advanced Technology
Libraries, Information Technology and Libraries, Online Review, Library
High Tech* and *The Electronic Library. IM* (Information Market), produced by the Commission of the European Communities, also covers CD
developments for time to time.

In addition, a number of personal computer magazines cover optical
media from time to time. Those that cover the media most often are
*Infomatics, Practical Computing, Systems International, Which Computer?,
Computer Weekly* and *Personal Computer World.*

Finally, *The Bookseller* maintains an active interest in the field. This is
no doubt partially fuelled by the fact that Whitaker's, its publisher, is an
active CD-ROM publisher in its own right. Whitaker's also publishes a free
newsletter, *Whitaker's CD-ROM Newsletter,* on its CD-ROM publishing
activities.

Market research reports

As might be expected in such a fast-moving and uncertain area, many
market research reports on the prospects for growth for the optical publishing industry are available. Link Resources, International Resource
Development Inc., Information Workstation Group, and Frost and
Sullivan, are amongst the better-known names in this area. These reports
are generally very expensive and make ambitious claims for the likely
growth of the marketplace. They are primarily intended for hardware and
software manufacturers and for publishers rather than for users.

Current awareness publications

The best sources are *Electronic and Optical Publishing Review* and *Library
Hi Tech News,* which offer useful scanning of other publications. Other
standard sources, such as *Library and Information Science Abstracts*
(LISA), *Information Science Abstracts* (ISA) and Aslib's *Current Awareness Bulletin,* are also useful. Perhaps the most useful single secondary
source, but not to be relied on alone, is Pergamon's *Electronic Publishing
Abstracts* (EPA).

If one were really keen, one could create an SDI profile on one of the library and information and/or computing abstracting services online, but this is not really necessary for someone wishing to keep generally up-to-date in the field. Services such as LISA, ISA and EPA are available online.

Corporate brochures and press releases

It is useful to enter the mailing lists of some of the major software houses, CD-ROM publishers and systems integrators. Receipt of their literature will ensure you are up-to-date with their products and services. Amongst the most helpful organizations are the following:

Archetype Systems Limited, 91–93 Charterhouse Street, London EC1M 6LN, UK

Dataware 200 GmbH, Garmischer Strasse 4–6, D 8000 Munich 2, West Germany

Online Computer Systems Inc., 20251 Century Boulevard, Germantown, MD 20874, USA

Silver Platter Information Services, 37 Walnut Street, Wellesley Hills, MA 02181, USA

Pergamon Compact Solution, 66–73 Shoe Lane, London EC4P 4AB, UK

In addition, the various CD-ROM publishers all issue brochures and descriptions of their CD products, and the various publishers of free newsletters noted earlier are worth contacting.

Finally, the July/August 1987 issue of *CD-ROM Librarian* (Vol. 2, No. 4) contains a useful bibliography of important articles in the field of CD-ROM.

Chapter 13

Conclusions

Charles Oppenheim

This book addresses some of the issues involved for both publishers and information users who have to evaluate the advantages and disadvantages of CD-ROM for distributing information. Robin Williamson's chapter gives much valuable information of the costs involved in creating CD-ROM, and Patrick Gibbins' chapter demonstrates just how much is involved in an integrator's function and why, therefore, such organizations are so important. The book also demonstrates (in Ray Walsh's chapter) the range of products currently available, and likely to be available in the near future. The book has examined some case studies in CD-ROM publishing from Barrie Stern, Bob Campbell and Christine Baldwin, and the role of the Commission of European Communities in encouraging CD-ROM developments in Franco Mastroddi's clear chapter. Chapter 5 by Martin Brooks looks at case studies in CD-ROM software, and Gordon Priestley examines why publishers should use CD-ROM. Finally, in Tony Hendley's and Martin White's chapters, the technology is put into perspective in relation to other optical technologies.

As was noted in the introduction to this volume, CD-ROM, like expert systems, has been the subject of much hype. The actual take-up of CD-ROM by publishers has been so far somewhat slow. Link Research, whose estimates are usually regarded as the most reliable in the information industry, has recently predicted that the number of CD-ROM drives in Europe will grow modestly, from 25 000 in 1988 to 284 000 in 1992. It predicts West Germany will have the most drives, followed by the United Kingdom, and that Italy will soon lose its early lead. These growth figures are far lower than those we were given by the proponents of CD-ROM two or three years ago. Why is this?

There are many reasons that can be advanced to explain this state of affairs; only a few microcomputer manufacturers have shown a commitment to the new hardware, and the attitude of IBM, always important, has not helped as the only interest it has shown so far has been in other optical media, such as WORM. A second problem, which follows on in part from the first, is the small installed base of CD-ROM players, which means that publishers have a relatively small potential marketplace at the moment — in other words, the classic chicken and egg problem.

If we combine these factors with the high initial cost for publishers (albeit balanced by low run on costs thereafter) and dissatisfaction with the performance of some CD-ROM information retrieval softwares, then the reason for the cautious approach is clear. The product was not helped by the hype either; CD-ROM is, contrary to early claims, totally inappropriate for fast-moving information typical of online databases, although the combination of an archival CD-ROM with the latest information either online or downloaded onto a local floppy disc is highly attractive.

There are reasons to be optimistic about the industry, though. The product is particularly well suited for European distribution because of the multilingual searching possibilities and because there is over-capacity at European CD audio replication plants at present. There is the model of Italy, that has taken to CD-ROM with considerable enthusiasm, perhaps because of the unreliability of online access in that country. Most CD-ROM products are based on print reference works, demonstrating that the publishing industry has recognized where CD-ROM is strongest. The ADONIS experiment is valuable, too, for the insight it gives into the costs and storage capacity of the new media, as well as for the insight into who borrows what.

As Ray Walsh's chapter demonstrates, pricing for CD-ROM is moderately random, and there is no clear correlation between price and update frequency or value of information, however one may wish to measure that. The best approach for such an immature product is to bundle the entire product — to throw in hardware, information and software into one subscription. In due course, as CD-ROM drives become prevalent, this strategy will become irrelevant. For the moment, this looks like the best way forward.

The problem for users is perhaps primarily the lack of perceived standards. (Will the hardware become obsolete? Will other discs be compatible?) Pricing may not necessarily be an issue, as long as the user can be persuaded that the medium will cost less in the long term than equivalent searching online or by other means.

So where will CD-ROM become important? It will grow as a means of disseminating non-time-critical information, especially to developing countries and anywhere else where online is expensive or unreliable. It will grow as a means for distributing technical documentation, parts manuals, and so on. It will grow as a means of distributing archival sets, and value-added subsets, to enhance online databases. It will grow as a means of distributing reference works. It will grow as a means of document delivery. Most of all it will grow when it is sold, together with the relevant hardware, by one or more information providers with a commitment to the technology. That commitment can only come when the provider is convinced the product can serve its ends profitably and users are convinced the product is for them. It is to be hoped that this book has made a contribution towards that end.

Index